BIRTH OR ABORTION?

Private Struggles in a Political World

ACKNOWLEDGMENTS

Since 1983, when we began our first interviews for *Birth or Abortion? Private Struggles in a Political World,* many people have helped us to find the time and resources to carry on with our work. We especially thank the Laurel Foundation and its president, Gregory D. Curtis, who awarded us a generous grant in 1990. We received further kind support for this book and for related projects from the Center for the Development of Educational Computing (CDEC) at Carnegie Mellon University. We were also given valuable time, respect, and flexibility by our respective associates and employers at Duquesne University and at the University of Pittsburgh's Learning Research and Development Center.

Early in our work, Fred Hetzel at the University of Pittsburgh Press steered us to the trade book market and to our agent, Arnold Goodman. This was indeed an important turning point, for Arnold had unwavering faith in our approach through good times and bad. We owe a similar debt to our editor, Linda Greenspan Regan, both for signing our book and for expertly guiding its development.

Birth or Abortion? would not exist without the many people who spent hours in interviews with us. Whether they shared their private experiences or their professional insights, they were extraordinarily generous and candid. Many opened their lives to us at great emotional cost. We want to express to all of them our affection as well as our thanks. They are the heart of this book.

For helping us find such people, and for recommending resources to support our work, we also thank Leslie Turner, Bobbi Menendez, Mary Littman, Barry Mitnick, the late Leah Sayles, Dr. Robert Stern, Dr. Robert Kaminski, Karen Kane, Ellen Gross, Ethel Landerman, Sue Berringer, and many others who must remain unnamed. Ed Blank, drama editor for the *Pittsburgh Press,* kindly shared his vast knowledge as well as the vast contents of his library of films on video.

Our dear friend Liane Ellison Norman deserves our special gratitude for always believing that we were on the right track, for introducing our project to the Laurel Foundation, and for reading and sensitively criticizing our work.

Marianne Novy also spent much time on a close reading of our manuscript, and her suggestions were invaluable. Our friend and fellow journalist Carol Hymowitz not only read sections of the manuscript but also offered professional encouragement and support. Maggie Jones Patterson's mother, Ruth Jones, cast her schoolteacher's eye over every page and pronounced our work remarkably free from errors. Other skilled and thoughtful readers who have earned our heartfelt thanks are Margaret McKeown, Jo Worthy, Father Jack Nantz, Jean Hunter, and Katie Esser. Jane Gardner, Mary Rapp, and Diane Clark, three of many people who transcribed hours of taped interviews, worked quickly and efficiently on short notice and often told us how moved they were by the material. Their services were indispensable.

Last, but also first, are our families. It would be impossible to explain how large a part Kate Maloy's husband, Preston Covey, and Maggie Jones Patterson's husband, Rob Ruck, have played in seeing this work to its completion. They pushed us to persist when we had given up. They endured and enlivened endless conversations that refined our thinking. They read our work, made our meals, and took care of our children so that we could travel and write. Our sons, Adam Covey and Alex Ruck, both born since we began this project (and both joyful distractions from it!), are happiest of all that we have finally finished. We thank them for their patience and their good hearts, and we dedicate *Birth or Abortion?* to all four wonderful males in our lives—our husbands and our sons.

CONTENTS

INTRODUCTION

Dilemma and Debate

[M]ost Americans think of abortion issues as involving individual rights—either the right to life of the fetus or a woman's right to privacy, choice, or control over her own body. Thus the two seemingly irrevocably opposed positions are actually locked within the same intellectual framework, a framework that appears rather rigid and impoverished. . . .

Mary Ann Glendon, *Abortion and Divorce in Western Law* (1987)

Birth or Abortion? Private Struggles in a Political World is a collection of almost fifty stories about women and men who have had to decide whether to continue or end an unplanned or medically troubled pregnancy. Some chose birth, some abortion. Some made peace with their decision, some say they never will. Their stories, however, can help to ease the pain and prejudice of a country divided for decades over the bitter issue of abortion. Together their diverse and richly detailed accounts encourage the possibility that the intense public conflict over abortion will give way to humane and rational discourse.

The heat of the conflict has, for all useful purposes, reduced a great many probing and subtle thoughts on the subject of abortion to just two antithetical positions. While thoughtful scholars, medical professionals, and conscientious citizens labor to explore and understand the issue, advocates of the inadequately labeled pro-choice and pro-life* positions have been able to capture the spotlight—whose glare has bleached any shade of gray. These two factions have come to represent abortion in deceptive black-or-white terms. Their arguments are directed toward preserving or overthrowing existing law, not exploring in

---

*We refer to both sides of the abortion debate in the terms they have chosen for themselves. Thus we use "pro-life" for those who want to see abortion severely restricted or made illegal, and "pro-choice" for those who want abortion to remain a legal option for individuals.

depth the truths and quandaries that surround the issue. As a consequence, little substantive dialogue has taken place in recent decades in the media or in legislatures. Rather, the rush to win votes, rights, or restrictions has clouded the controversy with hostility and even violence. Hardly a week goes by without television news coverage of shouting matches between the factions. Abortion clinics are under siege, some vandalized or even bombed. Their patients are harassed and accused as they enter to exercise a private, legally sanctioned choice. Those who accost them are sometimes attacked as well. In Youngstown, Ohio, two pro-life demonstrators, lying prone in the street outside a clinic, were deliberately run over by a man driving a light truck. The evening news captured the event in all its casual horror, showing the vehicle's front tires lifting and dropping over the horizontal protesters as if they were no more than speed bumps. (The protesters, a man and a woman, survived.)

Though individuals on both sides of the conflict decry the bitterness and acknowledge the complexities of the abortion issue, what comes across to most people is a fierce, forever shifting tug-of-war over the question, "Who decides, the woman or the law?" The very idea of compromise or common cause draws scorn. How, after all, can the political debate about abortion permit any more options than pregnancy itself does? An unwanted pregnancy, no matter how complicated or difficult its circumstances, can have only one of two deliberate outcomes; birth or abortion. Only one of the two beings* at risk can prevail— the woman or the developing child she carries. And only one of the two has the capacity to decide the outcome.

This inherent imbalance of power is crucial, all the more so because the fetus is always at risk of dying. The woman, meanwhile, faces risks that range from mere inconvenience to poverty, loss of opportunity, severe depression, or her own death. Some people believe the law should redress this imbalance by restricting or criminalizing abortion. Others counter that the claims of a fully capacitated woman, who can know and consciously suffer, must outweigh those of a partially formed being, who presumably cannot. But given two beings who cannot both be served, and disagreeing deeply about the relative worth and claims of each, people inevitably take sides, some championing the fetus, some the woman. Once they choose which of the two to protect, they are virtually bound by the all-or-nothing terms of the debate to abandon the other. Pro-life forces who would speak for the voiceless unborn child too often disregard the

---

*We choose this term because it is as close as we can come to a neutral word that applies to both the woman and the fetus.

woman. Pro-choice forces can fail to attend to the silent claims of the fetus. In the political debate, as in the private dilemma, only one party can "win."

Beyond "Who Decides?"

Where, between those who would protect the fetus and those who would champion the woman, is there any hope for fruitful dialogue? One premise of this book is that dialogue and even common cause lie dormant in the very dilemma that the debate, by insisting on simple answers, obscures. That dilemma lies not in "who decides?" but in having to choose at all. How is it possible to feel truly ethical, moral, and humane in a choice between two beings of value, whose claims vary in weight and validity from case to case? The public debate, with its emphasis on propaganda and persuasion, denies how painful that choice can be. Each faction, in promoting the interests of one being, minimizes the worth and the claims of the other, thereby damping the anguish of the dilemma. The pro-choice side, in its urgency to guard the interests of women who wish to abort, may betray other women who do not. Legalized abortion is too readily seen as a solution for poor or undereducated women, not as a loss they may mourn either at the time or later. Similarly, if the pro-life side fails to value the pregnant woman, to grasp the desperation she may experience, or to respect the lifelong loss she may suffer if she places her baby for adoption, then that side betrays both the fetus and the mother. Thus another premise of this book is that neither the pro-choice nor the pro-life faction—as they and their arguments are most commonly understood—truly represents or fully values either the woman or the fetus. Neither being *can* be valued—by the law, the individual, or society—at the price of disregarding the other.

Ultimately, the value we place on both the woman and the fetus must be attached to every positive aspect and capacity of each. Women must be respected and encouraged for intellect and professional achievement as much as for mothering and marriage, for directness, strength, and courage as much as for nurturance and tact. In a more ideal world, women's education and enculturation from early infancy would teach them to recognize and cultivate their own best qualities, whether their talents lead them to motherhood, a career, or both. They would be taught to strike a fair balance between their own interests and the concerns of other people, instead of too often being conditioned to unduly subjugate their desires.

Similarly, in a more perfect world, developing life would be valued for the full complement of human properties locked within its burgeoning cells and for the hope and continuity it represents in a society. Couples would be more likely to conceive only when they truly wanted to. When unplanned pregnancies did occur, they would be protected and nurtured under every appropriate circumstance. They would be sacrificed to the claims of others only in the last resort, when all other options, though fully accessible, somehow failed. For when fetuses are valued only if their mothers want to bear them, and when women are valued only for certain of their aspects, neither fetuses nor women are really valued at all. To assign worth to only part of a being, or to value a being only part of the time, reveals either a failure of imagination or constraining judgments about sexuality and lifestyle.

Inflexible Factions

Such constraining judgments are a major source of the hostility that pervades the public debate over abortion. The most vocal and visible activists in both camps not only disagree hotly over abortion itself but also regard each other's underlying attitudes about women, men, and sexuality as misguided and even immoral. According to sociologist Kristin Luker in her book *Abortion and the Politics of Motherhood*, there is a common belief on the part of pro-life activists that men and women are intrinsically different and are therefore best suited to different roles, the men to "the public world of work," the women to childrearing, homemaking, and caring for their husbands. Within this traditional gender division—which is uneven because it limits women to only one realm while permitting men to have influence in both—sex is valued most for its sacred, procreative purpose. Sex for pleasure alone is regarded as profane. Both contraception and abortion are wrong because they deny the primary purpose of sex, resist the "natural" roles of women, and either prevent or end the incipient human life that is the woman's highest calling to nurture.

Pro-choice activists, on the other hand, tend to regard women and men as more similar than different. People on this side value sex as much for pleasure and intimacy as for reproduction. According to Luker, they believe that unless motherhood is entirely voluntary, society will always see it as "a low-status, unrewarding role to which women can be banished at any time." The only way women can achieve their full potential is to be able to control their fertility. Given the inadequacies and the rates of misuse associated with every birth control method except sterilization, abortion that is properly performed provides the only 100-percent effective backup. Thus pro-choice people believe it is the only true biological equalizer, the only means for eliminating the risk of unwanted pregnancy—a risk whose full impact is felt only by women. Against the drive for full equality with men, many pro-choice activists minimize the claims of the fetus or refuse to acknowledge them at all.

It is not hard to see how two such inimical views might lead a nation to an angry, moralistic impasse over an issue that, like abortion, is inseparable from disputed matters of gender and sexuality. And yet, in the United States, those who hold the irreconcilable opinions outlined by Luker are only a minority. Not everyone who opposes legal abortion objects to contraception or to sex as an expression of affection or source of pleasure. Most see nothing wrong with women holding jobs outside the home. Some would even allow abortion in cases of rape, incest, fetal abnormality, or threat to the mother's health. Likewise, many people who favor legal abortion also recognize the need to value developing human life. They regard abortion more as an unfortunate necessity than a positive option. They understand that women can be torn between the desire for a child and the desire for personal fulfillment, but they are not so alarmed by the risk of unplanned pregnancy as to condone abortion as a means of birth control.

In fact, polls show that a majority of Americans are ambivalent about abortion, unwilling to join either faction yet agreeing with some points of each. They tend to believe women should be able to choose when and whether to bear a child, but they are disturbed by the 1.6 million abortions performed each year in the United States. Implicitly, their ambivalence derives from concern for both the women and the fetus, yet they seem unable to reconcile those concerns.

The factions have made efficient use of the majority's confusion. The two extremes have come to rule the public discussion and divide the country not only by speaking more loudly and passionately than those who find abortion a complex and ambiguous matter but also by putting forth arguments that seem unanswerable. For those who believe the fetus is a human being from the moment of conception, every point that follows from that belief is logically unassailable. The fetus, having committed no crime, cannot be killed—except perhaps to save the life of the woman—because killing it is murder. Arguments to the contrary deny that the fetus is a person. They hold that the woman, having attained full human status, can thereby claim full moral status to which the fetus, having only potential, is not entitled.

As long as the emphasis is on the arguments, the deadlock will stand and the premises will remain flatly contradictory. But the extreme views inherently lack balance. Those on one side would subjugate women's desires and interest to the claims of fetal life. Those on the other side, fearing the implications of anything less than total reproductive autonomy, would categorically reverse this priority. Neither side admits that in some cases the woman's claims are stronger while in others those of the fetus carry more weight. Their rigid positions offer little room for maneuvering toward common cause or feeling, even for the many Americans who would gladly move in that direction.

Two Moral Standards

While the debate has denied ambivalence, and the majority of Americans have quietly wrestled with it, millions of people have had to decide what to do about actual pregnancies. What we saw, early in our research for this book, was that these private, real-life choices bore almost no resemblance to the political struggle. The women and couples to whom we spoke rarely, if ever, mentioned rights to us. They did not base their actions on an explicit choice between the woman and the fetus; in fact, they did not even appear to regard the interests of one as separate from the interests of the other. In almost every case, the outcomes of these private dilemmas hung on practical and emotional matters— the quality of the connection between the woman and the man, the financial resources available, the number of other children a woman already had, the state of her self-esteem, the other important options that pregnancy might or might not foreclose.

Soon after we began to see this striking difference between the political arguments and the grounds for private decisions, we became aware of current research that has much to say about the conflict over gender roles, rights, and morality that underlies the abortion debate. For example, the work of Harvard psychologist Carol Gilligan explores the nature of women's experience and thought and finds that, although boys and girls behave similarly through toddlerhood, by age four their paths begin to diverge for life. Boys in Western cultures tend to push for independence and autonomy; girls, to maintain connectedness and intimacy. The common results for the two sexes are very different ways of viewing the world and other people and very different approaches to moral dilemmas. According to Gilligan, women typically focus more intently throughout their lives on relationships while men emphasize self-reliance and achievement. Women seek understanding, men solutions. Women tend to see acts and occurrences as parts of a patterned whole; men tend to see them as single and discrete. Because the male model, as Gilligan describes it, has defined and determined the conduct of business, government, education, the arts, and all public behaviors, the female model has been viewed as weaker, less valuable, and less healthy.

Traditional psychological research has only exacerbated this attitude toward women and their values. Studies of human development have focused almost exclusively on male subjects and have then applied their findings to women, whose own path toward maturity has not corresponded to these studies' definitions of the norm. Freudian theory, for example, maintains that for young boys to reach healthy manhood they must separate from their mothers and from the intricate web of relationships that women create and sustain. Boys in middle childhood must shift their allegiance and their ideas of selfhood to their fathers. To become adults, they must cultivate autonomy, decisiveness, fairness, logical clarity, and intellectual precision. Young girls, meanwhile, are seen as failing this challenge. They stay bound within the human web, and as a consequence they do not attain full maturity as it is defined in studies of men. Instead, according to psychoanalytic theory, women's sense of human connectedness and interdependence remains a mark of arrested development.

More recent psychological research challenges this belittling view of women and in the process enlarges the definition of adulthood that it propounds. By studying women's development directly, instead of extrapolating from findings about men, this newer work demonstrates that women reach maturity along a different developmental path. They are encouraged to follow a route through psychological territory that is dense with human relationships and defined by interaction with others. Their progress therefore fosters what Gilligan calls a "caretaking" moral standard, one that stresses the importance of human interdependence and defines morality and maturity in terms of people's responsibilities toward one another. In contrast, the road upon which men are typically guided runs through a developmental continuum in which they are expected to make fair but self-interested use of whatever resources they may find. Other travelers are free to do the same, as long as no one infringes unnecessarily upon the rights of another. This path, in Gilligan's terms, leads to the "justice" standard of morality.

The most important message in the newer psychological research is not that women and men proceed along separate but equally valid developmental paths. It is that each path leads to incompleteness, that people who consistently apply one standard over the other do not attain their full psychological and moral potential. The older research, conducted with boys and men, never grasped this. As long as women were measured only by the standards that held for men, they were seen as developmentally inferior. As long as men were measured without reference to women, psychological research remained blind to their diminished sense of human relationships. It was not until researchers examined women's concerns directly, compared them with men's, and then looked at both men's and women's moral decision making that they saw two different moral standards—one with a justice orientation, the other with a focus on caretaking. The researchers also saw that people of both sexes apply both sets of concerns, but usually in different proportions. Gilligan's studies in particular showed that men tend to lean more often toward a justice standard in moral dilemmas, but that they also consider matters of responsibility and caretaking. Women consult the caretaking standard more often than men, but they often apply the justice standard as well. The people who are viewed in recent research as the most morally mature are those who consistently try to balance justice with care. These are the men and women who understand that imbalance can lead to the hazards of either coldness or martyrdom.

Though adults of both sexes may strive for this balanced brand of moral maturity, it is more costly for women to attain, given prevailing cultural values and expectations. Gilligan, quoted in *Time* magazine's Fall 1990 special issue on women, explains that "for girls to remain responsive to themselves, they must resist the conventions of feminine goodness; to remain responsive to others, they must resist the values placed on self-sufficiency and independence." Gilligan might equally well have said that for women to feel sound and self-respecting they must actively foster *both* sets of values. The same holds for men, except that there is typically less dissonance in their imbalance. Though many men today are looking for more intimacy with others, their traditional values have been rewarded with prestige and power.

Critics of studies that probe gender differences argue that they could mean a step backward for women. They fear that discussions of women's interpersonal strengths and integrating perceptions will be taken by some as evidence that women belong exclusively in the personal realm. Counterarguments assert that these qualities suit women well for all endeavors, whether public or private. If many ills of the traditionally male domains—the economy, industry, international affairs, and management of natural resources—can be ascribed either to an overemphasis on autonomy and independence or to a lack of interconnected awareness, then women's ways of knowing, many believe, could mitigate those ills. Ultimately, since every person possesses every human quality in some degree, common sense suggests that members of both sexes, and the society in which they develop, should cultivate both traditional "male" and "female" strengths.

Listening to People in Crisis

Since the public and political realms of experience have been led primarily by men, it stands to reason that the justice standard, which reflects the values men tend to adopt, should define the discussion of laws, policies, and social controversies. It also seems reasonable that—as our interviews repeatedly showed us—private struggles might be resolved in somewhat different terms. For instance, people in crisis over a pregnancy must act. They may be just as ambivalent about abortion as most Americans or they may hold strong political views, but faced with the physical fact of an unplanned or risky pregnancy, they have no choice but to choose, finally and irreversibly, between birth and abortion. Given little help by the debate raging around them when they must meet, on their own, the necessity to decide, they are often surprised by doubts they never anticipated. In most of the cases in this book, they turn to the caretaking standard.

This book contains forty-nine of the ninety-five stories people have told us. The tellers are to some extent a self-selecting group. Though some were raped or experienced birth control failures beyond their control, and others planned their pregnancies only to be faced with medical or genetic problems, most became pregnant as a result of poor contraceptive practices. Within the limits of self-selection, however, the people in this book are diverse. From case to case, their resources, circumstances, wisdom, and values vary. They have different tools and talents with which to work. They come from all parts of the country, though most are from the northeastern and mid-Atlantic states. They come mainly from middle-class urban and suburban neighborhoods, but more than a few are from semirural factory towns, remote hills, ghettoes, or the streets. They come from intact, close families; from single-parent homes; from childhoods soured by abuse, addiction, poverty, or all three. They range from their teens to their seventies, from barely articulate to eloquent. To protect the storytellers' identities, nearly all names, places, and minor details in their accounts of struggle are changed. Each of their stories includes something the abortion debate has thus far avoided discussing—some element of ambiguity, complexity, uncertainty, loss, or respect for an opposing view.

Each story in this book is contained as if in a set of boxes nesting one inside the other and representing personal, interpersonal, familial, local, religious, national, and historical influences on human thought and action. Each story is set in a time and a place whose prevailing values the story reflects or rejects. *Birth or Abortion?* looks at each box and how it fits within or around the others. It looks at the values each box contains. How does a person's decision emerge from the beliefs and priorities communicated by parents, religion, peers, the law? How are women, children, men, the family, and work regarded in each time and place? What are the social realities and economic conditions surrounding each choice, and how do these—overtly or in unnoticed ways—affect the outcome?

As the stories in every section gather force, they convince us that no decision—legal or illegal, wise or ill-founded—is made outside the nest of boxes. Individuals are not totally isolated and self-made but shaped from birth by both the wide and the narrow worlds they occupy. We think we choose entirely for ourselves—when and whether to start having sex, to pursue higher education, to begin a career, to marry, to have children—until we look at the trends in our culture and perceive vast patterns of behavior in which our own is mirrored. We are defined by our culture, whether we lean with or against the trends of our time, and our culture, in turn, is defined by the sum of all our actions.

The Meaning of the Stories We Tell

Harvard law professor Mary Ann Glendon sees a country's laws and policies as stories it tells about its citizens, their values, and the country's imminent direction. Her book *Abortion and Divorce in Western Law* examines and contrasts American and European policies on these issues. As she explained in a television interview with commentator Bill Moyers, Glendon expected at first to find no possibility of compromise on abortion ("Conversation with Mary Ann Glendon, Harvard University Law Professor," 1990). Either the law would decide or it would permit the woman to decide. Instead, Glendon found it is only in the United States that the law leaves the private decisions about abortion entirely up to the woman through the sixth month of pregnancy. It is only in America that the larger question has been removed from the legislature and given wholly to the courts. Because the courts have almost total jurisdiction and because the abortion rights they have established effectively shut out the concerns of those who oppose abortion, the pitched battle is being waged between those who approve of the laws on abortion and those who want them overturned. With no process of give-and-take and no legislatures to lobby, the most extreme factions have turned on each other the full brunt of their mistrust and hostility. The caretaking standard is strikingly absent.

In Europe, by contrast, abortion statutes are written and refined through legislative processes. European nations typically proclaim the sanctity of life, yet they also, by statute or in practice, quite freely permit abortion early in pregnancy. Glendon admitted to Moyers that to many Americans such statutes may seem inconsistent. In her view, however, "If one tries to read the messages of those laws, it is that we have several important values in tension with each other. . . . " Europeans relieve that tension by providing for pregnant women, mothers, and children far better than we do in the United States. Glendon pointed out to Moyers that even the conservative Helmut Kohl "has said that German abortion policy is to increase maternal benefits, child allowances, to help people with raising children. We don't hear talk like that in the United States." Not only does the United States offer only minimal maternal benefits or other help to families, it leaves women and children much poorer after divorce. "[O]nly in the United States," Glendon said to Moyers, "can you free yourself from not only marriage but also substantially from the economic responsibility associated with marriage and children. . . . We have glided from 'no fault' into 'no responsibility.'" To Glendon this says "something puzzling about the message we communicate through the legal system about children and our attitudes toward neediness and dependency. . . . "

When Glendon ponders where women are better off, she acknowledges that they have more rights in the United States but are better protected as mothers and as members of interdependent families in Europe. She has no doubt that children are better off on the other side of the Atlantic, where far fewer live in poverty than our one in five—soon to be one in four.

Reflecting on her findings about women and children and about America's poor prospects for compromise, Glendon warned about the dangers of "becoming a society that can only think about individuals. The choices we make as individuals make us the kind of people we are. The choices we make collectively make us into the kind of society we are. If you put together a whole lot of decisions that let individual rights trump everything else, then that contributes to the shaping of society."

Glendon's remarks imply that the shape our society has assumed is an asymmetrical one, weighted too heavily on the side of individual autonomy (the "justice" standard), too lightly on the side of responsibility and regard for others (the "caretaking" standard). This might explain the message she finds so puzzling about our attitudes toward neediness and dependency. But, Glendon said, "I think we are better than the story we are telling ourselves through the law."

In a democracy, we are supposed to discover our story by listening to the people, no matter how difficult that task may be. We are required to set aside our assumptions, to think as well as to feel, to struggle with complexity and contradiciton, and to look directly at what disturbs and challenges us the most.

The stories that follow, taken together, *are* our nation's story, the one that does not get told, the one we enact, day by day, behind the scenes of battle. If we can bring this story forward and embody it in our laws and policies, we can prove that Glendon is right and that we are better than the story we now tell.

THE 1950s

From One Extreme . . .

The child (or children) might be absorbed in busyness, in his own dreamworld; but as soon as he felt me gliding into a world which did not include him, he would come to pull at my hand, ask for help, punch at the typewriter keys. . . . My anger would rise; I would feel the futility of any attempt to salvage myself, and also the inequality between us: my needs always balanced against those of a child, and always losing. I could love so much better, I told myself, even after a quarter-hour of selfishness, of peace, of detachment from my children. A few minutes! But it was as if an invisible thread would pull taut between us and break, to the child's sense of inconsolable abandonment, if I moved—not even physically, but in spirit—into a realm beyond our tightly circumscribed life together. . . . I did not understand that this circle, this magnetic field in which we lived, was not a natural phenomenon.

Adrienne Rich, *Of Woman Born* (1979)

Introduction

The word "abortion" was rarely mentioned in polite company during the 1950s; some said it was even "unthinkable." Nevertheless the unmentionable, unthinkable *practice* of abortion may have been no less common than it is today. While there were few reliable data, most estimates of U.S. abortions during the 1950s ran from 200,000 to more than one million abortions annually. Dr. Christopher Tietze, chairman of the statistical committee for a conference on abortion held by Planned Parenthood in 1955, thought 1.2 million abortions— or about one pregnancy in four—was the most accurate figure (Calderone, 1958). Dr. Albert Kinsey's 1953 study of more than six thousand urban, white, educated women showed that one-fifth to one-fourth of their pregnancies had been ended in abortion.

If Tietze's estimates were correct—and we will never know—illegal abortion was at least as widely performed on women in the 1950s as legal abortion is today. Today one pregnancy in four ends in abortion, adding up to a total of 1.6 million each year. Whatever the statistical truth about the period, birth-or-abortion decisions in the 1950s were made in a furtive and even dangerous climate. The prevailing cultural message was that female sexual activity belonged solely within marriage, where pregnancy was the always welcome—if sometimes inconvenient—outcome.

The 1950s provide a good starting point for our discussion of birth and abortion decisions because the era demonstrates how strongly the prevailing views of women affect both private decisions and public policy. So much of the change in attitude that followed that decade and eventually led to *Roe v. Wade* started in this post-war time when American women looked to the home for satisfaction and turned away from friendship, community, work, and creativity.

Today, poet Adrienne Rich would seem an unlikely candidate for the constricting domestic life she describes in *Of Woman Born*. She had had other plans. She had started writing poetry seriously in her early teens and had dreamed, in 1945, of "going to Europe as a journalist, sleeping among the ruins in bombed cities, recording the rebirth of civilization after the fall of the Nazis." Writing was her passionate pursuit as a teenager, although she also spent the requisite number of hours preoccupied, somewhat halfheartedly, with makeup, clothes, and boys. "There were two different compartments, already, to my life," she writes. In one, she prepared to become the independent writer. In the other, she was the ingenue, grooming for the role of dependent wife. How did Rich, who had felt throughout her teens that she was "only acting the part of a feminine creature," come to dwell almost exclusively in the compartment that had seemed less real to her, the territory claimed by "real women"? Why, by the late 1950s, was she unable to steal even fifteen minutes for the writing that defined her as a separate, adult person? And why, though she passionately loved her children, did they also cause her "the most exquisite suffering . . . the suffering of ambivalence: the murderous alternation between bitter resentment and raw-edged nerves, and blissful gratification and tenderness"?

The answers lie largely in the social values that prevailed when Rich made her choices about marriage, motherhood, and work. Between the end of World War II, when Rich dreamed her European dreams, and the 1950s, when she made her bed with a husband instead of in the ruins of cities, the pressure on women to renounce careers for marriage and motherhood had grown virtually irresistible. Rich succumbed. Her creative ambitions made her feel—perhaps more painfully than some—the tension between her domestic role and her "selfish" interests, but she was living in a time when that tension was not even supposed to exist. Truly feminine women were supposed to be entirely fulfilled by their family responsibilities. Even Rich, who later divorced and embraced a lesbian lifestyle, felt the strong cultural pressures back then. Because no possibility of resolving the tension was offered, Rich and millions of other women remained convinced that their needs would always lose to those of others.

Most middle-class women of the 1950s did not perceive this one-sidedness as unnatural. After all, an ideal of woman as a selfless nurturer and contented, stay-at-home mother had been around for generations, even though only a few had ever achieved it. For the first half of the century, the cult of domesticity had been countered by the ideals of feminism, which had urged women toward equality with men in public life. For decades the pendulum that swung between the conflicting appeals of the public and private domains had stayed in the middle range. Within this range a lively—if often paternalistic—dialogue about women and their proper roles took place in politics, periodicals, films, and fiction. The pull and counter-pull were reflected in the demographic trends of the century—in women's gradual tendencies toward more education, later marriages, fewer children, and increasing participation in the labor force. The world wars and Great Depression had pushed women—especially the poor— out of the home and into paying jobs. Children were no longer the economic asset they had been on the farm. Instead, they were mouths to feed on a tight budget.

Then, between 1945 and 1960, the gross national product soared 250 percent. In the affluent fifties, most of the century's earlier trends were reversed. Women began to marry earlier, have more children, and stay at home. Like Rich, they retreated from the larger world. They also had abortions—even the married women—despite the widespread belief in motherhood as woman's ultimate fulfillment. What is significant about the post–World War II period and its reversal of most demographic trends is the way in which that time sheds light on the real roles and capacities of women. Because it was a time of extremes, it provides a good place to begin an examination of women's decisions about reproduction. Nothing defines what is natural so clearly as something that is not.

What is natural for women, to varying degrees, is the pull toward both home and the outside world. This is also natural for men, but society has made it easier for men to accommodate both urges. For women, conflict between domestic and larger-world satisfactions may arise at every milestone in the choices they make about education, career, marriage, and motherhood. In the 1950s, many women felt uncompromising pressure to make all their choices on the domestic side. "The image of American women portrayed in the mass media during the 1950s was a well-groomed wife and mother. *She* was the American woman; any other kind was an aberration . . . " Carol Hymowitz and Michaele Weissman write in A *History of Women in America.*

These values seemed timeless. The cult of domesticity had been holding up this ideal to the American imagination for one hundred years as a counterpoint to the dreariness of the industrial world. Millions of women had longed for the luxury of domesticity but had been unable to achieve it until finally, at mid-century, peace and prosperity turned enormous numbers of women into domestic icons. In 1950, almost 60 percent of Americans were living in what was thought of as traditional families in which the wife stayed at home. The average age for women at the time of first marriage dropped to just twenty. The popular media glorified the luxurious new standard of living—the home in the suburbs paid for by a workaday, absentee father and tended by a homebound mother. People raced to achieve the domestic dream. During the 1950s, 1.2 million Americans moved to the suburbs each year, as massive a migration as any from Europe during the twentieth century.

Although feminism had picked up converts during the suffrage movement of the teens and twenties and inspired imaginations through the Depression and beyond, it went underground after World War II. As Betty Friedan explains in *The Feminine Mystique,* women's magazines in the "heyday" of the late 1930s and the 1940s had run fiction and articles about the "New Woman," about "heroines [who] were usually marching toward some goal or vision of their own, struggling with some problem of work or the world, when they found their man. . . . Often, there was a conflict between some commitment to her work and the man. But the moral, in 1939, was that if the New Woman kept her commitment to herself, she did not lose the man, if he was the right man." in 1949, Friedan "found the last clear note of the passionate search for individual identity in . . . a story called 'Sarah and the Seaplane,'" about a young flying student on her first solo, accompanied only by triumphant feelings of independence and delight.

"And then suddenly," Friedan writes, "the image blurs. The New Woman, soaring free, hesitates in midflight, shivers in all that blue sunlight, and rushes back to the cozy walls of home." Magazines that had carried feature stories on national or international affairs, economics, politics, literature, the arts, and ideas now closed their pages to the outside world. Instead they justified the world of the housewife to the housewife. They praised and encouraged her thrift and versatility, her talents as manager, seamstress, home decorator, gourmet chef, child development expert, chauffeur, community resource, secretary, and home financier.

The range of choices open to women has always been very much a function of the time in which they live, although some nonconformists have always struggled against convention. In the 1950s, according to A *History of Women in America*, experts from every corner communicated the message "that human personality and human sexual identity would be shattered unless they were channeled into an extremely narrow course. In their view almost any deviation from the norm, any form of unconventional behavior, was a sickness." Thus, women who "longed for the kind of 'masculine' satisfactions they had known in the job market prior to marriage" or during the war were doomed to behave in destructive ways—gossiping, making unwelcome waves in the community, or dominating their children and husbands.

During the 1940s, when economics and politics had assigned women to the work force to support the war effort, psychologists proclaimed their urge to work as "healthy" and the popular media created images of ideal women who could fill the country's economic needs. But when the war was over, the images reversed. Now that men were ready to reclaim their jobs, women who wanted to work suddenly revived ancient fears of emasculating harridans. The returning soldiers were in a position to do something about those fears. Not only did men take back their jobs, they also began to reshape the public image of women to suit their needs. In a period of hard-won peace made fragile by the threat of Communism, society was back in the hands of men who strove desperately to resolve the gender role confusion associated with earlier, unstable decades. If women were women, and men were men, and children were raised with clear, albeit inflexible, expectations, perhaps social and economic catastrophes could be held at bay. Tasks were assigned strictly along gender lines. It was assumed that women were nurturers by nature and could not handle the harsher realities of the marketplace. It was men who had the thicker skin needed for commerce. Husbands, in turn, seemed silly and emasculated in the kitchen or the nursery.

Thus an antidote to fear was the image of woman at home by the fire, with a child in her lap and bread in the oven. In the service of this comforting image, men engineered the disappearance of the New Woman from magazines and strong women's roles from the movies. For example, Betty Friedan was told by a woman magazine editor that "the old image of the spirited career girl was largely created by writers and editors who were women. . . . The new image of woman as housewife-mother has been largely created by writers and editors who are men. . . . " Friedan learned that "the new writers were all men, back from the war, who had been dreaming about home and a cozy domestic life."

The new images were made appealing to women with much the same language that had drawn them into the war effort in the 1940s. Then, they had been needed at the factories; now they were needed at home. They could ensure a safe future for their children by instructing them in the American way. In return, they were offered adulation, protection, material comforts, privilege, and clear, unquestionable values. Such rewards would not have seemed empty at first. There must have been something logical and irresistible about truly "feminine" roles being made affordable through the success of typically "masculine" pursuits. War and technological advances had evolved into peace and prosperity, which were managed almost exclusively by men. Women were now separated from the world in which they had found conflict between work and mothering. Increasingly, they were also separated from the richness of urban life, as families by the thousands moved to the suburbs. Once there, women also were separated from one another, atomized not only physically but also by the suburban psychology that ironically placed a high value on conformity and promoted deep and isolating fears of being different or malcontented.

The merging of economic opportunity with the ideal of womanly domesticity and the post-war threat of Communism was powerful enough to derail the 1940s' dreams of women like Adrienne Rich. This confluence persuaded a vast majority in a vast country that women could be satisfied by domesticity alone, with no need or capacity for larger-world roles. More educated women than ever before, including adventuresome dreamers like Rich, stayed home and had more babies than their counterparts in recent decades had ever had. The American wife and mother, supported by new effort-saving appliances, was supposedly the envy of the world and the rock to which American culture was moored.

American society vaunted and protected the nuclear family and the values it represented—honesty, resourcefulness, and individualism—but only within quite narrow norms. Those outside the charmed circle of these norms (the same circle Adrienne Rich soon found so tight) included the unmarried, the poor, the black, the brown, the powerfully creative, the nonconformist, and the dissident. The most visible and outspoken of these outsiders became the targets of the House Committee on Un-American Activities and Senator Joseph McCarthy, whose televised hearings entered the enshrined American household day after day, along with images of the ideal family reduced to bland comedy in television shows like "Father Knows Best" and "Leave it to Beaver."

Everyone was restricted in this age of conformity. Many middle-class men found their hearts and minds buttoned down into the gray flannel world of corporate America. They were the nine-to-five exiles from their families—five-to-nine strangers who scarcely knew their children. They were the lovable bumblers on the sitcoms. Nevertheless, men could express themselves in a range of pursuits. Women had only one very limited option. The 1950s mass media image of the ideal, all-giving wife and mother was actually a picture of a woman permanently stuck in what psychologist Carol Gilligan would later define as an immature stage. This stunted woman never reached the stages of moral and intellectual development in which she could consider her own needs in addition to those of others and develop a broader social consciousness.

Yet even this one, popular option was not open to every woman. Single women, for example, stood outside the charmed circle of the nuclear family. Without husbands and children to tend to, they were often objects of pity or scorn. They might have sought reward in their work, but they were impeded by the romantic notion that women were unfit for participation in the harsh reality of the marketplace. Supposedly, women worked only to fill in the economic gaps left by a man's absence or incapacity. The number of women working actually increased during the 1950s, however. The expensive reality of middle-class lifestyle contradicted the popular stereotype. As the post-war boom faded, more middle-class women returned to work to keep up their families' standard of living. But work seldom defined women as it did men. Many of these new working women were over thirty-five. They had waited until their children were well along in school, then returned to the workplace with rusty skills. Women's average earnings fell from 65 percent of men's in 1950 to less than 60 percent in 1960. When women lost the higher-paying jobs they had held during the war, they settled for the less interesting work men did not want, and they no longer took their work very seriously. Indeed, it was embarrassing not to be fully supported by a man who was, in turn, wholly dedicated to *his* job. Women's intelligence, ambition, and competence were best applied in the roles of help-mate, chef, attractive social asset. The number of female doctors, lawyers, and school superintendents declined. Jobs that were acceptable for women—sec-retary, teacher, or nurse—transplanted women's role of nurturing others to the workplace. But even in these fields, women who had real career ambitions were viewed as neurotic. Most women stayed low on the success ladder, while men took the management positions.

Propaganda against career women took on a scurrilous tone, Carol Hymowitz and Michaele Weissman write in *A History of Women in America*. "Women who sought careers were regularly depicted as 'castrating' and incapable of loving." In such an atmosphere, discrimination against women was widely accepted. If a woman was still single after the age of twenty-five, when her prospects for a husband seriously diminished, chances were good that her employer would still deny her equal treatment and a chance for advancement. In a 1961 poll, one-third of office managers admitted that they routinely paid men higher salaries than they paid women in equivalent positions.

Sex for the single woman was not discussed. The era's popular culture made it clear that women's sexual activity properly belonged inside matrimony, behind the bedroom doors, on twin beds. Babies were the welcome consequence. Yet, as Alfred Kinsey's studies would soon point out, single women did in fact have sex and married ones often liked it, despite the media images to the contrary. Nevertheless, women's magazines mentioned the delicate subject only in clinical articles about wives' frigidity or dissatisfactions with their husbands' sexual appetites. With a few wholesome exceptions like "Our Miss Brooks," popular television and radio heroines were married women who seemed to have children without sex. In the movies, the spunky New Women that Katharine Hepburn, Rosalind Russell, Barbara Stanwyck, and Bette Davis had portrayed in earlier decades began to fade.

Many films of the 1930s and 1940s dramatized a push-pull, bantering relationship between the sexes, with women always the ones who had to experiment, fight, change their minds, and meet new challenges. Gender-role confusion was everywhere, along with the conflict between domestic and professional urges. In *His Girl Friday* (1940), this conflict and confusion loads the comic dialogue with quips and gibes. The plot concerns Hildie (Rosalind Russell), who has divorced her former newspaper-editor boss and husband, Walter (Cary Grant), and is about to marry a good-hearted but colorless soul named Bruce (Ralph Bellamy). The story centers on whether Hildie will go through with this marriage.

"You can't quit the newspaper business," Walter tells her. "You're a newspaperman."

"That's why I'm quitting," she retorts. "I want to go someplace where I can be a woman."

The other reporters, all male, give Hildie's new marriage six months. "Can you picture Hildie singin' lullabies and hangin' out didies?" they ask. "She won't be able to stay away from the newspaper." They shake their heads at her willfulness. "Too independent," they call her, noting that she never even took alimony after her divorce.

Inevitably, Hildie gets hooked on her job again. Her fiance, Bruce, standing at her elbow while she frantically types a red-hot story, says accusingly, "You never intended to be decent and live like a human being!" Without even glancing at him, she mutters, "I'm not a suburban bridge player, I'm a newspaperman." Exit Bruce. Reenter Walter and the newspaper business, both of whom Hildie remarries.

The same themes appear in the 1942 classic *Woman of the Year*, starring Katharine Hepburn and Spencer Tracy. Again, it's the newspaper business versus domesticity. Tess Harding is an internationally respected columnist on world affairs; Sam Craig is a laid-back sportswriter on the same newspaper. They embark on a turbulent marriage, constantly disrupted by the demands of Tess's high-power career. Sam leaves her, telling Tess "she isn't a woman at all" on the very night she receives word that she has been voted "Outstanding Woman of the Year." Tess, finding her own successes empty, resolves to become the perfect, domestic wife. But she proves hilariously incompetent at even the simple task of preparing breakfast.

"I've been mad at you," Sam says, when he finds Tess in tears with the percolator erupting and the waffle iron overflowing, "but this is the first time I've been disappointed." The question of whether to change Tess's well-recognized name has persisted throughout the movie. He asks her "Why do you have to go to extremes? I don't want to be Mr. Tess Harding any more than I want you to be just Mrs. Sam Craig. Why can't you be Tess Harding Craig?"

Both *Woman of the Year* and *His Girl Friday* end with an articulation of the ideal—having it all, work and marriage—but without offering any practical guidelines for putting the ideal into practice. Neither Tess nor Hildie has to deal on-screen with the problem of children, for example. The business of Hollywood was to entertain and tantalize. It left real women—even those inside the movie industry, like an actress we call Lillian Miller—to deal with conflict as best they could.

Lillian Miller

Today, Lillian Miller is a lean, elegant woman in her late seventies. Her white hair is thick and wavy, her eyes deepset and still bright blue. It is easy to see in her face and carriage the Hollywood beauty that she was almost sixty years ago.

Lillian played young ingenues and feature roles in both 'A' and 'B' movies of the 1930s. She was Kate Hepburn and Rosalind Russell's contemporary, and she personally lived out some of the conflicts their roles portrayed. Throughout the 1930s and 1940s, she had basked in the glory of her own accomplishments, but she had also allowed her interests to be obscured in her husband's shadow. By 1952, after two children and years of his drinking and philandering, she had finally broken free of him. At thirty-eight, she was preparing to remarry, give up acting, and move to upstate New York to be a 1950s housewife. It was to be a new role for Lillian, a sharp contrast to the Hollywood life. She was also preparing for her fourth abortion.

Lillian had become pregnant by the man she was about to marry. Sam was an Easterner doing some work in California and they had met shortly after Lillian had left her screenwriter husband. Sam, she said, "was about the handsomest thing you ever saw in your life and very talented. He had been sent to California to direct a famous comedian's first year in television. We fell in love very quickly . . . and it was understood by all that we were going to be married. Anyway, I got pregnant and we had a long discussion about it. That was a pregnancy I wanted and so did he, but when we measured the problems, he had three children, I had two, and . . . we weren't married yet and had a lot of financial problems because I wasn't working now. I was depending on alimony and child support. So I got an abortion."

Though Lillian's abortion still was not legal, it was the next thing to it. "It was at a proper clinic," she remembered. "There was no subterfuge about it. I don't know if they were paying the police or getting protection of some kind, but it was very open. [The doctor] had a building of his own, and it was on a prominent street. There were nurses and he had assistant doctors, too. I had anesthesia and a nurse attendant."

Lillian's recollection is that this Hollywood clinic did nothing but abortions. There was virtually no effort to hide its purpose. She believes its openness was evidence that it gradually had become necessary—at least in Hollywood—"to somehow provide women with the ability to get abortions safely." Of course, Lillian readily admitted, it took money—about five hundred dollars in 1952.

After the procedure, Lillian and Sam married and moved to New York state. "We lived in the country," said Lillian, "and our children got along and I was president of the PTA and a very, very upstanding citizen of the community. I was very much in love and my ambitions had changed. I really ran a house and a family and did all the cooking and had no servants, and enjoyed it."

Not many 1950s housewives brought such a glamorous past under the roof of a suburban bungalow. But Lillian, like her humbler counterparts, settled into this new lifestyle as if she had finally been released from the hardship of the Depression and the war years to enjoy life's simpler pleasures. Indeed, like many women of the era, she had been buffeted by the financial demands of her times.

In 1933, at the height of the Depression, Lillian had been a nineteen-year-old under contract with a major studio. She earned enough to support her mother, who had been living with her in California. Lillian had just married George, a screenwriter seven years her senior who supported his own parents and could not afford two additional dependents. Lillian had to keep the new marriage a secret, even from family and friends. Had her employers learned of it, said Lillian, they would have canceled her contract "because I no longer would have been a romantic young lady." Fantasy and reality had to mesh; a leading lady had to be an available, if inaccessible, idol in the public mind. Rising stars who married lost their glow, flickered out.

Fear of losing her job and income was all the more reason for Lillian and her first husband to choose abortion when they learned she was pregnant for the first time. Lillian had been using a device called a pessary as birth control. Like the diaphragm, which Lillian found too big and uncomfortable, the pessary, she said, was shaped like a round derby hat. It was filled with spermicidal jelly before it was inserted over the cervix. When it failed to protect her, "I got the name of an abortionist from an actress who was under contract at the same studio," Lillian recalled. "It wasn't difficult. I called and mentioned her name."

Abortion was not frowned upon in a community whose business relied on its female stars being single, virginal, and alluring, Lillian said. Here, fantasy and reality diverged. Stars, though they were required to remain single, could have active sex lives as long as they were discreet. Some of this semi-liberal, confused attitude even crept into the movies that Hollywood produced. The same year that Lillian had her first abortion, Hollywood released *Ann Vickers*, an adaptation of the Sinclair Lewis novel. Irene Dunne played Ann, a social worker among doughboys heading off to World War I. Ann is torn between her commitment to social causes—women's rights, prison reform, and others—and her desire for love and a family. She falls for a frightened soldier who abandons her when she becomes pregnant. Ann travels to Havana for what the audience knows is an abortion, although the word is never mentioned. Later, when Ann falls in love with a married man, she bears a son to him at the cost of her reputation and her life's work. These were costs that Lillian and other women of the 1930s were not willing to pay.

Lillian's story contrasts in other ways to that of most American women of the 1930s. The Depression pushed some women out of higher-paying jobs that then went to men. Employers openly discriminated. Although women's overall employment remained fairly steady during the 1930s, they usually held low-paying clerical or service positions. A pamphlet released by the League of Women Voters in 1936 warned brides that many school boards throughout the country had "adopted a definite policy against the employment of married women teachers, and a similar attitude has been taken . . . toward employment of married women in any government position." But Lillian Miller was building a lucrative career. Female stars were necessary; they did work no man *could* do. Given every hope for success in this climate, twenty-year-old Lillian took abortion in stride, seeing that first pregnancy simply as "an obstacle that I was overcoming."

But Lillian soon lost her contract in spite of her careful secrecy about her marriage. She developed severe tics in her right eye and at the corners of her mouth, and she could not maintain appearances. "It was a financial disaster for me personally," Lillian recalled, "because my mother . . . had to return to Missouri. I could no longer support her." Lillian and George decided to marry publicly now, having no further reason to hide their commitment. His parents soon moved in with them.

Within a year, Lillian discovered she was pregnant again. Her pessary had failed again. This time it was George and his parents who chose what to do. "I was the youngest member, and they presumed that I would follow their advice. And as a matter of fact, I wasn't ready to have a child." Her agreement with her elders' choice notwithstanding, Lillian felt belittled by their preempting her choice.

Soon, however, Lillian recovered from both the second abortion and the facial tics and returned to work with a small independent studio, making westerns. Meanwhile, she had discovered that George was an alcoholic. She left him briefly and soon became involved with another man. At the same time, while she was working hard on a series of westerns, she was courted with renewed energy by George, who gradually drew her back into his bed. "So anyway," Lillian sighed, "I got pregnant and didn't know whether it was [by] my husband or the other man." So Lillian—faced with a third birth control failure—opted again for abortion. This third one was performed by a doctor, in his office, with little secrecy.

Afterward, Lillian went to New York to work in live theater. She intended to divorce George, but he followed her, promised to keep his meddling parents out of their lives, and eventually persuaded her to resume their marriage. "I fell for it," Lillian said. When her Broadway play closed, Lillian and George took a cruise together, and she got pregnant again. "This time," she said, "there was no reason not to have the child."

Lillian returned to California with George and eventually had two children. Lillian worked as George's collaborator on scripts. She received neither money nor recognition for her significant contributions to his success, because, she explained, "he argued that it would dissipate his importance—and that would have been quite true." Though Lillian had a cook, gardener, laundress, and nurse to run her big house and her family, she often stayed up until three or four in the morning working on George's material and entertained lavishly. "It was a very heavy schedule," she recalled. She did not resent the lack of acknowledgement for her collaborations, she remembers. "Isn't that incredible? I do resent it now, but back then I was just flattered as hell."

By the late 1940s, George had resumed his heavy drinking and had had several extramarital affairs, some of which he told Lillian about. What Lillian didn't know was that many of George's affairs were, and had always been, with men. "When he came home from this two-week thing I said, 'Who is she now?' and he said to me, 'What makes you think it was a woman?'"

The discovery of her husband's lifelong bisexuality sent Lillian into a deep depression. She checked into a sanitarium. Two weeks later, she went home to chaos. George had sold their house and soon began to threaten her with violence. She had to get a court order to get him out of their rented home.

"It is very hard to understand, I know, the kind of abuse . . . that I took, but women didn't expect to be equal in influence or anything else to men. I was happy to have someone so bright." Despite the exceptions and contrasts in her life, Lillian had always shared with other women of her time "the feeling that women measured their worth by their reflection in the man's eye." And George was "very intelligent. He was very comical. He was charming and he was handsome." Lillian's own gifts—her talent, her ability to earn a lavish income even in the Depression years, her own intelligence and beauty—none of these had been enough to convince her that she herself was worthwhile. Though she had been strong enough to make a career for herself, Lillian, like other women of her time, had no real language for describing the extent to which her life was controlled by others and their values. She had never been able to look inside and question the forces that shaped her life in other profound ways—her early marriage, her abortions, her inability to stand up to her in-laws, her repeated returns to a man who dominated and misused her. When her relationship with George finally ended, she rushed immediately into a second marriage and a fourth abortion.

From 1952 to 1962 Lillian tended house and raised children with Sam in upstate New York until the pleasures of suburbia soured and Lillian divorced again. The next year, 1963, Betty Friedan's *The Feminine Mystique* was published. It struck a responsive chord in Lillian, not because she had never worked outside the home but because she had. "All the years that I had worked," she explained, "there was no payoff for it. I was divorced and I was going to have to go to work again because my husband was refusing to pay alimony and I just wouldn't even fight for it." Lillian got a job in public relations and joined a feminist organization. "I was able to support myself, and I had freedom. It was the first time in my [adult] life that I hadn't been married. You are able to have a lot more fun if all you expect out of dating and sex is a relationship that's fun and pleasant and has no connection with your own financial security."

Asked about the years of quiet domesticity that she had relished, Lillian said: "Well you know, quite frankly, there is an awful lot to be enjoyed about what they call being a housewife or homemaker. I must admit I had a ball furnishing and finding antiques and being able to come in under the budget and being able to cook for forty people. There was a certain amount of satisfaction in that." Nevertheless, Lillian realized, the role of housewife earned no respect. "If I had it to do over again, I wouldn't," she concluded. "I would have pursued my own individual way."

Lillian might say the same thing about her first marriage, and even her film career. At the end of the interview, she grew reflective and said: "I'll tell you, in parting, that recently I looked at some old photographs and I saw one of myself at eighteen and I began to cry. And I tried to figure it out. It almost makes me cry now. I wasn't true to that person. I wasn't encouraged to be that person."

This, Lillian believes, is because "that person" was a girl. Not only did the conventions with which she grew up require her to be more docile than was her nature, they also denied her her first ambition. She never set out to be a Hollywood actress, she said. "No, I set out to make money so I could go to college and become a doctor." When she graduated from high school at fifteen, early in the Depression, she visited the dean at a large university to see whether she would be able to find a job to support herself through premed. But the dean, a woman, "said all the jobs were going to be given to the boys. There would be no opportunity for a girl and, being so young, she suggested I go back and make as much money as I could and come back in a couple of years." Then, after she was "discovered" through a job in radio, Lillian met and fell in love with George. She saw no hope of mixing love and medical school.

Had Lillian been true to herself, would she have gone to medical school? "Yes, of course I would," she said. "But I also would have offended many people. Do you know what I mean?" Lillian meant that she would have spoken up for herself, made her own decisions, taken none of the abuse she later took. She did not say how she would have felt about abortion. She did not speculate about other prices she might have paid instead of the ones she did pay. She had done what was expected of women of her time: She served the needs of others at the expense of her own. Although Lillian Miller's life had much more glamour than most women her age enjoyed, she brought to it the same insecurities and lack of self-definition most women her age suffered. When Lillian looks at the picture of herself at eighteen, she mourns the cost of what she—along with most women her age—denied herself and was denied by others.

Lillian sometimes sounds bitter today. She makes tart, unbidden comments to men in public places, reveling in the sassiness that old age permits her. Sometimes she goes beyond being sassy and at long last risks offending people. "I get my venom out," she said, and she related several incidents. One took place in a restaurant just after the Persian Gulf War broke out in January 1991. "The men were all watching the war at the bar. I passed them and said, 'Now I know why women live ten years longer than men.' They said, 'What?' And I said, 'So we can tend your goddamn graves!'"

A Matter of Time and Place

Ideas about morality are often defined by the company we keep. To the company Lillian Miller kept in the Hollywood of her day, illegal abortion was accepted as an open secret. But that attitude was not typical of the times or of the nation. Although abortion was practiced in most American communities throughout the first half of the twentieth century, it remained largely invisible. It was a furtive and hazardous act, and so most couples never considered it unless they were desperate. Instead, they accepted an unwanted pregnancy as their fate, meeting it with resignation, anguish or, eventually, joy.

Lillian had the support of her community for her career, though not for her marriage or pregnancy. In the world beyond Hollywood priorities were reversed. Few were likely to applaud women's ambitions or to give tacit approval for abortion. Yet, according to Dorothy O'Connor, a retired secretary we interviewed in Columbus, Ohio, women in the 1930s often were forced by their out-of-work husbands to end pregnancies they desperately wanted to keep.

Three of Dorothy's friends had had illegal abortions for just this reason, and they never spoke of them afterward, not even in their immediate families. Their silence, Dorothy said, "was not because of guilt but because of pain. They just could never talk about something so hard."

The women of the 1950s, even more than their mothers and sisters of the 1930s and '40s, still maintain a nearly impenetrable silence. The contrast to the openness of their counterparts in later decades is striking. In researching this book, we usually were gratified by the extraordinary candor with which people shared their stories and answered even the most probing questions in return for our guarantee of anonymity. We were therefore surprised when we found it so difficult to find firsthand stories of common experiences of the 1950s—house-wives who had chosen abortion and single women who had arranged a hasty marriage because of a pregnancy. One contact, whose mother had undergone two illegal abortions in the 1950s (one on the family's kitchen table), agreed to arrange an interview only to find her mother now feigned ignorance of the whole subject of illegal abortion.

Dr. Lore Reich Rubin, a psychoanalyst who started her practice in New York in 1958, told us how struck she had been by the number of her clients who had had abortions. "In the middle class, which is what my practice was involved with, I finally realized that almost every women that I had any contact with had had an abortion. . . . The quantity of it was so striking, when you got to know people intimately. I was amazed." Her recollections confirm the statistics of the time, but like obstetricians, social workers, and others who tried to help us, she was unable to lead us to women willing to talk about either abortions or hasty marriages during the 1950s. The silence might seem a natural response to feelings of guilt or shame aroused by having flouted the standards of society. Yet Dr. Rubin told us that her clients—women she treated at length in intensive analysis—had suffered no adverse reactions to their abortions. "I have only had two people in detailed treatment whose problems were precipitated by an abortion." In neither case, Rubin explained, was the abortion itself the root of the trouble; what caused the problem was the fact that these patients' mothers had forced the procedures upon them.

Some participants in a 1955 Planned Parenthood conference on abortion made similar observations. Dr. Theodore Lidz, professor of psychiatry at the Yale University School of Medicine, noted, "Although I have seen fairly serious psychiatric reactions on a very few occasions following an abortion, I have the impression that they are . . . certainly much rarer than severe emotional reactions to unwanted pregnancy, childbirth, and the responsibilities of mother-hood" (Calderone, 1958). Dr. Robert W. Laidlaw, chief of psychiatry at New York City's Roosevelt Hospital, had the same impression. He commented that "in the therapeutic field the guilt reactions—if such occur and I think they do rarely occur—come more from the type of antecedent psychiatric problem that the patient may present. In other words . . . it is not a new factor in the patient's psychiatric picture" (ibid).

Why, then, do the women of the 1950s refuse to talk about what so many of them were doing? Our best guess is that they may, like Dr. Rubin's patients, feel little personal guilt or shame, but that they still carry with them the memory of how shameful their actions would have seemed in their time and culture. If women in the 1950s could not admit to themselves or each other that their dream lives in dream houses were unfulfilling, how could they talk about illegal actions or out-of-wedlock pregnancies that, by the standards of the time, proved them unfeminine and unworthy? How could they risk their own children finding out, let alone their neighbors? The habit of secrecy is painful, and it dies hard. Those who did talk to us helped to explain how behaviors that were kept out of sight during the 1950s also dropped out of mind.

Daniel and Sidney Callahan

The Callahans (in this case we use their real names) are well-known as a couple who have agreed to disagree on the abortion issue. Sidney, a professor of psychology at Mercy College in Dobbs Ferry, New York, and the author of several books on parenting, abortion, and sexuality, was born in 1933. "I was a feminist from the time I was twelve," she says proudly. She had their seventh and last child in 1965 at the age of thirty-two, and her adamantly pro-life position makes her an enigma in her liberal, academic community. She is a petite, dark-haired woman, who is carefully groomed and has an erect posture and a high, clear forehead. Daniel, who was born in 1930, is a philosopher and director of the Hastings Center Institute of Society, Ethics, and the Life Sciences. A trim man with a slightly boyish face, he leaned back into the coach and spread an arm across its back. He told us that he reversed his initial pro-life position during the 1960s.

The Callahans listen attentively to one another. Their respectful disagreement on abortion policy has been widely aired in talks, articles, and books, but the question never surfaced during the decade from the mid-1950s to the mid-1960s when their own children were arriving at a rapid pace. For much of that time, they both pointed out, most people were still debating the issue of contraception. Abortion seemed unthinkable, although the statistics belie that claim. Though several of the Callahans' pregnancies were not exactly scheduled, neither were they entirely unplanned. In fact, Sidney reported that she and Daniel resolved their own ambivalence about contraceptive use only after the birth of the child they had decided would be their last. The couple thus welcomed each pregnancy, despite their circumstances. "We didn't have much money," Daniel said. "I was a graduate student and we lived in crummy places." Though a couple with an unplanned pregnancy in such circumstances today might say, "We just can't afford a family now," abortion never crossed the Callahans' minds. The mere suggestion of it, Sidney said, would have been "like saying, 'Maybe you should eat one of your children. . . . It would just not be something that would even be thought of."

Nonetheless, the resolution of the Callahans' own unplanned pregnancies both colors their views and enhances their ability to understand those who oppose them. Daniel explained, "I guess one of the things that has always made me soft as a pro-choice person is that I know from personal experience one can survive unplanned pregnancies. They are not the end of the world that some people think they are."

The Callahans had the advantage of truly wanting their children, however. "Sidney often joked that we would have liked to have had twelve children but she wanted to have a career," Daniel said. "Therefore, six would probably do." Moreover, large families were common in the 1950s. Friends of the Callahans had ten and twelve children. Finally, although Sidney and Daniel's children were born into poverty, the couple knew their future prospects were good. "I'm the only middle-class person I've known who's ever gone to a charity clinic in a hospital," Sidney reported with a laugh. But she knew at the time that she was not at the same dead end as the other women in the waiting room. "I had status and I had hopes. I wasn't really poor," she admitted.

When the Callahans identify the roots of their divergent views on abortion, their responses fall within rather traditional male and female territory. Daniel, who has left the Catholic religion of his youth, reached his pro-choice position through his work. He was affected, he said, by what he discovered as he traveled around the world researching his book *Abortion: Law, Choice and Morality*. Sidney converted from her family's halfhearted Protestantism to Catholicism, but as an advocate of both contraception and sterilization, she has shown herself to be a free thinker within the ranks. So she bases her views not on the church's dictate but on her own moral convictions and on her own reproductive experience, which has convinced her that the abortion of un-planned pregnancies, even those complicated by poverty, is not justifiable. She also believes the crib death of one of her children was a factor in her pro-life stance. She has noticed that many women in the pro-life movement have suffered a similar loss, "something that seemed to bring to their attention that the world is not a totally orderly, controlled world," she said. Indeed, Kristin Luker's book *Abortion and the Politics of Motherhood* indicates that pro-life activists tend to see much of life, including pregnancy, as rightfully outside the grasp of human control. On the other hand, Luker finds, pro-choice women believe that control of fertility is a human responsibility.

Just as Daniel admitted to soft spots in his pro-choice convictions, Sidney acknowledged a compassion for women who choose abortion. The feeling is rooted, she believes, in her own last pregnancy, the only one that she met with a sense of dread and remorse. Life was getting difficult with so many little children. Daniel helped when he was home, but he spent much of his time, even part of Christmas and Easter, in the library. Besides, she said with a laugh, she thought that at thirty-one she was too old to be pregnant. Ironically, she added, their youngest turned out to be the easiest to care for of any of their babies.

None of the now-grown Callahan children is pro-life, Sidney reported, nor is any of them a practicing Catholic. She believes that these young people are largely the product of their times and of the community in which they grew up. "I think it just goes with the fact that they were brought up in a very secular culture. . . . They were just upper-middle-class, liberal kids. They just thought like all the other upper-middle-class kids," Sidney said. She worries about them, she admitted, "but who listens to your mother?"

The Callahans have moved from the large home in which they raised their six surviving children to a two-bedroom apartment on the Hudson River. The hallways are filled with family photographs, framed awards, trophies, and in-vitations to graduations. The Callahans describe their young years with so many children as "busy" and "hard," but they are clearly proud and happy parents. Both wanted a family and a career, and they were able to balance their interests better and with more mutual respect than Lillian Miller could muster in her marriages. The Callahans enjoyed their nest when it was full and now relish the freedom of its emptiness.

Eva Schmidt

When Eva Schmidt became pregnant with her daughter in 1942 and her son in 1946 she never thought about abortion, although she and her husband had never wanted children. "Lord, no, [abortion] never entered my mind. Never gave it a thought. When I knew I was pregnant, that was it. I'm pregnant!" Although abortion was "unthinkable," Eva said, it was not unknown to her or to her small, working-class community along the Ohio River. In fact, both her experience and her town's show how abortion could be seen and not seen at the same time.

Eva's younger sister, Muriel, had two abortions. Her first pregnancy was the result of what is now called date rape. The rapist was a man Eva had introduced to Muriel in 1937. When Muriel, nineteen, discovered she was pregnant soon afterward, an older sister, Minnie, took her to the town's family doctor.

What went on in the office, I don't know," Eva said. "But this doctor, I've found out since, was performing abortions all the time." Many local women used this man's services. Some went to him for obstetrical care, others for abortions. And he was not the only abortionist. Eva remembered the town's midwife being arrested, but never jailed, when a local woman died after an illegal abortion. Yet Eva claimed she knew no one except her sister who had an abortion in her little town.

Muriel's second pregnancy came soon after she married in 1939. "I know she didn't want to get pregnant," Eva said. Muriel had to quit her job at a laundry because her morning sickness was almost constant. Then her husband was laid off. "They had a beautiful apartment, but they had to give it up and move into two dinky little rooms," Eva recalled. Muriel, then twenty-one, got pregnant again right after her first baby was born. "She didn't know anything about preventing. Neither did I," Eva said.

So Muriel had two children, and Eva had a four-month-old daughter herself in 1942 when she got a call from Muriel's husband. Her sister needed her, he said. Eva did not know what was wrong until she got there. "I think all she said to me was, 'I was pregnant and I went to see Dr. P.'" Eva knew what that meant: Muriel had had a second abortion. Now she was hemorrhaging badly. Eva's husband had been shipped overseas, so Eva settled in to take care of Muriel, Muriel's husband, and the three babies for the whole summer. Dr. P. came to see Muriel regularly. He must have been too afraid to put her in the hospital, Eva assumed. But the bleeding went on forever, and Eva just kept changing the sheets.

"All the neighbors kept asking, 'What's wrong with your sister?' I'd say, 'I really don't know.' But they knew. I'm hanging out sheets that I couldn't take all the stains out of. They could see that. But no one ever said anything to me," Eva recalled. That was the way such matters were handled in those days. Everyone knew abortion was happening but few talked out loud about it, least of all Eva. "I didn't want to hear any of that bunk." What she did detect despite her distaste for gossip was community scorn for Dr. P. Although the towns-people continued to seek his services for general family medicine, they con-demned his abortion practice as immoral. "I don't know why he did it," Eva said. Although many illegal abortionists were motivated by money, Eva is sure Muriel, at least, was never able to pay much. The women who had abortions— at least the married ones—were seldom blamed, she said. That was because not everyone had the emotional and intellectual resources or the future prospects the Callahans enjoyed. Eva does blame Muriel, however, especially for the second abortion, which Eva saw as an act of selfishness. Muriel was the baby of the family, Eva said, and their mother spoiled her. "I'm a Christian," Eva reported, "and I feel that if you don't want to get pregnant, then don't do things that make you pregnant." But in the next breath, Eva blamed Muriel's husband, not her, for the pregnancy, saying he never let his wife alone.

Eva remains opposed to abortion. A few years before our interview she had watched a slide show at church about what happens to babies during an abortion, and, she said, "I was just sick." She wondered how Muriel would react. "I wonder what she's thinking today when all this is coming out about how these babies die." Muriel and Eva had a falling out years ago. They have lost touch with each other, although they live in adjacent towns. "She'd kill me if she knew I told you about this," Eva said. She has never talked to Muriel about her abortions and she assumes she never will.

Molly Gelman

Molly Gelman is a retired teacher in her late sixties who lives in suburban Boston. She supported her husband through school after the war and then, like most women, quit working after the birth of their first child. "I wanted to continue working right after I had children," she said, "but I didn't because I was so worried it would make my husband feel like a failure. What kind of idiot was I! I was just plain stupid. But the prevailing mores affect one." Molly waited until long after she was ready to work but still went back to teaching while her three children were in grade school in the mid-1950s. "I was warned my husband would leave me and my children would become criminals," she said, laughing. She defied the patterns and predictions of her neighbors, though, and pursued her career.

Molly said she was not aware of housewives having abortions. "My single friends had abortions, especially during the war. You'd have a fling," she explained. "Sometimes you got pregnant. People had abortions. I never remember myself or my peers ever thinking of it as immoral. The people I knew were only affected by the physical danger." Though statistics indicate most illegal abortions were being sought by married women, Molly thinks single women, who were afraid of becoming social outcasts, were more prepared to brave the dangers inherent in abortion than married women. In her community, a notch or two upscale from Eva Schmidt's, another mouth to feed was less likely to cause a married woman to panic. "People thought . . . if you had an abortion you might die. If you were single maybe it was okay to risk dying because the stigma of an out-of-wedlock child was so awful. But if you were married you would rather have a baby than die. If you were married, a child was at most an inconvenience. We expected to be inconvenienced."

Molly was surprised to hear that some experts thought—perhaps inaccurately—that up to 90 percent of the estimated one million annual abortions during the 1950s were performed on married women. "I know a lot about unwanted pregnancies," she reflected, "but not about abortions. Maybe I just didn't know. I lived in a very typical suburban neighborhood, where the plan was to have babies."

Molly herself had two unplanned pregnancies. "I don't think I ever considered abortion," she said. "Not because it was abhorrent to me, but because it was not a thought that occurred." Instead, Molly continued to have children, giving birth to her third child and then being confronted with a dilemma about her fourth. That pregnancy was difficult, she remembered. "I was told to stay in bed. I did, for a week or so, and then I made a decision: 'If I lose the baby, fine.'" Molly disobeyed her doctor and lost the baby. "It wasn't fine. I grieved for it a long time. . . . My doctor said that it was just as well. It was nature's way of getting rid of anomalies. But my role in it significantly added to my emotional burden."

Molly lost her baby in 1957. That same year, a relative who was pregnant with her fifth child tried to induce abortion herself. "She didn't succeed," Molly said. "She had a premature baby that died at about six weeks old." That woman also grieved for her lost child, to the point of denying that she had ever tried to abort it. "She distorted the whole experience," said Molly. "To make [her version of it] true, she went on and had another baby. Then she could say, 'See, I really wanted five children.'"

Molly knew only one married woman who had had an abortion in those years. She thought for a while about asking this woman if she would interview with us, but then she decided she could not break the woman's own silence. "It was over forty years ago," Molly said. "[The abortion] was at her husband's urging. She was very resentful, but she did what he wanted. I don't think the marriage was ever the same. This woman is my close friend, and she has never brought it up in all those years. I think about it often when I see her."

Single and Pregnant

If popular opinion of the 1950s saw motherhood and housework as female destiny, then single women were a female anomaly. They did not seem to belong anywhere for very long. Being single was regarded as a temporary, unfortunate condition. Only about 25 percent of American women over fifteen had never married, a decrease from the 30 percent mark that had held steady for fifty years between 1890 and 1940. The ranks of single women were thinning, and so were their options.

After World War II the movies, like the magazines Betty Friedan researched, stopped treating women as multidimensional people and stopped offering complex role models. The Roz Russells and Kate Hepburns in search of challenge and independence gave way to Doris Day in search of a husband, willingly forgoing several careers in several films to catch and keep him. These 1950s movies seldom dealt with marriage itself, just with the quest for it. The few married women they portrayed were not agents in their own behalf but the power and nurturance behind their husbands' careers. There was no gender confusion, no conflicting attraction to the roles of both "real woman" and "newspaperman," only a single-minded determination to marry. Women were no longer offered the difficult balance—the chance to be Tess Harding Craig— but a choice between equally vacuous extremes: sugary Debbie Reynolds or sexy featherbrain Marilyn Monroe. For most, the choice was automatic. This is what was unnatural about the 1950s. It was a decade that denied half the population a vast range of human aspiration and experience. The message about sex was also clear, if rather tired: While healthy young men were tacitly allowed to fool around with "bad" girls, they married the kind who kept their virtue. The cult of domesticity and the double standard were as true a partnership as love and marriage.

Hollywood blessed this new flourishing of the old double standard. Toward the end of the decade, Doris Day starred in a series of popular comedies that prompted Groucho Marx to quip, "I knew Doris Day before she was a virgin." In *Pillow Talk* in 1957, Day plays Jan, a freckled, wholesome interior decorator of some accomplishment and perennial virginity. Opposite her, Rock Hudson is Brad Allen, the roguish but winsome wolf who lures dance hall girls to his bachelor pad, where his couch flips into a bed at the push of a button. In this comedy of mistaken identities, Brad wins Jan's affections by tricking her into thinking he is an innocent country boy just visiting New York from Texas. He is so respectful of her standards that she begins to wonder if he might be homosexual. Just as she is about to teach the sweet boy how to show some affection, the plot shifts; Jan sees through the scam, thereby saving her virtue and the audience's sympathy. This family fare teases but never violates the era's sexual norms. In the end Jan forgives Brad in a boys-will-be-boys spirit when he comes through with a marriage proposal, the reward of every single gal who kept herself pure for just such a payoff.

Although some of this public purity was pretense and hypocrisy, most women of the time apparently did strive to be the "good" sort, the kind who caught a husband. One study in 1960 indicated that 84 percent of men admitted to having sexual relations before marriage as opposed to only 41 percent of women. When Alfred Kinsey's *Sexual Behavior in the Human Female* made front-page news in 1953, one of its most startling findings was that nearly half of the nearly six thousand women that Kinsey had begun interviewing in 1938 had experienced sexual intercourse before marriage. Nonetheless, their behavior was conservative by today's standards. Almost half of the sexually active women Kinsey interviewed subsequently married their partners, usually within a year or two after sex was initiated.

Of the women in Kinsey's sample who avoided sexual intercourse while they were single, most (89 percent) cited moral considerations as a primary reason. Yet even these women were not entirely chaste. Kinsey found that 88 percent of his whole sample had engaged in premarital petting, and most had done so with at least a half-dozen partners. On the average of five to ten times per year, these women even used petting with a partner to reach orgasm.

Kinsey also found that about 18 percent of the sexually active women had become pregnant. Many, already or almost engaged, merely moved up the wedding date. Others hastily arranged "shotgun" weddings. In *Lover Come Back* (1961), Doris Day and Rock Hudson enact a plot similar to *Pillow Talk*. This time, both play advertising executives. She gets pregnant when the two unwittingly become intoxicated on cookies laced with rum. Afterward, they wake up in a Maryland motel, sharing one pair of pajamas. Their tryst is above reproach since their drunkenness is unintentional, but Hollywood makes doubly sure no one is offended by having them discover that they also got married in their stupor. Day's character has the marriage annulled because Hudson's is so disreputable. He, realizing he has fallen in love, mends his ways. As the movie ends, Day, about to give birth, finally remarries Hudson from her careening hospital gurney. They exchange their vows between her labor pains, heading through the double doors into the delivery room. In this and many similar plots of the time, the woman's virtue had the power not only to domesticate the man's sexual appetites but to change him from a dishonest, exploitative opportunist into a reputable breadwinner.

But marriage was not possible for all single women who became pregnant. Although there was little discussion of it, the United States did have 130,000 out-of-wedlock births annually in the early 1950s, about 4 percent of all births. Middle-class girls and young women commonly hid away in homes for unwed mothers, then gave away their babies for adoption. A few braved scorn and raised their children alone, and some families even pretended a daughter's child was really her mother's.

For other single women, neither marriage nor out-of-wedlock birth was an option. A hurried-up wedding meant both partners had to be willing and able to marry. If they were not, then giving birth, whether the woman raised the child or gave it up for adoption, meant facing an employer and perhaps family with shame or embarrassment. Pregnancy could cost a woman her job and humiliate her family. Some women were willing to risk their very lives in an illegal abortion to escape these consequences. In fact, Kinsey also found that 20 percent of the nearly six thousand women he interviewed had had abortions.

Whatever a single woman did about unplanned pregnancy during the 1950s, she made her decision in an atmosphere that handicapped her twice over. First, the pregnancy itself crippled her progress on the only path really open to her, her climb to the pedestal reserved for sexually virtuous wives and mothers. Even if she married, the hasty wedding and "premature" baby branded her with disgrace. If she aborted or gave up her child for adoption, she always carried a terrible secret even if she eventually attained the appearance of virtue. Second, the prevailing view of a woman's nature as fragile and childlike left her little confidence in her ability to act with integrity and autonomy. She was supposed to want motherhood above all, and she was also supposed to be taken care of and protected from difficult situations. If the man abandoned her she had only herself to blame, because she had lost the virtue that, according to romantic mythology, could convert the rogue into a hero, the frog into a prince.

It is not surprising, then, that many single women relied heavily on others, especially the man involved, in making decisions about an embarrassing, un-planned pregnancy. They worried about their reputations and the effect of their pregnancy on their relationships with family, friends, and employers. Their decisions were complicated by the fact that unless they could afford to go outside the country, abortion would take them outside the law and quite possibly into the hands of unscrupulous abortionists. Some feared the illegality and hazards enough to go ahead with pregnancies they did not want, while others risked the offices of unqualified butchers. Most estimates on abortions performed before *Roe v. Wade* agree that the majority (some claim up to 90 percent) were done on married women, but the figures are hopelessly unreliable. Certainly most legal, therapeutic, hospital-based abortions were performed on married women. But no one will ever count all the women, married and single, who self-aborted or underwent illegal procedures performed by amateurs in dirty kitchens or physicians in secret, sterile clinics.

Lois Duncan Harris

In 1956, Lois Duncan was a petite, pretty twenty-year-old who shared an apartment in Cleveland with a girlfriend. Lois worked at a good secretarial job in a large international engineering firm that had just chosen her as its candi-date in a citywide beauty contest. During that charity pageant she attracted the attention of a local mogul, Sy Harris, twenty-seven years her senior.

Sy dallied shadily and with great financial success in entertainment, sports, and organized crime. Lois, the ninth of twelve children in a poor Kentucky hill family, was dazzled by him. She had already moved far away from her origins— from a mother who had married at fourteen, from a drunken, womanizing father, and from sisters who had all become pregnant in high school. She was the pride of the family—the first to graduate from high school and the first to land a decent job. But she had never seen the likes of Sy or his world.

As soon as Lois started seeing Sy he took control of her life, acting as much like her father as her lover. He taught her about sex but not about contraception. He simply told her to go home afterward and douche as a precaution against pregnancy. His method didn't work.

Lois, at fifty-three, talked while sitting in the conference room of a Cleveland abortion clinic. She was there to help escort patients past anti-abortion demonstrators. Her short, graying hair was feathered around her delicate features and large brown eyes. Her voice, which can be strong with conviction, began to crack as she recalled her growing fear that she was pregnant. "I spent anxious moments running to the bathroom, you know, every time I felt a little bit of moisture between my legs," she said. But she never saw the spots of blood she so desperately hoped for. She was indeed pregnant.

Sy, who "was very much married, with children as old as I," reacted nonchalantly. "'Well, you know,' he said, 'there's no problem about that. You'll have to have an abortion.'" Lois paused for a moment in her recollection. More than thirty years after these events she was still overcome in the telling. "Abortion to me was a whispered word, and the whispered word meant knitting needles and coat hangers and dying," she went on, tears welling in her eyes. "But he said that I wasn't to worry about that because with all of his connections, he knew of a place in Youngstown where all the mob guys took their girlfriends." And so Lois comforted herself with the thought that anybody doing a procedure on mob girlfriends would certainly be careful.

As it turned out, Sy took Lois to a dirty, back-alley operation. She rode through the night in the front seat of a "gigantic black car" between Sy and his mobster buddy. Over the top of her head, they talked about "gambling and boxers and beer sales—men's talk," while she stared into the stream of oncoming headlights. Eventually, the car meandered down back streets in Youngstown to "an old deserted house. . . . They sat in the car, and I got out and walked in to this back part of the house. . . . What I remember in that room is a table. I remember a black man with real frizzy white hair, and he was small. And he put me on the table, and I looked up, and on the wall was an old calendar that had 1936 on it, and that's the year of my birth. I just concentrated on that calendar the whole time that I was in that room, and I don't know what happened to me."

Lois has tried to bring back the events of that night, but the trauma and its aftermath have blocked her memory. She thinks she was in her twelfth week of pregnancy and that she was given an injection, perhaps of saline. "I remember leaving and the doctor saying something like, 'You'll probably have some pain, but take some aspirin and you'll be all right.' " Her memory of the trip home is a blur.

"I remember . . . going into my apartment, and then I don't know how much time passed, but I went into labor," Lois said. The labor went on for hours, and her roommate became frightened. "Call your mother. Call a doctor," she begged. "And I would say, 'They'll put me in jail. I can't. . . . If you commit crime by having an abortion, how can you go to a doctor and say *Treat me?* He's gonna put you in jail and your name's gonna be in the paper and you'll lose your job.' So I convinced myself that I had to tough this out on my own. And I did . . . I just kept bleeding and bleeding and bleeding." Eventually Lois delivered the fetus in the bathroom, and the bleeding stopped. She went back to work.

But something had gone wrong. Lois lost weight, her complexion grew sallow, and a foul-smelling discharge seeped out of her. She had not been seeing Sy since the abortion; he had called but she put him off, angry that he had gotten her pregnant and then taken her to a place that could have killed her. Finally, her roommate, the only one who knew how sick Lois was, convinced her to see a doctor. Lois could not bring herself to tell the physician what had happened, but he diagnosed an infection and severe anemia. He ordered her to go to the hospital for a D&C (dilation and curettage) and blood transfusions. After, she recalled, the physician leaned over her bed with tears in his eyes. "'Why didn't you tell me?' he asked. And I said, 'I was afraid you'd put me in jail.' He was very sweet. He just said, 'I would never have done that; you needed care much before you came to me.' And he gave me this little lecture about birth control. He said, 'You've gotten pregnant once, and it's very easy to get pregnant again.' However, I never did." Lois paused in the interview and wept.

Sy had sent flowers after the abortion and begged Lois to come with him on fancy dates. Finally she gave in. A couple of years later he divorced his wife and married Lois. They tried to have a child together but never succeeded. "I'm not sure why. Probably something as simple as a blockage in the tubes from the severe infection," Lois speculated. Doctors suggested the problem might be Sy's age, but he refused to be tested. Lois even tried having secret affairs with younger men, hoping they might get her pregnant. Finally, in 1966 and '68, Lois and Sy adopted two daughters, Margot and Meredith, whom they came to adore.

Meanwhile, Lois had begun to change. She had undergone psychotherapy and discovered how much she had looked to Sy to replace the inadequate father she'd left behind in Kentucky. She also had become active in the National Organization for Women, which had awakened in her another kind of consciousness—a feminist awareness. Lois had met the 1950s standard for womanliness. She had been docile and childlike with her husband. But in the 1960s, when she finally began to grow up, the price of staying in that relationship seemed too high to keep paying. In 1970 she divorced Sy, who remained a wonderful father—more like an indulgent grandfather, Lois said.

Lois had never really considered going ahead with what turned out to be her only pregnancy. She had depended totally on Sy, and she knew he never wanted that baby. "All I did was wait for him to tell me what to do," she said. Although he later married her, "at that time I was just, you know, some cute little secretary. . . . I don't think he had any idea in the world then that he was going to end up marrying me."

Even if Sy had not arranged the abortion, Lois said she would have found a way to get one on her own. Few companies would let a pregnant, single woman keep her job in those days. Besides, she said, "I was my mother's hopes and dreams. . . . I would have just let her down tremendously if I would have gone back and said, 'Well Mom, here I am; my life's over, too, just like my sisters' lives.'" If Lois considered her own feelings in making her decision, she never mentioned them. She probably never thought about them. She had kept herself sensitive only to the needs of others.

Not long before the interview, Lois had begun to talk publicly about her abortion as part of her political commitment to abortion rights. "The feeling like I was outside the law and a criminal stayed with me for a long time," she said. It fell away in small pieces. She remembers seeing an edition of Ms. magazine in 1971 that contained a legislative petition calling for abortion rights, signed by fifty-three women who acknowledged their own abortions. "I remember picking up that magazine and looking at each one of those women's names. . . . It was a real breakthrough for me and for other women to come out and say they had had illegal abortions."

Lois never thought of her infertility as punishment, although others have suggested that possibility to her since she began to speak publicly about her experience. "I wasn't punished," Lois responded. "I was rewarded with two lovely daughters." Her daughters' convictions are also strong. Margot and Meredith too have marched for abortion rights, carrying signs that say "I'm adopted *and* pro-choice."

Dangerous Practices

Lois Harris probably did pay for her illegal abortion with her fertility. Many others had been paying that price and a higher one for years. A 1944 article by Maxine Davis in *Good Housekeeping* magazine estimated that abortions were the cause of 30 to 35 percent of all deaths associated with pregnancy. In an article about her own illegal abortion that was published in *Reader's Digest* in August 1941, Jane Ward quoted Morris Fishbein, editor of the *Journal of the American Medical Association*, who had said in 1941 that "twenty to forty percent of pregnancies terminate in abortion." Fishbein called for "serious consideration of this widespread sociological and economic problem." But for more than two decades, most of the medical profession ignored his call.

"Nice people pretend it doesn't happen," Ward wrote. "Yet every minute of the day some woman in the U.S. has an abortion. . . . Fifty thousand women a year become sterile as a result of illegal operations." Ward, a young mother of three whose husband had died when she was two months pregnant with her fourth child, had no income. "An abortion seemed imperative," she wrote. Ward went to "a medical pariah plying his trade in an upstairs office on a back street." For one hundred dollars he performed an excruciating, middle-of-the-night curettage, occasionally offering her a whiff of chloroform. He instructed her not to get in touch with him, or with any physician, if she experienced any aftereffects. When she developed severe abdominal pains she "suffered alone, pulled through."

Ward's advice to other women was clear in the title of her article, "Don't Have an Abortion." She cited moral opprobrium, the high medical risks of all illegal abortions—including self-induced ones—and the number of unnecessary procedures performed by opportunists on women who only thought they were pregnant when they were not. She quoted Dr. Frederick J. Taussig, whose research was sponsored by the National Committee on Maternal Health. He estimated that 9 percent of women undergoing illegal abortions became sterile and that the rate doubled for those having more than one.

Although the estimated number of abortions being performed in the 1940s and 1950s was close to one million a year, the public paid scant attention to the problem. Abortion was a whispered word, as Lois Harris noted. Movies, television, and radio never touched the subject, and until the late 1950s only one or two articles per year appeared in popular magazines. Those that did appear sometimes took a rather hysterical tone. In 1944, Maxine Davis wrote in *Good Housekeeping* that studies from Russia showed that even legal, therapeutic abortion could cause everything from malfunctioning endocrine glands to sterility and that the procedure commonly resulted in "depression, hysteria, neurasthenia, and loss of all desire for love. . . . " Davis claimed the reasons for abortion were gradually disappearing. "Factories [in the United States] are becoming less prudish about the presence of pregnant women," she wrote. But she failed to note that such broad-mindedness was prompted by economic necessity. The country was at war and was suffering a serious shortage of male labor. Employment for women had jumped from 27 percent of the work force in 1940 to 35 percent in 1944. Women had rushed past fallen barriers to don the workshirts and overalls of Rosie the Riveter, a popular media creation with a wide, triumphant smile and a blue bandanna in her dark hair.

But Rosie's babies were another matter. Half of the 6.5 million working women during the war were wives. And by the mid-1940s, these women contributed to a new baby boom—and an accompanying abortion boom. The federal government helped to build and operate almost three thousand child-care centers, but they were unpopular and inadequate. During the war, one social worker reported counting forty-five babies locked inside cars in a munitions plant parking lot in Los Angeles.

Gretta Palmer, writing for *Woman's Home Companion* in October 1943, did not find employers so tolerant of pregnancy among their women workers as Maxine Davis had claimed in her article. Palmer said many working wives in war jobs ended their pregnancies in order to stay at work. Many already had children farmed out to baby-sitters and wanted no more. Others "bootlegged" their pregnancies, hiding their bulging bellies in order to keep their jobs. Palmer reported that, because of absenteeism and the high cost of maternity benefits, "half the war factories discharge women as soon as their pregnancy is reported." Palmer interviewed women in factories across the country and found them pitching in to help one another when pregnancy occurred, just as they were pitching in to help with the war effort.

"A friend of mine," said one of Palmer's sources, "managed to stick it out through the sixth month without getting reported. The matrons are good sports—they pretend not to see. We all help cover up the pregnant woman. We know she needs the money." But the women also helped one another get abortions, according to Palmer. Though Palmer referred to "the universal moral opposition to abortion," it was solidarity, not judgment, that prevailed among the women she interviewed. One aircraft worker in Buffalo reported, "There are only three subjects we discuss in the women's rest room: 'my operation'; how to keep from getting pregnant if you aren't; how to get rid of the baby if you are."

Another young woman in Rochester had no trouble gathering a list of nine illegal abortionists from her co-workers. Palmer cited an estimate by Dr. Fishbein, the *Journal of the American Medical Association* editor, that "the number of abortions has increased 20 to 40 percent during the war."

One midwife in the Midwest told Palmer she had done forty-five abortions the previous Saturday. "The girls like Saturday because that gives them the weekend to rest," she said. Saturday abortions led to Monday absences, since most women needed a minimum of three days to recover from the procedures, which were more complicated than the simple suction method used in modern abortions. Thus, in the factories, "three-day absence" became a euphemism for illegal abortion.

The whispers about abortion grew louder in the middle and late 1950s. Magazines and newspapers began to carry stories about abortion policies and ethics, about other countries' policies, and about American abortion laws and their strikingly inconsistent applications. Although abortion ran counter to every strict American value of this period in which having babies was women's primary occupation, people began to notice that married women remained the major source of demand for the procedure. Those with means could usually obtain either legal, therapeutic abortions or safe, illegal ones, or abortions in other countries. Those without means, who tended not to live within the neat, tight circle of the American dream, were at greatest risk, hazarding the back streets, possible infection, or death. Very few of them were ever granted therapeutic abortions in hospitals; those who were sometimes had to agree to sterilization as well. This, according to a participant in the 1955 Planned Parenthood conference on abortion, was known as a "package deal" (Calderone, 1958). Its purpose ranged from punitive to racist. Many women who were granted legal hospital abortions on psychiatric grounds—a practice that grew in the 1950s—were convinced or forced to accept sterilization to ensure that they would not come back with the same request a few months later. Others were sterilized as part of a larger pattern that affected poor women of color throughout the country—an effort to control the fertility and "promiscuity" of people who were regarded by the white establishment as overly and irresponsibly sexual and fecund.

Kinsey reported to the 1955 Planned Parenthood Conference on abortion that he found the incidence of abortion in the black community was considerably lower than among the white population (ibid). He speculated that the difference was partly a "matter of sociology," because a child born prior to marriage was "not the social disgrace among the socially lower-level Negroes that it is among college girls." He added, however, that the lower incidence among blacks held true even if the sample was adjusted for comparable age, education, and marital status.

But many poor women, black and white, would never be counted because they had learned how to self-induce abortions and keep quiet about it. They had been doing it for generations. Dr. Hilla Sheriff of the State Board of Health in South Carolina told the 1955 Planned Parenthood conference about a study she had done of contraceptive practices in her state. "I was very much impressed with a white patient I saw," she recalled. "She had had I don't know how many pregnancies—maybe a dozen. I was young then. I was showing her from a little chart how she was made inside."

She told the doctor: "Child, I know more about how I'm made inside than you do. Three or four times a year I just take a coat hanger and end the whole thing!"

Most women were too afraid or ashamed for such bragging. Sheriff did not know how many of her patients had perfected such techniques without telling her. Stories about herbalists and midwives, about shots that would bring on a late period, and about women taking the herb pennyroyal to abort were common in the South and elsewhere, but they were often told in whispers.

Inside the white establishment, the number of abortions performed on "respectable" wives and mothers was alarming. Despite the return of prosperity and the imposition of strictly traditional female roles, those numbers had not declined since the abortion epidemic of the 1940s. Estimates rose past one million abortions a year, even at the height of the baby boom. The numbers gave the lie to a central myth about abortion, that it was the last resort of a low class of single women.

In most states abortion had long been legal only to save the life of the pregnant woman; in three states and the District of Columbia it could also be performed to save her health. But doctors and hospital review boards interpreted each states' laws in any number of ways. For some, "life" also meant quality of life; "health" included mental health. Others adhered to the letter of the law, avoiding any risk of investigation or censure.

An article by Morton Southeimer in *Woman's Home Companion* in October 1955 vividly illustrated this legal haphazardness. The article began with short profiles of four pregnant women who wanted legal, therapeutic abortions: a young married woman who was likely to give birth to a physically deformed child; a menopausal grandmother with a heart condition; an emotionally disturbed wife who threatened suicide; and a thirteen-year-old rape victim. The grandmother and the suicidal woman were granted abortions; the other two were not. "But," the article commented, "in other cases with exactly the same circumstances, sometimes in the same cities, the decisions have been just the opposite."

In 1953, when Mary Steichen Calderone, medical director of the Planned Parenthood Federation of America, began preparing for the conference of medical practitioners and policy-makers that met in 1955, she invited participants to address all aspects of abortion, including the overwhelming inconsistencies. "The plan was made in absolute secrecy for fear of a hostile press," according to *American Women in the 1950s: Mothers and More*, by Eugenia Kaledin. "Calderone knew that sex education, like fluoridation and day care, was often considered a Communist plot to undermine American health." Calderone and Planned Parenthood published the conference proceedings in 1958 as *Abortion in the United States: A Conference Sponsored by the Planned Parenthood Federation of America, Inc. at Arden House and the New York Academy of Medicine*. "Medical journals," according to *American Women in the 1950s*, were uneasy "about even reviewing the book."

Most of the conference participants were East Coast physicians and public health experts who specialized in women's health—people who may have been more liberal than their counterparts elsewhere in the medical community. The conference was remarkable not only for being held at a time when public opinion was so easily outraged, but also for its odd combination of paternalistic language and enlightened insight into the realities of women's lives.

Though several countries, including Sweden, Denmark, Finland, Austria, Japan, and Cuba, permitted abortion for quality of life as well as medical reasons, the United States did not generally recognize financial hardship, number of other children, physical or emotional exhaustion, marital instability, the possibility of a deformed child, or even rape and incest as legitimate grounds for abortion. Nevertheless, the rising number of therapeutic abortions granted for "psychiatric" reasons in the 1950s indicated an increasing latitude in the medical community's response to injustices and inconsistencies. As Dr. Alan Guttmacher, chairman of the Planned Parenthood conference session on illegal abortion, said in his opening remarks, "abortions are being recommended by some psychiatrists for a variety of situations that very closely match the indications written into the Scandinavian laws."

Psychiatrist Robert W. Laidlaw of New York City's Roosevelt Hospital, who was also attending the Planned Parenthood conference, posited the case of a hypothetical patient, an overworked, low-income wife and mother confronting her fifth pregnancy with feelings of exhaustion, depression, and morbid dread. Laidlaw said: "Our patients do not live in a vacuum. We have to consider them in their own particular personal environment. . . . Therefore, we are thinking as psychiatrists, 'What will be the effect upon my patient's physical and emotional well-being when she is exposed to this additional stress, since at this time the patient is at the very limit of her endurance?' "

Most of the participants at the conference clearly favored the liberalization of abortion laws, but not all arrived at this position through the kind of compassion Dr. Laidlaw demonstrated. In the case of Dr. Iago Galdston of the New York Academy of Medicine, an argument for liberalization was a direct outgrowth of his extremely conservative views of women. "A woman," he declared to the session on psychiatric aspects of abortion, "is a uterus surrounded by a supporting organism and a directing personality." Because he felt that the "uterus is the main rationale of the *biological female*" and because the feminine drive toward motherhood is so strong, Galdston concluded that "if and when a so-called adult woman, a responsible female, seeks an abortion, unless the warrant for it is overwhelming—as say in the case of rape or incest—we are in effect confronted both with a sick person and a sick situation." Abortion might be the best treatment for this sickness, Galdston reasoned, it if would help to mend the patient's sexuality as well as her relationships with males and her family.

However they viewed women, the conference participants agreed that, unless laws and conditions changed, "the difference between an illegal and a therapeutic abortion [would continue to be] three hundred dollars and knowing the right person!" This, they concurred, was deeply unjust.

During the 1950s, the number of abortions performed in hospitals had risen quickly but quietly across the country. Dr. Thomas E. Allen, who began practice at Pittsburgh's Magee-Womens Hospital in 1948, told us in an interview that for years hospitals had performed abortions on mostly married, middle-class patients who suffered, in most cases, from acute renal or severe cardiovascular diseases. In some hospitals, exposure to rubella measles, the only widely recognized threat to fetal health at the time, was considered sufficient reason to abort. Even severe vomiting could sometimes justify ending a pregnancy. But social or psychological justifications were never considered, Allen said, although doctors were certainly aware that some women were desperate to end their pregnancies. While the doctors themselves were helpless in the face of such desperation, they treated the aftermath of botched illegal abortions every day. Eight to ten beds in Magee's "septic ward" were regularly occupied by patients—many of them indigent—with severe pelvic infections resulting from illegal abortions.

During the 1950s, when psychiatrists urged that justifications for therapeutic abortion be broadened to include threats to women's mental as well as physical health, Magee-Womens Hospital, like maternity hospitals in many urban areas, set up an Abortion and Sterilization Committee of doctors to consider abortion requests. According to Allen, the hospital wanted to protect physicians from prosecution under Pennsylvania's nineteenth century statute that made performance of abortion a felony. The committee, adopting standards applied in a number of other states, began to require any woman who requested an abortion for reasons of mental health to consult with two psychiatrists. Their fees, along with the cost of surgery and a hospital stay, all boosted the cost of an abortion. "Threats to mental health" were broadly construed, and the number of so-called legal abortions grew.

Nonetheless, the new bureaucratic procedure was cumbersome, expensive, and generally available to only the metropolitan well-to-do, who had the additional option of going abroad. Havana, where "Ann Vickers" had gone in the 1930s movie, had long offered safe abortions to wealthy Americans from the East Coast, but that avenue was closed after the 1959 Cuban revolution. The removal of that option, combined with a crackdown on American physicians performing illegal and surreptitious abortions, left many women in the hands of untrained amateurs. As a result, the mortality rate from illegal abortions soared until, in 1962, over half the maternal deaths in New York City resulted from criminal abortions. But Japan, which had passed permissive abortion legislation in 1948, and the Scandinavian countries were beginning to provide opportunities for legal abortions.

Selma Pentes

Selma Pentes, twenty-three years old and about ten weeks pregnant, boarded a plane in San Francisco for Tokyo in the late summer of 1962. A graduate student in art history, she already had arranged to spend a year at a Japanese university when she found she had conceived during a brief liaison with a fellow student. There had been little agony over the decision to abort. Selma and the young man involved had no serious intentions, and they agreed abortion was their best course. But Selma cried on the plane, afraid of what lay ahead and sad about destroying the developing life inside her.

The daughter of immigrant Jews from Eastern Europe, Selma had grown up on the edge of poverty in a large East Coast city. Her father was a scrap-metal dealer who sexually abused his daughter; her mother was an oblivious, self-centered beauty. But in eighth grade, Selma explained, she was plucked from her neighborhood grammar school to attend the city's special high school for gifted girls. She met intellectual and artistic challenges there, along with brilliant and accomplished women who became her role models. She praised the school for opening doors to girls like herself. Without its guidance, she said emphatically, she might never have stepped beyond the limited possibilities defined for women by her family and her times.

Selma recalled her abortion experience more than twenty-five years after it happened. She sat cross-legged on the floor of her Michigan apartment, surrounded by the Japanese art she collected and the silk screens she made and sold throughout the country. She said she had never talked so fully about her trip to Japan. She clutched a pair of earrings that one of her sons had given her, talismans in case long-untouched emotions flooded forth. Her tale emerged as an odd mixture of precise detail, still vivid to her artist's eye, and memory gaps created by the strange language and culture she had encountered while in an anxious and vulnerable state.

It was hot and humid when Selma landed in Tokyo. She remembered people in the streets wearing only what appeared to her to be their underwear. She recalled a hotel with long, red carpets. Selma had with her the name of an obstetrician/gynecologist given to her by a faculty member in California. She found the doctor at a hospital in Tokyo. He spoke little English, and communication was difficult. He had trained for a short time in the United States and liked Americans, he told her as he filched a few of her Marlboros. He indicated, however, that he could not perform the operation in the hospital itself. Selma was frightened, but she was also ignorant about Japanese laws and customs regarding foreigners, so she accepted his word and put herself at his mercy. He was sympathetic, he said, and he promised to call her. She walked back to her hotel feeling frantic and isolated. On the hot Tokyo streets, vendors peddled live turtles and crabs that scuttled across the sidewalks and steps.

A few hours later, the doctor called and came to her hotel room. Selma gave him all her Marlboros and pinned her hopes on what he told her. He could get in trouble for helping her, he said, but he would perform the surgery at his clinic in his country home for one hundred American dollars. She handed over the money immediately, although it nearly wiped her out. The next day, she remembered, she put on her favorite Jonathan Logan bandana-print sundress and got into a cab with the doctor.

"We were sitting in the cab and he tried to kiss me," Selma recalled. "He kept talking about how unlike other Americans I was because I was interested in his soul. . . . He thought all Americans had super gobs of money. . . . I fended him off by kind of making light of it." Although Selma's faith in the doctor wavered, she was afraid to make him angry. At his country home, they were joined by his wife, who acted as a nurse. She took Selma to a small room with a bed and gave her a cotton kimono and an injection of anesthetic. Like Lois Harris, Selma, too, concentrated on a wall calendar. "It had a Japanese landscape of some kind. I focused on that. That's all that I remember at that point. When I woke up, I was in a different room. . . . The wife, who spoke not a word of English, was a very sweet person. I don't exactly know why, but I sensed this was hard for her. . . . I remember the radio being on. . . . It was American music, which struck me as not funny but tacky somehow, that there was this attempt to be Western," Selma remembered. "I cried and I cried and I cried. I was not relieved in any way."

The wife/nurse came in with a cold, yellow watermelon on that hot night. Selma asked the doctor if the fetus had been a male or a female, but he said he could not tell. He refused to show it to her when she asked. When she wanted to know what happened to the remains, he told her that the "offal" was collected and buried in a kind of potter's field for unborn souls. "He said that once a year the doctors who performed these abortions were obliged to go to a ceremony. I think it is Shinto or Buddhist." At a ceremony, the doctors prayed for the aborted souls. Selma asked him to mark her baby's grave and say a special prayer for her.

"So I've thought of this little soul . . . buried in Japan. . . . I never felt relieved about having done that. I wouldn't do it today," said Selma, who still marked the anniversary of her abortion with a little thought and prayer.

Now married and the mother of two grown sons, Selma believes the baby she aborted would have been her daughter. Twenty years after the abortion, while teaching at a small college, she befriended a talented art student who was the age her aborted child would have been. The young woman confided to Selma that she felt like a child in search of her true mother. She had been adopted by a woman who had been kind and attentive but who did not share or understand her daughter's artistic inclinations. The girl had recently tracked down her natural mother in Illinois, but she had been disappointed to find that the woman was more "a flake" than the fulfillment of the girl's fantasies. Selma became the young painter's mentor and confidante and has remained close to her over the years. "I found it interesting not only that she should come into my life . . . but that she should have shared her story with me," Selma said. She felt she had supplied some of the nurturing the young woman had failed to find from her own mothers.

Our society does not offer women a chance to grieve the loss of a pregnancy, Selma contended. She felt she mourned an abortion that was never acknowledged as a loss. She argued that we need a ritual of penance and grieving like the one the Japanese doctor described to her. "You never get over such a thing, in my opinion, no matter what the reason is. . . . There is something very wrong with that—the way we do not let people grieve."

The Loosening of Controls

Sometime during the middle of the 1950s, the pendulum that had come to a stop in the cult of domesticity began to move again. Women had been returning to work all along. Many waited until the children were grown or took part-time jobs while they were in school. Most of the new working women were married and over thirty-five. Few pursued professions or saw their jobs as much more than a means to a paycheck. Post-war growth had begun to slow, and the nation headed toward the 1958 recession. With men's income less and less able to meet rising expenses, the values that kept women at home began to wobble. Women's income was necessary for many families to sustain the middle-class lifestyle that men alone had supposedly supported since the war. If these wives hadn't worked, the standard of living in suburbia would have slipped.

Discussion of careers for women crept slowly back into the public forum. In 1956, Sloan Wilson, author of the best-selling novel *The Man in the Gray Flannel Suit*, took a patronizing stand against women donning similar work garb. Writing in the *New York Times*, he claimed that women's lives were much more enriched when they wore a housedress. "I know plenty of women who, as the wives of successful men, learn more about investments, accounting, and upper-bracket public relations than 99 percent of the women in the offices. There's happiness and money in marriage, girls!" Two weeks later, Bernice Fitz-Gibbon, the head of her own advertising agency and the 1955 Woman of the Year in Business, responded. Wilson was spineless, Fitz-Gibbon said. He'd even admitted "most women *could* have careers: women without children, women with grown children, spinsters, women whose families needed the money to stay together, women who had extraordinary abilities which should not be kept from the world." Wilson had worried about the effect on the family if mothers of young children left the nest. Fitz-Gibbon, who had worked while she raised two children, retorted, "Well, I say it's young women with small children who definitely *should* have careers." She went on to make a claim—far ahead of her time—that a career could actually make a woman a better wife and mother. Hers was a small, prescient voice, but it was too little and too late for those, like Adrienne Rich, who had seen no alternative to full-time domesticity. A couple of years later, however, the *New York Times* was carrying stories about experts who endorsed work for women. A significant gap between the popular culture's view of the idealized housewife and the reality of the working wife was beginning to close. The 1960 census confirmed the trend, reporting that more than one-third of women of working age were employed.

As usual, the economic shift was accompanied by a change in attitude— not only about working women but also about sexuality and reproduction. In our interviews, the Callahans, Eva Schmidt, Molly Gelman, and others remembered contraception, not abortion, as the great reproductive controversy of the 1940s and 1950s. As late as 1968, 60 percent of the states had laws restricting the dispersal and use of contraceptives. Frequently, these restrictions denied birth control distribution to the young or unmarried. Throughout the century, however, the notion that the sex act could be separated from pregnancy had gradually infiltrated the American consciousness. Molly Gelman's generation had believed: "If you were married, a child was at most an inconvenience. We expected to be inconvenienced." But younger couples no longer agreed. Planned parenthood—the notion as well as the federation—began to grow. And once contraception was accepted, questions about abortion inevitably arose. A small minority began to argue that an unwanted pregnancy was too high a price to pay for a mistake in judgment or a mishap of nature or technology.

Peace and affluence had increased the measure of control Americans expected to have over their destinies. The American dream of a good salary, shorter work week, greener lawn, shinier kitchen floor, and pampered children had come within the grasp of the masses. Yankee ingenuity and capitalist investment were building a technology that could conquer nature, and just about everyone was sharing in the profit. The appearance of technology in the bedroom, as a means to control natural reproductive processes, was no longer shocking or foreign. Anthropologist Margaret Mead pointed out in *Male and Female: A Study of the Sexes in a Changing World* that modern society had come to think of children as expensive luxuries. She observed that the tragic fairy tale of the king and queen who could not have children had been replaced by jokes about contraceptive failures. By the 1960s, some demographers had even begun to warn the world about overpopulation by the early 1960s. Books like Paul Ehrlich's *The Population Bomb* (1968) popularized the notion that having more than two children was recklessly irresponsible.

Meanwhile, Dr. Benjamin Spock's *Baby and Child Care*, first published in 1945, promoted a more indulgent and permissive attitude toward the rearing of children. By the middle of the 1950s it had become America's bible of childrearing. Spock both reflected and promoted the idea of children as the precious center of their parents' loving attention. As America's affluence allowed hopes and aspirations to grow, children began to be given an enormous investment of time and money. Suburban mothers chauffeured their children to Little League games, dancing lessons, Scout meetings, and slumber parties. Each child had a savings account for college before he or she started grade school. The birth of a child became too major a commitment to be left to chance. Middle-class America began to accept birth control—natural or artificial—as a personal and social responsibility and necessity.

Such acceptance, however, planted the seed of discontent. The uncoupling of sex from reproduction and female biology from female destiny had always been at the heart of the feminist movement. But this acceptance had even larger implications, which the pampered children of the 1950s were quick to grasp. The very control of nature allowed by contraception—and by extension abortion—could lead to a new freedom of behavior for women and men. As the ties that had connected sexual morality to a fear of pregnancy began to loosen, so did the carefully protected and promoted values of 1950s America.

The parents of the 1950s, who had suffered the travails of war and economic depression, had worked hard and passionately to gain control over the fearsome unknowns of life and to provide for their children the material luxuries they themselves had lacked. They had worked to give their baby-boom offspring safety and security. What they failed to see was the blandness of the comfortable world they had created. Powerful and creative forces lay outside that controlled world, carefully held in check by its values. The House Committee on Un-American Activities (HUAC) and the McCarthy hearings in the Senate patrolled deviants among artistic and political minds. But Senator Joseph McCarthy and his followers were about to meet their comeuppance. The Civil Rights Movement was beginning to stir against the conventions that told blacks where they could work, live, eat, sleep, and go to the bathroom. The popular media, which had tried to fence out any divergence from the sexual norms, were beginning to loosen their standards.

Meanwhile, the children of the post-war baby boom were not inhibited by the fears that their parents had forged during difficult decades. Communism proved too abstract and far away to threaten them directly. The rigid conformity and double standard of the 1950s restricted their curiosity and, for some, their self-indulgence. The security blanket had been wrapped too tightly. They took a peek outside suburbia and were intrigued by the force of what lay beyond. They wanted to raise questions and take risks. They wanted to act out, and sex offered them a stage. When Elvis Presley performed his pelvic gyrations on "The Ed Sullivan Show" in 1956, American parents knew that he was also thumbing his nose. They began to suspect what was coming.

In 1960 about 224,000 babies were born out of wedlock, a 72 percent increase in a decade. Most of these babies were still being given up for adoption, but many other unplanned pregnancies were ending in abortion. In 1963 the Planned Parenthood Federation of America again estimated that 1.2 million abortions—or one to every four births—were being performed annually in America.

Young women growing up in the 1950s saw something inconsistent in their mothers' world. "It was hard to reconcile the self-denying 'essence' of woman's nature with the cultural atmosphere created by a consumption-centered economy," Barbara Ehrenreich and Deirdre English write in *For Her Own Good: 150 Years of the Experts' Advice to Women*. In a society that valued individualism and exhorted everyone to search for personal gratification, "one-half the population seemed to be committed, by their very anatomy, to a life of renunciation and self-denial." Since the 1930s, the psychoanalytic theory that females had an inherent need for self-denial had found mounting acceptance. By the 1950s, Ehrenreich and English write, belief in the Freudian notion of female masochism was almost undisputed. But not for long. It is not surprising, really, that the young women of the 1960s threw off this too-tight definition of womanhood along with the uplift bras and binding girdles that had been pinching bodies into an unnatural hour glass shape. The tight control was about to snap.

. . . TO THE OTHER

The 1960s and Early 1970s

Coitus can scarcely be said to take place in a vacuum; although of itself it appears a biological and physical activity, it is set so deeply within the larger context of human affairs that it serves as a charged microcosm of the variety of attitudes and values to which culture subscribes. Among other things, it may serve as a model of sexual politics on an individual or personal plane.

Kate Millet, *Sexual Politics* (1970)

I read *Anna Karenina* when I was sixteen. I didn't hear of Grace Slick until I was twenty. Somewhere between the two of them, my life and the life of my generation lies—with our expectations, beliefs, and behavior shaped by the nineteenth century values of our parents, our sense of defensive necessities shaped by the clash of romanticism and vulgarity in the fifties, and our adult life (what there has been of it) lived out in the egalitarian antiromanticism of the sixties, when every pattern of existence that I had struggled to adapt to, promptly became obsolete and was replaced by its near opposite.

Ingrid Bengis, *Combat in the Erogenous Zone* (1972)

Introduction

During the 1960s, abortion went from being barely mentionable to the hot topic of the new decade. While the issue itself sizzled with controversy, it also borrowed some heat from the general friction between men and women. Attitudes were shifting dramatically. A new generation was growing up which had radically different expectations about sex and sexuality. Domestic bliss had soured. Women began to resist the idea that they should be totally fulfilled by family life. The strength of their reactions moved the pendulum of many lives far away from the post-war extreme—the cult of domesticity—toward a new one in the other direction.

Ingrid Bengis, born in 1944 near the end of World War II, was rich in experience by the time she published *Combat in the Erogenous Zone* at the age of twenty-eight. She had traveled the world, driven a taxi, waited tables, written for a newspaper, slept with many men, and flirted with lesbianism. She had felt little of the societal pressure that, less than a generation earlier, had driven Adrienne Rich to betray her dreams and settle into traditional family life. Bengis had followed a highly individualized course in her young life. Still, something profoundly important was missing: She longed for emotional connection and commitment. At the same time, she feared that such needs might fetter her freedom. She felt so pulled by the ideological currents of her time that she longed to reconnect with genuine feelings that were "not ruled by social decree."

Social values had changed radically during Bengis's youth. Her generation had been brought up to believe that women love and men screw; that men have affairs and women don't; that men want to marry virgins; that if, like Anna Karenina, she let her passions run away with her, she would wind up, as Anna did, dead on the railroad tracks.

By the time Bengis was old enough to apply these standards, however, they had turned inside out. In the 1960s, sex among the young broke free of traditional moral entanglements. Women became liberated. Some radicals proclaimed monogamy and even romantic love obsolete. Larger concerns loomed. Social justice was supposedly more important than personal intimacy. Bengis had lived by some of these radical notions, even as a part of her resisted them. "When Grace Slick said, 'People are getting killed, so who cares if John gets Mary in the end,' I wanted to agree with her, even though basically I knew that no matter how important deaths all over the world were, lives and loves were not less important," Bengis wrote in *Combat in the Erogenous Zone*.

The youth of the 1960s resoundingly rejected the notion that sexual promiscuity was bad. They exclaimed: "If it feels good, do it," "Make love, not war," "All you need is love." The "love" they talked about was large and encompassing, not exclusive. Above all, it allowed people to move freely in and out of sexual relationships. No one "owned" anyone else. Sex was good, and brief liaisons were healthy. Multiple orgasms and fellatio became permissible—if not always comfortable—topics in mixed company. The members of this generation set out to reclaim the importance of human connection, which they thought their parents had suffocated inside the suburban split-levels and corporate boardrooms. But Bengis found herself unprepared for the consequences of so much freedom and with it the pain of ending relationship after relationship. Making sexual contact had proven much easier than making emotional connections. Rejection and loss still hurt.

After a decade of "liberated" sex, Bengis felt jaded. She knew she could never adopt her mother's life, devoted to buy-and-exchange trips to department stores and neurosis. Bengis's mother had been so insecure that she often called her husband five times a day to ask what she should prepare for dinner. No woman who had developed an independent focus in her life, as Bengis had, could willingly turn all her best talents to domestic interests alone. Bengis stubbornly held on to the hope that she could have everything—love, commitment, children, and her work. But she could not find a man willing and capable of trying it with her, and, worse, she could not find female role models to assure her it was possible. Her heroines were women writers who lived in open revolt against conventions—George Eliot, Virginia Woolf, Doris Lessing, Simone de Beauvoir, and Sylvia Plath. But not one of them had succeeded in merging marriage *and* children *and* work.

The New Woman heroines that Betty Friedan found in the women's magazines of the 1930s and 1940s had asked questions similar to Bengis's. So had Kate Hepburn and Rosalind Russell's characters when they had clashed and bantered with men over whether a woman might marry and still be true to herself. Now the tense, lively discussion about women's conflicting roles, which had fallen silent during the 1950s, reentered American life with a thunderclap. In 1963, Betty Friedan's *Feminine Mystique* blew the cover off what she called "the problem that has no name." Housewives who had been maneuvered into strictly traditional roles felt their very souls had been bound like the feet of ancient Chinese women, and they blamed men for the bindings, the pain, and the distortion. They were not wholly wrong, since, as Friedan had discovered, men had done so much to reshape the post-war feminine image until it fit inside a new, much narrower sphere. Now these women, who had been taught to pursue nothing more zealously than a husband, reacted with passionate relief and anger to the news that they were not alone in their unhappiness at having caught him.

Friedan reintroduced the old ideals of feminism, molded anew to the modern world. She called on women to escape what she called their "comfortable concentration camp" and urged them to return to the marketplace, to indulge new professional ambitions, and to demand equality with men. Although Friedan herself foresaw the need for women to find balance in their lives, many of her followers heard only a call for women to aspire to success as it had been defined in traditionally male domains. Friedan rejuvenated the feminist movement in a world already abuzz with social change. The carefully constructed walls that had kept men separate from women, blacks from whites, and capitalists from communists were beginning to crumble. *The Feminine Mystique* came out the same year that 250,000 people marched on Washington, demanding action on civil rights and cheering to Dr. Martin Luther King's "I have a dream . . . " speech. Those outside the tight circle of middle-class privilege had begun to demand a place in the American dream. They challenged America with America's own ideals. Exclusivity and privilege were un-American, they said; "Freedom!" was their cry.

Television had brought the civil rights struggle into American living rooms, and white suburban youngsters had watched when black children were taunted and cursed as they tried to enter Little Rock Central High School in 1957. During the post-war era, parents and teachers had told their privileged young baby boomers that they were growing up in the best country the world had ever known. But it was exactly this carefully instilled idealism that led the young to question just what this wonderful nation was so afraid of. They watched blacks in the South brutalized for such simple demands as the right to vote, eat, and ride side by side with whites and to use the same bathrooms and water fountains. They saw a nation falling short of "liberty and justice for all" and they heard a President exhort them to "make a difference." In 1964, as the early baby boomers went to college, the Berkeley Free Speech Movement inaugurated a decade of campus unrest. Activists with political sympathies ranging from Students for Goldwater to the Young Socialists joined a common protest against the Berkeley administration's ban on the distribution of non-campus political literature. They were the "antithesis of alienated and cynical," recalled Jackie Goldberg, one of the early protesters, in Mark Kitchell's documentary *Berkeley in the Sixties*. These students believed so much in the ideals of the Bill of Rights and the Declaration of Independence that they were willing to risk their academic careers to enforce them. When their parents' generation—in the form of the Berkeley administration and the California Board of Regents—saw the students' protest as more of a threat to American ideals than a fulfillment of them, what became known as a generation gap began to form. Gradually this gap was widened by a seemingly endless number of issues, from the civil rights movement and the war in Vietnam to long hair and marijuana.

Passionate, opinionated action and reaction were the rule of the 1960s and early 1970s, and they blew the lid off the seemingly simple world of clear values, prescribed roles, and unquestioned expectations. What lay beneath the lid were diversity, dissent, and resentment. Never again would the United States seem as homogeneous as it had in the 1950s, with as great a consensus for the white, male, middle-class vision of American life. Not one of the values of the American dream went unchallenged or unchanged in the tumultuous years of the 1960s and '70s.

But nothing divided the generations as much as sexual issues. Radical women's liberationists formed women's caucuses within the free speech and student anti-war movements. Through counterculture books and underground newspapers, these groups spurred women's anger and condemned the career ambitions that the (mostly older) feminists advocated. Soon many of them left the male-dominated movements and abandoned traditional relationships with men as well. Because the radical vanguard of the women's movement evolved within the other political movements of the day, it carried much of their flavor even as it split off from them. These highly politicized younger women sought more and different changes than those pursued by the readership of *The Feminine Mystique*. Though some radical feminists were married, few had the same image of marriage that Friedan's audience had had. Friedan's followers, who formed groups like the National Organization for Women (NOW), began to push for women's *rights* within the existing structures—the workplace, public office, higher education, the professions. The movement women, on the other hand, pushed for women's *liberation*, which required rebuilding the entire social structure upon a new foundation. Coming out of the New Left, the radical liberationists called for a new economic order to end all oppression based on sex, class, race, or age. They wanted to restructure a new America that would stand for greater social justice and less individual ambition.

By the end of the decade, radical women, like radicals in general, no longer sounded fresh and hopeful. Their voices grew shrill and even cynical. They began to despair that America would ever live up to old or new ideals. As John D'Emilio and Estelle B. Freedman, authors of *Intimate Matters: A History of Sexuality in America*, observed, the women's liberationists "disputed the possibility of equality in marriage or in other sexual relationships when women were economically dependent on men or had internalized values that made them doubt their self-worth. To them, the oppression of women had contaminated the sex act itself, while the sexual ideology of modern America reinforced female inequality. Women's liberationists expected that only a revolutionary transformation of society could remove the corruption that attached to sex."

Women's liberationists correctly perceived that the range of choices between NOW's feminism and the cult of domesticity were inadequate. Deeper change was called for. Coming out of the New Left, they used radical rhetoric about oppression and class struggle, and they also called for the abolition of the traditional family because it supposedly institutionalized sexism. But recent history provided few attractive models as alternatives, and the liberationists groped blindly, unable to describe their vision of a new society in a way the general public could grasp or adopt. Women's rights within the existing society were much easier to understand than vague ideas about what would come after a "revolution."

The whole range of feminist discussion—from rights to revolution—had evolved in reaction to the extreme confinements of the post-war era. All feminists wanted to throw off the old constraints, and few seemed to feel that women's traditional roles had any parts worth saving. No one seemed to have a clear idea of where sexual egalitarianism should lead. But feminists had no trouble stirring up a great wind of resentment against the way things had been. Like many young women coming of age during this feminist reawakening, Ingrid Bengis found it easy to set her sail with this wind. But navigating her own course proved difficult and lonely.

Each external event had its corresponding internal effect in the lives of women living through this upheaval. No woman was left untouched, whatever her age or social class. But no one was more affected by these turbulent times than those in the massive population bulge whose members were just growing up. Middle-class baby boomers, born during and after the war, both experienced and contributed to much of the whiplashing change during their formative years. Raised by the totally feminine—and sometimes totally frustrated—women of the 1950s, they matured during the sexually liberated 1960s and began making life decisions as the 1970s ushered in the new anti-sexist militantism. Many carried within them—as Bengis says she did—vestiges of all the shifting values they had lived with. At the same time, each young woman had individual needs that would not be denied, no matter what the social decree of the moment. Bengis felt pressured to conform to each new model, just as her mother and Adrienne Rich had felt pressed into the mold of the 1950s housewife. "The personal is political" became a slogan of the 1960s, as many young women tried to shape their private feelings into a new political ideology. When, in some inchoate, inarticulate, and private place, some found it impossible to have sex without emotional attachment or desire for commitment, they tried to set aside such "obsessions" as obsolete. But the prescribed political persona was shallow. Sex easily penetrated their efforts to maintain emotional distance. "What I discovered in the midst of my drive toward emancipation," Bengis writes, "was that sex, love, hurt, and hate were the real stuff I was made of; that fairness, rationality, and the willingness to share or to give away [a relationship] one had never been sure of possessing in the first place were all secondary characteristics, carefully cultivated to be sure, but capable of collapsing the moment stronger passions reared their heads."

Bengis could no more accomplish the emancipation she strove for than she could shed her skin. Like most of the women later studied by psychologist Carol Gilligan, Bengis felt and thought in a characteristically feminine way. Caring and relationships were more important and more immediate to her than abstract, political principles. Whether this feminine priority was inborn or cultivated by sexist socialization, willpower and political coercion could not easily change it. But that did not stop Bengis and many other women from trying, then and later.

The first two stories in this chapter—those of Leigh Barken and Anne Londino—are about women of Ingrid Bengis's generation, born during or shortly after World War II. Each was raised in a stable, middle-class, post-war home. Each wanted a career and independence. Each demonstrated her confusion about the role of men, children, and work in her life. Each also demonstrated both how much and how little women's attitudes about sexuality had changed during what came to be called the Sexual Revolution. Contradictions cut deeply into their most intimate choices about the kind of men they found attractive, about their need for romance, and about their sexual conduct. Like Bengis, they found themselves caught between conflicting desires. Although they wanted their own identity, they still sought, in part, to live vicariously through men. Although they wanted independence, a man transformed by romantic love reassured them of their feminine powers. Although neither of these women was ready for a child, neither used birth control methodically. Neither did their partners. Since the introduction of the pill in the early 1960s, men had increasingly come to think of contraception as the woman's responsibility. Marketers of the pill had assumed that because women were the ones who got pregnant, they would be highly motivated to prevent it.

But as Kristin Luker reports in her book *Taking Chances: Abortion and the Decision Not to Contracept*, women's motivation was not so simple. For many women throughout this book, pregnancy seemed only a remote possibility, while the romantic moment was powerful and immediate. To prepare and plan for sex was to rob it of its spontaneity and passion. Sex should be something that just happened. Besides, as Luker points out, pregnancy can have benefits. It can provide proof of womanhood and test the relationship. Even so, when the relationship failed the test, some of these women felt as if they had contracted a "life-threatening disease," as one woman who aborted in 1966 told us. Then, perceptions shifted; it was the pregnancy that seemed quite real and immediate and the romance that receded into obscurity.

Leigh Barken

Leigh Barken decided to go ahead with a pregnancy in 1967. Leigh, who was single, gave her baby up for adoption, but her decision, as she explained to us, was not based on any moral objections to abortion. In fact, she had already undergone one without guilt or regret. Leigh's story indicates just what a complicated web of factors can affect a woman's decisions about pregnancy.

"To be pregnant, to have an illegitimate child as it was called then . . . was probably the worst thing that could happen to a girl. It would brand you as the wrong type of person" said Leigh, who was forty-nine at the time of this interview. She apologized for the fact that some of her memories of pregnancy and childbirth in 1967 were beyond her reach. "There's just a lot of it I don't remember anymore."

A native of New Zealand, now living near Detroit, Leigh has bright blue eyes and fair skin, a small pointed nose, and a sharp accent in her highly expressive voice. The home she shares with her French-born husband and their two teenage children is a renovated vacation cottage near Lake Erie, filled with artifacts of their travels around the world. Leigh sat in the airy family room addition looking out toward the water, the mid-summer sun highlighting her fair hair.

Leigh had been what was called a free spirit in the 1960s, traveling to the Orient and living in Hong Kong for three years. "The idea of having liaisons and affairs with people didn't worry me at all." She had been raised with traditional values but had drawn her own lines—or thought she had—after she went away to school. She had a long-term relationship with a Chinese man and had gotten pregnant when she was switching from high- to lower-dose birth control pills. Although abortion was technically illegal in Hong Kong, the man's mother had arranged a quick, clean medical procedure, and no one, including Leigh, gave it much thought. "Neither of us was particularly interested in getting married, although he was a very nice person and we were both genuinely very fond of each other. But I was off to see the world . . . . Having a child meant a great sort of commitment that I didn't want, but there was not a moral value on [the abortion]."

In spring 1966, Leigh stopped to visit her family in Wellington and to say goodbye to her father, who was dying of cancer. Then she moved to Ottawa. The move was an exciting one, "like coming to a new world and a new start, a new part of my life," she said. "So I was very optimistic and happy about the whole thing." Nonetheless, when she got the news of her father's death that summer, it seriously set her back. Her family told her not to travel all the way back home for the funeral. Though the advice was practical, it isolated her in her grief.

Leigh began substitute teaching in a high school and very quickly met a man there who clipped the wings of her free spirit. Peter, as she remembered him, was a dark-haired, handsome young man with a winsome, somewhat quizzical expression. Leigh is now convinced that her grief over her father's death and her loneliness for her family got caught up in her relationship with Peter. She stressed several times that the connection between her father's death and her pregnancy with Peter were quite important, although she admitted she had never seen the way one had affected the other until she began to prepare her thoughts for this interview.

Her relationship with Peter was highly romantic, she said in a tone that implied she now found that romance somewhat silly. The tough-minded, independent, world traveler acted like a moony school girl. "I wasn't young," Leigh said. "I was twenty-five or something, so I wasn't a starry-eyed little girl. I should have had far more sense. That's what has always puzzled me: why I didn't have more sense. Looking back, I think it was just an emotional vulnerability." Her father's death brought out in her a need for intimate connection and commitment that had been dormant but not dead during her traveling years. Peter was mysterious. "There were always unexplained absences . . . and times he wasn't available," she said. Perhaps because he kept a lot of himself hidden, she ended up seeing what she wanted to see in him, not what he really was.

When Leigh became pregnant that fall, "I wasn't disturbed about it," she said. In fact, her feelings were closer to euphoria. Pregnancy seemed a natural outcome of this intense romance. She had not been using birth control. "I don't want to say that I deliberately set out to become pregnant. . . . I think there is a lot more in our actions than we can put up front. And I think when I look back that it was definitely the fact that my father had died and that I really wanted to see in myself a perpetuation of life. . . .

"I don't know if I believed or I hoped to believe that Peter would come along and we'd get married and live happily ever after. But it was that sort of thing," she said. Though she thinks, in retrospect, that she was filling the void left by her father with a new life, she never consciously had such thoughts in 1967.

When she told Peter about her pregnancy, "I can't say he was indifferent. He talked a good story. . . . The story was that this was a wonderful thing that had happened between us. [He had] just a very silly, immature approach. When I think about that time, I find it hard to believe that this was me operating then, you know?" Leigh does not remember that Peter specifically mentioned marriage, but she is sure the implication was there.

Then slowly—almost imperceptibly—Peter's ardor began to cool. "Oh, it must have been a couple of months into my pregnancy—he started not to come around. He started to make appointments, make arrangements, and he wouldn't be there . . . just wouldn't be there," Leigh recalled. One of Peter's friends came to see Leigh, upset because Peter had told him Leigh was pregnant with someone else's child. When the friend saw Leigh's astonishment, he tried to arrange a reconciliation with Peter.

"By this time I was getting distraught. The reality of it was coming in on me—the reality that Peter was not going to be around," Leigh recalled. The reconciliation never happened. In fact, Peter just disappeared into one of his unexplained absences and never returned. Leigh was devastated by the loss and frightened by what lay ahead. What saved her, she felt, was the support of a half-dozen women friends she had made in the city. "They didn't push me or question me. They didn't say you should have an abortion; they didn't say you should have the child; they didn't say you should get married. Nothing. They were just very supportive." The experience marked the birth of her commitment to feminism, Leigh recalled, and she remains close to all those women today.

By the time Peter disappeared, Leigh's pregnancy was four months along. Abortion was not legal in Canada, and none of her friends knew where to look. On the other hand, she admitted, no one tried very hard. Abortion was legal in some parts of the United States by then, and someone had also suggested she could fly to London. But Leigh never pursued these options, and she still cannot explain why. She did not recall having any moral qualms about abortion at the time, though she acknowledged that today, as the mother of two teenagers, her feelings have become more complicated.

In December, Leigh told the vice principal at her school about her situation. He was shocked and upset for her. "S-s-sh! Keep your voice down," he warned her. "We don't want the principal to hear." But he made no moral judgments, Leigh felt, and in January he found her a place in another school where the staff assumed she was married.

The fact that no one outwardly condemned her allowed Leigh to act decisively on practical matters. It may also have allowed her to continue a pregnancy that she otherwise might have felt desperate to end. Such compassion had been scarce a decade earlier—when more vociferously judgmental attitudes prevailed—and it reflected some of the profound changes that had swept in with the 1960s. Nevertheless, Leigh said: "I was ashamed. I was ashamed for my family's sake." Back in New Zealand, her family had status. "It was only a limited status, but they were very moral, middle-class, respected people. When I was growing up, if a girl got married quickly, it was spoken about in sort of hushed tones. There was a very clear distinction between good girls and bad girls," Leigh recalled. And bad girls were the target of bad jokes.

Leigh handled her shame by never telling her mother or her two sisters about her pregnancy. At the time, she saw no need to burden them so soon after her father's death. Since then, she has thought often about telling her mother. What has always stopped her is the fear that her mother would be hurt to think Leigh had gone through the experience without her family's support.

Leigh knew as soon as she realized Peter was gone that she would give up the child for adoption. She considered keeping the child only in fleeting "four-in-the-morning dreams about an ideal world. . . . But in the reality of the time, there was still a stigma, definite stigma" that she could not face. The visibility of her pregnancy embarrassed her. "I had been so silly and stupid to be taken in by this fellow and by a romantic view of the world which I knew existed only in those stories, those paperbacks." During the months she had been seeing Peter, Leigh said, the intensity of their romance "just seemed to stop my mind from thinking sensibly about things. I think it stopped me from thinking about having an abortion."

Leigh quit teaching in her seventh month and went on welfare until after the baby was born. She deliberately kept her distance from her pregnancy by avoiding childbirth classes and even refusing to read books about labor and delivery. "And when they asked me when the baby was born what name—she had to have a name—I just gave them my name, so I didn't give her a special name." Leigh saw her daughter in the hospital but not much. Seeing her was too painful. Leigh's voice filled with emotion as she described her baby.

"She was beautiful, you know, and you look at life and you think, 'Gosh! what a miracle. This is part of me.' I didn't care about Peter anymore. He was gone, and I got over that. In fact by that time I was thinking, 'Silly man, he's missed out on something miraculous.'" Leigh halfheartedly tried to serve Peter with an injunction to force him to help her with her medical bills. She even briefly considered an offer from the husband of one of her friends to see that he was beaten up. But in the end she just wanted to let him go, be rid of him.

Leigh's obstetrician knew of an infertile couple who were looking for a child. The family he described fit the right image for Leigh: similar coloring, same religion, a good family eager for a child. So she agreed to let them take her daughter home from the hospital.

Leigh's women friends, in turn, took her in, seeing her through a period of acute depression that followed the birth. "I think I was very unstable. I don't think I knew how to cope with things. But again, whatever I did, my friends never complained," she said.

When Leigh went to sign the final papers for adoption, the woman lawyer who handled the case let her cry and talk for a long time. "I was feeling worthless, absolutely worthless. . . . She talked to me about how I was young and I was an attractive person. You know, just built me up, saying that I was giving great happiness to other people. Oh, I can remember just sitting in her office and crying and crying and crying." Leigh knew that once the papers were signed she would never change her mind, and she never did.

Nonetheless, the feeling of worthlessness lasted for a long time. "Maybe it was my upbringing—that shame coming through finally. . . . I had let down my morals that I had been brought up with." Like Ingrid Bengis, Leigh found that the values of her upbringing had remained an important part of her. She thought she had set her own, more modern course until the death of her father and the birth of her child truly tested her. Jean-Paul, the man she later married, turned out to be an important antidote to her depression. She had met him while she was pregnant. When he came around after the delivery to court her, she was moved that he could love and accept her for what she was, knowing she had borne another man's child.

The overriding feeling Leigh recalled was loss. She feels it still, although she seems to have come fully to terms with her decision. "I was determined that I wasn't going to go after the baby. . . . I had quite decided that the life that she was going to go into was better than the one that I could have given her then, because twenty years ago society was not conducive to bringing up children on your own." And although society is more tolerant of single motherhood now, Leigh expresses no regrets about her decision. "I felt it was a wonderful alternative for this child to go to a place where she was wanted and cherished, and I still believe that."

Anne Londino

Anne was a twenty-one-year old mathematics student at Florida International University in 1969. She was also a violinist, and in her teens she had scarcely dated because she spent most of her free time practicing. She continued her violin lessons in college and was always drawn to other people in the arts. Anne met Miguel, a thirty-two-year-old Latin American artist, at a dinner party given by her violin teacher. "I was in awe of Miguel," Anne recalled, sitting in a friend's backyard in Virginia almost twenty years later. She wore a sundress and sandals, her long dark hair tied back with a green scarf. "He was much older than I was and he knew everyone in Miami, from the millionaires on the beach to the artists in Coconut Grove. I fell in love with him. I couldn't see what he was, and I couldn't see that he was just using me. I don't think that's putting it too strongly, to say that he was using me."

Anne had an on-and-off relationship with Miguel for several months. She was living at home with her parents at that time but spent many nights at Miguel's house. "He never asked me what I was doing about birth control," Anne said, "and once, early on, when I worried about becoming pregnant, he just laughed it off and said, 'Oh, but I'd love to marry you. Don't worry about it.' I did worry, but I wasn't too careful, so what happened was really my fault," she said, placing no blame on Miguel.

What happened was that Anne got pregnant. "I went to Miguel immediately and told him. He said, 'Well, you'll just have to do something about it.' I panicked. Abortion was illegal, and I didn't have any idea how to arrange one. Miguel investigated, but we had a terrible time. We actually made about six appointments with six different doctors, and every single time the doctor was arrested right before I was scheduled to see him. I was even planning to go to Puerto Rico."

Finally, though, Miguel and Anne learned of Dr. G., who practiced in a small town near Chattanooga, Tennessee. They traveled there together. "It was a one-horse town," Anne said. "The only place to eat was the drugstore, and they didn't even have hot tea. This doctor had an office right next to the Elks or Masons.

"The doctor used no anesthetic," Anne went on. "The procedure was like a D&C without any numbing. During the abortion, I must have made too much noise—it hurt!—and he must have chosen to stop before he had finished because he was afraid he'd get caught. It was nighttime and there was a meeting going on at the lodge next door. When I left his office, I was still bleeding heavily.'"

Anne and Miguel stayed at the town's hotel the next day, with Anne vomiting and in pain the whole time. After they returned to Miami, they parted and did not stay in touch. Miguel had treated her badly throughout the ordeal. Anne said in disgust: "Yes, he arranged the abortion and went to Tennessee with me and paid the bill. But it was all under coercion. I had threatened to tell my father, who is a hot-tempered, protective, Italian Catholic, if he didn't help me. So Miguel didn't really have a choice. But all he said to me when I was feeling sick and desperate was, 'You can't cry over spilled milk.'"

Back in Miami, Anne continued to feel ill and distressed. "I took a lot of tranquilizers, both Librium and Valium. I got them from a friend. My school-work was not good. I had a clerical job, and that was suffering too. I looked like hell. I wasn't having periods, and I didn't even wonder why, I was so out of touch. But I was living at home, and my mother *was* in touch. I was skinny, but my belly was growing. My mother insisted that I go to the doctor."

Anne's mother had known about her pregnancy almost from the beginning. "When I first told her, she got very angry, said terrible things, ran out, and slammed the door. In about an hour she came back with a little present for me, put her arms around me, and said she'd help me through this—we'd get through it together. She even offered to help me bring up the child, if that's what I wanted. I told her it wasn't."

Anne complied with her mother's wishes to see a doctor, even though she was sure it was unnecessary. The doctor she went to told her she was pregnant. "That's impossible," she said to him. "I've had an abortion."

"You're pregnant, and you have to have this child," the doctor insisted. "It's too late. You would die if you had an illegal abortion now." Anne had been six to eight weeks pregnant when she had gone to Dr. G. She was now at least eighteen weeks pregnant.

Anne told the doctor about the drugs she had been taking, which, even if the abortion attempt had not harmed the fetus, she was sure would cause other serious damage. Her doctor would not listen to any questions about abortion, although by then it was legal through the second trimester in several states, a fact Anne and Miguel did not know. Anne felt the doctor was passing a strong moral judgment when he reiterated that she would have to face the consequences of her actions.

"I would rather have died," Anne said, leaning forward in her lawn chair. "I didn't care about anyone or anything. I had one goal, and that was killing that baby. I didn't like the baby; I didn't like Miguel. I was not going to have that child." Her eyes glittered with defiance and pain as she recalled terrible emotions. This was the moment at which her memory seemed to come most intensely alive.

Anne reluctantly got in touch with Miguel, who called Dr. G. "He refused to finish what he'd started, so I called him and threatened to turn him in."

Anne and Miguel went back to Tennessee. They tried to be civil to each other, just to get through what lay ahead of them. "We met Dr. G. at six that evening, and he explained what he would do later on, when I came back at ten. He would insert a balloon [and then fill it] with air, or fluid of some kind, and that would cause an abortion. He said it would be like giving birth. I was so relieved that I thanked him and kissed him. I have no recollection of the next four hours."

At ten o'clock, Anne went back to the doctor's office alone. This time, he administered a shot of the anesthetic sodium pentothal. Because of the drug, Anne's recollections were hazy and confused, but she had a distinct memory that he had asked her "dirty questions." Less clear was her impression that he may have raped her while she was on his examining table. "When Miguel picked me up, Dr. G. told him that I'd been babbling about rape. He said not to pay any attention." Anne reflected for a moment and said: "In truth, it was rape anyway. The fact that he asked those questions, that he put me through such hell."

Dr. G. woke Anne up before the sodium pentothal had time to wear off. He had inserted the balloon while Anne was unconscious, but the effects of the procedure would not start for some time. Still groggy from the drug, Anne vomited in Dr. G.'s office, in the car, and in the hotel. Miguel insisted on leaving on an early flight the next morning so that he could keep a tennis date the next afternoon. "I was vomiting as we were running through the airport. I never knew how I could have so much in my stomach; it seemed I'd never be empty again. By the time we got to Atlanta, though, where we had a three-hour layover, I'd started to feel a little better. I even got hungry, but Miguel wouldn't let me eat. He didn't want to put up with any more vomiting."

They went to Miguel's apartment as soon as they landed in Miami. He left for his tennis match, and a friend of Anne's picked her up to take her home to her parents' house. "I fell apart," Anne wearily recalled. "My mother told my father I had a terrible virus."

The next twenty-four hours are a blur in Anne's mind. She went into labor entirely unprepared. The doctor had given her no guidance or instructions. "I didn't expect the pain. I didn't know what it would be like or what I should do. I started pushing right away. My mother was panicking. I don't know how long that labor took, but I remember that I had to deliver both the inflated balloon and the fetus. I was sitting on the toilet when the fetus dropped out. My mother tells me it was much smaller than I thought. Its eyes seemed very large to me. I think it was a boy. To me it was Miguel, and I muttered awful things like 'Die you fucker, die.' I was hysterical. I hated him. I hated it. It was not part of me." Anne took a breath and then said: "Dr. G. was wrong. It wasn't like giving birth. I gave death."

During the next two weeks Anne bled heavily and became anemic. When she returned to school, she would go two or three days without bleeding and then would hemorrhage. One evening, on a date, she stood up from a chair and saw she had been sitting in a pool of blood. She managed to get home and then fainted. She didn't want to wake her mother, so she put ice on her stomach to ease the pain. By morning she had gone completely white. Her doctor (not the one who had insisted she have the child) ordered a D&C just before she would have required blood transfusions. She was laid up for another month.

"When did I deal with it?" she wondered, pausing in the interview to think about this question. "I don't know if I ever did." Over the years since her abortion, Anne has had nightmares about it and has talked to counselors about it. Even the interview made her slightly nauseous. Yet, she said: "It's as if it happened to someone else. When I hear my own story, I can't believe it. I can't feel about it; I have nothing left to feel. It's as if I'm sitting in a tunnel when I talk about it."

When Anne got pregnant again a few years after her abortion, she married the father and went ahead with that pregnancy. "I would never even have considered another abortion, legal or otherwise." Anne's daughter, Laura, is now twenty and a musician like her mother. The two are very close. "Laura has made up for a lot of it," Anne reflected. "She was a gift, a chance for me to be a good mother, to love a child. Maybe she wouldn't have been so important to me if I hadn't gone through that abortion. Laura was what was supposed to happen, the way it was supposed to happen." Even so, when Laura was born with a kidney infection and had to be hospitalized, Anne thought: "This is where I pay. I'm going to lose this one."

Pulling her legs under her in the lawn chair and leaning a little into the shade, Anne sounded resigned and tired. "Maybe that [abortion] experience will always be unresolved for me. . . . But I accept responsibility for what I did. I think abortion is murder, and yet I know I made the right choice. I know that's inconsistent, but it's the best I can do. I wouldn't have loved that baby, but I couldn't have stood having it in the world without taking care of it," she said. "That abortion was not a well thought-out decision. I was an impulsive, flighty twenty-one-year-old. I wanted my freedom. . . . When I think about my life then and the people I was involved with at that time, I can see that we wanted gratification without paying any prices. But there are heavy prices to pay for an attitude like that. The price I paid changed me a lot."

Anne will never face another unwanted pregnancy herself. When her marriage to Laura's father broke up almost ten years ago, Anne feared she might be pregnant. "I had wanted a second child," she remembered. "I even wanted to be an Earth Mother; I wanted a bunch of kids." But she was horrified at the thought of being pregnant while her marriage was dissolving. "I knew I would never have another abortion, so I imagined being alone with a ten-year-old and a newborn and trying to work at the same time. When it turned out I wasn't pregnant, I was so relieved I had my tubes tied right away. I gave up on having any more children. Now I teach music, and have dozens. I just have to work with children."

Anne admits that her views on abortion remain inconsistent today. "I make contributions to pro-choice groups. I don't want anyone, ever, to go through what I went through. And whether it's right or wrong, some people will always choose not to have babies. I don't even feel that they should have them and give them up. There are already enough needy babies in the world for everyone who wants one. We just haven't figured out a way to channel them to the right parents. All the same, there's still a very Catholic side of me that thinks abortion is murder."

Such ambivalence, while confusing to Anne herself, resembles the mixture of feelings expressed by the majority of Americans, who tell pollsters they want legal abortion but hate the need for it. A reasoning and compassionate person like Anne, applying the principles of justice and human rights, can find abortion unjust. At the same time, that person can feel that it is sometimes permissible when he or she looks closely at particular circumstances with a sense of caring and responsibility. Anne's own thinking seems inconsistent to her because she thinks it should conform to the black-and-white debate on abortion. But that debate closes out exactly the moral shadings that are brought forth when principles of caring temper those of justice. In fact, the oversimplification of the public debate often causes people like Anne to regard the complexity of their own thinking as moral weakness. Instead it can be seen as moral strength and sophistication. It is the struggle of people like Anne, who refuse to lose sight of either justice or care considerations in the face of ethical dilemmas, that may be the real measure of moral maturity. This is what Carol Gilligan and Jane Attanucci suggest in their article "Two Moral Orientations: Gender Differences and Similarities." Gilligan and Attanucci discuss the neglect of the care perspective—the one used more commonly by women—in analyses of the ethics of abortion.

> The language of the abortion debate . . . reveals a justice perspective. Whether the abortion dilemma is cast as a conflict of rights or in terms of respect for human life, the claims of the fetus and the pregnant women are balanced or placed in opposition. . . . Framed as a problem of care, the dilemma posed by abortion shifts. The connection between the fetus and the pregnant woman becomes the focus and the question becomes whether it is responsible or irresponsible, caring or careless, to extend or to end this connection.

While many women have always applied the moral perspective of caring and responsibility to their private birth or abortion decisions, the public debate has rarely given them confidence that such a perspective is legitimate.

Splits in the Sisterhood

In the late 1960s, arguments between the National Organization for Women and more radical thinkers over whether women should fight for rights or revolution grew more vehement. But both camps were largely made up of college-educated women from middle-class backgrounds. Most Americans, especially working-class women, remained largely impervious to disagreements within the movement. Nonetheless, every woman found herself affected by it and by the new attitudes toward sex and sexuality. As a generation, baby boomers of every social class were in much less of a hurry to settle down than their counterparts in the 1950s had been. Between 1960 and 1975 the number of single adults between the ages of twenty and thirty-four increased by 50 percent. The age group was larger because of the population bulge, but the proportion of singles had risen because of changing attitudes. When couples did tie the knot, it often came loose. The percentage of divorced individuals in the population rose 200 percent between 1960 and 1979. By the 1970s, being single was no longer a way station on the road to or from marriage. It was a way of life. The very word "single" began to sound positive. It replaced "spinster," "bachelor," and "divorcee," all of which had long implied that the unmarried were deviant, unhappy, or maladjusted people.

In 1962, author Helen Gurley Brown assured pink-collar career women—secretaries, clerks, copywriters, and the like—that they need no longer consider themselves outcasts. In her controversial book *Sex and the Single Girl*, Brown laughs off the notion that "nice" single women are Doris Day virgins. There is nothing premarital about the sex she advocates. "What nonsense!" Brown writes. The single girl "need never be bored with one man per lifetime. Her choice of partners is endless." Just eight years later, in a 1970 update to her book, Brown notes that the sexual climate had changed dramatically. The double standard had become a single one, but, as Ingrid Bengis says, it was still the male standard. Women could use men as freely as they had been used by them. The rhetoric of liberated sex failed to recognize the legitimacy of emotional needs. Brown sometimes sounds like a female Hugh Hefner or James Bond, the ultimate love-'em-and-leave-'em capitalists of sex.

In some quarters, motherhood came to be seen as the greatest single deterrent to women's equality with men—at work, in marriage, and in sex. Some women, out of a defensive urge against the suffocating motherhood of the 1950s, threw the baby out with the bathwater. For example, author Ellen Peck vituperatively dismisses the whole idea of motherhood in her 1971 book *The Baby Trap*. Though Peck's views are extreme, respect for the domestic and maternal concerns of women, never high to begin with, waned noticeably, not only among some wary feminists but also among some nonfeminist housewives and their husbands, in the media, and in the mind of the public at large. The pressure to perform was on, and women who resisted it, choosing to stick with traditional roles, were made to feel less interesting and less strong than their more worldly and ambitious sisters. Many felt no sisterhood at all. Many who chose marriage and motherhood exclusively held the feminists in contempt and were in turn dismissed by some of them.

Splits began to develop, not just between the generations but among women of all ages. Women who forsook the traditional path felt threatened by those who chose it, and vice versa. Some who intended to follow a traditional path found it closed to them. Economic growth had slowed, and a gradual decline in the American wage earner's buying power meant more and more 1960s families required two incomes, whether the wife wanted to work or not. Some women's gains offset others' losses. Many women found themselves torn between careers and domesticity. These internal splits were the most painful ones.

Maxine Bonner was a fully independent career woman when she weighed the prospect of motherhood. Her story demonstrates how women had begun to think of their readiness for parenthood in a new way, one that balanced career and parenting—an option that had previously been available only to men. Women like Maxine, confronting unplanned pregnancies, now took into account their ability to earn a living as part of their decision. They considered whether they could be both nurturing mother and the breadwinner.

Maxine, a contemporary of the 1950s housewives, bucked the trends of her time. She simply followed her own career desires, despite the strong prevailing norms. Yet it was the gradual change in social attitudes that allowed her to choose, somewhat uncomfortably, to become a single mother in 1971.

Maxine Bonner

When Maxine became pregnant in 1971, she was forty-three years old, in love, and deliriously happy. But within a few short weeks of confirming her pregnancy, that happiness turned to anxiety and despair. She faced the possibility of losing the man she loved, her job, and her parents if she proceeded to have the baby she wanted.

"I'll never understand how people can go out on the streets and march against abortion," she said as a frown creased her high forehead. "How can they be so sure? I don't think anyone ever knows what they'll really do until they face the situation."

Born in 1928, Maxine had forgone marriage and family well into her thirties without apparent regret. Today, in her sixties, this former model is still stunning. She has a tall, slim figure and wears her silver-streaked, chestnut brown hair in a stylish bun. Her high cheekbones have kept her skin taut, though her face is webbed with delicate wrinkles. Now a magazine editor in New York, Maxine was the public relations director for a midsize New England television station in 1971. In 1965, she had married a doctor from her hometown, about fifty miles outside her New England city. Jeffrey, a divorced father of three children, was a dashing but unreliable and even emotionally abusive spouse. Their stormy, on-again, off-again relationship produced one miscarriage before it ended in divorce in 1970.

Then, for six months early in 1971, they began to see each other again, spending a lot of time in Maxine's apartment in the city. "It was the best six months we ever had. We were talking about getting remarried, so I was delighted when I found out I was pregnant," Maxine recalled, rolling her brown eyes. Jeffrey was not pleased. "He never had been too interested in having any more children. When I started talking about getting married again, he suggested I should wait to see if I could actually carry this pregnancy, since I had had that miscarriage. Then he started raising questions about what kind of a mother I would be, trying to break down my confidence. He was a master at that." Finally Jeffrey started dropping hints about abortion.

"Suddenly it hit me that he was backing out," Maxine said. Abortion had just been made legal in New York. A friend gave her the name of a gynecologist there, so she made a quick appointment. It must have been his day to see obstetric patients, she recalled. His office was filled with pregnant women, some of them with other small children in tow. It was hard for Maxine to watch their warm and simple interactions. The doctor brought her into his office after the examination. Although he was willing to perform the abortion, he had heard confusion and doubt in Maxine's report of her situation.

"I don't think you want to be here," he told her. "I don't," she answered, "but I don't know what else to do." He counseled her to think about the fact that, at forty-three, she was probably facing her last chance for a child and to call him again with her decision. She walked the streets of New York City, familiar from her years as a model. Before she boarded the train back to New England she had made up her mind: She would have this baby.

It was not an easy decision. Maxine was fairly certain that she would face parenthood alone. Jeffrey seemed intent on walking away from both fatherhood and their relationship. She also thought she might lose her job. One secretary at the station had been rehired a year after her baby was born, but that was no guarantee the station was willing to hold Maxine's job while she gave birth. Besides, the management might find it improper for a woman in such a public position to be having an out-of-wedlock baby. Then there were her parents, whom she adored. They had never even liked Jeffrey. Could they accept the embarrassment of her pregnancy in the small town where her father had been a bank president? Two years earlier, her father had suffered his first heart attack, and she really feared the news of her pregnancy might kill him.

"I can't explain this," Maxine admitted, "but despite all of that, I felt very at peace with my decision on the way home." She is not even sure why she made the decision. She had never longed for motherhood; indeed, she had given up on it. She had never felt jealous when her friends had babies, had never even played with dolls as a child. Although she had always had lots of dates, Jeffrey had been the first man she had ever slept with, and she had always known he was not too keen on starting another family. Yet the reality of this last-chance pregnancy stirred in her a desire she had not experienced before.

Prenatal testing was not widely available yet, and Maxine, because of her age, did worry about the risks of genetic abnormalities. But after skimming through a few books full of statistics and dreadful possibilities, she decided to put anxiety aside and not let it spoil the pregnancy.

She did not lose her job, although the company refused to give her any time off beyond the normal two weeks of sick days and three weeks of vacation. She did not tell her parents until she was in her seventh month. "I wasn't just avoiding the issue," she said. "I didn't want them to worry the whole time about the baby because of my age." What was remarkable, however, was that although she saw her parents nearly every weekend, they never noticed her bulging belly. "It just shows you that people only see what they want to see," Maxine said. Her father didn't have a heart attack at the news. In fact, her parents were thrilled at the prospect of the grandchild they had given up on.

One cold evening in late 1971, Maxine left work at the usual six o'clock, feeling some cramps. In the wee hours of the next morning, she delivered a health baby boy she named Doug. With occasional help from her parents and a steady rise in her own income, she was able to buy a comfortable home and hire a nanny who stayed with Doug until he finished high school. Doug is now a tall, handsome sophomore away at college. He and a pack of pals frequently invade Maxine's otherwise quiet home for the weekend, filling up all the spare beds and mattresses she can muster. Doug is doing well and is dating a girl even this doting mother can approve of. "He is truly the joy of my life." Maxine said with a proud grin. "I so often think, what if I had . . . " She paused without finishing the sentence. "How lonely my life would be now!"

After our interview, Maxine resolved to find the doctor she had seen in New York who had been so instrumental in her decision. She intended to thank him and give him a picture of Doug. Abortion had been new in his practice, Maxine recalled, and she wondered if, as it became more common, his sensitive counseling of patients diminished. Today's clinics, especially those that do a large number of abortions, rarely explore with women the implications of their choices or the possibility that they are being coerced. If they did, they could broaden the avenue toward real choice on a matter as serious as abortion, which requires reflection and psychological freedom. Maxine said that while she is thankful that legal abortion was available to her, she is afraid that the large number of abortions today indicates that many women abort—as she herself almost did—before they have truly explored their options.

Changing State Laws

By the middle of the 1960s, state legislatures had begun heated debates about the liberalization of statutes, inching the United States toward the Supreme Court's 1973 *Roe v. Wade* decision. The medical community began to insist that the law align with modern medical practice, which saw hospitals performing abortions in rising numbers. Yet in 1966 forty-two states considered abortion legal only to save the life of the mother. In a 1966 *Newsweek* article entitled "The Abortion Epidemic," Dr. Robert E. Hall of Columbia University College of Physicians and Surgeons estimated that half of the eight thousand to ten thousand abortions being performed yearly in U.S. hospitals were done because the mother's mental stability was threatened or because she had contracted rubella, which commonly led to birth defects. Nonetheless, Hall noted, state laws still made such practices illegal. Besides, Hall added, the precautions physicians were taking—such as demanding two psychiatric consultations to establish mental instability—made abortion a privilege of the rich. *Newsweek* cited one study done in New York City which showed that one hospital abortion was being performed for every four hundred deliveries among private patients while the ratio among the poor in the wards was one to fourteen hundred. Most physicians knew problems of "mental stability" now covered just about any hardship. A survey in the April 1967 issue of *Modern Medicine* showed that 93 percent of non-Catholic and almost one-half of Catholic physicians responding approved of liberalizing abortion laws (Kerby, 1967).

Early in 1967, Colorado passed a legislative amendment permitting abortion when there was a threat to the mother's mental or physical health, when the pregnancy resulted from rape or incest, or when there was the likelihood of lasting physical harm to the baby. California (where a new law was signed by then-Governor Ronald Reagan), Florida, and North Carolina quickly followed suit. By 1970, ten states had relaxed their abortion laws and several were considering repeal measures.

Nonetheless, the new laws had strict limits and quasi-legal hospital abortions were getting harder to obtain in some of the states that had old statutes. Hospital committees, trying to control what *Newsweek* called "the abortion epidemic," had grown stricter and were granting fewer requests for abortions. With illegal procedures and trips abroad the only alternatives, many people, especially in the medical community and in the women's movement, began to push for legalization.

Attitudes were in flux. In some urban areas, abortion came out of the back alleys and into an aboveboard social service network. For example, the Reverend Howard Moody began operating the Clergy Consultation Service (CCS) from Judson Memorial Church in Greenwich Village in 1967. He referred as many as fifty or sixty patients a week to physicians willing to perform abortions. Within months of its inception, CCS membership had grown from two dozen ministers and rabbis to fourteen hundred clergy who shared referral information from coast to coast. Eventually, CCS had enough clout to get abortionists to lower or occasionally to waive their fees. The service investigated the doctors it sent women to, and periodically Judson Memorial Church would issue a nationwide list so the referral services around the country would know which doctors were incompetent or unkind. Operating quietly through word of mouth, CCS was able to avoid any great outcry from those opposed to abortion. Perhaps, one rabbi speculated, that was because neither the clergy nor the opposition saw what CCS was doing as a political movement. Theirs was a service organization.

Many compelling practical and emotional arguments for abortion were not obvious to most people, but some of the stories publicized by pro-legalization activists began to influence people's thinking. One of the most influential activists, Lawrence Lader, wrote magazine articles and books that catalogued story after story of women overwhelmed by pressures that made pregnancy intolerable.

In a January 1969 issue of *Look* magazine, Lader described some of the five hundred women who had written to him pleading for his help in obtaining abortions. Although Lader's sample was unscientific, his report provided one of the first glimpses into the types of women who were having abortions. Lader found that the largest number of women, 62 percent, were single. This finding challenged earlier estimates by Planned Parenthood and other experts that 75 to 90 percent of abortions, legal and illegal, were being performed on married women. Lader speculated that "The reason for this is probably the literate background of the survey group. Two-thirds of them spent at least a year in college, which means that the proportion of students and young career women was above normal." It may also have reflected the increase in sexual activity by single women during the 1960s.

Whether married or single, women were considering abortion more openly than ever before. But their chances of obtaining a safe and legal procedure were wildly uneven. Lader managed to find some physicians who were willing to abort any woman who came to them, but some women, who were less literate, farther removed from sophisticated urban medical centers, or too poor to afford the high cost of safe abortions, were beyond the reach of these physicians and were driven to more desperate ends.

In Lader's sample and in the recollections of practitioners, it was nearly always practical and emotional matters that drove women to consider abortion. Pregnancies associated with rape, incest, fetal deformity, or serious health risks aroused the most sympathy, but these were rare instances. Advances in medical science had greatly diminished the number and severity of health risks that had, at one time, been cited to justify abortion. Hardships caused by financial stress, depression, problems with men, or the needs of existing children were common-place reasons for seeking an abortion. These practical problems often had to do with relationships and women's beliefs about their ability to care for a baby properly. Women from the ghettoes to the suburbs, the prairies to the moun-tains, had always sought abortions for such reasons. Now these reasons were being labeled as "threats to the mother's mental health" in order to provide a medical reason for some privileged women to abort legally.

We talked to a woman named Nancy who grew up in rural Georgia in the 1960s. She knows, from her own recollections and her mother's stories, how frequently her neighbors chose between birth and abortion. "One time my mom's friend Raylene came over from the next farm. She already had six or seven kids. And she told my mom, 'I'm messed up again. I'm just gon' have to find an old quack.' It was too soon after her last baby," Nancy explained. "Farming season was coming on."

"I think anyone could get an abortion," Nancy told us. "I had a cousin who was a doctor, and he did abortions. He was run out of one town, but he just went away for a while and then came back to practice in the next town over."

These rural women often had large families, and they generally welcomed children. But with little birth control information available, their pregnancies sometimes came too frequently or at times when the women's energies were required elsewhere. Those who couldn't find a doctor to perform an abortion could always find someone else, Nancy said. "There was always a lot of people you could go to for things if you didn't think the doctor was going to do you right. Like black women, herbalists. There were people to take care of this, do away with things. That was a term people used—'do away with things.' "

Most of the stories Nancy heard were only whispered. "I even think my mom had an abortion," she speculated. "A brief remark passed between us once." That brief remark is the closest Nancy will probably ever come to knowing her mother's story. Nor would her mother ask friends like Raylene if they would talk with us. "The way people had to deal with it then is why they won't talk," said Nancy. "It was too awful." They shared their secrets only with those they deeply trusted.

Women like Raylene and her neighbors were far removed by class and geography from the legal or quasi-legal hospital abortions or the organized abortion underground that existed in many large cities. They formed their own network. Others, however, had no one to turn to. The cases of Sylvia Rakow and Julia Henning are about young women whose poverty was compounded by isolation and abuse. They were baby boomers who missed out on the Ozzie-and-Harriet security that others in their generation took for granted. Raised by drunken and abusive parents, each sought in sex a solace they never attained. In some ways they were even more ambivalent about contraception and repro-duction than their more stable counterparts. They demonstrate how young women who led lives outside the American mainstream were more vulnerable than many of those within. On the rare occasions when they were able to voice their own concerns, no one seemed to listen. If their families and communities provided safety nets, those nets often failed to hold.

Sylvia Rakow

Sylvia never actually decided to become a single mother. She fell into the role by default, despite her inadequacies as a nurturer and a provider. She is an example of what has come to be known as the feminization of poverty: poor women left alone with children.

In 1968, at age twenty, Sylvia left the man she had married at eighteen and went to Richmond to start college. She had grown up in a difficult home, the oldest daughter of a depressed mother and a father who slapped his wife around. Her father worked for the railroad near Macon, Georgia, and her mother was a secretary who came from a family of "Bible-beating Baptists," according to Sylvia. All three of Sylvia's sisters ended up having babies out of wedlock, and their brother committed suicide.

Sylvia met a boy in Richmond after she had left her husband. "He was just like a regular college boy. A real dumb guy, too. I was like miles ahead of him in life experience by then because I had already been married a couple of years and my husband was like real crazy." We interviewed Sylvia in the living room of a large, once luxurious home in Austin, Texas. She was forty and had thought of herself as society's victim for so long that she almost wore it as a badge. The house embarrassed her. "A slum apartment costs the same," she said with a shrug. Although she has pulled herself out of the immediate grip of poverty, Sylvia is deeply scarred by it. Her experience has led her to believe that no woman—especially one with children—is ever far from poverty's grasp.

Sylvia has jet-black hair. Her broad cheekbones, brooding mouth, and startling gray-green eyes give her the look of a Gypsy. She put her feet—in frayed, black espadrilles—up on the coffee table and slouched down in her chair as she talked. The tables and bookshelves around the living room were cluttered with strange and colorful paraphernalia of the supernatural and the super-stitious—tiny carved and brightly painted creches from Peru, crystal balls, and Tarot cards. She is a collector and a dealer, not a believer, she explained.

If Sylvia ever did see men through romance-colored glasses, her vision, including hindsight, has long ago been darkened by disappointment. The college boy in Richmond got her pregnant in September and then ran away to the army before the school term was over. "I couldn't believe he was such a coward about it," Sylvia said. Her grandmother, who lived in Richmond, called the boy's father and threatened legal action. "The dad said that if we tried to press it that Timmy would get all his friends, who were also my friends—just some boys in the school—to come and testify that I was a real whore and that I had fucked all of them, which was totally untrue."

With that avenue closed, Sylvia's grandmother began to call her friends trying to get the name of an abortionist. Sylvia was shocked; her "real Baptist" grandmother had always been staunchly opposed to abortion. But the search was fruitless, and Sylvia began to resign herself to the pregnancy. A campus beauty from a well-to-do family was pregnant at around the same time, Sylvia recalled with scorn, but she simply ducked away for a weekend and returned to school with her problem taken care of.

At Thanksgiving, when Sylvia was three months pregnant, a man broke into the apartment she had rented near her grandmother's home and raped her. She reported the incident, but the police officers wisecracked and as much as told her, Sylvia claimed, that she deserved what she got for living on the edge of a black neighborhood. The doctor who examined her told the police he thought she might have made the whole thing up in an attempt to get an abortion. "It was just typical," she shrugged, as if to convey that she was destined to be victimized by cruel or insensitive men.

At Christmas break, Sylvia returned to Macon, where her mother took her to a nearby abortionist. "It was just like a regular person's house. . . . My mother sat with me, and he explained that since I was four months pregnant by this time the only thing he could do was give me a shot in my uterus and they would take me to this motel room. It was like right out of a movie, all this corny stuff. My mother couldn't be with me. I had to be all by myself." Maybe the doctor was afraid of witnesses, Sylvia speculated. He told Sylvia and her mother that a nurse would come to the motel room when Sylvia went into labor. Lastly, he told them that the procedure would cost seven hundred dollars.

"We didn't have seven hundred dollars and couldn't get it," Sylvia said. "When we left we said that we would come back, but we didn't. My mother took me to another lady, a black lady, who didn't want to do it, but she told us how to give me an abortion: Straighten out a coat hanger and put it in a catheter and then you put it up and pop it. I don't know what you pop. That was what was so scary. . . . We went and bought the catheter and then I said, 'I don't think so.' My mother really wanted me to, but she wouldn't do it. . . . I was too afraid."

Sylvia considered adoption "for about a minute. I didn't want my child to be raised by Southern Baptists." So after her failure to obtain an abortion, Sylvia returned to Richmond, in part to escape her father's anger. She imitated his deep, gravelly drawl: "Every time I look at that stomach it makes me want to throw up." She stayed with her grandparents because she was afraid to be alone again after the rape.

At the welfare clinic, the doctors liked to joke with her, she said, because she was white and pretty. But she believed the doctor-patient relationship actually was one of mutual contempt. "One doctor saw on my chart that I'd taken LSD. He asked me: 'Why did you take LSD? Don't you care about your baby?' I told him I didn't know I was pregnant at the time. 'Really?' he said. 'Do you know how you got pregnant? Heh, heh, heh.' . . . People assume that if you're poor you're ignorant and stupid."

At ten o'clock one spring evening, Sylvia entered a Richmond hospital alone and in labor. She recalled being put in a dark labor room lined with extra gurneys and medical supplies, perhaps a storage or utility area. When she screamed obscenities during her contractions, a nurse came in and slapped her and told her, "Shut your filthy mouth, girl." Sylvia was strapped down to the bed until the baby was delivered at eight o'clock the next morning.

Sylvia's grandparents took care of the baby. Sylvia couldn't stand to hear her cry. "I didn't like her very much. I think I was mean to her." She remembered slapping the infant, shaking her, and throwing her down in her crib. "When you do that stuff, you're not conscious of what you're doing. It's instinctive. I remember wondering if that was what people meant by child abuse."

When Carrie was only five months old, Sylvia decided to hitchhike to San Francisco. To raise money for the trip she applied for a job as a barmaid, but the bar owner offered to give her money for sex instead. "In a way, it did seem better because if you're barmaiding, you have all these guys hanging around yelling at you and touching you. . . . I've done some really rotten jobs for quick money," she said, being coy about whether she accepted the bar owner's offer. She and the baby got a ride from a man who said he would take them as far as Missouri. But when Carrie began wailing with an ear infection, the man dropped them in the rain at a clinic in Indiana.

"We were hippies when we lived in California. . . . I kind of felt that was the only alternative to being poor. You could be a poor hippie," Sylvia said. Over the years she has had her chances and turned them down. She did marry a young lawyer briefly, when Carrie was about five, and she had another daughter, Danielle. She has also had several abortions and a number of bouts with chronic depression. Except for her short second marriage, she has spent the rest of her life as a poor, single mother.

Sylvia came to think of herself as the "poor, white trash" her grandmother used to look down upon, the people who lived along the river. Before she was thirty she felt "washed-up and hopeless," alone in a cold-water walk-up with two young children. "When I was feeling good, I saw my life alone with the children as courageous," she said. She called herself a pioneer, a new kind of woman. But when the heat was shut off and the pipes froze, she hit rock bottom. She remembered listening to a psychiatrist on the radio talking about women and depression and screaming, "They need money, not tranquilizers, you creep!"

Poor women are always treated as if they are dumb, Sylvia told us. But they are not stupid, just demoralized. "All the poor women I know are depressed. You get really lethargic and you really can't face things." She has read articles about depression and has found all the same symptoms occur in poverty. Guilt, hopelessness, constant anxiety—the checklist for depression applies equally to "dead-end, poor persons. . . . Does that mean all poor people are depressed? Does that mean poverty is caused by depression? They are just so similar." Sylvia was convinced that poverty made her easy prey for sleazy men. Yet she contended men are the only way for women to ever get out of poverty. Ten years ago, she had hoped to follow that path herself by throwing off her scorn for middle-class values in order to marry a "rich Republican. . . . He really wasn't my type. But anyway he was real in love with me—I think he was. . . . I got pregnant by him. I sort of resigned myself to being with him. I was always like thinking: 'Well, it wouldn't be so bad. We could live in Palm Beach and have a nice car and the kids could go to a private school and even though I don't agree with this and that, he would always provide for us.' . . . See, I don't know for sure if I wanted a baby as much as I wanted that myth of the 'happy family with a baby.' " But the rich Republican insisted that she have an abortion. "I was pretty hurt by that." She even claimed that the private clinic he took her to gave her a sedative to quiet her when she tried to change her mind at the last minute.

At times Sylvia has felt paralyzed by hopelessness. "I'd always keep the house clean, but the idea of going out and looking for a job, no way. I just couldn't, even if I did get somebody to take care of the kids." She couldn't imagine mustering the energy to put her clothes on. Sylvia has often wondered in the worst of times what her life might have been if one of the failed abortion attempts in 1968 had succeeded. "I can hardly see myself really working my way up in a career," she said with a mocking laugh. "But I'm sure I'd probably be happier. I think I would have done more things."

Opportunities may still await her, Sylvia admitted. Her children are almost grown and she is still relatively young. Yet she wonders if she could respond to opportunity, since she has been crippled so often by anxiety and depression. Her illness has caused her children to suffer as well. They have had to grow up too fast, their well-being stalked by Sylvia's problems. She recalled an instance when Carrie, at twelve, stayed up all night putting cold compresses on her mother's forehead because Sylvia was "freaked out." What Sylvia had bought on the street as a tranquilizer had turned out to be a powerful psychedelic.

When we spoke with her, Sylvia was running a rare books store, where she also sold occult objets d'art. She had also begun acting in some local theater productions. Carrie had just graduated from high school and was working part-time as a receptionist while attending art school. Danielle was still at home. They all had a good relationship now, Sylvia felt. Because of her acting, she often moved now in artistic and academic circles, but she still felt that single mothers were social pariahs. Wives did not trust Sylvia with their husbands, she told us. Men felt uncomfortable when they discovered she still had boy-friends.

Sylvia had harsh advice for women who find themselves faced with an unwanted pregnancy. "Mostly what I really think is that if you don't think that you can handle having a baby, you probably can't. . . . I hate to bring up child abuse and all that kind of stuff because I don't want to just add that stigma to [the single mother]. But the truth is if you don't have any money, you're freaked out, and you don't have any friends, you're hysterical and there's no one around but that child. . . . Well, I see it all the time."

Sylvia admitted that she abused her children. The society whose laws and policies put abortion out of her reach did little to help her with the child she was therefore forced to bear. According to Henry David, clinical psychologist and editor of *Born Unwanted: Developmental Effects of Denied Abortion,* such a society may be building problems into its own future. David *et al.* claim that their study of Czechoslovakian children whose mothers had been turned down repeatedly for abortions demonstrates the long-term effects of forcing women to give birth. In a longitudinal study using matched pairs of children, David *et al.* found that unwanted children fared poorly. By age sixteen, many had dropped out of school. Although their IQs matched those in the control group and the study controlled for factors of poverty and broken homes, the unwanted children had not measured up to their potential as well as those who were welcomed by their mothers. As a group, the unwanted children had higher instances of drug and alcohol abuse, psychological problems, criminal behavior, and court sentences.

Although David *et al.*'s study may hold for Czechoslovakia, it is difficult to transfer their conclusions to the United States. In the twenty years since abortion first became available here, the United States has experienced a steady rise in drug and alcohol abuse, poor learning habits, and criminal behavior among the young. Such problems, in this country at least, appear to emerge from more complex causes than David *et al.*'s study might imply.

Sylvia's case also raises questions about what happens to women who become mothers as a last resort. Her bitterness and depression turned much of her talent to cynicism, and her once-spirited rebellion against the middle-class mire became little more than a shoulder shrug. Though she admitted to depression and child abuse, she scorned the value of psychotherapy. Her deeply ingrained negativity made it difficult to speculate how Sylvia's life might have gone had she not had the child she tried to abort. Julia Henning, whose embattled background resembles Sylvia's, was not as burdened by bitterness and was more willing to search for therapeutic resources.

Julia Henning

Julia Henning's face has a serenity that belies the struggles in her life. She leaned back in her bentwood rocker, handmade by Swedish farmers whose rolling fields lie just twenty miles from the midsize Minnesota town where she has lived all of her life. Minneapolis is thirty miles in another direction. There, Julia has found groups for adult children of alcoholics, psychiatrists in training, and other forms of free or low-cost therapy. Settled between the bucolic quiet, where her great-grandparents came from Sweden to farm, and the sophisticated bustle, where she found expert help, Julia seemed to have broken the stranglehold of her difficult past.

Julia was born forty-two years ago, the younger of two daughters born to hostile, alcoholic parents who never wanted any children. She was small, with delicate bones and eyes the soft blue of forget-me-nots. Her father sexually abused her when she was very young, but he was still capable of expressing some love and warmth. Her cold and negligent mother favored Julia's older sister and resented her husband's attentions to the younger girl. Julia became pregnant as a teenager and married the child's father, another alcoholic who walked out on her a year later.

She was a nineteen-year-old mother, raising her daughter Ginger alone, when her sister talked her into going dancing at a local club. There she danced with a former neighbor she had not seen since childhood. "I felt rather safe because he was someone my family knew and I had a wonderful time with him, just dancing all night," Julia remembered. Toward the end of the evening, Julia's sister pulled her aside and whispered, "I think Eddie is quite smitten with you and I think he's married." She was right on both counts, but her warning came too late. Julia was already smitten as well. Eddie, who was fifteen years older than Julia, told her sad stories about his terrible marriage. "I didn't realize he was snowing me. I was much too young," she said.

Julia and Eddie saw each other on and off. When they began to have sex, Julia tried birth control pills but had a terrible reaction to them—headaches and swelling in her legs. Sometimes Eddie used condoms and sometimes he tried to withdraw before ejaculation. "Sometimes that worked and sometimes it didn't. It was a very careless approach. There were attempts, but careless ones," Julia said. After two years of this hit-or-miss method of contraception, Julia became pregnant. Eddie panicked. He had talked about leaving his wife, but he had two boys whom he adored. "I remember him saying that he would sit down and try to talk to them to tell them that he was going to leave. But he would come back with these sad stories about how they would respond. Of course, I would be devastated and say, 'Oh God, you just *can't* leave.' So he had a wonderful setup. He knew exactly how to play the cards. . . . There would be no way that we could have a life together. This was just not a consideration at all."

It was 1971. Many large hospitals were performing abortions with approval from two psychiatrists, but Julia knew nothing about that. She had a small sales job, doing house calls and telephone solicitations from her home. When she told her boss that she might have to quit and why, he gave her the name of a doctor with offices in a large Minneapolis hotel who might help her.

Eddie borrowed money from a loan shark for Julia's abortion and then was so nervous that he wrecked his car trying to get it to her. The doctor, who had answered his own phone, set up a nighttime appointment. He was an older man, perhaps retired from regular practice. He was alone in his office. "Everything was cold and gloomy," Julia said. The doctor refused to answer her questions and told her she was too upset and unprepared for the procedure the first time she went. When she returned within a week, chemically calmed by Valium, he performed a suction abortion, took her envelope with three hundred dollars cash, and quickly ushered her out of the office.

Her sister drove her home, and Eddie waited for her at her apartment. "Eddie and I were up all night just talking about it. I was angry. I was crying, and it was very hard for both of us." But the physical effect of the abortion was minimal, and that helped Julia to put the experience out of her mind fairly quickly. She and Eddie resumed their relationship, no more cautious than before about contraception, although Julia cannot explain why. About a year later, she was pregnant again. In the meantime, the relationship had progressed—or so she thought.

"Actually, I was not at all unhappy about the pregnancy," Julia said. Eddie had been complaining constantly about his miserable marriage and mean wife, who now knew about their relationship. He was finally ready to leave. "We were going to have our child. We were going to start our life. My daughter would have a good dad, because he was a good dad to his sons, and he liked my daughter. So I wasn't unhappy, and he wasn't willing for me to have an abortion again, either. We started to make plans."

Eddie left his family at last. He had been renting a room for about a month when Julia called him on Easter morning to invite him to come over for her daughter's Easter egg hunt. Instead of Eddie, the landlady picked up the phone and announced that he had moved out. Julia knew right away that he had gone back to his family.

"I was about seven months pregnant. It was real, real painful, real scary and awful. So I just decided to call and talk to his wife and ask her if she would come to my home. It was time to get this aired out." Julia does not think Eddie's wife knew about the pregnancy until she arrived that afternoon at Julia's apartment with Eddie.

It appeared they had been crying. "They both came in wearing sunglasses.

They never took them off the whole time they were there," Julia said. The wife sat in a chair and Eddie stood beside her with his hand on her shoulder. "He really appeared to be very supportive of her. They were a couple," not the embattled and estranged pair Julia had been hearing about. But that was not the worst of Eddie's betrayals. In front of his wife, he denied that Julia was carrying his child. Devastated, Julia argued with them briefly, then gave up and showed them the door.

"I had to go through some real difficult decision making," Julia said. A cloud crossed her face and she leaned forward. She had no choice but to go ahead with the pregnancy this time; yet she could not see how she could care for another baby. "All I could think about was this second baby not having a dad to say, 'I'm your dad' and who would not provide financial support." She was already providing the sole, meager support for Ginger. "I couldn't imagine any more deprivation," she said. But at least Ginger's father acknowledged her and visited from time to time. "I just couldn't understand what I was going to do on holidays when my girl got things from a dad and this child wouldn't." She decided to give this baby up for adoption.

But there were complications. Her divorce from Ginger's father had never been made final, and Julia discovered that under Minnesota law a husband was considered the father of his wife's child if they were married at the time of conception. For years, Julia's only contact with her husband had been indirect—her repeated attempts to elicit child support through the courts and his rare visits with Ginger, which he arranged through his mother. Now she had to get him to sign papers that would relinquish his claim to a child he had nothing to do with. "Well, he had his opportunity to ride me to the lowest part of the earth," Julia recalled. "I knew then that this was going to be hard."

Julia retreated from the world, sticking close to her apartment and wearing big muumuus to cover her pregnancy on her occasional trips to the grocery store. The loss of both her relationship with Eddie and her dream of having this child with him hit her hard. "I remember feeling as close to losing it as I think I have ever been. The best I could deal with it was just rocking in my rocking chair for hours and hours and hours," Julia said. "I guess I was wishing my life away, just wishing I could wake up at another point in time."

Maureen, a woman Julia used to clean house for, popped in one day to drop off some of her daughter's old clothes for Ginger. "My God!" Maureen exclaimed when Julia got up to fix her a cup of coffee. "You're pregnant, Julia!" Maureen was so upset that her reaction shook Julia out of her emotional paralysis. Maureen convinced Julia to seek counseling through the Christian adoption agency where Julia had already agreed to place her child. "I wish I could take this baby myself," Maureen kept saying, but she already had three sons of her own.

A month later, Julia gave birth to a healthy boy who was whisked away and into foster care until the legal paperwork could be completed. She had been advised not to see him and she didn't. She went back home to her rocking chair, until one day she got a call from Maureen. Maureen had found a couple who had been on the adoption waiting list for six years. Maureen's husband knew the man through his law practice and knew that his wife had finally conceived, only to deliver a stillborn boy a few months earlier. The couple lived in a wealthy suburb and desperately wanted a child. If Julia was willing to give them her son, Maureen promised he would have a loving home and she would be able to keep Julia posted on how he was doing.

"She promised to be my informant, which was such an act of grace that I just felt very grateful," Julia said, clasping her hand over her heart. "I really believed God was very much in my life, and knowing how painful this could have been for me, He provided this opportunity." There was another blessing, Julia said in a whisper. "I got to see him."

Between the foster care and his delivery to the family that would adopt him, Maureen brought Julia's son to her apartment. He was two months old. "Really cute. *Really* cute," she said with a grin. "It was so nice. I got to give him a bath, change his clothes, talk to him a little bit." She paused. "But I do remember that I made a conscious decision to stay detached."

Over the years, Maureen has kept her word. "You know, you just need to hear a word or two. I'm sure I would not have made it through the years as well if I hadn't had that information," Julia said. The boy has started college. He rides horses, plays baseball, and has an interest in law, like his adoptive father. "To this day, I have never felt that I made the wrong decision," she said. But she wonders if her son will ever know why she did what she did—"That it was really done so that he would have opportunities. I could never give him the full family that he has, loving parents, opportunities for education."

The only troubling aspect of Maureen's reports has been news that the family has never told the boy that he was adopted. "I wasn't really surprised," Julia said. When the adoption so quickly followed the loss of the couple's own son, Julia had harbored a suspicion that the mother might try to forget the substitution. Julia is troubled by the fact that the adoptive parents have allowed their relationship with their son to be based to some extent on fear and on a fundamental dishonesty. "I think they've done a terrible injustice to him as well as to themselves. . . . But I would not force myself into that situation. I can stay in this position until the day I die. The only thing I want to do is look at him. That is one of the things that I just continue to pray for is that I will at least get to set eyes on him once. If it's at some distance, that's okay." She knows that he lives near her but she has never tried to find out where he is and never will, she said. She has never seen Eddie since the day he left her apartment with his wife.

"I've noticed as I was telling you this story," Julia said, as the fading rays of sunset streaked through her window and glistened in her hair, "what a different feeling and experience adoption was than abortion. And I'm sure that is directly connected to my moral values about it." She thinks of her abortion as the murder of her own child. "That baby could have been like my Ginger or like my son, who has given joy to other people. I feel like I violated something that's very dear and precious. I compare that to what the adoption experience was—there I feel I gave something very good. It was blessed and honored."

Julia has always considered herself a pro-life person, and she regretted her abortion decision, although she was not sure that she was capable of seeing another way to go at the time. "I feel a great deal of pain about how many abortions are performed on a daily basis. . . . I think sometimes abortion can harden people's hearts." She was deeply troubled by a woman she had seen recently on public television who talked about her abortion as a "joyful" experience. Julia could think of her adoption experience as joyful but never abortion. She did not believe that anyone has a "right" to abortion, but she said, "I also realize that sometimes there is no other way out." She is struggling to find some kind of middle ground on the issue. "I don't know how all of us women can connect to find an answer in all of this. I just don't know."

Throughout her thirties, and even today, Julia has sought individual and group therapies that have helped her understand how her abusive, alcoholic parents left her inadequately prepared for what she faced as a young woman. The early incest at the hands of her father, the only parent who ever showed her affection, left her feeling that her own sexuality was not within her control. "It didn't belong to me; it belonged to the man," she said. The early abuse was covered with a "gray fog of denial" until the memory of it came back during therapy a few years ago. Julia shifted herself forward, put her hands on her knees, and sought the right words. In therapy, she was able to realize that the abuse had left her feeling "helpless, vulnerable, like a victim. In other words, I didn't have control over my sexuality. That didn't belong to me. I wasn't the owner, and so that power is what I gave to the man . . . someone I thought I could love and trust," as she had thought she could love and trust her father.

While Julia was growing up in the 1950s, she said, the popular image of women as fragile and vulnerable to the whims of men only confirmed her image of herself. By the early 1970s, when she made her three decisions about pregnancy, feminists were urging women to assert their own interests. But to Julia, at the time, such ideas were a threat. She saw feminists as hard-core man-haters whom men hated right back. "I was so needy that it all was just too scary. . . . The approval of men was too much to lose. . . . If I lost that, I would lose hope, because that was the only way I knew how to go. . . . No, I didn't buy feminism. I more or less stood on the opposing end."

Today, in her forties, Julia has completed a bachelor's degree while working as a full-time clerk in a dry-cleaning store. She plans to become a full-time graduate assistant in a Ph.D. program in social work soon. Julia said she thought that if anyone could help other women break through the fog of unconsciousness, she could. "I know I can't change and take total responsibility for each woman that I work with, but I can contribute pieces," she said. Julia ran her fingers through her hair and leaned back in her chair. She hoped her most important asset in her work would be her approach. "Because I remember what turned me off back then, when the women's movement first came out. The feminists were just so unappealing. Not just to men, but they were unappealing to me." And the negative image of feminism was still around, Julia was convinced. She had recently had a conversation with Ginger, who had finished college and begun working in a male-dominated field, about some women's issues. Julia suggested a few books. Ginger's response was: "Mum, I'm not going to be a dyke and wear army boots. I'm sorry." That image, Julia pointed out, is a holdover from the 1960s; she was hearing it not just from Ginger but from the young women whom she met in undergraduate classes. The militancy of the early feminists divided women and made them afraid of one another. And the damage remains unrepaired today.

A Search for Balance and Dialogue

In their passion to escape the restraints of domesticity, many feminists failed to find a balance between what had been traditional masculine and feminine values. The imbalance leaned toward the masculine, and some appeared to be advocating that women should simply emulate men. The media grabbed on to belittling images of feminists wearing combat boots and burning their bras, and these images became shorthand references for this perceived imbalance.

The folding of the sexual double standard into a single masculine one, where sex was easy and without obligation, had omitted the need for a connection between sex and affection, affection and commitment. Women were much more successful in entering the marketplace than they were at getting men or the marketplace to care about domestic concerns. Women who had chosen traditional roles began to lament that they were the only ones left to nurture the children, and they rightly complained that society undervalued that function. Some feminists also worried about the homefront; they felt that men underestimated the importance of domestic concerns and of women's contributions to home life and childrearing. But compared with attempts to open the male-only world to women, there were relatively few efforts to sort out what had always been valuable and worth preserving about women's traditional roles. Middle-class feminists bonded with one another in new consciousness-raising groups, but their sisterhood seldom spanned political differences. Consequently, women split off not only from other women but from parts of themselves that now seemed contrary to their causes.

By the late 1960s, abortion was a burning social issue. It was discussed vigorously and robustly but not yet with great rancor. The arguments—pro and con—began to attach themselves to all the shifting and inchoate views on the proper role of women. Traditionalists saw legalization of abortion as a last straw in the devaluation of women's domestic concerns. Many feminists, on the other hand, insisted that women could not be free without total reproductive freedom, including abortion. As ideas about revolution faded, feminists focused increasingly on the winning of rights—to equal pay, to education, to jobs, and to abortion. In response, opponents began to argue for fetal rights.

But the issue was not yet reduced to only these positions. To some socially concerned women and men, the increasing number of abortions was a symptom of deep inequities in America. To them, the issue of abortion represented matters of human relationships—and not just that of the woman's relation to the child forming within her. People who maintained this focus saw decisions about birth, abortion, and public policy as reflections of how men and society valued women and children and whether American society cared for the individuals within it. They argued that this network of relationships—the private as well as the political ones—should be characterized by care and responsibility. President Lyndon Johnson's 1960s Great Society program was a part of this thinking. Within this frame of reference, the civil-rights concepts of social justice were being extended to include—however paternalistically—a helping hand to the poor and oppressed. For a time, America seemed to be grappling with the connection between rights and responsibilities.

In the context of so much social change, America seemed ready to tackle the abortion issue in a spirit of give and take. In April 1968, *McCall's* published what the magazine implied were conflicting views on abortion. On one side was Eunice Kennedy Shriver, founder of the Special Olympics and of the Joseph P. Kennedy Jr. Foundation and sister of the late president. On the other was Dr. Alan F. Guttmacher, obstetrician and subsequent founder of the research institute that bears his name. But their disagreement was hardly a simple pro versus con debate on legalization. In fact, they agreed that the movement to legalize abortion was unstoppable.

In her article, Shriver was sympathetic with the reformists. "I do not approve of using the criminal code to impose my personal moral standards—or anyone else's—on the whole of society," she said. But she warned that "mere changes in the abortion laws constitute a terribly inadequate response to the conditions that motivate the advocates for reform." These conditions included poverty, suffering, and the social costs of unwanted children. "Instead of being content with legalistic tinkering," Shriver pleaded, "I would urgently propose that we try to change the conditions that cause people to seek abortion. . . . I think we should be *intolerant* toward anything that makes it difficult for a woman who has conceived a child to bring him or her into the world in joy and gladness—confident that if some problems arise that are beyond her capacity, she can trust her community, like a larger family surrounding and supporting her, to provide the assistance she needs."

Shriver estimated that 80 percent of abortions had nothing to do with the dire circumstances (e.g., rape, incest, fetal abnormalities, or a threat to maternal health) under which the majority of people would approve of abortion. Her suggestions for reducing this 80-percent figure indicate that she was sensitive to factors that our interviews have shown actually do affect birth-or-abortion decisions. For example, Shriver recommended counseling for women seeking abortions, more involvement and accountability of fathers, education on parenting in the schools, birth insurance to help parents with the heavy financial burden of a child with birth defects, and a family allowance plan similar to those in other industrial democracies. She also argued for some recognition of the value of the fetus, which many European statutes now include, and she pointed out that "We have not begun to do enough to make birth control universally understood, universally available to anyone who truly needs it."

Shriver maintained that her policy suggestions showed "respect for human beings as they really are, for the sexual act in all its implications, for parenthood, and for community." She contrasted her ideas with what she saw as a "drift into what I would call the 'Hard Society' "—one without love, in which everyone takes care of himself or herself and people too frequently use one another to satisfy their desires without assuming the responsibilities of permanent relationships. The Hard Society was characterized by "separateness between rich and poor, between whites and blacks, between an intellectual elite and the unlearned masses, where both individuals and blocs are concerned solely with maximizing their own comforts and enforcing their own prejudices."

Dr. Alan Guttmacher argued different points in a very different style. Citing opinion polls and the inconsistencies and injustices of current law, he focused on evidence in favor of legalization, a point Shriver had conceded, early in her discussion, was an inevitability. Guttmacher predicted—rather rashly as it has turned out—that legal abortion would go far toward making every child a wanted child. He also believed it would eliminate the racketeering aspects of illegal abortion, reduce discrimination, save lives, and lower the birthrate.

Finally, Guttmacher advised that abortion reform should progress slowly, predicting that most states would have liberalized laws by 1975. He did not favor the total repeal of abortion laws. Abortion on demand for women, Guttmacher argued, would reduce the need for birth control, which he believed was preferable to abortion, and would absolve men of all responsibility for birth control. With amazing prescience and error, Guttmacher said, "To be sure, by 1990 [reform] may no longer be necessary, for if before then a safe, effective pill is discovered that any woman can take on the twenty-fifth day of a menstrual cycle and it will bring on her period three days later, whether or not she is pregnant, the matter of repealing abortion laws becomes strictly . . . academic." Guttmacher foresaw a medical development much like the French pill RU-486, but he failed to see that it would by no means render the abortion question moot.

What Guttmacher did favor, as an evolutionary step, were laws that would permit abortion where there was a risk to the mother's mental or physical health, grave danger of fetal impairment, or rape or incest. He also recommended legal abortions for teenagers or older women and for couples facing extraordinary hardships, including the kinds of conditions Shriver thought the nation must address along with abortion reform if it wanted to avoid becoming a Hard Society.

Shriver's language was full of her concern for the welfare of society, women, and children. Guttmacher also supported those interests, but he focused more narrowly on the injustice of denying women access to safe, legal abortion. He did not raise questions about society's responsibility to welcome children or to provide for them a better world than the one that existed. He dealt with the world as it was and pointed out the failures of current law. Shriver's recommendations reflect a standard of human responsibility and caring, which Carol Gilligan identifies as the approach to moral and ethical dilemmas often used by women. Guttmacher used a standard of justice, more typical of men's decision making. It was the latter that characterized the *Roe v. Wade* ruling five years later, when the Supreme Court established a woman's right to abortion without any of the moderating language both Shriver and Guttmacher advocated.

Shriver's fears about the effect of legalization seem prescient today. They describe what Mary Ann Glendon, author of *Abortion and Divorce in Western Law*, fears we have already become: a culture in which individualism reigns unchecked by sufficient concern for other people, by respect for their needs and views, or by a regard for the good of the larger community. In fact, Shriver argued that mere change in abortion laws "evades the core problems instead of solving them—or at best treats symptoms rather than the underlying conditions." As a nation, she added, echoing the words of her brother, the late President Kennedy, "I think we can do better."

The 1968 Shriver and Guttmacher articles indicate that had these two faced one another in person they would have found their arguments more complementary than oppositional. Like Shriver and Guttmacher, most Americans in the late 1960s were not prepared to divide neatly into two camps—one for the woman and the other for the fetus. The results of an October 1967 poll by *Good Housekeeping* of its one thousand–member consumer panel, reported in the article "Should Abortion Laws be Eased?", showed overwhelming support for legalization of abortion under certain conditions. These included cases in which the woman's health was in danger (84 percent in favor), when she had been the victim of rape or incest (86 percent), or when her baby was likely to be born with defects (79 percent). But these readers were unsympathetic, to about the same degree, to women seeking abortions because family income was too low, because they were unmarried, or because they were married but wanted no more children. Only one in ten of those polled supported abortion on demand. Few readers saw the matter in black-and-white terms. "In fact, they find it so complex that replies are often laced with seeming contradictions," *Good Housekeeping* reported. "Not a single reader approached this subject in a casual or frivolous manner," the magazine found, describing the process for most respondents as "soul-searching." Perhaps such a process would have led to legislative compromises and to policies designed to allow abortion in some circumstances but also to encourage pregnancy to go forward in others.

In *McCall's* and *Good Housekeeping* and in other public forums of the time, there was an appreciation of the complexity of the abortion issue. Churches were not yet cemented into positions on abortion law. Religious leaders spoke in modulated tones. "Catholics do not need the support of civil law to be faithful to their religious convictions," said Boston's Richard Cardinal Cushing in an article in *Life* entitled "Abortion Comes Out of the Shadows." Then, as now, opinion polls contained "seeming contradictions" that *Good Housekeeping* concluded were indicative of the public's willingness to wrestle with moral and emotional complications. It is anyone's guess where such discussions might have led. Shrill voices were heard before *Roe v. Wade*, but they were not the ones that carried the day—yet. For a brief period of time, the public discourse on abortion left room to consider both the principles of caring and those of justice. For a brief time, the public dialogue on the legalization of abortion began to resemble the moral and emotional complexity of private experience.

3

THE MORE THINGS CHANGE . . .

When feminism took root in the late sixties, a movement was already afoot in a number of states to reform abortion laws by giving doctors more room to recommend abortion. But feminists quickly transformed the debate, recasting the issue as one of "rights" over one's own body. . . . Responding to the pressure, a few states soon revised their statutes along lines closer to feminist models. Then, in January 1973, in the case of *Roe v. Wade*, the Supreme Court . . . declared unconstitutional any prohibitions on abortion in the first trimester, and made second-trimester abortions easily available. Feminists, caught unawares by this unexpected boon, hailed the decision as a major victory. . . .

For Americans who objected to abortion, the Supreme Court's *Roe* decision . . . appeared as a "bolt from the blue," catching them off-guard and unprepared. Though local anti-abortion groups formed almost immediately, the Court's ruling seemed clear and incontrovertible, leaving little room for action.

John D'Emilio and Estelle B. Freedman,
Intimate Matters: A History of Sexuality in America (1988)

Introduction

Roe v. Wade surprised everyone in 1973. Its suddenness engendered hot dispute and disrupted the more careful and probing dialogue that had taken place in the late 1960s. Though many voices had been strident then, too, they did not drown out the calmer ones until abortion abruptly became legal.

Insofar as *Roe v. Wade* granted women more of the reproductive control that is crucial to equality, women's rights advocates were correct in calling it a victory. But euphoria blinded them to the dangers of this boon. The Supreme Court's decision, which implicitly sanctified the feminist call for an abortion "right," also exiled opposing and moderating views to an unconstitutional wasteland. It permitted abortion without also promoting the value of pregnancy and childbirth. And in doing so it split American society as if with a cleaver.

What many feminists of the early 1970s were not in a position to see was that the Supreme Court had devalued women's reproductive function even as it gave them one-sided control over it. *Roe v. Wade* did not grant full reproductive freedom, just the freedom *not* to reproduce—assuming a woman could afford an abortion. This was in vivid contrast to the liberalizing abortion statutes

97

of other Western democracies, most of which had been worked out in leg-islatures instead of being handed down by the courts. Nearly all of those statutes, which permitted abortion under varying circumstances, also contained measures to prevent unplanned pregnancies, promote alternatives to abortion, or otherwise acknowledge and institutionalize the state's concern for life and its interest in supporting childbirth and families.

Even Sweden, which enacted the most liberal abortion laws of all the Western European countries, carefully intertwined those laws with efforts to make abortion a genuine last resort. For example, although it allowed un-restricted abortion in the first twelve weeks of pregnancy, the Swedish govern-ment limited the need for that option through generous maternal benefits and the aggressive enforcement of child support rulings. It mandated sex education and promoted contraception, making the latter widely available and affordable. It required women seeking second-trimester abortions to meet with a social worker. Finally, says Mary Ann Glendon in *Abortion and Divorce in Western Law,* Swedish law—like the laws in many American states—prohibited abor-tion if the fetus was likely to be viable. Exceptions were made only when the mother would be seriously endangered by continuing the pregnancy.

The more moderate French statute, Glendon says, permitted abortion until the tenth week of pregnancy for any woman "whose condition place[d] her in a situation of distress." The woman herself was the judge of this, and so the statute, written in 1975, effectively granted early term abortion on demand. It is important to note, however, that it did so without directly saying so. Glendon holds that the effect of designating abortion only for women in distress was to convey "a message which *may* enter, along with other social forces, into the way in which French men and women think—and teach their children and each other—about how one should conduct one's life." The French statute further upheld respect for "every human being from the commencement of life" and proclaimed, "There shall be no derogation from this principle except in cases of necessity and under conditions laid down by this law." In 1979, Glendon reports, the statute's message was strengthened by new language that defined as a "national obligation" the acceptance, support, and education of children and the enactment of strong family policies.

The 1973 United States ruling identified no similar national obligation. Coming out of a long tradition of individualism and a corresponding emphasis on rights, it held strictly to the justice model of moral decision making that psychologist Carol Gilligan ascribes to men and their cultural conditioning. The *Roe v. Wade* decision focused on the individual woman's right to privacy, unqualified by any expressed concern for the value of pregnancy and childbirth. It contained no suggestion that human interdependence and responsibility, the hallmarks of the caretaking standard that women learn to consult in moral dilemmas, were as important as privacy and autonomy. Many women who celebrated the ruling were straightforwardly pleased to hold legal proprietorship over their bodies; they perceived no dangers in the one-sidedness of the Supreme Court's decision. Others were appalled by what they saw as society's abandonment of its weakest members, unborn children.

Roe v. Wade's model of moral and ethical choice was there for Americans to emulate in their personal lives. The message it still conveys to the American people—though with even greater opposition today—is that abortion is permissible for any and all reasons through the first and in many cases the second trimester of pregnancy and that the state is not responsible for helping people to find other options. None of the supports that are offered in this country— such as welfare or occasional job-training programs—is sufficient to overcome a generations-old pattern of family breakdown and dependence on social programs.

Few women's rights advocates in 1973 saw any downside to Roe v. Wade, however. Some of the most vocal feminists, given their passionate reaction against persistent, belittling views of women, were naturally suspicious of traditional female roles. In their haste to throw off the bitter constraints that had bound women's lives so tightly, they were unlikely to protect motherhood in the abstract or to push for alternatives to abortion. Instead, they hailed the Supreme Court's ruling and often turned their backs on the traditional values and attitudes still cherished by millions of women. In effect, they adopted the justice standard that had ruled in favor of reproductive "rights" and in many cases rejected not only old constraints but an entire set of values traditionally associated with women—the values reflected in the caretaking standard, which included nurturance, relationship, interpersonal responsibility, and the refusal to abandon the needy or weak.

Some women who still held these values or aspired to strictly domestic roles became ardent, pro-life adversaries of feminism through avenues largely defined by class. Middle-class feminists who supported Roe v. Wade—many of them thinking it would benefit poor women by letting them end pregnancies they could not afford—failed to recognize that pushing reproductive matters beyond the reach of public policy actually made life harder for poorer women. What if they *wanted* to continue a pregnancy? What if they wanted both a family and the opportunity to learn a skill and end their dependence on welfare?

What if they needed help collecting child support? What if they needed high-quality, affordable day-care so that they could work or go to school? The question for American society was, and still is, which will be the last resort of its public policies: birth or abortion?

These economic realities, obscured from some feminists' views, slowly began to define the two sides of the abortion debate. As Kristin Luker found in her studies of pro-choice and pro-life activists—reported in *Abortion and the Politics of Motherhood*—higher education levels were more common among middle-class women, who could afford to reach them. Their academic accomplishments were associated with lower levels of religious commitment, greater independence from men, and more earning power. For these women, the privatization of reproductive choice was unquestionably an asset.

The same could not be said for women of the poorer classes. They were less able to afford an education and less likely to value what came with it. Many opted freely for domesticity as a career, their choice sometimes bolstered by religion or by traditional gender views. Others may have drifted into marriage and motherhood because they lacked other options. Many of these women were threatened by feminism, either because they did not have the means to achieve independence or because they equated feminism with man-hating and were afraid of the effect such an attitude could have on their relationships with men they loved, valued, or relied upon. As a group, these women were much closer to the edge of poverty, where private choice was more harshly constrained, and public policies of care would have eased the hardship.

Eventually, in this and more subtle ways, the victory that feminists celebrated—in the battle between "constitutional" and "unconstitutional" positions on abortion and between advocates and opponents of women's rights—would conspire with other trends and attitudes to leave a majority of women out of the women's movement. Feminism, at least as it was popularly portrayed and understood, was interested primarily in equality *with* men; it paid less attention to equality *among* women. Feminism belonged to women who wanted careers, equal respect (and equal pay) for their intellects and skills, and a fifty-fifty division of child care and labor at home. To a great many Americans, such feminism had a clear tendency to disregard women who were "only" housewives and mothers.

The first effect of *Roe v. Wade*, born in this split between feminists and traditionalists, was to polarize and politicize the abortion issue. In place of conscientious exploration, there arose on both sides the need to campaign, convince, and convert. Dialogue became debate, complexity gave way to propaganda. Activists could not afford to wrestle publicly with the moral or ethical questions raised by their adversaries. Women who faced unplanned pregnancies might struggle in private with doubts and with the pain of having to choose, but few admitted it openly for fear of harsh judgments or accusations of political defection. The troubling, difficult, paradoxical issue of abortion, often a source of anguish in private, thus became in public a subject of simplistic but impassioned rhetoric.

Paula Welsh, a nurse practitioner who worked in a Detroit women's clinic from 1978 until 1983, sat in her living room on a hot August evening and talked about the bitter national debate over abortion. Pushing her damp red hair off her forehead, she said, "People on both sides may in their private thoughts admit that it is a very complicated moral, personal, psychological issue, but when it comes to activism . . . they tend to exaggerate their position and not admit there are any [other valid] views, because that would give the other side ammunition."

Paula saw this defensiveness daily in her work at the clinic. Though the facility offered a range of services to women, Paula dealt mainly with abortion cases. In an environment where political feelings and commitment to a cause ran high, probing discussion was suspect. "[W]hat I went crazy about was that nobody wanted to talk. I got on my little pedestal and I yelled, 'Why don't [we] talk about it? Instead of talking about statistics and how many people went through this clinic on Friday, why don't we talk about what each one of us is feeling about abortion?'"

What Paula felt was a complicated mixture of the political and the private. She was dedicated to the belief that legal abortion was essential to the quality of women's lives, and yet, she said, there were times when the work could be "just totally dehumanizing. You do thirty pelvic exams in four hours. It is a horrible experience. To see a patient every three or four minutes no matter what. . . . " Although she came to understand a lot about the circumstances, attitudes, and feelings of the clinic's clientele through frequent staff meetings, she seldom talked with individual women about their choices. "I basically saw a pelvis, and in the face of what I considered a very big moral question, and being pregnant myself at the time, it was really hard to deal with." Seeing a waiting room filled with women "all waiting to have their uterus scraped out" depressed her. "Again, I believe it should be available, but when you don't have any honest-to-God contact with patients other than feeling the size of their uterus, and not even knowing what went on in that decision, it is too hard."

In this, Paula described precisely the dilemma of most Americans: They believe abortion should be legal and the decision left to the individual, but they are afraid, given the high numbers, that some women resort to abortion lightly or for dubious reasons.

Staff meetings and reports from counselors at the clinic reassured Paula on this count. Asked about the number of women for whom abortion is a casual choice, she had the impression "that that's really, really the exception. That it is nine out of ten much, much more complicated."

On the other hand, Paula could cite troubling cases. One involved a black teenager who had had a baby only because she had delayed her decision making and could not afford a second-trimester abortion. Paula saw her when she visited the clinic for contraception after the birth. "She was so in love with this baby," Paula recalled, "and her boyfriend had come through. . . . This young woman and young man were ecstatic about this little baby, who was getting very good care. . . . But, you know, everybody in the clinic would have lined up thinking, 'This baby shouldn't come into the world. This kid needs an abortion.' "

If clinic workers could make poor judgments, so could patients. Paula remembered one who wanted to be sure of the date on which she had conceived so that she would know whether the father of her child was white or black. If the father was her white lover, Paula recalled, the woman wanted the baby. If he was her black lover, she wanted an abortion. "The worst of it was that she had had a four-month-old child she had left with the landlord [while she had] gone to Texas the year before, and the child had died." Paula, who could not be sure when the woman had conceived, remembered saying to the social worker at the clinic, "I wish we could lie to her exactly and say 'It's the black guy and you better abort,' because this kid is going to be battered or left in some crib with the landlord." To us, Paula added vehemently, "The pro-lifers don't think about that shit."

Paula, despite her daily exposure to the complexities of the abortion issue and her own ambivalence, still held a narrow, undifferentiated view of "the pro-lifers" They were the ones who failed to think hard about troubling cases. Yet interviews with volunteers at three pro-life organizations did not support Paula's perception. Those we spoke to described at length the care with which they avoided judging or influencing their clients. They discussed their close scrutiny of their position and its possible limits and they talked about cases they had found difficult or challenging. One volunteer, a plump, cheerful mother of four named Ellen Schaeffer, said: "We've had the kind of call saying, 'Can you just pinpoint when I got pregnant? If it's my husband's baby I'll carry it. If it's my boyfriend's baby I'll abort.'" To Ellen, it was important to understand that "There's got to be more to this baby than who fathered it." Where Paula might add that who would mother the child, and how well, was equally important, Ellen would likely have offered the pro-life argument that the potential for neglect or abuse did not justify abortion. By Ellen's standards, a choice made using Paula's criteria would amount to a life-or-death call based only on a possibility. Its message would be that a hard life was not worth living or that the human spirit should not be given the chance to prevail over adversity.

Ellen differed from Paula not in the amount or depth of her pondering but in her conclusion. To Ellen, the fetus had a real and separate identity that deserved protection. She would have protected the fetus by urging that it be born; Paula would have protected it from being born into a life she believed would be ghastly. Both women were concerned for the unborn child. Both acknowledged the terrible quandaries presented by unintended pregnancy. Yet neither could see in the other the conscientious questioning that each engaged in.

Paula's account of her experience in the clinic and her resentment of the pro-life position suggest how readily judgments about birth and abortion were made along political lines. Years after *Roe v. Wade*, women who faced unplanned pregnancies continued to fear such judgments from both sides of the issue. Many paid for the politicization of the abortion issue in feelings of isolation. Often, they told no one about abortions that caused them sorrow, regret, or remorse, keeping their feelings to themselves for many years.

When something that touches people's personal lives arouses such passion and hostility in public, it silences those who most need to talk. It also excludes from public discussion the viewpoints people most need to hear. Because *Roe v. Wade* was handed down by judicial fiat instead of evolving through dialogue and legislation, the abortion question remained couched in the language of the law, defined as a matter of rights and justice alone. This emphasis was misleading, for it left out a whole set of standards and concerns that, in their focus on human responsibility and relationships, were particularly appropriate in this deeply human matter. This one-sidedness exaggerated political feelings and moral judgments about abortion in this country to such an extreme that many people were discouraged from thinking deeply about the subject or admitting their thoughts openly. Thus a matter of grave importance became oversimplified in public debate while remaining complex in private. The oversimplification, in turn, allowed some of the worst and oldest judgments about women and their sexuality to persist in spite of the societal changes that women had thought would weaken those judgments.

For example, legal abortion, which many women had expected would bring them closer to equality, instead, or in addition, kept negative views of women alive. As the abortion rates rose yearly after *Roe v. Wade*—partly because a new sexual tolerance meant more women were sexually active, partly because baby-boom women had come of age sexually, and partly because the pill and the IUD did not greatly diminish the large numbers of unwanted pregnancies—those rates appeared to uphold the notion that women were irresponsible and untrustworthy.

Kristin Luker's *Taking Chances: Abortion and the Decision Not to Contracept* illustrates the insidiousness with which such an assumption came to seem self-fulfilling. As Luker explains, "virtually all contraceptives prior to the pill were intercourse-related," which meant there was "an invariant threshold at which the male must acknowledge [the contraceptives'] presence and involve himself more or less directly in the decision not to contracept." Some men could and did countermand women's desire to prevent pregnancy. But, Luker says, the pill and the IUD marked a turning point: "Not only are both these methods used outside the context of intercourse . . . but they are both exclusively female-oriented methods."

This, Luker contends, was the plan behind contraceptive research in the United States: to separate birth control from the act that made it necessary and to put all responsibility for it on women. The argument for this approach was that "only women are motivated to contracept because only women get pregnant, and that women's motivation tends to be higher and more committed outside of the emotionally charged context of intercourse." The flaw in this argument, Luker explains, is that it confuses "value judgment with scientific fact." In this case, the value judgment—namely, that men need not worry about contraception—directly contradicts the scientific fact that both men and women play an equal part in conception.

What Luker fails to address is that equal responsibility does not mean equal effect. Men do not get pregnant, nor, in this country, are they often held accountable for their sexual acts. Though several European countries succeed in establishing paternity for nearly every child, in enforcing strict and aggressive collection of child support, and even in supporting single parents while attempting to collect from their derelict partners, the United States' efforts in these matters are notably ineffectual. Though European policies show a measure of respect for women and refrain from judging their sexuality, American policies that permit men to shuck responsibility end up being punitive toward women.

All this would seem to support the assumption that women in the United States would be doubly motivated to use birth control consistently and well, whether at the moment of intercourse or well in advance of it. But Luker found—as we have also discovered—that women often do not practice contraception effectively in either context. The forms of birth control that on paper are nearly foolproof do not work nearly so well in practice. Instead of accepting the popular conclusion that women are irresponsible at *both* rational and romantic moments, Luker set out to investigate the possibility that they have good reasons for their behavior. What she discovered is that women who forego contraception are often not abdicating responsibility but instead making reasonable choices in the pursuit of complex goals that may conflict with the simple desire to prevent pregnancy.

This is precisely what we saw repeatedly in our interviews—not only those that we have referred to in this chapter but many others that do and do not appear in this book. In nearly every case of birth control neglect or misuse that we came across, women exhibited mixed feelings about pregnancy and about their own sexual identity, values, and self-esteem. They ignored birth control because they wanted, consciously or not, to prove they were fertile, to test their relationship with a man, or to avoid acknowledging that they were fully and intentionally sexually active. They were unable to use any contraceptive method themselves—perhaps because of side effects or infections—but they did not dare insist that their partners use condoms. They stopped practicing birth control because their parents found out and disapproved, because their lovers objected, or because they had ended an affair and did not expect any sexual encounter. They ended up pregnant because they wanted attention, because they believed a man was more committed than he was, or because pregnancy would satisfy a rebellious urge or a desire to retreat from other challenges. As Luker observes, "Pregnancy connotes fertility, femininity, adulthood, independence, and many other meanings." It also permits women to retreat to the "female prerogatives to be passive and protected."

Thus women's reasons for not using birth control have to do with complex matters of relationships and of attitudes toward women and their sexuality. The failure to practice contraception is often grounded in, and perpetuates, inequality and poor self-esteem. Matters only grow worse once a woman is pregnant, when the man who has been absolved of all responsibility for contraception can turn to her and say, "Well, it's not my problem." Luker maintains that to use birth control effectively women "must feel at ease with themselves, their bodies, and their lovers and accept some less romantic aspects of bodily functions." Yet little in United States social policies or in prevailing attitudes toward women encourages or even permits most women to attain such feelings of acceptance and self-regard.

The negative views of women that are tangled up with legal abortion and with birth control explain to some extent why the sweeping social changes of the 1960s and 1970s did not bring with them robust new standards and values or true equality between the sexes. The changes in women's lives—in sex, work, marriage, motherhood, and levels of education and independence—were wide but not deep. Women's rights were expanded, but sometimes at great cost. In general, women who wanted to succeed in new endeavors had to adopt and adapt to the established terms of public and professional life. They had to prove themselves the equal of men by men's own standards, which often meant they had to deny and disown lifelong, deeply acculturated impulses toward inter-personal responsibility and caretaking. They had to prove themselves to be as decisive, autonomous, and tough-minded as their male competitors.

One reason for the shallowness of social change, and for women's wide-spread inability to incorporate some of their strengths in their new pursuits, lies in the schism between many feminists and traditional women. Had the 1960s dialogue about abortion proceeded without the cataclysm of *Roe v. Wade*, it might eventually have examined the crucial question of reproduction in rela-tionship to every other aspect of women's lives. Such an exploration might gradually have encompassed all women and all their concerns, both traditional and new. It might have encouraged women to break free of old and belittling constraints without rejecting wholesale the pursuits or values associated with those constraints. Thus marriage, motherhood, and other domestic concerns might have remained—or become—worthy of respect even in the eyes of women who wanted other things instead. Had dialogue about women's options and priorities been conducted in a give-and-take spirit among all women, perhaps it would have led to a broad winnowing of what was positive from what was negative in women's old and new experiences. In preventing or discourag-ing a total rift between groups of women, it might have enabled those with worldly ambitions to hang on to humanizing values, and it might thereby have led to social policies regarding women, children, and reproduction that were more like Europe's. Women might have been offered more genuine choices. They might have been nearly as able to proceed with pregnancy as to end it.

They might have been able to achieve both domestic and larger-world goals with the help of quality child-care, family allowances, parental leave, and other social supports. Instead, because some women came to view worldly aims as more valuable than domestic ones and others were made to feel defensive about their enjoyment of marriage and family, the two factions drifted warily and mistrustfully apart.

Although some women in both groups saw how damaging the rift was, the division persisted. The prevailing picture of feminism never convincingly included women who wanted traditional roles and found them rewarding. It did not recognize how dangerous it was to devalue *any* aspect of women's lives, even those that had been so tightly wrapped in propriety and propaganda. By the time the *Roe v. Wade* decision was handed down, even a good many feminists with children were unwilling to be thought of as "maternal." They rejected idealized views of maternity. They accepted and then insisted on abortion as a "right," not as a woeful necessity or a lesser evil. They held to a politically dictated denial of any value or emotion that could lead back to the oppression and total domestication of women. With good reason for suspicion, but with their vision fogged, they denied the importance of much that Carol Gilligan's work has found to be characteristic of women's ways of knowing—their moral grounding in human relationships, their interweaving imaginations, their pattern-making perceptions, and their constant reference to care as a moral and ethical standard.

With silence or denial surrounding the true complexity of women's choices in all matters of sex—from intimacy and affection to contraception and abortion—it is no surprise that sexual relations perpetuated a double standard. Except for a few who chose politically motivated celibacy or lesbianism, women became more heterosexually active than ever. But sex was more on men's terms than ever, especially with the separation of birth control from intercourse. No-strings, recreational sex was the new ground on which many women sought liberation from constraints and false standards. Women who wanted more intimate relationships were often afraid to say so.

Male values—or values associated with maleness—prevailed in the workplace, too. If a man could hire and fire, campaign and lobby, litigate and operate, so could a woman. The idea that women's hormones and emotions unsuited them to public and professional life was a bogey that needed killing. Feminism forged the ax. The notion that women were too tenderhearted to make tough decisions had to be disproven. Feminism provided the opportunities and arguments to refute that notion. Many women who had been starved for space and challenge seized hungrily upon new opportunities without questioning or examining them closely.

This chapter and the next focus on the effects of change in women's lives and on their decisions about pregnancy. The stories that follow illustrate the breadth of social change in the years after *Roe v. Wade*, but they also reveal much sameness underneath. In the stories of Judy McInnis and Denise Gage, what is new is their pursuit of careers and independence; what is old is the extent to which they had to deny what was most female in them in order to achieve their goals.

Judy McInnis

Judy McInnis is a busy, family-practice physician in Baltimore. She has a wide smile and a rangy, athletic build. She wears her curly, dark-brown hair short. As she looked back on 1978, when she was twenty-six, her naturally strong voice dropped almost to a whisper from time to time. "It was during my junior year of residency," she recalled. "I became pregnant using the diaphragm with somebody I had been seeing for a period of about three months. And by the time I knew I was pregnant, the relationship was over."

Judy never told the man involved that she was pregnant. "He was out of my life," she explained. "And, in a way, the decision itself, intellectually, was not at all difficult. There was no way I could be pregnant." The demands of a medical residency did not permit any breaks. "I mean," she said, "I couldn't be sick a day."

Judy didn't talk to anyone about her pregnancy in the beginning. She felt, despite her faithful use of a diaphragm, "like such a jerk for being pregnant" that she didn't want anyone to know. She also did not want to introduce a crisis among her female friends in residency, who were under the same pressure she was. All were working desperately hard to prove themselves in their field. "You've got to picture," Judy explained, "that this is a relationship in which, yes, you're close, but it's in the context of being thrown into a hellhole together." The hellhole of residency, with its intensity, thirty-six hour shifts, exhaustion, and competitiveness, did not encourage intimacy or permit lapses in control or confidence. So Judy discovered her pregnancy and decided on abortion with no support from anyone else.

Already, Judy's story bears the marks of large-scale social change. In 1978, remarkable new options were open to women in every dimension of their lives.

Judy had choices her mother had never thought of. She could have sex without strings, she could have money (or earning potential) without depending on a man, and she could build a career far beyond the borders of the pink-collar ghetto. In her level of education, achievement, and independence, Judy exemplified the women of her generation who were growing in autonomy.

By the 1980s, there had been a dramatic rise in the number of women who were independent, accomplished, and wholly self-supporting. With so many women increasingly able to earn their own living, more were able to leave unsatisfying marriages, and this contributed to a steadily rising divorce rate. Because more women aspired to careers and were free to separate sex from marriage, many of them married later or not at all. Because they had other commitments they had fewer children, so family size diminished. In all of these ways, women like Judy and her peers accelerated trends that had been started by their grandmothers in the 1920s and '30s. The changes that their choices represented, however, looked dramatic because they departed radically from those of their 1950s mothers.

And yet, Judy's generation did grow up in that odd-decade-out, when the cult of domesticity flowered and then, for so many women, grew rank with discontent. Women Judy's age, fearing that kind of discontent, became more individualistic and less constrained by relationships than their mothers had been. They embraced change, espoused political positions, and demanded reproductive rights. In all these trends, a part of them moved away from the caretaking standard of moral action and closer to the application of justice alone. Some, like Judy, were surprised by the pain they felt when the exercise of their rights came at the expense of relationships or options for caretaking.

The decision Judy had thought was intellectually straightforward turned out to be emotionally wrenching. Once she had made it, she broke her isolation by confiding in an old college friend who had had an abortion a few years earlier. The friend wanted to accompany Judy to the clinic. "I initially played proud and said, 'No that's not necessary. I can handle this myself,'" Judy recalled softly. "And she insisted on going. And I was so happy to have someone there. You just don't anticipate the impact that it's going to have."

Judy believed she would be able to steel herself for the procedure. She expected to control her emotions, as she had done at other difficult moments in her life, and then to go about her business. She maintained her resolve through obligatory counseling at the clinic, keeping her face a mask. "It had been hard enough for me to open up to a friend," she said. "I wasn't about to rehash it with a stranger."

It wasn't until the moment the abortion began, with the counselor still at her side, that Judy's emotions surged past her resolve. "It was just one of those gut-wrenching feelings of your insides and this developing organism being sucked out of you. . . . It was at that moment that it really all came crashing in."

Judy's counselor never knew. "I'm sure if someone looked at me, I would have been a woman who was showing no emotions when I had my abortion. . . . I was feeling this desperate need to somehow hold it in, and maintain control."

This, more than anything, encapsulates Judy's story. Under stress and in a time of great change, she felt she had to deny or avoid emotion. This was true not only during her abortion but in her lack of attachment to the man with whom she had conceived. Keeping her affair light and brief—previously the privilege of men more than women—was necessary in Judy's high-pressure life.

Judy's situation symbolized social change and at the same time women's need to control their feelings. The change was that four out of six new physicians in Judy's residency program were females in a formerly all-male domain. But to succeed in that domain, these women had to observe its standards. So, although feminism urged women to further their aims through sisterhood and solidarity, Judy did not feel she could call upon her female colleagues for support when she needed it. Furthermore, the female nature of her need made her feel vulnerable and embarrassed, as if pregnancy revealed her to be weak when she most needed to be strong. The demands of the career that feminism had in some measure won for her were so great that they put feminine values and concerns on hold. As Judy told us, it wasn't until "later on" that her friendships with her female coresidents grew or could be tested.

Thus, although Judy was unquestionably privileged in her ability to pursue a lucrative and respected career, she also paid for that privilege. Abortion was emotionally much harder than she thought it would be, not only because of the loss it represented on its own but because of something larger, too. Referring to the potential that her pregnancy represented, she said: "I interrupted it. And it was a part of me . . . it was part of my own potential. And it didn't hit at that level until the time at which it was being done."

What Judy's abortion "sucked out" of her was her potential for motherhood and other close human bonds. Judy, pregnant in an environment in which standards had been developed and defined by men, was isolated from those bonds, not because a given man had let her down but because she had accepted the consequences of no-strings sex and a demanding job. In doing so, she had left herself no room for intimacy, trust among colleagues, pregnancy, or the exploration of emotion. The time and place in which Judy pursued her goals could not be expected to accommodate those qualities. Yet the imposition of harsh, inflexible standards in a proving ground for a caring profession seems inconsistent at best. Had changes in women's lives established true equality, striking a balance between the standards of justice and caretaking, Judy's residency might have been less hellish.

Today, Judy feels she has resolved the pain of her abortion. Though she has had four miscarriages in the years since then, she also has a healthy three-year-old daughter and a happy marriage. She enjoys family practice and feels no resentment for the choice her profession forced her to make. "Life is full of hard choices," she said. "If I were a fundamentalist, I suppose I would look at my miscarriages as punishment for my abortion. But I really don't feel that way. And I think my experience has made me more sympathetic to patients who have to deal with this decision."

Denise Gage

Like Judy McInnis, Denise Gage had an abortion because she wanted a career. Unlike Judy, she was married and had three children at the time of her decision. Now thirty-nine, Denise is a dark-haired, hazel-eyed woman with slender hands that are never still. She told us her story in a quiet corner of a park on Long Island, sitting at a picnic table.

Denise had her first child in 1971, at eighteen, after refusing the abortion that her mother and boyfriend urged her to have. She had grown up in a troubled family, with an alcoholic father, and had quit high school at fifteen. Frank, her twenty-two year-old boyfriend, was a drug addict trying to stay straight. He, too, had limited job skills and not much education. Nevertheless, when he agreed to marry her, Denise was filled with romantic notions of motherhood and domesticity.

The romance was surprisingly sturdy. It never entirely died, even under the pressures of parenthood and the pain of dead-end jobs and poverty. Denise adored Frank and their daughter Sally, but she was still lonely and miserable for the first four years of her marriage. "I just wanted Frank to like me," she recalled. "That was my fantasy. That he would care more than he did." Frank never fulfilled Denise's fantasy. Though he stayed free of heroin, he remained addicted to alcohol, and his addiction left little room for caring or companionship.

Denise hit bottom herself after she was fired from her job as a K Mart cashier. The shock and humiliation roused her from depression and challenged her to confront an almost total lack of confidence. Motivated largely by fear, Denise forced herself to pursue an education. She had to buck her own painful misgivings and Frank's scornful objections, but gradually she earned a two-year degree in psychology. After seven more years, with time off for two more babies, Denise completed a bachelor's degree and even went on to graduate school in clinical psychology. She was the only student in her demanding program who had three children to raise, a dying father to care for, and a husband who behaved less rationally all the time. Denise called Frank a "dry drunk." He no longer drank, but he continued to indulge in "the same wild, erratic behavior binges" without the "excuse of alcohol" in his system. She compared him to the charming, unpredictable, but morbid character Nick in the movie *Sophie's Choice*. "It was as though he were my fourth child. I had three natural children, and then my husband was even more of a child than they were."

Frank attempted suicide several times. He drove a car head-on into a bridge abutment, overdosed on pills, and made superficial cuts on his wrists. "Most of it was manipulation," Denise explained. "Finally I said: 'If there are any more suicide attempts, I'm sorry, I will not come to the hospital. I will not be there for you.' And he put me to the challenge. He tried it again, and I didn't go." To the rest of the world, Denise was a monster. Frank was furious. His family disowned her. Then she learned she was pregnant again.

"When the doctor told me, I refused to believe it," Denise said. "I was just in shock. I left the doctor's office, came out to the car, and cried and screamed. Just pounded the dashboard—'This can't be!' "

Denise's youngest child was three years old. Denise's father had died a short time earlier, after a long bout with cancer during which she had done much of the caretaking. Her mother had recently been diagnosed with the same disease. Frank had just been released from the hospital after the last melodramatic attempt on his life. In an edgy voice, near tears, Denise explained that she had reached her limit. "I just thought that life would never get any better if I went through with that pregnancy." So Denise, who had been raised a Catholic and had, with righteous determination, refused to abort her first pregnancy, decided to end this fourth one—but the choice cost her an arduous internal struggle.

"I didn't wait that long to have the abortion," she recalled. "It was probably no more than three weeks. But looking back on it—what I went through—it seems like it was months. To do that amount of thinking and that amount of changing my mind and that amount of looking at things from different angles—

but it was only three weeks." What finally stilled the wavering in Denise's heart was the thought of her three other children. "Certainly it would be wrong to have the abortion," she explained, "but it would be wrong not to have the abortion. Because if I didn't have that abortion, I would probably lose my mind, and the other children would suffer. My decision was for the betterment of the most. The least wrong. The least amount of harm done. The least number of people that would suffer."

Denise's sad acceptance of her dilemma, and her choice of the lesser evil, was a measure of how far she had come since her first pregnancy. "I didn't have that strong anti-abortion position that I had had when I was eighteen," she said soberly. Sitting at the table in the park, twirling a small twig between her fingers, she reminisced. "I had something of a self-righteous attitude at one point in my life. I was kind of on a high horse. I was faced with this decision when I was eighteen years old, and I didn't do it. I dealt with it. [I thought] why can't other people deal with it? It was very easy to be judgmental of other people when I was so naive about life."

This time, Denise said: "I was a little more realistic that life is not so simple. [W]hen it happened to me, I was humbled. It was the most humbling experience. To this day, my ideas about what's right and wrong have changed entirely. I don't believe that there is a black-and-white distinction between right and wrong anymore. I think that one incident in my life has completely changed my view of the world."

Denise not only chose something she had once sworn would be impossible for her, she also opened herself fully to a range of terrible emotions as she came to her decision and dealt with its aftermath. This, she believes, made recovery possible. "I went through such excruciating, unbelievable [pain]—I think I lost my mind during that time. I felt every feeling about it so intensely that I think I got it out of my system." Though guilt and sorrow overtook Denise for the three weeks in which she struggled to make her choice, they faded for good once she carried it out.

So did her quick judgments of other people's moral decisions "about anything, not just abortion." If emotional cleansing dissolved her pain, the humility she spoke of knocked her off her high horse. She took full responsibility for a morally troubling act. "I made the decision entirely on my own," she said. "There was no coercion, no persuasion on anybody's part. It was my own."

The final ingredient in the balm that healed Denise was communication. "There were about eight of us that were having the procedure that day," she said softly. "We had to be there at about eight in the morning, and the doctor didn't get there until about noon. We were left in a room. . . . At first we sat there for a half-hour. Nobody said a word to anybody. Then finally somebody opened up and made comments. Then we talked intensely. We told each other about our lives. Perfect strangers."

Most of Denise's companions "were in pretty bad shape," she recalled. "We were all struggling pretty equally." The sharing of that struggle had a miraculous quality to Denise. "It was intensely therapeutic to find out that I was not alone, that there were people going through the same thing at the same time."

Only one woman in the room "was very casual about it, at least on the surface," Denise said. "That was her second abortion, and she just said, 'I wasn't cut out for motherhood.' That's all there was to it. She planned on going back to work after the procedure." Denise thought the woman seemed "a little too calm. . . . I think if you don't suffer before, you suffer afterward, because it's not a natural act."

The Woman in the Waiting Room

Abortion is often viewed as unnatural or as a cause for mourning by women who already have children or who desire to do so when better circumstances arise. The woman in the waiting room, despite Denise's expectations, may never have suffered. Feeling no emotional attachment to her pregnancy and believing herself unfit for motherhood, she may have experienced no loss or guilt, especially if she also weighed her interests carefully against those of the fetus before concluding that hers took precedence.

If she chose abortion on these grounds, the woman in the waiting room was merely following the same model of moral decision making that the Supreme Court applied in Roe v. Wade. She was acting in accordance with the message implied by United States policy on abortion—that it is purely and simply a matter of rights and justice.

And yet, according to polls, a majority of Americans are unsettled by the image of a woman whose abortion interrupts the normal workday no more than a dental appointment would. Even Denise, with her new sense of humility and her reluctance to presume about other people's morality, still judged the one woman at the clinic who was not visibly in pain over her choice.

An obvious source of people's uneasiness over the idea of a woman choosing to have an abortion without an emotional struggle is that such a choice fails to align comfortably with the popular image of women as nurturers.

A less obvious but even more persuasive explanation for their discomfiture is the sense that there is something amiss in applying a strictly logical, rights-based standard to a matter that is so tightly bound up with notions of relationship, responsibility, and caretaking. People who accept the justice standard in a ruling on an abstract social issue may instinctively be repelled by the use of that standard in an individual case. The implication is that the majority of Americans—the ones who find this disjunction unsettling—understand that the abstract issue and the personal dilemma are one and the same and cannot be judged so differently. What is a matter for care and human responsibility in private should also be considered in those terms—as well as in terms of rights and justice—on the broader scale. What the majority of Americans seems to want is what most people in crisis usually strive for—a sense of balance between the justice and the caretaking models of moral action. As the stories in this book repeatedly suggest, very few people take abortion to be as simple a matter as politics and propaganda imply. Those who must choose between birth and abortion, between fetus and mother, seldom do so lightly. Instead, they end up wrestling with complexity and trying not to be thrown off balance by it.

As Carol Gilligan and Jane Attanucci explain in an article on moral standards and gender: "Two moral injunctions, not to treat others unfairly and not to turn away from someone in need, capture these different concerns. From a developmental standpoint, both inequality and attachments are universal human experiences: All children are born into a situation of inequality and no child survives in the absence of some kind of adult attachment. These two intersecting dimensions of equality and attachment characterize all forms of human relationship. . . . Because everyone has been vulnerable both to oppression and to abandonment, two moral visions—one of justice and one of care—recur in human experience."

Gilligan and Attanucci regard an equal consideration of justice and care as the mark of "mature moral thinking," pointing out that when only one of the two standards is applied, the other, though it represents an equally important moral perspective, is sacrificed. What Gilligan and Attanucci found, in their studies of how thirty-four women and forty-six men had resolved real-life dilemmas, was that about two-thirds of the male and female subjects either strove for or achieved a balance between justice considerations and caretaking considerations. Gender differences showed up only in failures to achieve balance. Although women were almost as likely to overbalance toward the justice standard as toward caretaking—perhaps because justice is the prevailing standard in our culture—men had a strong tendency to focus mainly or exclusively on concerns relating to individual rights and justice. In fact, only one man focused more intently on care than on justice, which led Gilligan and Attanucci to observe that "if women were excluded from a study of moral reasoning, [the focus on care] could easily be overlooked."

Given Gilligan and Attanucci's definition of mature morality, it begins to look as if the American approach to the abortion dilemma is stuck in a juvenile stage of development. Not only does *Roe v. Wade* apply the justice standard without reference to care, but the most broadly communicated arguments of both the pro-choice and the pro-life activists also disregard the care model. Although each side pays some lip service to the care standard—pro-choice advocates by discussing quality of life, pro-life forces by appealing to women's traditional role as nurturers—neither side weighs it equally against the concerns of rights and justice.

The trends that have led more and more women away from traditional roles—and from the traditionally female values that support those roles—have perpetuated the imbalance between the care and justice standards. The rise in the number of autonomous, self-supporting, independent women has been accompanied by what many see as an alarming decline in the stability of marriage and the family. This trend seems to confirm the worst fears of traditionalists—that no one will do the nurturing if women leave the home to go to work—thereby reinforcing their notion that the quality and importance of family life are determined exclusively by women. Feminists, of course, would argue that the trend merely reflects women's return to a range of choices and experiences that the 1950s and the cult of domesticity denied them. They would maintain that both men and women must shape their private lives together. And so the split remains.

In the meantime, beyond the arguments, most people plug along looking instinctively for ways to accomplish both the nurturing and the pursuit of other ambitions. Denise Gage and Judy McInnis are good examples. Both sought independence and careers but not to the exclusion of relationships. Both wanted rights and justice, yet both wanted intimate human bonds and responsibility to others, too. Denise went back to school so that she could provide a better life for herself and her children. Judy, though she felt no need to consider anyone else in her abortion decision, kept sight of her emotions and of the importance of relationships in her life.

Both Denise and Judy felt that the pain of abortion would sooner or later catch up with nearly everyone who had one. Denise referred to the woman in the waiting room; Judy, to her own attempts, and those of other women, to seal off emotion in order to accomplish hard necessities. One way or another, Judy believes, "most people who are in touch with themselves will acknowledge that there is some degree of difficulty with having an abortion." The following stories, about two young, single women faced with multiple unplanned pregnancies, subtly bear out Judy's notion, for both women underwent abortions without much questioning, yet both indicate a lingering uneasiness with their choices.

Karen Ellis, born in 1949, is the only daughter of an unmarried mother who worked as a hospital orderly and a housekeeper. Karen is black; she grew up in a poor, urban neighborhood in Gary, Indiana, near warehouses and a factory. She never went to college, but she has built a career as administrative assistant to the head of a large university research center.

Isabel Martin was born in 1961 to white, middle-class, educated parents who divorced while Isabel was still in grade school. Isabel lived with her mother, a medical librarian, in a comfortable apartment near Riverside Park in New York City. She has a master's degree in education but has given up teaching to work for a landscape architect, helping to plant and tend the grounds of commercial and institutional buildings.

These two women could not be more different, and yet both have had multiple abortions. Both are aware that there is a moral dimension to their choices, and both nonetheless seem unable to grope their way toward a clear moral standard in their lives. Although they appear to take abortion casually, sometimes that appearance fades; a shadow of doubt and guilt looms behind it, as when they allude vaguely to notions of punishment or atonement.

Karen Ellis

Karen is a big, pretty woman with smooth brown skin and an easy laugh. She had her first abortion in 1965, at sixteen, after her mother noticed that the supply of tampons was not dwindling and confronted Karen with her condition. About five years later, Karen became pregnant again, even though she had been using an IUD.

"That's supposed to work, right? Wrong!" she exclaimed, laughing out loud. She remembered her conversation with the doctor she saw after missing a period. "He said, 'What are you here for?' And I said, 'To have my IUD checked.' And he said, 'You don't have an IUD.' I said, 'Yes, I do.' Me being silly, I said, 'Maybe somebody took it with him, I don't know.' He was a resident. His face got all red." The doctor gave Karen a free abortion.

Karen's methods of birth control worked for the next fourteen years, but then another failure meant another pregnancy and a third abortion. She decided to have her tubes tied. "I couldn't take the pill anymore. That diaphragm—I'm scared of my body anyway. I'm scared to put things up there and make sure they're right. At thirty-five, I said, 'Am I gonna have kids?' "

Before she went through with the operation, Karen talked with Joyce, a social worker she knew, who worked at the same hospital as her mother. She had gone to see Joyce about her abortion, too. "She said: 'Karen, everyone wants to have a baby. Do you want to be a parent?' See, that's the difference. Oh, yeah, I want a baby. But I said: 'No, I need things. When mommy needs shoes and baby needs shoes, you know who gets the shoes. No, I don't want no kids.' "

Karen's experience had taught her that mommy sacrificed for baby. Her own mother had always gone without in order to satisfy Karen's wants and needs. But something more was going on with Karen, who actually could have afforded a child with far less struggle than her mother went through. First, she was not in love with the man she lived with. Second, the baby was not his. "It would have been different if he hadn't been with me and I wanted to have this baby. I would have had it." With this man in the picture, though, she said, "If I would have had a baby then, I would never have gotten rid of him."

Karen paused briefly and then said, "Now I'm worried about my tubes being tied." Looking up from her hands, which moved restlessly in her lap, she laughed again. "Someday God's gonna send a man to me and he's gonna love me and want me to have his children and I won't be able to. So I always think about that." Doubts stirred in her about the advice her social worker had given. "I only went to Joyce. She's never had a baby. She's never been married, so what does she know? I didn't even talk to my mother. I didn't tell her about the last two abortions [because] she would've said, 'Yeah, go ahead, have the baby.'"

Karen sought the advice she wanted, avoiding counsel to the contrary, yet she had doubts about having followed that advice. "I always think about having a baby," she admitted, and she remembered that she had not slept the night before her third abortion. Joyce had asked her if she was ready for an eighteen year commitment, and Karen had said no. But Karen asked the doctor if she could still change her mind once she was on the table. He said she could, but she said, "Nah, go ahead."

Karen felt she made her abortion decisions selfishly and rashly, yet she also felt she had a certain right to do that. "I just feel like this is my body. [But] I'll probably be punished for it someday. In fact, I'm being punished for it right now. Because God gave me all these mechanical things to reproduce. And I'm not. Sometimes I feel bad about that, but it was my body and it's my decision and if it happened again, I'd probably do it all over again."

Today, just as Karen predicted, she is married to a man whose children she wishes she could have. She continues her career and is happy in her marriage. She has all the shoes she wants. But, she says: "I knew this would happen. Didn't I tell you?"

Isabel Martin

Isabel had her first abortion after a summer affair in her late teens (see Chapter 5). Her mother, a pro-choice activist, had strongly supported her choice because it kept her education goals on track. Isabel next became pregnant at twenty-two by a man she had been seeing for two years. She was a graduate student; John was a faculty member. Throughout their affair she had thought she wanted to marry him, but by the time her diaphragm failed, despite her regular use of it, she knew John was not serious about her. When Isabel told him she was pregnant, she recalled, "He didn't want to marry me, but he was proud of having impregnated a woman." Two weeks after the abortion, John began an affair with another student. "That, to me, was the bitter end," she said. Again, Isabel's mother gave her support.

Altogether, Isabel talked about four pregnancies, three of which ended in abortion. She sat with us in a small cafe in Philadelphia, where she now lives, slowly sipping wine as she told her story. Yet even the effects of alcohol did not bring warmth or expression to her voice. She spoke flatly, so that even "the bitter end" did not sound bitter at all. Her long, fair hair was loose, her skirt and tunic top graceful and flowing. She used her hands expressively, lifting them now and then to trace languid or abrupt gestures in the air. And yet her voice remained uninflected, almost stolid.

Aborting Isabel's pregnancy with John "wasn't a hard decision to make, but it was a hard decision to accept." Like so many other women in similar circumstances, Isabel's sexual self-esteem was wounded by John's ready dismissal of her pregnancy and his quick defection to another woman. That "and knowing that I still was in school, I still wasn't working, I still wasn't able to provide" made her feel somehow maneuvered by circumstances into a choice she probably would have made in any case. Adoption was out, too. "I have a friend who gave a child up for adoption. I don't think I could bear that, because every time she saw a child she just looked at it and wondered."

Though Isabel, like her mother, strongly advocates abortion rights and thinks *Roe v. Wade* is "lovely" because it "just balances the different rights involved as well as possible," she also perceived a dark, serious side to her experience. She determined she would not conceive again unless she meant to. "I really admonished myself to be careful. This time it was a failure of birth control, but . . . if you make a mistake twice, that's more stupid than making it once."

Four years later, though, Isabel was pregnant again. Rudy, the man she was living with, was a weight lifter, she said, "and he was taking steroids at the time, which made his sperm count so low he shouldn't have been able to impregnate anybody. He had been to the doctor and had it checked. So we hadn't been using birth control. But I did in fact become pregnant." Rudy, who had thought the combination of steroids and a damaged testicle had made him permanently sterile, "was thrilled. He was very excited. He really wanted to keep the baby."

Isabel thought seriously about going ahead with the pregnancy. She had graduated by that time and was working as a substitute teacher. Rudy was still finishing a graduate degree in bio-ecology. Their income was sporadic at best, and their relationship was still maturing. Though Isabel knew there was a chance Rudy might never again be able to father a child, she said: "I finally decided that it just wasn't quite time. I found this wonderful fellow, but we had no money and with a child we couldn't do it. A thousand dollars a month just doesn't do it." Rudy reluctantly agreed. "He said, 'Do what you think is best.' But he was very disappointed."

If Isabel was surprised at Rudy's desire for a child, which was so much stronger than her own, her voice did not register it as she recalled her decision. She did not think Rudy's boyhood Catholicism played any part in his feelings. She just thought he loved children and wanted one of his own. "He's also a scientist," she said. "He knows exactly what that fetus is doing. I think that very clear picture in his head makes [abortion] difficult."

After the abortion, and after Isabel and Rudy had stopped feeling careful and solicitous with one another, Rudy confided that he was, in fact, uneasy about abortion on moral grounds. He had not told her so before because he had not wanted to influence her decision.

Rudy and Isabel married a year later. She went back to her diaphragm, and there were no more mishaps for the next three years. Then, one night, after "a few beers," she miscalculated how long ago her period had been and they made love without protection. When she learned she was pregnant, Rudy again eagerly pressed her to have the baby.

This time, both Rudy and Isabel were teaching high school. She had just moved to a new school district, and Rudy was hoping to do the same. Their budget was still tight, though. They were paying off graduate school debts, and their car insurance had doubled after an accident. Their relationship was solid now, but the other reasons Isabel had cited for her earlier abortion were still in place. Nevertheless, she agreed to go ahead with this pregnancy.

"I think in some ways I had this baby for my husband," Isabel admitted. "He wanted it so badly and was so excited. . . . I also sort of felt like three strikes you're out. Like this time just go for it. It's almost like . . . I don't think retribution is the right word for it. It's almost like paying dues or something. It's time to stop fooling around and take responsibility. . . . I don't know. That all sounds sort of Puritan and too harsh to describe what I'm feeling. I guess what I'm saying is that it didn't bother me to decide to have this child."

When Isabel wavered sometimes during her pregnancy, "Rudy was just lovely. Every time I was ill or worried and would say, 'Oh, this is so stupid. I really don't want to do this. The timing isn't right,' he would say, 'Everything is gonna be fine.' "

Today Isabel and Rudy's daughter, Chloe, is eighteen months old. Her father is mad about her. "He is so happy to be a daddy," Isabel said, flashing a smile for the first time in the interview. "And he keeps saying, 'Look, if you make enough money, I'll stay home.' " Isabel herself lacks passion for her child. Resuming her flat tone, she said merely, "I have been growing more and more fond of Chloe." She wishes she and Rudy could have waited another year or two "so we would have our savings account and we wouldn't have to worry so much of the time."

Nevertheless, Isabel is not sorry she had Chloe. She feels about Rudy the way Rudy feels about both Isabel and Chloe, and she is glad she has made him happy. But she does wonder about her own feelings. "I guess it's really hard in these situations to know what *you* think. I mean, I knew what my mother thought. I knew what Rudy thought. I knew what other people thought. I understood what they were saying. I could see the value of it and I could agree with it, but, I don't know . . . I mean, if my mother had been a strict Catholic and had said [about my first pregnancy], 'Oh, keep the baby or put it up for adoption'—if my mother's strong voice had said something different, maybe I would have gone along with that. I didn't, and maybe I still don't, divorce what

I think from what those people around me are saying. That was hard. I would sit and I would think, 'Well, what do I want to do?' "

Listening Women

Despite her words, Isabel did know what she wanted to do. So did Karen Ellis. The uncertainties these women express about their choices derive, we believe, from their inability to take full responsibility. When they wanted to abort, they sought and obtained support for that action, Isabel from her own past experience and the lingering effect of her mother's "strong voice," Karen from the social worker, Joyce. Karen never told her mother about ending her second and third pregnancies because she did not want to confront her mother's likely objections. Isabel never took Rudy's pleas for a child fully to heart the first time she conceived with him, partly because she had the strain of circumstances on her side. She never really looked him in the eye and said plainly that she was serving her own desire instead of his. By the time she was pregnant by him the second time she could no longer justify abortion, yet she maintained that she had the child for Rudy, not for herself.

In their unwillingness or inability to accept full responsibility for their choices, Karen and Isabel resemble a category of women described in *Women's Ways of Knowing*, by Mary Field Belenky, Blythe McVicker Clinchy, Nancy Rule Goldberger, and Jill Mattuck Tarule. This book delineates a range of qualities that characterize women at different stages of moral and intellectual development. Though the authors draw clearer boundaries between the stages than we have observed in the stories we present, we see in both Karen and Isabel certain aspects of what Belenky *et al.* call "listeners" or "receivers." These are women who, having little or no confidence in their own thoughts, take both knowledge and direction from outside sources. According to the authors, listeners "have little confidence in their own ability to speak. Believing that truth comes from others, they still their own voices to hear the voices of others. . . . [They] are frequently surprised and relieved to hear others saying the very same things that they would say."

Unlike Belenky *et al.*'s "silent women," who have no voice or sense of self at all and who usually come from abusive, neglectful families, the typical "listeners" are women who simply have not learned how to speak with authority. They tend to come from families in which communication is one-way; parents hand down knowledge and rules without inviting discussion. Inequality within family relationships is seen as permanent, and the duty of children is to do exactly as they are told. Rebellion and independent thought are forbidden.

Karen and Isabel came from families in which they were loved and carefully guided, but neither seems to have been encouraged to communicate intimately with her parents or to question parental values or prescriptions. As adult women faced with multiple unplanned pregnancies, they both avoided a full confrontation with views that challenged their own. As a consequence, they may not have explored or even fully understood the choices they made. Without a strong sense of their own authority or their reasons for their actions, neither could make a fully mature moral decision. Though they both seemed aware of moral concerns, they were also unable to grasp them fully enough to be guided by them. They remain plagued by doubts because they relied on others, blamed their circumstances, or only sought opinions that would confirm their own.

Karen wanted the rewards of freedom and autonomy but feared punishment for being selfish. She wondered what would happen with the man God would send her, whose children she would not be able to have. She knew that a child demanded real devotion and care, and she based her choice of abortion on her inability to muster that commitment. This choice required her to deny her maternal urges, however. She admitted that she thought about babies all the time and wondered what hers would have looked like.

Like Luker's subjects, whose ambivalence about birth control use is rooted in its social and emotional costs, Karen may have had more reasons for abortion and sterilization than she knew or stated. Though it would be presumptuous to claim any certainty about those reasons, Karen's reference to her childhood might offer a clue. "I would have wanted my baby to have double what I had, and I had everything I wanted," she told us. Her mother made sure Karen got all the new shoes she needed, but in her struggle to provide, she worked night and day. "Double" what Karen grew up with would have meant two parents who could give time and attention, not just one parent who adored her daughter but was hardly ever home with her. If Karen later looked after her own needs to the exclusion of anyone else's, it is possible that she doubted her ability to do more than her own mother had done. She had a model for hard work and material support but not for availability, extended periods of intimacy, or close parental guidance. Without such a model, and without a strong inner voice, Karen was not likely to choose birth over abortion.

Isabel was not as concerned with rewards or punishments as Karen was, but neither was she able to balance her desires with those of others and achieve

real clarity in her actions. Even though she had Chloe without wanting passionately to be a mother, childbirth led her to think a little differently about her
abortions. She described a method of dealing with her feelings that sounds like
what Judy McInnis called "sealing off." It may be the explanation for her
expressionless voice. "I have all these things in my mind, like abortion is a
terrible thing and you just murdered three children and you're a murderess and
all that kind of stuff. But I just stop it. I don't want to do that to myself." Still,
she saw a recurring image in her mind. "You know," she said, "I have three little
ghost children. My child has three brothers or sisters."

What is new in the stories of Karen and Isabel is the extent to which they
took for granted opportunities to explore their sexuality, follow career paths,
and exercise reproductive choice. What is old, and undermines the new, is their
inability to feel in control of their choices and to understand fully the reasons
for which they made them. The next story, about a young woman determined
to proceed with a pregnancy under difficult circumstances, demonstrates
change and sameness from a different perspective.

Jenny Willard

Jenny Willard is a twenty-six year-old single mother who works as a
hairdresser in a large department store salon in Atlanta. She met us at closing
time in the deserted employee lounge, telling us her story as security guards
toured the premises. One of them had agreed to escort us out when we had
finished.

Jenny settled nervously into her story, speaking rapidly in a marked Southern accent. Her shoulder-length dark hair fell into her eyes repeatedly, and she
tossed it back with a practiced lift of her chin. Beneath her salon smock she
wore a lime-green linen sheath with cut-glass beads and earrings. Her smile and
makeup were professional; she never fully relaxed. Her manner, polite and
self-consciously poised, was very much in keeping with her story and her
account of the maturity she felt she had gained in recent years.

Jenny was nineteen the first time she faced an unintended pregnancy. It
was the summer after her disastrous first year in college, and she was tempted
by thoughts of marriage and motherhood as alternatives to school. But the
hometown boy who got Jenny pregnant "wasn't much of a catch," and her
parents disapproved of the relationship. She miscarried before she had to make

a decision about her pregnancy, but she is sure she would have aborted.

Jenny went to a new school the next fall to study cosmetology. There she became involved with Charlie, a somewhat older man who was "handsome and good to be seen with." This time, when Jenny became pregnant, she again wanted to marry and have the baby. Charlie refused, and Jenny was once more deprived of "the whole family scene, being like everyone else" in her hometown. Nevertheless, she did not think of this abortion as "taking a human life." Her pregnancy was "a situation, not a child."

In both relationships Jenny had used birth control pills, which, she said wonderingly, "failed with the least little slip." Given the high reliability of the pill, it is likely the slips were more than little. Jenny, in Kristin Luker's terms, had probably made a not-quite-conscious "decision not to contracept." This likelihood looks almost certain in light of Jenny's third pregnancy, which followed the same pattern under different circumstances.

By the time Jenny was pregnant again, at twenty-four, her father had died and left her enough life insurance to pay off a small bundle of debts and make a down payment on a ranch house in a development near Atlanta. She had finished school and was making a good living selling salon products and giving cosmetology workshops. She finally felt in charge of her life. She saw herself as ambitious and responsible, a homeowner and a hard worker.

Then Jenny met Ron, who was charming but "looked no further ahead than Saturday's beers." He was going through a divorce, halfheartedly continuing his education, but mainly marking time. She tried to settle him down, but Ron was a grasshopper, impervious to her ant-like persuasions. Still, when Jenny's birth control pills "failed" for the third time, she felt, once again, that she wanted the relationship to work. "I had a house and enough income to support him till he finished school," she said. "I didn't want him financially, I wanted him emotionally." Ron, though, "had hometown Southern values against such an arrangement." He stuck around at first and then, by degrees, drifted away from Jenny and showed no interest in the pregnancy she decided to carry to term. "The time was right for me to have a baby, even if not to marry," Jenny said. "This was always a child to me, not a situation."

Jenny was full of pride and determination. She knew many women in her circumstances would choose abortion freely, and she felt that was "sometimes the best solution." But it was not for her. She was more mature and independent now than she had been at nineteen and twenty. "I felt like I had, I guess you'd say, sowed my wild oats," Jenny said. What was important to her now was to act like an adult and to accept responsibility. To her, that meant observing the standards that prevail for men in our culture—being a good provider, paying the bills on time, being firm and decisive.

This was easier for Jenny with her father gone. He had been a merchant seaman, away for months at a time and often drunk or abusive when he was at home. "He was very conservative," Jenny explained. "He would have rejected me and the baby and would've chased Ron down with a shotgun." Jenny had no such apprehensions regarding her mother and sisters, to whom she had always been close. She knew they would be upset at first but would quickly rally around her. She was right. "They've been *very* helpful and *very* supportive, in every sense." Jenny's mother, however, was quick to accept Jenny's offer to stay away from their hometown while she was visibly pregnant.

Jenny ran rapidly through the details of her three pregnancies and her reactions to each. What was most immediate to her, and what she wanted desperately to tell us about, was what it was like to live every day with the consequences of her choice. "You hear so much talk about abortion and antiabortion," she said, "but what do you hear of support for women who decided *not* to?"

Support was what Jenny "yearned for the most" after she had Danny. She wanted relief from both financial and emotional stress. "I incurred a lot of debt," she said. "Being better off . . . actually puts you at a disadvantage sometimes. . . . I'm still paying my hospital bills, because my insurance wouldn't. And I was not eligible for any kind of help, because I was better off."

With debt deepening the stresses of caring for a newborn alone, Jenny went looking for other kinds of help. "I called different clinics and centers," she remembered. "I told them my situation and their answer was, 'Do you need clothes? Do you need shelter? Do you need food?' Well, like, no, I don't need those things. They said, 'We can't help you.' "

What Jenny wanted was human contact. "I wanted a group. I wanted other mothers that were in the same situation with me. Just so I'd know, 'cause I felt so alienated. I felt like I was something nobody else was. I was a—an unwanted mother. I thought I was doing this wonderful thing . . . giving a man a child, and *he* didn't even want me. So who would want me, who would want—I felt so unwanted and so unloved." Even when she tried to organize a group for single mothers through her church, Jenny met with indifference. "Unfortunately, our single minister does not put this on top of his priority list," she sighed.

Even if Jenny could find other single mothers to talk to, she admitted that finding time to spend with them would be difficult. Her days are consumed at both ends by Danny, in the middle by work. The loneliness, she told us, was "overwhelming." Nevertheless, she explained how careful she was not to take the loneliness out on Danny. "I know what it was like to be among abusive, screamy adults," she said. "I never scream at him, never. . . . He's a very happy child, so it makes me happy to be around him, and that makes a big difference. If I discipline him a little, it's usually only a pop of my hand—you know, a mad face. But it's never a yell or a scream."

As if to be sure there was no mistake, Jenny added: "Danny has just been a true joy since the day he was born. He has never been one bit of trouble. He is easy-go-lucky. He is always completely and totally happy. And I do not regret having him one bit." On the other hand, she sighed, "I do get frustrated at him at times—when he's ill and I'm tired and I've got to get up and go to work the next morning and there's nobody here to take my place. But I just remind myself he's my child and he has no control over what situation is around him."

Jenny's real anger is aimed at Ron. "It angers me [that] Danny's father [could] *rob* me of a good home environment with someone who will share this responsibility with me," Jenny declared. "It bothers me. I told Ron that, too. I said, 'You are a shit for denying him that.' " Still, Jenny accepts Ron's absence. All things considered, she said, she is "very glad he didn't marry me, because he obviously has a drinking problem. Some people are not meant to be parents . . . and he was one of them. At least he was mature enough to realize that."

Asked for words of advice about single mothers, Jenny said: "One thing I just cannot stress enough is, don't let society turn away from them and shut them out. Be proud of them because they have made a big decision and it's something they should be proud of. And they need to have group therapy, they need to have support, they need to have acceptance. Just, I can't stress that enough."

Abortion: A First Resort of Public Policy?

In an earlier age, coming from a small Southern town, Jenny Willard would never have dared to have a child without a husband. But today, what is not dished out to her as opprobrium is dished out as indifference, which may be more painful still. Jenny is living between old values and new ones, neither of which reflect the kind of human connection, recognition, and nurturance that Jenny longs for. In the hometown of her childhood, an unmarried mother would have been condemned to loneliness for being "immoral"; in the modern city where she struggles to raise Danny, pay her bills, hold a job, and keep her hopes alive, she is serving the same sentence for a choice she made out of her desire to be mature and responsible. She stressed repeatedly how important it was to her to be financially secure and to provide for Danny, but even that struggle—which is usually rewarded in our society—has not made Jenny feel respected.

In this regard, Jenny is a casualty of the worst aspects of our national policies on abortion, birth, families, and children. Her case demonstrates the extent to which abortion has become the first resort of those policies, for—childlessness aside—Jenny might have been better off in many ways had she chosen not to have Danny. She would, in all likelihood, have been less isolated, less financially strapped, less exhausted, less hurt.

Regardless of how people feel about out-of-wedlock childbirth, the only alternative to aiding women like Jenny is to abandon them, which is what our society has done. In doing so it has also abandoned its own best interests, since any society that fails to shore up its families at their weakest points is less likely to remain vigorous, competitive, or unified. Women who proceed with unplanned pregnancies constitute families, whether they marry or not. Strong family policies would help these women to become good mothers, would hold the fathers responsible for child support at the very least, and would see to it that the children are fed, clothed, protected, and given both medical care and good educations. Families are the fundamental units of nations, and nations that maintain the health and strength of families reap the benefits. Moreover, when families are supported—not just by the government but by all of society's institutions—instead of abandoned, their members begin to feel valued in ways that might gradually diminish the forces that lead to high rates of unplanned and out-of-wedlock pregnancies. These forces can include family breakdown, dysfunction, violence, or neglect of children.

The next two stories are about couples who attempted to achieve or sustain the strength and honest communication that healthy families depend on. In each case, the woman and man disagreed over the fate of an unplanned pregnancy. Alarmed and threatened by the power of their feelings, they faced the possibility of serious harm to their relationships. In each case, and against the initial odds, they found a way to preserve both the relationship and their own integrity.

Lisa Hodl and Peter Beaudry

We talked with Lisa Hodl and Peter Beaudry together and in separate interviews. Most of the time we sat in a bright breakfast area of their kitchen, with a view of the backyard garden in high summer. Zinnias and snapdragons flourished; Pittsburgh's ubiquitous impatiens lined a shady paved path in every hot color. Lisa and Peter share a passion for gardening that took them five years to discover. There had been times when it looked as if they had nothing in common.

Lisa Hodl is Jewish; Peter Beaudry is Catholic. She is direct, open, emotionally expressive; he is reticent, private, contemplative. She is small, dark, and plump; he is tall, light-haired, light-eyed, and lean. She is a clinical psychologist, at home with her patient's intimate disclosures and her profession's nuanced concepts of human relationships; he is a radiologist who interprets peoples' innermost—but strictly physiological—images while having little direct patient contact. She has always championed abortion rights; he believes abortion is wrong.

This odd couple had been dating less than six months when Lisa walked into Peter's kitchen one night and announced, "Peter, I'm late with my period."

"It didn't register for a few minutes," Peter recalled. "And then I turned to her and I said, 'Well, what should we do?' "

Peter's question, which was strictly practical, launched their conflict. He meant, what was their next step? How and when could they know for sure if she was pregnant? "I didn't feel like there was an issue yet," he said. He knew if Lisa tested positive for pregnancy he was in for a rough time. "I could see myself going through a lot of head hassles and mental trauma if that was the case," he explained. "So I just said, 'Let's just wait and find out.' I don't know if that's strictly male or just part male and part how I was brought up."

Lisa had wanted to talk immediately about what they would do if she was pregnant. She wanted to explore her feelings and Peter's. When he would not open up, she became impatient and strongly defensive. "He had told me a long time ago that he didn't believe in abortion," she recalled. "But I have run into people who say that, philosophically, and then change when they have to deal with it on a personal level. So I never really took it that seriously when he said that to me. I remember coming back really hostile and just saying: 'Well it's too bad. This isn't a time to be theorizing. This is real life and if I'm pregnant, I'm going to have an abortion.' "

Like Judy McInnis, Lisa was then on a tight, straight career path that permitted no flexibility and no surprises. She was finishing a closely timed dissertation based on experiments at a mid-Atlantic university and she was soon to begin a demanding internship more than a thousand miles away in Wisconsin. Peter, who had just finished his residency, was planning to go with her.

Soon after Lisa's pregnancy was confirmed the plan was put on hold. Neither she nor Peter was sure their relationship would survive this crisis.

Lisa never anticipated the crisis, for one thing. She had used a diaphragm without fail, or failure, for ten years. For the last five years she had been combining birth control methods. She charted her cycles, which were very regular, and used the diaphragm during her fertile times and for a week or so on either side. She got pregnant after taking a calculated risk. "It was the eighteenth day of my cycle," she said. "I'd usually wait until the twentieth day before I'd stop using my diaphragm, but Peter and I had been fighting and it was a night we felt we wanted to have sex and I was out of diaphragm cream. So I thought, well, it seemed I was pretty regularly ovulating around the thirteenth or fourteenth day. I really felt that I was safe, so I just went ahead and had unprotected intercourse."

Lisa and Peter had identical fleeting first reactions to the news that she was indeed pregnant. They were standing outside the women's clinic where she had been tested, looking at each other in the weak, early-spring sunlight. "There was this moment that we both were happy," she recalled, "even though I think we both knew that it wasn't going to last very long." Peter independently admitted that "Initially, I felt really happy to find out she was pregnant. It was . . . the power of being able to bring life into the world. And then it just struck me that, 'Well, wait a minute, this is probably not going to happen.' And then I just said, 'Well, where do we go from here?' "

Peter had abortion in mind from the moment he knew Lisa was pregnant. Lisa was never aware of that. "We both had other appointments to keep," she said, "so we really didn't discuss it until later that night. I said I didn't think I had a choice. The path that I was on academically was going to get really screwed up if I chose to have this baby. Peter kept saying 'I don't believe in abortion,' but he never said 'I want to have this baby' or 'Let's figure out some way of having this baby.' "

Lisa's interpretation of Peter's remarks and actions angered her. "I think the fact is that he wanted to have an abortion, but he was sort of laying the responsibility for that on me." Lisa also thought Peter blamed and judged her for the morally doubtful choice he had more or less cornered her into making. "It really created a big hassle between us," she said. "We nearly broke up."

Because she was only about sixteen days into her pregnancy and the clinic she called wanted her to be further along, Lisa had to wait three weeks before she could schedule her abortion. During that time, she and Peter became estranged. "I didn't want to see him, and he didn't know how to help me—plus

I was really violently sick," she sighed. Lisa was also depressed and anxious over the loss of this opportunity for motherhood. She was thirty years old and far from being able to offer a child what she wanted to give. "There was no support system for having a baby," she said. "There was no day care, there was no financial help, there was no flexibility in the internship, there was nothing that would have allowed me to have that baby other than Peter." Adoption was out of the question: "There is no way I would ever give up a baby."

Lisa talked about her feelings with several people—her family, her women friends, even faculty members. She never felt isolated or alone; everyone was supportive. Her dissertation adviser sympathized with her bitter observations that career preparations left no room to "do something human, like have a baby." He even confided that he thought his own work had cost him his marriage. Yet Lisa felt that Peter gave her nothing. She and a friend, who had had an abortion eight months earlier, agreed that "the men in our lives were absolutely no help during that time, even though we said the same things to them that we said to each other."

For his part, Peter was put off by Lisa's willingness for everyone in their world to know about her pregnancy and abortion. "I'm a real private person," he explained. "I really felt the need to keep it between us, and she felt the need to share it." Peter tried to make allowances for Lisa's emotional style and requirements. Lisa tried to get Peter to change his approach. "She would say, 'Well, you need to open up and you need to talk to people. How come you're not talking to people?' And my response was, 'Well, I don't need to. I don't like to.' She would say, 'Well, you really need to.' It wasn't a healthful kind of interchange."

Peter thought his reticence was part maleness, part guilt, and part doubts about Lisa. "I didn't feel at that time that I would want to get married to Lisa," he said. But his doubts, her circumstances, and her unwillingness to consider adoption meant there was not much chance of avoiding an abortion.

Peter remembered philosophical discussions about abortion with friends in college. "When is life? It was fun to talk about. But that was in an atmosphere of conjecture. Then, all of a sudden, the situation presents itself. It's no longer conjecture. You begin to realize that there are other variables that come into play, whether or not they're good or moral or whatever."

So, for different reasons, and with different causes for pain, Lisa and Peter agreed on an abortion without fully understanding each other. Despite their estrangement, Peter went with Lisa on the day of the procedure. He spent hours in the waiting room with other men while the women were shepherded through their paperwork, counseling, abortions, and recovery. None of the men spoke to each other. Most of them read. A few smoked or drank coffee from a vending machine.

Lisa disliked the clinic where she had her abortion. She found it impersonal, and she resented the long wait for the procedure. Peter, too, criticized the clinic for its standard refusal to allow men to stay with the women. "Because I didn't see the abortion," he explained, "it's still, to some extent, theoretical." He admitted he would be nervous and perhaps tempted to decline, but he did think, "If I was given the option, I would go [in with Lisa]."

On the night of the abortion, Lisa went to Peter's house. She stayed up late, watching TV. "Then I went to bed," she remembered, "and as soon as I shut my eyes I was having visions of the abortion and I just started to cry hysterically. This is one of the few things Peter handled well. He came in and just wrapped his whole body around mine and just held me until I stopped crying. It was a long time. I can't remember how long it was. I don't remember crying like that after my mother died. I don't remember ever crying like that before." It was as though Lisa, beyond words herself, could in that one instance accept and be comforted by Peter's wordless way of caring for her.

Soon, though, Lisa herself began resorting to Peter's silent method of coping. "I put [the abortion] in the back of my mind," she said. "For a long time, I just got involved in my work."

Peter also kept his feelings in check. "I had this belief, and then I did something that was counter to it," he explained. "Something had to adjust." What adjusted was the tightness of his control. Though he told his brother and a friend about the abortion after the fact, he never confided his anguish. "I just sort of tucked that away," he admitted. "I think if I really started to get into that, it would be bad news."

Although Peter was not a practicing Catholic, his betrayal of the Church's position on abortion troubled him. "I don't actively pray a lot," he said, "but after the abortion I felt that that channel was just sort of cut. And that's hard." He was cut off from Lisa, too. He didn't try to talk to her about his spiritual pain because she does not believe in God. "I just didn't think that she would understand. I knew it would create just more hell between us. That's why I never got into the religious aspects of it."

Gradually, with their truest feelings masked, Lisa and Peter began to get along better. The tensions between them eased up in an apparent return to normal, and they revived their plans to move to Wisconsin together. In the weeks before Lisa began her internship their relationship improved, and the abortion receded as an issue.

"Then I started the program in September," Lisa said, "and I think the hardest time was then, because one of the staff members was pregnant. I also started thinking that the baby would have been due soon." Lisa, still unconsciously adopting Peter's tactics, denied the source of her sad and edgy feelings. "I would just write it off all the time, thinking 'No, no, it can't be that.'"

More as a matter of form than of need, she decided to participate in a therapy group that was offered for new interns. At the very first session, the pregnant staff member showed up with her husband, one of Lisa's colleagues. "They started chitchatting about this baby and their expectations and all this stuff. And all of a sudden my heart started pounding and my face got hot and I became hysterical. I sat there and tears just started pouring out of my eyes, and so the leader, who was a psychiatrist, turned to me and said, 'What is going on with you?' I told him about the abortion and how I was feeling. . . . I realized I was starting to deal with some of the emotional stuff that I had pushed aside for all those months and that a lot of what I was dealing with was my anger toward Peter and the feeling like he hadn't shared it with me and that I needed to talk to him about it."

At long last, Lisa and Peter began to communicate honestly about what each of them had been through. They began explosively. Lisa told Peter what she had felt at the therapy session, and he said, "Well, you're not going to like what I have to say if we talk about it." She asked, "Well, what's that?" And Peter said, "I still feel that it was wrong."

"I just really blew up," Lisa remembered. "But then . . . he clarified a couple of things that helped me. He wasn't saying he thought *I* did something wrong. He was saying he thought *he* did something wrong." Peter felt he had betrayed his beliefs, while Lisa had been true to hers. Once she understood that, she could forgive his unwillingness to talk. "[Talking] made him sad and angry," she said simply. "Whereas, when I talked about it, it made me feel better."

Peter and Lisa's sudden and simple revelations to each other cleared the air between them for a long time. They did not discuss the risk of another pregnancy, because Lisa had switched to the pill right after the abortion. She used it for three years. But when she began tracing depression and a lowered sex drive to that source, she decided to go back to the diaphragm. She could not return to a less secure method of birth control, however, without knowing what she was going to do if it failed. She went to Peter and said: "There is a chance that I could get pregnant again, and I've decided that I wouldn't have another abortion. He said that was good, because he had decided the same thing."

This determination, which had grown in each of them from a different seed, "was the most comforting thing," Lisa marveled. "We both went through a lot of pain with that abortion, and part of [it arose from] questions about commitment to each other. [Some of] those questions were finally resolved in some way."

Peter, although he acknowledged the riskiness of having a child before a relationship is really strong enough, still said, "If I went back to that time with the knowledge I have now . . . I think we would have gone ahead and had the baby." Lisa did not exactly second Peter, but she did say, "I've always known that I will feel, when my first child is born, that it is actually my second."

Today, seven years after the abortion, Peter Beaudry and Lisa Hodl are married and have finally had that "second" child. It is unlikely they would still be together if they had not been able to share the pain that each had experienced alone—the pain at the heart of the abortion dilemma.

The Pressures of Social Change

Peter and Lisa's conflict and its resolution were very much influenced by the broad social changes in attitude and options that we have discussed in this chapter. Lisa's career ambitions were only one manifestation of those changes. The couple's choice of abortion, in a society that had freely permitted the procedure for almost half their lifetime, was another. Both Peter and Lisa admitted that abortion sprang almost instantly to mind when she became pregnant. So did the likelihood that their relationship would end. In fact, the two were surrounded by social forces that promoted greater individual autonomy but did little to encourage commitment, especially in the face of hardship or profound disagreement. Sex had long been separated from marriage and even from engagement. Pregnancy was less of a reason for marriage than it had ever been. Though religious differences were no longer an obstacle to love, they could exacerbate problems and provide an easy way out of a relationship that grew troublesome. And professional necessity was more likely than ever to put geographical distance between two people. All of these factors operated between Lisa and Peter. Had the couple allowed their wrong assumptions and resentment of each other to persist, any one of the forces described here offered an exit. Had they taken the offer, choosing strict autonomy over the harder challenge of connection, they would have lost all opportunity for the satisfying life they share and the trust they have developed.

Anna and David Jacobi

Anna and David are another study in contrasts. She is Danish, the tall, fair, elegant daughter of musicians. He is a red-haired American Jew from Manhattan, a criminal attorney and the third son of a high school biology teacher and a nurse. But their differences were no barrier to an instantaneous attraction. They met at an outdoor concert in Copenhagen in the summer of 1977. "You know," Anna laughed, "my heart started to beat. It was love at first sight. It's crazy."

They married two months after their first lovestruck encounter, exchanging "a plastic turtle ring and one of those that you get out of the bubble gum machines," Anna remembered happily. "We did not have a penny to our names." They moved to New York together, and Anna converted to Judaism. With a convert's enthusiasm, she outdid David's casual observance of his religion by becoming "an Orthodox woman. I lived that life for maybe two years, and it became too damned hard," she said. "Whenever I traveled I almost starved to death because I couldn't find the right foods to eat. . . . Then I decided, 'Oh, shrimp tastes good!' " Anna laughed at the memory of her zeal and its easy downfall, but she is still a more observant Jew than David.

Religion, though, played no part in the conflict that tried their marriage two years ago. By then Anna and David had two sons, ages six and three. A third pregnancy had ended in a late miscarriage at twenty-five weeks. There had been no warning, and there was never a firm explanation. Anna learned she was pregnant again just as she was beginning to think seriously about pursuing a graduate degree in musical composition. Her ambitions and her fear of another loss made pregnancy no longer seem a wholly benign condition.

"I've never gone through anything of its like in my life," she said, her laughter gone from her eyes, "You know, when you can't sleep through the night, when you wake up and kick in the bed and you feel like, 'I'm trapped, I'm trapped in this. I'm trapped in my own—Help!' It was horrible. I could not have foreseen that, you know." Anna knew without question that she wanted an abortion at the first possible moment.

David was appalled. In their time together he had changed from a footloose young man with no interest in children to a delighted and intensely involved father. "When I expected Alan," said Anna, "I wasn't quite sure how [David] would be as a daddy. He never talked about kids, [and] he never behaved like he was crazy about kids. It was something that was innate in him and that came out through the kids, that indeed he was a terrific daddy. He's very tender and wonderful." Laughing, Anna added: "The kids just say, you know, they like their daddy, but mom, she's a witch. Really, that's true. And I tell David often, often, I could not have found a better dad."

When Anna told David she wanted an abortion, he was hurt and shocked. "You know, he really couldn't understand it," Anna said. "And for me, it was very, very hard to deal with somebody that I respect and that means so much to me—I mean, to make him so unhappy. I shouldn't have his child? He just couldn't understand."

Other people did not always understand either, Anna said. No one presumed to judge her desire for an abortion, but many, including her mother-in-law, were surprised. "I don't think it's very easy to admit it when you're married," Anna speculated. "When people hear that you're pregnant, automatically they go 'Oh, congratulations!' It's not so easy to say, 'But I'm not very happy about it.'" Anna thought many married women must hide such feelings the way they would hide marital problems. "Everybody wants to give off a nice facade," she said. "And this is just one of those things that you can hush-hush very easily."

David and Anna did not feel compelled to 'hush-hush' their conflict. They talked to friends and family, and they went for counseling. She had already made an appointment for the abortion and could not imagine she would ever change her mind. She wanted to find a way for David to accept her decision. "We both looked like we just got through a funeral," she said, recalling their visit to a counselor. "I just—I cried, because I said, you know, 'I want an abortion, but he wants the baby.'"

The counselor listened carefully and neutrally to both David and Anna. "Everybody turns into the little Freud," Anna smiled. "They sit there and they say 'Hm' and they nod their heads, you know." The counselor parroted back to them what they had said. By Anna's account, the woman said: "Well, I hear clearly. Anna is convinced that she's not going through with this pregnancy. And David is convinced that she must have this baby. You're not changing your attitudes."

Although David "swore to God" that he would not bear a grudge against Anna if she kept her appointment for the abortion, she did not entirely believe him. She suspected his emotions were too powerful for him to control. That made the next week all the harder. "Day and night I was thinking about this," she remembered. "I mean, you have to decide quick or it's going to be a little baby there, you know, soon."

Throughout this period of conflict and pain, Anna was always aware of a life beginning inside her, and the thought of abortion always meant to her the taking of that life. She began to have nightmares, which she described in her lilting, oddly cheerful Danish accent. "I dreamt I was in the clinic, and there was everything there, and there were five or six ladies lying there on the operation tables, and you hear this clink-clunk of like metallic instruments and everything. When I looked down into these stainless, sterile plates—basins—I saw fetuses and blood and placentas everywhere. I had not had an abortion, myself."

Anna's other dreams were less graphic but still represented her growing torment. "I was flying over oceans and mountains, and I was scared of the person that was going to make an abortion on me . . . a man that looked like a murderer or something—that threatened my life. And I . . . started to think, 'Goddamn, it is a life in there.' You know, I can't even kill a mouse."

Anna also remembered her miscarriage, but with somewhat altered feelings. Though her fears of another inexplicable loss were a major source of her reluctance to continue this pregnancy, they also inspired her to reexamine her feelings. "I had gone through the process of grieving that baby," she explained. "I saw him. I mean, he had all the fingers, lips, everything was there, you know? And I was thinking, 'I'm now going to do this, of free will, [after] how hard it was for me then?' I think that had a big impact."

Soon Anna found she had undergone a total change of both heart and mind. She felt she had been tested, morally and ethically. Her decision came down to: "How do I think about my family? How do I think about my husband? Am I responsible a little bit, maybe, for his happiness in life? Will this make his life less fulfilled?" Though Anna believes strongly that legal abortion should be available to women and that it is impossible to judge another's decision, she herself was relieved to be free of the urgent desire to end her pregnancy.

"It was all my decision," she said, even as she confided her belief that David "would have thought about the abortion for the rest of his life." The matter is perfectly clear to her. She made a free, wholehearted choice not only because it was the choice David wanted her to make (although it was) and not because she feared his bearing a grudge (although she did), but primarily because she loved him and trusted herself to love this third child. "We very much respect each other," she explained. "We are very much in love with each other, and we want to see that both are happy." That desire could not be served by an abortion, so Anna set about reversing her feelings about her pregnancy to make them harmonize with her feelings for David.

"It was not easy for me," she admitted. "It did not mean that all those assumed . . . or real hindrances were gone. It took a couple more weeks of feeling depressed and still not sleeping through the nights, and it put me to the decision that, well, now I just have to do something . . . about this. I have to sit down and think how I can make this work out really nice for me. . . . I planned a plan for myself—you know, how I could go through this with a lot of carrots on the road." Anna laughed. "That's how it worked for me. I never once thought, 'I did it because of you, damn. Male pig chauvinist.'"

David treated Anna with gratitude and tenderness throughout the rest of her pregnancy and beyond. "Anything you want," he kept saying to her. But Anna did not want David to bear guilt for urging her to have this baby against her initial desires. Instead, though she was quite happy with his extra attentions, she made it clear to him that she now wanted the baby as much as he did. "I wanted us to be straight about it, [so] that he was [not] suffering."

David and Anna's daughter Katina was one year old when we met with Anna a second time. Unlike her brothers, one with red and one with dark-brown hair, Katina has her mother's blond hair and delicate looks. She also has her father's sense of fun and pealing laugh. Anna has never looked back, never once second-guessed her choice. Today she pursues her scholarly ambitions. She studies part-time and has recently won an academic honor. She is very happy. The whole experience, she says, "brought me and my husband even closer. It has helped us to break through and penetrate another level of existence, you know. We have worked through a problem, and that enriches anybody. I think that shows strength in our relationship."

The Value of Hearing and Being Heard

The strength in David and Anna's relationship is the strength of balance. It has been tested by the same social forces that strained the newer and more fragile bond between Lisa and Peter. Marriage today, perhaps even more than more tentative sexual relationships, has been influenced by women's desires for fulfillment outside the home and the ease with which these desires are served by abortion. Married women no longer expect, as they did decades ago, to have to take unplanned pregnancies in stride. If they do not want more—or any—

children, they can abort. If they want to work or go to school they can end an inconvenient pregnancy. But in Anna's case the ready availability of abortion only made her struggle all the harder to choose wisely. Her decision, far from being a foregone conclusion, came as a surprise to her, especially in these days of heightened individuality.

Perhaps it is only when the desire for human connection and intimacy is stronger than the desire for autonomy that truly balanced choices can be made, choices that carefully consider and respond to the wishes of both the self and important others. Both Anna and David tried, even when neither could accommodate the other, to find a way to reconcile their differences. David promised he would not blame Anna forever. Anna asked herself what she owed David and weighed that against her responsibility to herself. She even compared him to infertile women in his desire for a child he could not bear himself. Finally, in Anna's mind, her well-being and his were so inseparable that to injure him was to injure herself. The only way to avoid the double wound was to turn herself around emotionally. She could see that having another child would simply postpone her plans, whereas having an abortion would permanently deprive David. She was very definite that no coercion was involved in her final choice. In fact, it was only after she had realized that her desire for harmony was stronger than her desire for an abortion that she stopped feeling trapped.

Anna and David both had strong voices and feelings. Anna was able to change hers only because she could listen to David compassionately and be heard by him in turn. This compassionate listening was not possible between Lisa and Peter until after their abortion, but as soon as they could hear each other, their defensiveness and judgments dropped away, revealing their love and concern. For each couple, compassion brought relief. They were, as Lisa put it, comforted by their ability to understand each other, not diminished by it or forced to give ground against their will.

These examples, of course, are in marked contrast to the public wrangling over abortion, in which compassionate listening is rare if not entirely absent. In fact, society as a whole does not listen with care to the voices of women. It tends to hear what women say only if they speak in the public arena, using prevailing terminologies of rights, justice, or power—which tend to be the terminologies of men. This is how they have won sexual liberties at the frequent expense of intimacy and have gained professional success at high cost to their personal lives. This is how women in the feminist movement became divided against more traditional women. It is how the pro-choice movement became identified with women's rights, the pro-life movement with fetal rights, and neither with the importance of exploring fully the human concerns of women in crisis or the quality of life they can offer to children.

Although both women and men privately apply the standards of both care and justice, public voices in America speak mainly about justice and the rights of individuals, not about compassion, nurturing, or human interconnectedness and responsibility. Thus the public discussion can never acknowledge what people who experience the pain of the abortion dilemma discover. What individuals learn by being torn over their choice is that the concerns of both sides of the issue are legitimate, that care is as important as justice, and that one can see the need for legal abortion and yet mourn every case in which it is chosen.

All of the women in this chapter felt the pain of the abortion dilemma. Those who could make their voices heard by those close to them found their pain diminished or removed. Those who could not make themselves heard by others suffered longer. And those who could not heed or even hear their own voices have never stopped feeling uneasy in their hearts about doing what others advised them to do. It is impossible even to speculate how many abortions might be avoided each year if women could hear their own voices, if they could sort out the wisdom from the poor advice in what others have to say, and if society paid more attention and showed more care. But if the women in the next chapter are any indication, problems of identity and self-esteem may account for more abortions than birth control failures do. Only one of the five stories in Chapter 4 ends in birth, and even that outcome is compromised by the loneliness of closed communication.

4

...THE MORE THEY REMAIN THE SAME

First, Freud focused on bodily, sexual, and childish experience and said that these are of determining but hidden importance. More recent psychoanalytic theory tends to emphasize ... feelings of vulnerability, weakness, helplessness, dependency, and the basic emotional connections between an individual and other people. ... [T]hese areas of experience may have been kept out of people's conscious awareness by virtue of their being so heavily dissociated from men and so heavily associated with women.... Women, then, become the "carriers" for society of certain aspects of the total human experience—those aspects that remain unsolved.
Jean Baker Miller, *Toward a New Psychology of Women*, 2nd ed. (1986)

Introduction

The lack of compassionate listening that characterizes the abortion debate has many old and new sources. The hostile political division created or exacerbated by *Roe v. Wade* is only the most recent. A much older source of deafness is the persistent view that women are inherently inferior to men, their concerns less substantial than masculine ones. This view is at the bottom of the schism between the home and workplace, women and men, private life and public life. It has changed little, despite the fact that, as we discussed in the last chapter, women have made deeper inroads into the professions, public affairs, and politics than ever before.

The idea that women are somehow derivatives of men, and by definition less complete than men, is as old as Adam's rib, but in more recent times it has been perpetuated by traditional psychological research. The Freudian view of male psychological development centers on the Oedipal crisis, whose resolution depends on a boy's ability to separate from his mother and, implicitly, from feminine concerns with human interdependence and care. A boy's initiation into full maleness is marked by his achievement of autonomy, independence, pragmatism, and the pursuit of individual rights; it comes at the expense of the early intimacy, empathy, and interconnectedness of his first human relationships.

As some feminist scholars have recently pointed out, women have suffered greatly under this measure of masculine development. As we noted earlier, most psychological studies have been conducted with men and boys as subjects, and their findings have then been superimposed without adjustment or reinterpretation onto women and girls. When the images fail to align, women are blamed. Because they do not follow the same developmental path as men but stay closely bound to their mothers and to other intimate human relationships, they are seen as having "failed" developmentally. The failure is not their fault; being female, they could not do otherwise. Thus femaleness in and of itself is incomplete, and the qualities that women develop through their persistent connectedness to others—that is, an ability to see far-reaching consequences of human interactions, an awareness of interdependence, an insistence on responsibility to others—are subordinated to the more commonly male qualities bred by separation.

Because men have dominated the worlds of work and policy, those worlds have typically institutionalized "masculine" qualities and rigid perceptions of female inferiority. Women, meanwhile, have traditionally been held responsible for maintaining the well-being of their families and other intimates, often with little regard for their own interests. They have taken on, almost exclusively, the emotional, sexual, bodily, maternal tasks that society has regarded as the tedious necessities of life rather than as the fundamental challenges upon which its whole character is built. In the 1950s, in particular, women were given hollow adulation—but no respect—for assuming these tasks. According to psychologist Jean Baker Miller in *Toward a New Psychology of Women*, society has perilously ignored the fact that humanity's "highest necessities" came to be seen as its "lowest needs." Women, in taking care of those needs, were by association only confirmed in their inferiority.

Thus the traits that have traditionally been most valued in male psychological development are also the traits that have dominated American public policy and the marketplace, leaving little room or regard for the concerns that women have been raised to value. Not only have women remained second-class citizens, dominated by men and by the values associated with men, but they are still, in more cases than not, the keepers of a domain that society as a whole has belittled. The rigidity of the structure has permitted little change in its underlying assumptions. Miller says: "it is quite clear that there is an inherent tendency for societies to maintain themselves and for those in positions of prestige and power to believe in and seek to maintain fixity. . . . Some societies, particularly ours, attempt to divert the need for change by entertainment, and a rapid succession of fads. All of these 'circuses' may convey the illusion of change, but in fact they accomplish the opposite."

Though the lives of women have changed dramatically on the surface, as we saw in several stories in the last chapter, the changes have failed to touch the culturally induced sense of worthlessness that, for many women, remains in place deep down. The women who experience self-doubt and self-dislike most intensely are often unable to grasp the root source of their pain. They have trouble hearing their own voices or making themselves understood by those around them. In times of crisis, their fragile stability may disappear. The symptoms of their malaise grow severe and the women become anguished, self-destructive, or immobilized.

The effects of women's silence and of society's deafness to their concerns surface frequently in decisions about unintended pregnancies. This is because so many women who become pregnant without consciously meaning to (unless they experience a straightforward birth control failure) do so because they lack self-esteem or a strong identity. Once pregnant, few women who have fully absorbed the cultural message of their lesser worth succeed in making their own clear, informed choices about their pregnancies. Either they are unable to make themselves heard above the voices of others or they cave in to pragmatism and convenience, attempting to dismiss emotions and desires that cry out against those easier values. Every story in this chapter reveals a degree of voicelessness, depression, or powerlessness in the woman who tells it.

Some of the men in these stories exploit the women's inability to assert their own interests. These men do not always do this manipulatively or even consciously but more as if by habit. Women's self-denial and uncertainty are a part of the landscape. Many men would not question using it to their advantage any more than they would question using a road instead of beating a whole new path to their destination. Yet the stories of these decisions—some of which resemble the public debate about abortion in their lack of attention to responsibility, relationships, and care—suggest that a whole new path is necessary. This path must wind its way through a territory in which women's voices and the content of their concerns are heard with compassion and respect. The incidence and outcome of unplanned pregnancies might change in that unexplored space. It may be more than just an accident of our sample that only one of the five stories in this chapter ends in birth instead of abortion or that that story like the others, is darkened by a failure of compassionate listening on the part of both the woman and the man.

Beth Nichols

We interviewed Beth early in our research and again during the writing of this book. When she first talked to us about the abortion she had had in 1974, at twenty-six, she relived it alarmingly, feeling anguish and rage that she had thought were long extinguished. Her hazel eyes filled repeatedly, and more than once she wept out loud as she recalled events almost twelve years past. She was thin, pretty, and intense, as susceptible to pain as an exposed nerve.

Beth was living in Cleveland at the time of that first interview, but we met with her in Pittsburgh in her aunt's big, high-ceilinged living room. Her aunt had gone out for the day, and Beth's husband, Todd, had stayed in Cleveland with their children. With privacy guaranteed, Beth launched into her narrative.

She had been living in Baltimore, working as a pediatric nurse, when she met Todd, a general surgery resident. They had been together nearly three years when she got pregnant. Her gynecologist had taken her off the birth control pill, for reasons she could not remember, and she had turned to the chancier use of foam, without the added protection of condoms. "I knew Todd didn't like to use anything," she recalled, "which was probably why I was on the pill anyway." She conceived during her first cycle after the switch.

"We weren't married," Beth went on. "Todd hadn't made any commitment to marry me, although we were living together." Todd did make his feelings about the pregnancy plain, though. "He did not want this pregnancy. He really believed it was important to plan a pregnancy. It was important to really want a child. Also, I had been conceived out of wedlock, and my sister had gotten married because she was pregnant. I knew I didn't want to do that. I didn't want to have to . . . say to myself that this person had married me only because I was pregnant."

Beth was not sure she would have believed Todd was sincere even if he had proposed that they marry and have the baby. "How would you know?" she asked. It was clear to Beth that she wanted to preserve the relationship, even at the expense of the pregnancy. "I probably could have worked out raising a child as a single parent. That could be done. But I think we were at a decision point in the relationship—whether we were going to stay together or not. And the relationship was very important to me."

So Beth made an appointment for an abortion, talking about it to no one but Todd. "Once you make up your mind to do something," she explained, "sometimes it's easier just to go ahead than to get a lot of input and become even more confused—especially when you might not want to do what you're doing."

In retrospect, Beth could see that sealing off her emotions in the interest of getting things done was a mistake. At the time, she figured there was no other way. Todd drove her to her appointment and left until it was time to pick her up again. She had a hard time. "I thought it was a perfectly hellish experience. . . . The people were pleasant, but they were cool and detached. The physician was nice and I thought seemed sympathetic. The actual abortion hurt. And the sound of the machine and everything, and realizing what that machine was doing to a baby, was just awful. Afterward, in the recovery room, I thought I was the only person shaking. I thought I was going to lose my mind right then. I just could not stop shaking."

Still, when Todd came to take Beth home, they did not talk. "He had no concept of it," Beth said, and she herself ended up "filing it away."

A month later, while Todd and Beth were trying to work out the fate of their relationship, he traveled to Boston for a medical convention. While he was there, he visited a former girlfriend. A few days later, he joined Beth in Maine, where she was vacationing with a cousin. "I'll never forget it," Beth told us, starting to cry. "Somehow or other, someone brought up Boston, and I remember looking at Todd and saying, 'You slept with Karen, didn't you?' And he said 'yes,' and I lost it. I just lost it. People were there, and I was screaming, 'I killed a baby and you're sleeping with somebody!' I flipped out and stayed flipped out. I got a ride to the airport and went back to Baltimore. I hated him."

Beth also hated the realization that her scene with Todd had forced upon her, which was that she had immersed herself in him and in his interests, forsaking her own. The abortion was only the most devastating in a series of sacrifices she had made to hang onto Todd. "I probably would have kept the pregnancy if it had been, maybe, a more casual relationship," Beth said, wiping furiously at her eyes. "It will always be a mistake. I don't think women are meant to destroy their babies. It is totally against something that is within you. You cannot really voluntarily do that. Pressure can do it—when you have to succumb to medical or financial pressure. But I think when we get right down to it, it's just totally alien."

Beth paused in her narrative to explain that she thought abortion was wrong but "necessary." She wanted to make it plain that she would not condemn women who were forced by circumstances into ending their pregnancies. "I would never judge them," she said. "My heart aches for them." On the other hand, she continued: "It is hard for me to think that someone can sit and be very calm and cool and say, 'I did this because, A, B, C, and D and just walk out the door. I would like to meet this person and talk with her." Echoing some of the women in the last chapter, Beth said, "It has to be a harrowing experience if there is any kind of sensitivity to what they are doing, and perhaps that sensitivity doesn't come until you are thirty-five. But sooner or later, it has got to be dealt with."

Beth did not deal directly with her own abortion. When she got back to Baltimore from Maine, she said: "I came real close to being totally self-destructive. I wasn't coming out of my room for days and days at a time. I wasn't eating or taking care of myself or anything. I had walked out on my job. I couldn't do it. I couldn't do anything." Finally, Beth said: "I remember thinking I was going to throw myself through a window and coming terribly, terribly close to it. So I called my mother and talked with her. She was totally nonjudgmental. I remember that it was just, 'Beth, if you would like to come home, you can come home.' And that was it."

Beth's mother's response steadied her, but what jolted Beth out of her paralysis was a call to a psychiatrist. "I got an appointment with somebody at the hospital, and he said he thought I ought to [check] in," she recalled. "And I thought, no way in hell am I ready to do this. I've got to be better than this. I remembered, from the psych nursing I did for a while, what a trap that was. It was so safe to have someone take care of you and do everything for you and not have to worry at all. I remember thinking it was the ultimate in security, but what a price you would pay for it."

Rather than pay the price, Beth pushed aside the pain that her abortion had triggered. She never again confronted it fully until she met with us. By then she and Todd, with whom she had reunited a few months after the scene in Maine, had been married ten years. They had two children, but Beth had gone through years of infertility and three miscarriages before her successful pregnancies. Those ordeals had raised the specter of her abortion, but it wasn't until she prepared herself for our interview that Beth began to reel under the impact of long-repressed emotions. "I wanted to destroy Todd last week," she said. "I hated him all over again. I hated myself all over again. He still believes we made the right decision under the circumstances."

By the time she met us in Pittsburgh, Beth said: "The thing I feel now is that I can talk. . . . Perhaps my biggest mistake all those years ago was isolating myself. Perhaps if I had found a group of women who had been through the same thing, it would have been the best thing in the world. . . . We share [our experiences of] childbirth. We share the joy of creating, and everybody gets all this attention and all this love. And if there ever was a time when you need love and to be touched and to be made to feel like a real person again, it is after you have destroyed something."

A year or so after we first spoke with her, Beth began to deliberately probe the pain that went far deeper than her anger with Todd or her sorrow over the abortion. It took three years of twice-a-week therapy to bring her to terms with her anguish and its source, which lay in the wild disorder of her upbringing.

"Both my parents were alcoholic," Beth explained. "My father died of cirrhosis when I was fifteen. My mother is still drinking at seventy-three. I no longer have any contact with her. In our house, when I was little, someone was always striking somebody or screaming or isolating themselves. As the oldest child, I was always the caretaker. After my father died, my mother was extremely verbally abusive. She would wake me up at night to call me names and tell me I killed my father or that my father had hated me."

Beth's need for a good parent drove her into Todd's arms. "He was the first man who sort of made me laugh a little," she said. "He was a father I never had. When the abortion crisis came along, he failed me, and that was what was so devastating. . . . Our marriage only began to work when I began to separate Todd from my father. Then I could acknowledge that the abortion was my decision, too. It is probably not the one I would have made if I had known what I know now."

What Beth knows now is who she is. "I insist I was born a year ago," she laughed. "By the end of therapy, I could stand on my own two feet. I had learned skills I never could have learned as a child in that house." Asked to describe those skills, Beth answered: "I think of them as parenting skills, because it is with my children that I use them the most. I have a new ability to let go, to look at a situation and not feel threatened by my child choosing something different than what I would choose. I give them choices and leeway. I am able to validate them and love them, yet I am able to claim my own space, time, and boundaries."

It had been the loss of her boundaries that had sent Beth into therapy. She had begun to act like her own mother. "I wasn't drinking," she recalled, "but I was doing everything else. I was becoming violent, yelling and screaming all the time." One day, Beth said, she went into her bathroom and locked the door, fearful and alarmed. "I was terrified I was going to dissolve," she said. "I couldn't feel my edges. I literally, physically, could not feel myself touch myself. I had no boundaries."

Today Beth has redefined her edges; she knows just where she ends and others begin. That clarity allows her to grant her children their own identities, an enterprise that takes work but no real struggle. Beth wants to help her children gain self-knowledge, in part so that they will not have to define themselves by opposing her as she has had to oppose her own mother. "My mother has no power over me," said Beth. "I'm forty-three years old and still need to reinforce that every day. But as a result I see in my daughter someone who knows who she is. She was the only girl in her class who went winter camping with a group of boys and counselors, who played boys' soccer, who took up speed skating. Now other girls are getting interested. These are not things I would have encouraged, once."

The final step in Beth's liberation from her past came when she announced, after a brief return to nursing, that she hated it. "It felt wonderful," she said gleefully. It represented a final break with her childhood, a repudiation of the caretaking career she had begun in her parents' house and followed into her relationships with Todd and her children. That caretaking role had been a radical distortion of the moral standard that women are typically guided by. It cost Beth her childhood and her identity. What she has achieved in its place is a kind of creative separation. She has balanced the exaggerated need to care for others with a healthy degree of independence and self interest. Her new skills allow her to foster relationships without being consumed by them. Now that she no longer devotes herself entirely to others, she ends up doing both them and herself more good.

This balanced awareness has led Beth to believe that her abortion decision was wrong for her. It led another woman we talked to, whose story and background were remarkably similar, to the opposite conclusion—also after extended therapy. But any woman who learns to respect herself may gain what society so often fails to foster or respect: a sense of connectedness with others and a feeling of health and proportion within herself.

Silent Women

In *Women's Ways of Knowing*, Mary Belenky and her colleagues describe women who, having no inner voice or no trust in it, look outside themselves not only for confirmation of their desires but for identity, truth, and direction. According to Belenky and her colleagues, the most seriously incapacitated women, the "silent women," often come from deeply troubled families whose members communicate little except through blows and cruel words. Such women, write the authors, live "in silence or din, looking for nourishment in the most barren soil." When they find none, they tend to withdraw. This is what Beth did after her abortion stirred up such pain. She retreated to her room, isolating herself in despair. She tried to reach out to her mother—the same mother who had neglected her emotional and developmental needs in childhood. And, in both her suicidal impulses and her willingness to deny her own desires in order to serve Todd's, Beth was self-destructive.

For silent women and others with no trustworthy inner voice, relationships are based on the power of others to command or guide them. These women rely on others not only to tell them what to do but to give them an identity. Beth had no voice with Todd. From the beginning, theirs was a stereotypical doctor-nurse, father-child, dominant-subordinate relationship. She looked to Todd for what she could not find in herself and had not received from her parents. Cold and violent as they had been, she had craved their love, and in Todd she saw a loving father for whom she could be "a perfect little girl." When she became pregnant, she had to do as Todd wished. "If I didn't, he would leave me," she explained. She could not face another abandonment after living abandoned all her life.

When women like Beth become pregnant at an inconvenient time, abortion may be dictated by male-associated standards that are manifest everywhere: in some people's strictly pragmatic approach to unplanned pregnancy, in circumstantial imperatives, and in the desires of the men themselves. Such women are left to grieve alone, as Beth was. What rescued her was initiation into an acceptance and celebration of female values, which she reached through her strong, intimate connection to her therapist, to herself, and eventually to Todd and her children. The psychological trouble she needed to repair had arisen from her attempt to satisfy prevailing standards of autonomy and pragmatism by isolating herself and disregarding the messages her emotions struggled to convey. The attempt led her deeply into grief and rage from which she could emerge only when she could speak and be heard in her own voice.

Beth was wise in describing her new strength as a source of better parenting skills, for as Belenky *et al.* write, "It is through the ability to ask and hear answers to 'What are you going through?' that the reality of the child is both created and respected." Beth was able to do this with her children—helping them to discover and nurture their identities—only after her therapist had done it for her. Today, she feels she has received a gift. What she once saw as her weakness and vulnerability have become sources of strength. As Jean Baker Miller says, "By acknowledging their weakness, women are undertaking, first of all, a vast act of exposure. As soon as women add, 'I feel weak now, but I intend to move on from that,' they are displaying a great strength."

Miller also maintains that the kind of vulnerability that Beth experienced can "in its extreme form . . . be described as the threat of psychic annihilation." Another term would be loss of identity, which women like Beth suffer when they take to heart demeaning and abusive attitudes. They learn to please others before themselves, to strive for conventional feminine goodness at the expense of personal growth, and to take undue responsibility for parents, mates, friends or children. In all these aims, they unwittingly distort and corrupt the care-taking standard. When, like Beth, such women stop overbalancing so pre-cariously, they gain equilibrium and great strength.

The next story is about a woman who had a greater ability to hear her own voice than Beth did at first. Yet she too experienced many of her best qualities as weaknesses. For reasons her story will make clear, she could not act confidently on her instincts, nor could she trust her inner voice to advise her well.

Linda Pedersen

We interviewed Linda, a textile artist, in her studio in Bucks County, Pennsylvania. She had just turned fifty but looked younger in her worn jeans, peasant blouse, and scuffed leather thongs as she led us through a vast vegetable garden that she told us accounted for her farmer's tan. We followed her into what looked like a shed but contained a bright space dominated by a loom and hung with colorful woven, embroidered, or quilted works. She was preparing for a show, experimenting with different ways of displaying her art. She served us lemonade and then perched on a stool beside the loom, running her hand through her thick, salt-and-pepper hair.

Linda looked very much like what she was, an early 1950s baby boomer who had been deeply influenced by the social upheaval that arose in her young adulthood. Even in 1990, she had the look of the 1960s or early 1970s, and she surrounded herself with books on meditation and spiritualism, goddess worship and holistic healing. She had woven herself an exquisite prayer mat on which, she told us, she spent the first and last hour of each day.

In 1970, however, Linda was not living the life of a flower child. She had already been married for four years and was the mother of two girls. For all of those years, except for the weeks just before and after childbirth, she and her husband, Joe, had had sex "once a day, twice a day, seven days a week." Linda derived no pleasure from Joe's frequent urges. "I never was turned on," she said. "I never had an orgasm." A fundamentalist Christian minister's daughter who was raised to be obedient, Linda said: "I was just doing what wives were supposed to do, being turned over at four o'clock in the morning and being screwed. I never questioned things until much later."

By the time Linda began to register an unconscious protest against Joe's violations and her own compliance, another four years had gone by. "I just was really exhausted," she said. "I ended up with viral infections and had to have surgery for prolapsed organs. My doctor finally said: 'You have to talk to your husband. Something's going on.' She meant that the infections weren't true infections. She definitely felt it was more emotional."

Even surgery, though, did not take the sexual pressure off Linda. She never really confronted Joe with her doctor's message. Instead, she took a radical step for a preacher's daughter by encouraging the fashionable, mid-1970s idea of open marriage. At first it was a joke. Several of her friends in the small town where she still lives and works found Joe attractive and made playful, flirtatious comments. Linda started turning their jokes back on them. "'Take him home for the weekend,' I'd say. 'Just bring him back. It would be a relief.'" She laughed but watched our expressions closely. "Finally," she said, "I was serious."

Joe and a few discreet friends took Linda up on her suggestion, and Linda enjoyed a respite for the first time in nearly nine years. She recovered her health and energies. For a while, that was enough; she wasn't interested in pursuing the same freedoms she had granted to others. Gradually, realizing she had a choice at last, she began to think it was time to learn something about her own sexuality. She had some friendly affairs with men she had known a long time. She and Joe kept their sexual forays strictly within a circle of friends, so they did not worry about the opinions of other people in their small town.

It was in the course of her only truly passionate liaison that Linda became pregnant. An old friend, Tommy, visited for two months, and in that short time Linda conceived with him. "I was using the diaphragm," she said, "but I wasn't being real careful. I didn't use it every time . . . he said it was uncomfortable." Tommy also devised a marvelously illogical, manipulative argument against the diaphragm. He said to Linda, "You know, sometimes when people are really in love, no matter what they use as prevention, there's still a child that comes out of it." If the diaphragm was powerless against the force of love, why bother?

Joe, meanwhile, had had a vasectomy. The whole town knew about it,

Linda said with a giggle, because "he had complications and could barely walk." If Linda continued her pregnancy, "the whole town would know it wasn't his."

To both men, there was only one course of action. "They had a hard time hearing that I was even making a decision," Linda said. "They didn't act like I even had a choice. They just assumed I would get an abortion." For Linda it was not so simple, and the men's attitude made her "just totally livid," even though she herself felt "stupid for letting it get to the point where there was only a possibility for an abortion or a child." Looking back, Linda thought her pregnancy was not exactly an accident. She thought, if she got pregnant, something "would shift." She wasn't sure what, or in which direction. Her feeling is a good example of how intuitive and complicated decisions about birth control can be.

Though Linda did end up having an abortion, she felt "a real big sense of loss" along with her anger. She was sure the baby she chose not to have would have been a boy—that she had given up her only chance to have a son. Though in the long run she did not regret her action, she felt forced into it to some extent by the men's attitudes and by her fear that Joe would try to take her daughters from her if she had another man's child. Still, she said, "having another child at that time in my life would have been the craziest thing I could have done."

Linda stayed married to Joe for another eight years after the abortion. The state of their marriage, which they had agreed would no longer be an open one, was never very strong. Nevertheless, she was momentarily surprised when Joe announced one night, while she was reading in bed, that he wanted out. She quickly recognized her opportunity. "It takes nothing to trigger it, when we need to make a change," she said. "So I leaned back in the bed, and I heard this little voice that said: 'This is perfect. Don't fight it. Just go with the flow.' And I just picked up my book and started reading."

In the years since she and Joe divorced, Linda has had few relationships with men, and only one with someone she believed did not want to exploit her. Like other women in this chapter, she has gone digging into the past, trying to discover what had prevented her from "speaking up and being heard." For several years now, she has been excavating her Texas childhood and her fundamentalist upbringing, which permitted no comic books, no dancing, no movies—no wild oats. Though she felt safe and cared for as a child, watched with both tenderness and a critical eye by her father's flock, intimations of dark incidents haunt her. She has grown sure, as have two of her sisters, that there was sexual abuse. She remembers sitting in church at only three years old, knowing in her bones that God was not there. She thinks it was a sexual incident that prompted her infant cynicism. Though she suspects one of many uncles, and desperately hopes it was no one closer, she is not sure who her abuser was.

Linda has come to feel that secrets, abuse, scrutiny, and the perfectionist standards of her childhood community robbed her of her voice. She believes spirituality and feminism restored it to her, and that her open marriage and her abortion made room in her life for those healing forces. This was the "shift" she had dimly intuited might come about if she got pregnant. "Without those experiences," she said, "I would have just maintained the pretense." Instead, she has learned to take care of herself. "I used to just go along until something hit me with a brick in the face to get me to realize, 'Hey, you've got to take care of yourself.' . . . Men don't usually need to be hit with a brick. They were taught to take care of themselves, or to have us take care of them."

Linda was convinced that, had she learned this lesson earlier, she would not have had sex without using her diaphragm "no matter how uncomfortable Tommy was." She would not "have gotten swept away with the romance."

Adulthood versus Womanhood

The dominant culture's views of adulthood differ greatly from its views of womanhood. Under the continuing separation of values for men and for women, the characteristics of adulthood generally match only the qualities that men are urged to cultivate: the capacity for independent thought, logical clarity, and decisive action. Women, under a persistent double standard, continue to be held in high regard not for achieving these qualities—though they are as able as men to do so—but for putting the needs and views of others before their own. They are too often encouraged, whether tacitly or overtly, to retain childlike qualities of dependence and obedience. Though strong models of female adulthood are provided by the work of Carol Gilligan, Jean Baker Miller, and Mary Belenky *et al.*—models that actually serve both women and men by bringing the values of each into balance—many women in our society have either had to remain immature or to adopt the image of adulthood that evolved for men. Both of these conditions can put clear-headed, balanced decisions about sexuality and pregnancy far out of reach. And in the absence of clarity and balance, women are likely either to serve the needs of others at the expense of their own or else to block the caretaking impulse and adopt a strictly pragmatic standard.

Linda Pedersen was strongly affected by the conflict between womanhood and adulthood. Outwardly a product of seemingly changed attitudes toward women and sexuality, Linda was a very unliberated woman during the time of her most radical behavior. She was so little able to consider her own desires that for years she never objected to what might be called daily marital rape had it not been for her helpless compliance. Open marriage was not a daring thumb-of-the-nose at traditional social mores but the only escape she could devise. Even after she had begun to enjoy her own sexuality, she could not risk embarrassing her husband with her extramarital pregnancy or losing her daughters to him in a custody battle. Never mind that Joe, too, had been having sex outside their marriage; the risks were never the same for him.

In retrospect, Linda believes she made the right choice about abortion but that she depended too heavily on what the men in her life expected. She continues her struggle with the problem of how to be both grown up and female, a struggle that, in Belenky et al.'s terms, is a search for an authentic voice, one that a woman can trust to inform her of her own worth and desires and to help her assess what other voices have to say.

If Linda had had such a clear inner voice, she would have insisted on birth control despite Tommy's objections. As it was, the best Linda's voice could do was to whisper the vague possibility that something would "shift" if she got pregnant. As Kristin Luker reports in Taking Chances: Abortion and the Decision not to Contracept, it is all too common for women to end up with unintended pregnancies when they are trying—usually only half-consciously—to serve conflicting emotional purposes through sex and the risk of pregnancy.

Today, Linda avoids rather than wrestles with the persistent, demeaning attitudes toward women that lay beneath many of her experiences and choices. She stays out of relationships with men, not only sexual ones but also others that would pit her against their world. She pursues a feminine art at the edge of her garden. She shuns the judgmental religiosity of her father in favor of spiritual exercises that promote healing, connection, and an awareness of life's fine, intricate web.

For now, Linda is shaping herself in defiance of the standards of a male-dominated society. She no longer engages in conflict or tries to come to terms with the world around her. In this she is like some of the women in Belenky et al.'s studies who, in searching for greater self-definition, walked away from their pasts, rejected the teachings of their parents, left constricting relationships, and ended up knowing more about who they were not than who they were. For every woman who defines herself in this way, there are others who try to meet the standards of the dominant culture by achieving success and professionalism on that culture's terms. They strive for unflappable poise, cool rationality, and unwavering control. And so they, too, are ruled by the values of male-led society.

So far, the stories in this chapter demonstrate how difficult it can be for women to be clear, authentic, and adult, especially in their intimate relationships with men. The next three stories—two of them about the same couple—expand on that theme. At the same time, they show how little concern there is in our politics or social policies for women who would like to proceed with unplanned pregnancies. In these stories, social disregard mingles with a lack of compassion and a lack of respect between individuals to create a sorrowful amalgam of loneliness and frustration.

Tina Morgan

Tina heard about our research soon after we began interviewing people, and she volunteered her story. We talked with her at her apartment near Pittsburgh while her husband was out. She cried steadily as she told her story, her grief and frustration as fresh as on the day two years earlier when she had discovered she was pregnant. It was as if, at that time, she had been sentenced to prison for a crime she did not commit.

"I've always been really, really, really careful about birth control," she began. "I read everything I could so I could make good decisions about it. I used a diaphragm until the year before I got married, and then I switched to an IUD." Tina's single-minded determination to avoid an untimely pregnancy set her apart from the majority of women we spoke to, and yet she did not come across as a strong or confident woman, more as a frightened one. She was small, light-haired, disheveled from crying, and helpless to overcome her pain. She seemed to shrink beneath its weight, curling ever more tightly into an over-stuffed couch as she told her story.

Tina's parents and in-laws knew nothing of her abortion. "For my mother and my mother-in-law," she explained, "the decision I made would be a terrible, terrible thing. Both my husband and I come from very large families. Jack has four sisters and two brothers; I have two sisters and two brothers. So it's just a way of thinking about families, I guess, that . . . that makes it hard. It makes me very sad," Tina sighed. "I feel that I've betrayed a basic value of having a family, even though it's not what I want right now. I haven't changed my feeling about that."

What seemed to be hurting Tina most was how relentlessly irreconcilable her family values were with her certainty that she was not ready for children herself. She was crushed between her right to choose abortion and her feeling, despite her flawless record of responsible birth control, that she had been irresponsible in doing so.

At first, when Tina's period was later than it had ever been before, she disregarded it. She knew the IUD was supposed to have a 97 or 98 percent success rate, and she did not believe she could fall within the tiny group who suffered its failure. Finally, with her breasts aching and her eyelids always heavy, she went to a drop-in clinic around the corner and had a pelvic exam. The clinic did not offer pregnancy testing, but the doctor "rudely and roughly" dismissed her dawning fears. "Oh, oh, he was such a jerk," Tina recalled, crying harder. "He told me I wasn't pregnant. He should have told me to get tested, but he just didn't think I could possibly be pregnant."

Tina went away thinking something else must be wrong with her. When she confided in a friend who worked with her at a day-care center, the friend urged her to have a pregnancy test right away. Tina did so, and the test was positive. "I wanted so much to believe that doctor, to believe that I was not pregnant. It was the worst thing that had ever happened to me. I never wanted to feel that way about being pregnant. That was why I was always so careful about birth control. I always wanted pregnancy to be . . . " Tina broke off, sobbing, and then said ruefully, "That was two years ago, and I still do this."

Jack agreed with Tina that their circumstances left them no alternative but abortion. They were living a bare-bones life. He had recently quit a graduate program in public health administration and was looking for work. "When he was idle for that length of time," Tina said, "there was a lot of strain on both of us, emotionally. And financially, it was terrible. I was making about nine thousand dollars a year, bringing home six hundred dollars a month. Half of that went for rent. I didn't have any medical coverage. We were at a very low point in our marriage. Money—money was a big factor. Which is sad to me."

Neither Jack nor Tina felt their marriage was in trouble. They just needed to weather a black spell. Had they tried to proceed with the pregnancy, though, they feared it would be more than they could handle. Adoption was out, too, Tina said, "because I couldn't have had the baby and then given it up when I was married. People would have thought that was even worse than what I did."

The people who made Tina feel judged for her decision were some of the very ones who supported *Roe v. Wade* most strongly. Though Tina was hesitant about telling others about her pregnancy, she did seek out some women she had met though a feminist discussion group she belonged to. Quite reasonably, she expected sympathy and solidarity. Instead, she found politics and opinion. One woman, who Tina knew had had several abortions herself, simply said, "Oh, but I never had to do that when I was married." Tina had not thought of this woman as a judgmental person, and so she wondered if she had misinterpreted the tone of the remark. "But what came across," she said, "was that this wasn't the kind of decision [a married] woman made."

Others in Tina's women's group were politically in support of abortion but had never chosen it for themselves. One had had a child without being married. Most others had never faced the question. They did not suggest that her choice was wrong. Mainly, Tina said, they wanted to know what Jack thought. That infuriated her. She thought: "Politically, you're not supposed to ask me that question. What the hell difference does it make what Jack thinks? But that's what they wanted to know."

What Tina concluded from these women's curiosity was that, to them, "getting married—you know, signing up with this guy—was not really the politically acceptable thing to do. So . . . what they wanted was for me to have to kind of fight him to do what I wanted." That way, Tina surmised, she would be wresting her rights from the male oppressor, and the women in her group could be more sympathetic. Abortion, on the other hand, "wasn't supposed to be something that was a struggle." Politics had taken away empathy and replaced it with rhetoric and the one-sided concern for rights that has characterized most of the debate on this issue.

For Tina, meanwhile, the decision to abort was wrenching, and the procedure, a menstrual extraction, was worse. Though physically easy, it left vivid and painful impressions on Tina. "Jack took me down to the hospital and waited for me. The doctor had to remove the IUD first, and she was—my feet were in the stirrups, and she took the IUD out and held it in her bloody tweezers. And she said, 'You know, you don't have to terminate this pregnancy because of this.' And I thought, 'How can you even present that? How can you think I can make a decision like that when I'm right here?' I just said, 'No, don't say that.' And she went ahead. It was a very brief procedure." Immediately afterward, the doctor performed a test on the minuscule fetus to make sure the pregnancy had not been lodged in a Fallopian tube. "She took the . . . you know . . . what she extracted, and she examined it. That was terrible, when she did that."

Tina felt, about medical professionals and about her women friends, that "they didn't think it was really a big deal. They don't acknowledge that there's pain, that there's trauma." To Tina, both groups seemed so used to the terms and language of the public discussion, with its emphasis on black-or-white answers and its arguments framed mainly as matters of rights, that they could not perceive any other reality. In the meantime, Tina's "right" to an abortion did nothing to address her pain or loss.

Soon, as if to confirm that her pain was valid, Tina began dwelling on thoughts of infertile women. "You know what bothers me?" she asked. "When I hear about women who can't have children. I feel so terrible. I feel like I've robbed them. I really feel like I . . . hurt them. I've never said, to anybody else, this thing about infertility. But I feel it every time I read an article . . . or read the little personal ads. You know, 'Happily married professional couple desires white infant.'" Crying and laughing a little, Tina shrugged and looked confused. Yet her thoughts, considered in the light of women's concerns with responsibility, care, and interdependence, make sense. Tina, though she was not in a position to have a child, wanted children someday. She knew in her blood and bones what she had learned as a loved child in a large family: that a fetus has value in and of itself. Doing away with something of value was dreadful to her. "The whole idea of choice—it's not a choice," she said. Infertile women, perhaps more than any others, would be the ones who would share and understand Tina's feelings. They would recognize the value of what Tina had destroyed; they would share her grief; they would understand the unfairness and the lack of control she had experienced. She felt she had done everything right and responsibly, and yet she was left with sharp, persistent guilt and sorrow.

At the end of our interview with Tina, we asked her why she had called to volunteer her story. "I think, in a way, I needed affirmation," she answered. "I still need to know that what I think is a problem, is a problem—that it's not something I made up." She felt that the interview, and her tears, had been "cathartic." And yet, she said, "I don't know if I'll ever feel quiet in my soul about this."

The Pain of Powerlessness

The source of Tina's unrelieved anguish over her abortion may be powerlessness of a different sort than the other women in this chapter experienced. She relied on one of medical technology's most effective forms of birth control, and it failed her. She turned to medical professionals for help and found them insensitive. She anticipated support from women friends who could not provide it. She was prevented from turning to her family by her feeling that she was betraying their values. And she did not expect Jack, to whom her early pregnancy remained rather abstract, to grasp the immediacy of her grief. Finally, she turned to two strangers doing research on people's struggles with birth-or-abortion choices in the hope of seeing in them an acceptance of her own reality. Tina's story, uncomplicated by any background of abuse, addiction, or parental failure, still illustrates the heartache that widespread deafness to women can generate, especially when a woman has done everything possible to avoid both pregnancy and judgment but is still forced to suffer.

The final two stories in this chapter are about two people who, through deeply ingrained differences in outlook and background, are often unable to hear each other. But their differences and deafness are greatly exaggerated by social institutions that offer them no care and no real choice.

Nancy and Jim Shaler (1)

Nancy Murray and Jim Shaler met in 1983 while both were working part-time for a weekly newspaper near Richmond, Virginia. Nancy took photographs of local weddings and events, a sideline to her main effort, an unpaid internship that would qualify her to teach emotionally disturbed children. Jim wrote book reviews and a column on sports. He also drove a taxi. She was twenty-eight, and he was thirty-four. Both were far from settled down.

They found each other odd and irresistible. Nancy was pure Tidewater country: rangy, freckled, blue-eyed, and slow of speech. She still had about her an air of the scabby-kneed girl who had grown up within a dusty bike-ride of three grandparents, six aunts, four uncles, and eighteen cousins. Jim was a rootless Yankee, most recently from Manhattan. He was dark, curly-haired, and abrupt in speech and manner. He had moved a half-dozen times in childhood and had scarcely met his extended family. He had stayed on the move as an adult, living on both coasts and in several places in between. "The whole sense of family and the whole sense of place is entirely different for Nancy than it is for me," Jim said.

Nancy had not been involved with anyone at all for three years before Jim came along. In fact, she had had few relationships since her late teens, when she had become pregnant in the aftermath of a family disaster. Her father, a successful salesman, had lost everything when he was disabled in an automobile accident. Financial misfortune wrecked Nancy's careful plans for college and a career and sent her to work in a local textile mill. Despondency carried her without resistance into bad friendships, drug use, pregnancy, a listless suicide attempt, and an illegal abortion. In the wake of those disasters, Nancy was determined to regain her emotional health and restore her plans. She worked hard at a variety of jobs, saved money, and went to school.

"Years passed," she told us. "My life was on track. Every now and than I would have a relationship with a person [but a lot of times] I didn't even have sex. I was pretty responsible." Nancy tried several methods of birth control, but the most reliable ones never worked for her. "I had a lot of trouble with the pill," she said. "I had an IUD and it came out. My body just pushed it back out." In her infrequent sexual encounters, she usually relied on condoms or a diaphragm.

Nancy had been working at the newspaper for a year when Jim started contributing his column and reviews. She and Jim began dating gradually, each of them a little wary of the differences that were also so attractive. They dealt with the usual issues that arise early in a relationship, most of which concerned style more than content. For example, Jim urged Nancy to be less self-sacrificing and less conscientious on others' behalf. "I don't know where she gets that," he said. "Her mother does the same kind of thing, though. . . . Like one night Nancy was trying to find something in a catalog and [remembered] that the catalog was at her mom's and [she called her mom and] said, 'I don't know which catalog it's in, but could you see if you could find it?' So her mother spent the next four hours looking for this thing. That's the sort of thing Nancy would do—and then feel pressured because of the time it took [away from] her own business."

The emotional patterns and mild tensions Jim described gathered into a crisis a year after he and Nancy met. They were living together by that time, but for her parents' sake they maintained a genteel pretense to the contrary. "Her mother never indicated that she knew otherwise," Jim said wryly, "but she knew otherwise. . . . People in the South do that a lot. [They] don't deal with the actuality. . . . If there's a story [they] *can* pretend to believe, [they] *will* pretend to believe it."

Nancy knew immediately when she became pregnant. She remembered the symptoms. She and Jim had been using condoms, but not with perfect regularity. Looking back on that time, Jim mused about the ways that he and Nancy had evolved for meeting problems together. "There's always a seeking of balance," he said. "Sometimes it feels like we are at opposite ends of a teeter-totter, and here's the issue in the middle, and here's me, and here's her, and eventually, with a lot of ups and downs, it sort of balances out and stabilizes." He thought the two of them were equally practical and equally emotional, but in different ways. "My practicality goes along very nicely day to day, but I'm capable of a big flight of impracticality—the big moment of saying, 'Oh, screw it, we'll just do it.'" That was what Jim felt when Nancy told him she was pregnant; he was eager to proceed and happy at the thought of becoming a father.

Nancy was skeptical but apprehensively agreed to go along. "We decided to go through with it," she said. "I guess we were going to get married. I don't remember that as a specific. I do remember telling Jim to check into the insurance. I was afraid insurance wouldn't cover it."

In retrospect, Jim thought Nancy was just guiding him gently toward a faceoff with reality. Sure enough, his investigations yielded one disappointment after another. He was the only one with health insurance, having gone full-time with the paper a few months earlier, but it would not cover Nancy's pregnancy even if they married. Their incomes were small. Nancy could not supplement hers without violating the terms of her internship; Jim had dental bills and a legal debt from a car accident the year before. Nevertheless, their combined paychecks, had they married, would have put them over the limit for assistance.

"It was kind of like doors closing, you know." Nancy said. "We were thinking: 'This is what we're going to do and everything's going to be fine, we're going to have this baby. Everything will be fine.' But doors were closing."

Jim sighed. "I think Nancy was just willing . . . to let me prove to myself that it wasn't a good idea." He felt all along that Nancy was hoping his findings would support her unstated preference for abortion. He was pretty sure she did not want to put her professional plans on hold after spending so many years restoring the hopes that her father's disability had shattered. "I ultimately agreed that [abortion] was what we ought to do," he said. "But I was very sad about that. I really was."

Still, Jim admitted that their lives, had they had the baby, would have been unmanageable. "We would have had a lot of debt and no wherewithal to pay it off. We would probably have had to rely on some kind of social services." Even if Nancy had given up her teaching internship to take a full-time job, the kind of salary she could expect would not have covered day-care. Her extended family lived more than an hour's drive away, so all those aunts, uncles, and cousins were only wishful resources, not real ones. Nancy would have had to stay home with the child, stretching Jim's income far past its limits. In the end,

Jim agreed with Nancy that they would have to abort. She was at least as relieved as she was sorry; his disappointment was undiluted.

"There was a black moment in our relationship as a result of this [decision]," Nancy recalled. The worst of the trouble arose in the aftermath of the abortion, which her doctor performed in his office. It was brief, but, said Nancy, "While it's happening, it's intense, painful in every way imaginable. It's like you're being killed, I guess. Abortions are horrible things, the way they feel, the thing that happens when that life is separated from you. It's devastating. It's, it just feels like . . . your life has been ripped out of you."

Though a part of her had wanted the abortion, Nancy could not get over it. She was depressed; she developed pneumonia, and she had to take a leave from her internship after all. "I always think I get sick when things get too tough emotionally," she said. Jim, on the other hand, "is the kind of person who believes, when you make a decision . . . [that's] the way it is, and you try to put it behind you. You try not to have guilt and frustration. We were really frustrated with the insurance companies and things like that, you know."

As soon as Nancy's abortion was over, she said, "[I was] kind of in shock, you know. You go behind a mask . . . and you get through." Though she relied on her mask to cover the intensity of her reaction to abortion, she could not maintain her emotional disguise. A few days after the procedure, Nancy's mask slipped. "I was . . . being haunted by what it was like, by the whole experience. And I tried to talk to Jim about it. I was, I guess, too graphically describing what had happened and the way it felt, and he was sitting there listening with no expression at all. And when I finished telling him, he just jumped all over me. He just started yelling about the emotional bludgeoning I had just given him. . . . [But] I wanted him to know, just as I knew, what it felt like. I felt like he had a responsibility to know what I had been through."

For his part, Jim had been unable to adhere to his own prescribed way of dealing with decisions. Just as Nancy was haunted by the abortion, he was haunted by sadness at the loss of the pregnancy. "Her nature is that things . . . affect her very strongly and tend to have a lingering effect. They tend to lay a claim on her that takes a long time to fit into her life. . . . for me, I think I have an easier time putting things behind me, but I was really sad about this. . . . I really wanted to have that child. I really did. I really looked forward to being a parent." From Jim's perspective, it was hard to sympathize wholeheartedly with what Nancy had suffered or to feel the sense of responsibility she wanted him to feel. "I don't think Nancy in any way wanted to have the child . . . but at the same time I think the process of the abortion . . . was a very saddening one for her, and I don't think it helped her to know that I didn't agree with her feelings [of reluctance about the pregnancy]. I think she was somewhat emotionally scarred by the experience."

In the end, as Nancy and Jim both said in their separate interviews, they never could talk satisfactorily about the abortion they both, for different reasons, had chosen. Jim felt they never shared their different kinds of sadness. Nancy said: "There are some things Jim refuses to discuss, and [the abortion] was one of them. I mean, we can talk about it in some terms, but not . . . what it felt like—that horrible, stripping-everything-inside-of-you-feeling. We can't talk about that."

Public Policy Failures and Private Pain

From the outside, it is easy to see both Nancy's and Jim's points of view in this story. It is easy to regard Nancy's emotional, graphic account of her abortion—her urgent need to talk—as a means of coping that women resort to more commonly than men. Jim did not have the same impulse to describe to Nancy the details of his sense of loss. In the abstract, both people may have had a responsibility to acknowledge each other's pain, but both were surfeited with their personal sorrow. Nancy's anguish over the abortion was too tightly bound to the very source of Jim's pain for him to bear her account of it. She could bear his reactions no better, since his grief contained within it a tacit accusation against her for having had the abortion at all. Though Jim had agreed it would be impossible for them to proceed with the pregnancy, the abortion represented the loss of a child to him. To Nancy, it was more a personal ordeal than a loss. Their emotional differences obscured the merely practical accord they had reached through necessity.

Given enough time, Nancy and Jim might have found voices in which they could communicate about the abortion without making matters worse. For example, they might have transferred some of their frustration with each other back to the original source of frustration—the insurance companies, the lack of affordable day care, their ineligibility for assistance. Like so many people in their circumstances, though, they never really questioned the absence of support. They took that as an unpleasant given and proceeded to a conclusion that even Jim had to admit was the only one left to them.

Had Nancy and Jim really attended to the message society sent them in their dilemma, they might have realized that what had become a last resort for them was a first resort of public policy. They might have turned to each other for comfort in a cold world. They might have been able to see that, privately, they were in agreement, if in pain, at every step toward a decision that felt forced upon them by a lack of public care and concern. Nancy initially agreed to have the child, but she was afraid it would be at the cost of her other pursuits and the quality of their lives. She was relieved when they resorted to abortion, not because she was unwilling to become a mother, but because she did not want to do so without resources. Jim, after other doors had shut in his face, felt forced to agree to an abortion. Like Nancy, he could see no other way. In fact, they both were glad they had that legal option. In their relief that it was available, they never wondered why they did not have as strong an option to have their baby.

Had Jim and Nancy lived in one of many Western European countries, their pregnancy could have proceeded without costing them everything Nancy feared. They would have had access to a national health program that would have covered their expenses, and they would have benefitted from strong social policies aimed at promoting childbirth, supporting families, and making abortion a more genuine last resort. Having a child would not have meant such long-term debt and so many lost opportunities.

Nancy and Jim (2)

Like most people, Nancy and Jim had no perspective on this broad view. Eventually, they put the incident aside. They recovered from their shock at the depths of their emotional differences and put their energies into understanding and accommodating those differences. Two years later, after many more ups and downs, they married. A month after that, Nancy was pregnant again.

"We hadn't anticipated a pregnancy quite that soon," Jim admitted. "I think Nancy was disappointed to be pregnant so quickly. But we never did sit down and say, 'Are we going to carry this one to term or not?' It was pretty much assumed."

Both Nancy and Jim were working full-time, though neither was making much money. Jim had been promoted to the position of managing editor of the newspaper and Nancy, despite her training in special education, was working for a political organization in Richmond. They still had debts. They had bought a new car, and Nancy was paying off a tuition loan. Despite the hardships, Jim relied on their stronger commitment, the medical coverage that would now apply to pregnancy, and the security of their jobs in his unquestioning pleasure over the prospect of a child.

Nancy's version of their decision to continue the pregnancy differed a little from Jim's. She struggled, and she questioned things that Jim did not. "We thought we . . . would like to have a child. And we knew it was going to be hard, because we still didn't have much money, and all those kinds of things. But that's the way it always is when people are going to have children. It's always hard. . . . But I got scared. I was feeling really frightened . . . and I began to wonder if I really . . . could go through with this." Nancy had helped to raise several of her youngest cousins, and she knew exactly how much energy and time went into parenthood. On the other hand, she said, Jim's idea was "you have a child and it fits into your life." She laughed. "*You* fit into *their* life. . . . I mean, they just consume your life."

This was largely what Nancy had found in her brief stint of work with disturbed children. She knew many people in special education eventually burned out and switched careers, but she had never expected it would happen to her so soon. She had quit after only a year and a half, and she was now managing crews of political canvassers. The job was stressful and paid little. Canvassers came and went before she could learn their names. Many were college students, but even more were representatives of harder times than her own—single parents, addicts, abuse victims, even street people. She spent most of her time on recruitment, troubleshooting, and paperwork. She wanted to rethink her career plans but had no idea what new direction she wanted to take. "In the back of my mind I kind of wanted to go to graduate school. I wanted to do a lot of things. I wanted it to be a few years before I had a child."

Nancy tried taking her anxieties to Jim a few days after she first tested positive for pregnancy. "I had not decided I wanted to have an abortion. But I had decided I wanted to talk about what all this meant in terms of my life. And he just blew up and said—he said something like, 'If we don't have this child, it'll be a long damn time before you have one with me.' Something like that."

Nancy dropped the attempt to communicate with Jim. She went ahead with the pregnancy, but she felt his ultimatum pushed her into a choice she probably would have made more willingly had he listened. Though she had been determined she would never go through another abortion, she said, "I thought, well, an abortion is physically minutes of pain, and having a child you're not prepared for is forever pain." Nancy, in going to Jim with her doubts, was trying to prepare. "I was questioning my ability to be a mother," she explained. "It wasn't that I was saying that I didn't want to have the baby. But I needed to talk about it. I didn't work it through. I may have come to the same decision, but I will never know." Jim's refusal to let her explore her fears made Nancy feel "rejected as a person." But she added, "Of course I'm very glad we have Lily."

Nancy's feelings about motherhood were mixed, though. She was no closer to a real career, and she was holding a second job to supplement her income. "The hardest part for me," she explained, "is [that] I always wanted to be successful at work. And I feel like I'm so drained by motherhood and working two jobs that that may never happen. . . . I don't have the time or the energy to further myself . . . because I have to do all this just to maintain."

What made matters worse was that overwork also robbed Nancy of time with Lily, leaving her with constant guilt. "I'm always aware that I need to be doing better," she sighed. "I need to eat better. I need to feed Lily better. I have a ton of guilt right now. Like Lily with her allergies and constant ear infections. She doesn't feel good a whole lot of the time. And Jim and I have both been sick since Lily's been born. We've been sick more than we have ever been sick in our lives."

In her fog of exhaustion and discouragement, Nancy sometimes resented Jim, who made more money in less time at a job he liked pretty well. Though his salary was modest and he had occasional fantasies about starting his own newspaper, he felt challenged and respected where he was. Jim also loved being a father. He had long wanted a child, and he felt he was a good parent without quite understanding why. He himself had come from a home in which, as he said, "There wasn't a lot of family warmth, really. My mother just wasn't demonstrative. I think my father had some real warmth but didn't know how to express it. And it always came out awkwardly, so it had a tendency to repel rather than endear." Jim thought perhaps he had "a desire to do well for a child what wasn't done especially well for me." He also had always felt comfortable with children. "I really like the play aspects," he grinned. "It allows me an opportunity to play as a child, which certainly in adult life we don't get any more. And the processes kids go through as they get older are just thrilling, really. I'm fulfilled by having Lily as my daughter in the ways that I thought I would be but also in ways that I never really imagined. Of course, the frustrations are there, too. It just gets to be a real pain in the butt sometimes, and you don't always imagine that in advance."

Nancy was glad about Jim's wholeheartedness toward Lily and grateful for his total involvement with their daughter. He spent more time with Lily than she did herself, picking her up from day-care and spending the evening with her when Nancy worked her second job. But her long hours and continuing ambivalence about motherhood made her feel guilty and sad. It hurt her that, as she told us, "Lily loves Daddy a lot more than Mommy." She knew that young children inevitably—and almost always temporarily—show a preference for the parent who is most involved in their care, but she also feared that Lily sensed her lingering uncertainties and frustrations. "I'm crazy about Lily," Nancy said. "But I'm crazy about her the way I was crazy about my cousins I helped bring up." As if to clarify her evident confusion, she added, "I felt like they were mine, too, I guess. I had a tremendous amount of feeling for them. . . . I'm just so tired and so overburdened," Nancy sighed, "that I don't think I'm totally in touch with what I'm feeling."

Intimate Conflict and Surrender

On the surface, Nancy and Jim Shaler reversed many "typical" masculine and feminine concerns. Nancy had never longed for a child the way Jim did. Her mother had had "horrible pregnancies and deliveries" yet had gone through the ordeal six times. Though Nancy always felt loved and even favored by her mother, she said, "I was the kid that said I would never have a kid. . . . I had hopes and dreams, and I wasn't sure that motherhood was the most fulfilling thing in the world. I knew how much work was involved." Nancy's large extended family grounded her and gave her the sense of home and family that Jim found so attractive, but it did not give her a whole sense of self. After her father's financial disaster bankrupted her hopes and dreams, she vowed she would never again depend on anyone else for her security. The daily grind of her life represented defeat to her. A satisfying career would have spelled success.

Jim defined success in different terms, not the way Nancy—and most people—would define it. As a boy he had watched his father, an ineffectual and insecure man, put in long hours for little return. He had keenly felt the absence of a strong male's time and attention. Perhaps as a consequence, Jim was not drawn to hard work, but he did feel a tug toward children. "I have taken a lot of jobs purely because I thought they would be fun for a while," he said. "I've never really sought out a career. . . . I didn't get married until I was nearly thirty-eight. So a lot of things that people routinely do early in their adulthood I have put off for a long time. A lot of it is that I never really felt like I was particularly good at any of those things I was doing. And yet being a father is something that I've felt like I'm pretty good at right from the start. And I expected to be. I don't know why."

In both pregnancies, Jim and Nancy's reversals of certain gender-asso-
ciated values and desires became an intimate ground on which their deeper
conformities played out. Both feared being thwarted in what was perhaps their
most passionate desire. Nancy wanted a career; Jim wanted a child. But they
also behaved in ways strongly associated with their genders. Nancy was overly
responsible, self-sacrificing, and sensitive to pain. She did not seem to balance
those common female qualities with a strong ability to assert the needs she felt
so keenly. She did not even seem sure that those sharp needs outweighed her
willingness to have a child. She needed to communicate her emotional struggles
and hardships, but she readily dropped the attempt in the face of Jim's anger.
To Jim, she was someone who could "internalize a hurt and hold it for a long,
long time, more so than anyone I have ever known." He did not put the same
stake Nancy did in discussion; he did not believe it was possible to "talk out the
truth. I mean," he explained, "you can never really get to all the nuances of
somebody's emotional processing system. . . . That old saying about the un-
examined life is not worth living—I think examination is important, but I think
the living of it is a lot more important." Jim, being male, preferred decisive
action in a crisis, and he expected action to resolve emotion. What's done
should be done with, too. That had not been so easy for him after the abortion,
because he had felt coerced by circumstances into a decision that was not really
his. After Lily's birth, there was nothing to resolve. Jim was thrilled.

Someone had to surrender in Jim and Nancy's intimate conflict; their
heart's desires were incompatible. Nancy, who had had her preference supported (or her fears allayed) by circumstance in the first pregnancy, felt that to
a degree she gave in to Jim in the second. "I guess this is part of being female,
to some extent, and part of it is the way I was raised, and part of it is the person
I am," she said. She admitted to resentment, which she tried to control. Instead
of viewing her hopes for a career as temporarily shelved, she feared she would
never find fulfilling work. She worried that there would never be enough money
to send Lily to college. Had she been able to see that the decision to have Lily
was really as much her own as Jim's, her anxieties and guilt might gradually have
lifted.

Jim, meanwhile, with his fondest wish granted, saw his horizons expanding,
modestly but in a satisfying way. He had a new commitment to his work and
a new sense of interconnectedness in all his endeavors. "I got into the newspaper business because I thought it would be fun to do," he said. Now, for the
first time, he has made a commitment to a career, in order to provide for his
daughter. "I don't feel any resentment about that, and now I really am inter-

ested in managing this paper and making it better." Pausing for a long moment, Jim added: "I would have to say that I lived, probably, a fairly selfish and isolated life . . . and that is different now. I find myself making decisions in terms of their effect on my daughter, on my relationship with my wife, and on the effect that has on Lily. Everything has an interrelatedness that it didn't used to have. While I find it trying and wearying sometimes, I don't regret it at all. I like being a parent, and I like the peripheral effects that that has on my life. It ripples outward into other parts of my life. That's okay, too."

Women, Men, and Powerlessness

Jean Baker Miller, in *Toward a New Psychology of Women*, sees women as better able than men to understand and tolerate vulnerability. This quality, she maintains, can generate a strength whose roots lie in the fact that all human beings are unavoidably vulnerable. "In that sense," she argues, "women . . . are more closely in touch with basic life experiences—in touch with reality. By being in this closer connection with this central human condition, by having to defend less and deny less, women are in a position to understand weakness more readily and to work productively *with* it." But women's familiarity with weakness also costs them.

It is reasonable to interpret what happened between Nancy and Jim as arising in part from culturally determined attitudes toward powerlessness and concessions. Jim could not tolerate Nancy's power over his fondest wish; she could not resist his intimate coercions. When Nancy—or, actually, inflexible circumstances—denied Jim's desire for fatherhood in their first pregnancy, he reacted furiously to her attempt to make him understand the horrors of the abortion procedure. It must have felt to him as if she were twisting a knife in the wound that his powerlessness had made. The interdependence that he later found fulfilling once Lily was born must at that time have terrified him. By the time Nancy was pregnant again, Jim—no doubt fearing another loss—squelched any mention of doubt. He threatened to end their relationship unless she did as he wanted her to do. Nancy fell into silence because she could not assert her need for communication and support, but she seemed to regard her concession as a far greater one: the sacrifice of all her aspirations.

As a consequence, Nancy gained little from the decision that pleased and profited Jim. The sense of family that he celebrated became, for her, a chief source of guilt and discontent. Her disproportionate sense of responsibility (the very quality that Jim had so often urged her to modify) explains why Nancy consented to remain the more vulnerable of the two. It also explains both her fear that she would never have a career and her feeling that she had been "rejected as a person" by Jim's unwillingness to let her talk. As Miller says, women who sacrifice in this way "provide all sorts of personal and social supports to help keep men going and to keep them and the total society from admitting that better arrangements are needed. That is, the whole man-woman interaction thus dilutes the push to confront and deal with our societal deficiencies."

In other words, private and public inequalities perpetuate each other, and fear of weakness keeps the cycle going. Men tend to fear vulnerability—as Jim feared emotional devastation if Nancy had a second abortion—because men are taught to place a great personal stake in self-sufficiency and independence. Women commonly have different fears—of rejection, abandonment, isolation—which make them aware of vulnerability all the time. Thus Nancy chose silence over the prospect of losing Jim.

But when women are aware of vulnerability and also lack a counterbalancing sense of strength, they pay too dearly to keep their human bonds intact. And when men deny or avoid weakness—with no sense of its universality—they exploit women's sacrificing tendency and remain blind to their own dependence on others. This explains why Jim could not afford and Nancy would not insist on the discussion of her doubts, even though communication was the one thing that could have shown them that they were both heading voluntarily—though with cause for apprehension—in the same direction. Nancy did not want an abortion; she only wanted to talk. Jim did not want an abortion, either, but he was afraid to talk. His fear of talking and Nancy's fear of losing him conspired to obscure their common cause.

Miller writes, "Authenticity and subordination are totally incompatible." Had Nancy and Jim been able to tell each other the truth—he about his fear of loss, she about her doubts but also her sense that communication could ease them—she might not feel today that her desires had been subordinated to his.

Miller's concern with authenticity meshes well with that of Belenky et al. in *Women's Ways of Knowing*. These authors describe a continuum along which women learn to know and act authentically. At one extreme are the silent women, who have no voice or identity of their own and so look to others—often fearfully—for truth and guidance. Further along are women who can recognize their own voice only when they hear others say what they believe; women for whom truth resides only in the subjective promptings of emotion and intuition;

and women who cultivate a voice of reason, relying on books and institutions to substantiate their views and knowledge.

At the most advanced end of Belenky *et al.*'s continuum are women who achieve authenticity by "constructing" knowledge from every internal and external voice, by "weaving together the strands of rational and emotive thought and . . . integrating objective and subjective knowing." In confronting moral dilemmas, constructivist women attempt to respect all the voices wanting to be heard, whether they are male or female, whether they speak of justice or of care.

This moral model is absent both from our vituperative national debate on abortion and from the rugged individualism that makes us resist strong policies of care and nurturance. On a public scale, as in private relations such as the Shalers', we are ruled by fears and judgments of vulnerability and need. We tend to scorn people who cannot "bootstrap" themselves into a comfortable life. We give to them only grudgingly and inadequately. We do not provide people like Jim and Nancy with the resources—better insurance, a family allowance, benefits to children, high-quality, affordable day care—that would have let them proceed with their pregnancy and still maintain some quality of life. Jim and Nancy have not shunned hard work; in fact, each has held two jobs when necessary, but always at the expense of their family relationships. This is the hard choice that a hard society presents. It reveals the lack of care and connection beneath our proud individualism.

TEENAGERS AND PREGNANCY

Older than Their Years

Security as provided by society is fine, but it cannot give one inner security—neither emotional warmth and well-being, nor self-respect, nor a feeling of worthwhileness. All these only parents can give their child, and they can do so best when they also give them to each other. And if one fails to get them from one's parents, it is extremely difficult to acquire these feelings later in life, and they will remain shaky at best. Thus everything depends on whether the modern family can provide this emotional security based on personal intimacy and the mutual love and respect of all its members.

Bruno Bettelheim, *A Good Enough Parent* (1987)

Introduction

The reasons any individual develops an authentic sense of his or her own worth, or fails to, are always complex. But some patterns common to many women may be traceable to childhood—especially to an important turning point at childhood's twilight when a girl first finds she is becoming a woman.

Sometime between the ages of eight and ten, a girl's hypothalamus, the peanut-size gland deep inside the center of her brain, sends a crucial message to the pituitary gland telling it to begin pumping out hormones. These messenger hormones, in turn, trigger a cascade of sex hormones that start the physical transformation of puberty. Soon afterward, the growing girl will notice the budding of her breasts, the first outward sign of the approach of womanhood.

As these changes begin, many girls, even those who have been making good progress socially and academically, will begin to stumble, according to Carol Gilligan, Nona Lyons, and Trudy J. Hammer in *Making Connections: The Rational World of Adolescent Girls of Emma Willard School.* Gilligan *et al.* studied how and why so many girls suffer setbacks in their moral and intellectual development at about the age of puberty, and they have found answers that are sometimes surprisingly simple. They conclude, for example, that although girls grow up side by side with boys, they actually live in a culturally separate world.

Therefore, boys and girls follow different paths to adulthood—an observation known to most parents but highly controversial in the psychological community and among some feminists. Gilligan *et al.* believe that girls define themselves much more fundamentally in terms of their close relationships than do boys, and so the changes in those relationships, precipitated by puberty, affect the two sexes quite differently.

Although parents, teachers, and others who work with adolescents may perceive gender-related differences, few are likely to understand their complex manifestations. Adolescent behavior often throws both teenagers and the adults around them into a stormy transition phase. This situation is worsened by the fact that almost all psychological models of what adolescence is supposed to be like are based on studies done exclusively with males. Until quite recently, research on and knowledge of female adolescence was virtually nonexistent.

Freud, and most psychologists after him, defined adolescence as a painful time in which the child completed the task of separating from his or her parents. Freud observed that some individuals, notably girls, failed to complete their withdrawal from their parents' affection and authority. In subsequent studies that used Freud's model, therefore, girls and women were often found to be developmentally deficient, with 'weaker' ego boundaries. In the 1970s, Gilligan notes in her book *In a Different Voice: Psychological Theory and Women's Development,* Nancy Chodorow challenged the Freudian model. From the time boys are toddlers, she notes, separation and individuation are critically tied to gender identification, because separation of boys from their mothers, their primary caretakers, is essential to the development of their masculinity. For girls, however, femininity is developed through an attachment to their mother. "Consequently, relationships, and particularly issues of dependency, are experienced differently by women and men," Gilligan explains, citing Chodorow's influence on her own work. "Since masculinity is defined through separation while femininity is defined through attachment, male gender identity is threatened by intimacy while female gender identity is threatened by separation. Thus males tend to have difficulty with relationships, while females tend to have problems with individuation."

Psychological researchers, Gilligan argues, have failed to see a second path of adolescent development, one that usually predominates among females. Girls often are reluctant to break affectionate bonds. In fact, to them emotional attachment may be morally compelling. While boys often come to view ethics in terms of abstract principles, girls believe that ethical responsibility resides within relationship bonds. Therefore, Gilligan theorizes, girls resist complete autonomy from their parents, which they see as immoral. For girls, healthy development involves changing the form of parental attachment by voicing their own needs and values and renegotiating the relationship in those terms. Psychology's inattention to girls' development has meant researchers have missed these issues of attachment and intimacy, which play an important role in the lives of all adolescents, female and male. By acknowledging only the characteristics predominant in boys, researchers failed to see their secondary characteristics. It is only when we look at what is predominant in girls that we see issues of attachment that are present in both sexes and that may be dominant or secondary in any individual regardless of gender.

Blinded by ignorance, adults set inappropriate expectations. For example, at a time when girls—and many boys—need deepening attachments, most "expert" advice tells them that becoming an adult means detaching from their childhood bonds and becoming independent. Instead, many girls cling to the notion that relationships are paramount. In extensive interviews with girls in two exclusive private schools and with others in poorer, urban environments, Gilligan and her colleagues found that many girls reach a pinnacle of outspokenness around the age of eleven, when they claim their own sense of female authority and honesty in relationships. For example, Gilligan's group told a *New York Times* reporter about twelve-year-old Tanya, who bravely challenged a camp's rule against calling home (Prose, 1989). With strong conviction, she spoke out on behalf of a young, homesick cousin who needed to talk to her family. "People," Tanya argued, "are more important than rules."

But soon after this assertive stage of girlhood, the sharp clarity fades. By age fifteen, Tanya's moral conviction had slipped, and her concerns were more petty. The moral sense of caring and responsibility for the well-being of others that girls began to develop in childhood falters. They see a world governed by men in which the mature adult is defined as tough-minded, independent, and detached. As girls look ahead toward the institutions and professions in which they will one day work, they notice the relative scarcity of women and feminine values, and many become withdrawn. By age fifteen or sixteen, Gilligan has found, girls' hardy resistance has turned to uncertainty. Their speech becomes peppered with "I don't know" and "This may sound silly. . . ."

Adolescent girls believe their close relationship with their parents can change and adapt through negotiation, Gilligan says. But this succeeds only if the child is able to acknowledge her developing sexuality and express her distinct personality, and only if adults accept these changes. For many girls, such negotiation proves difficult. They lose faith that their voice is one that their parents—or anyone else—want to hear. In a world where sex is used to peddle everything from toothpaste to car batteries, teenage sexuality often threatens parents. Few, if any, adults garner the courage to talk straight to teenagers about sex, and when teenagers look around for comforting models of mature sexual love to guide them they see many in their parents' generation abandoning partners and tearing one another's marriages apart.

Many girls turn to early sexual activity when the key adults in their lives are unable or unwilling to recognize their sexuality and their need for relationship. The situation is worse among girls who have never been encouraged to develop strong family bonds, especially if their childhood development was thwarted by poverty, abuse, or dysfunctional homes. When their hormones disrupt their sense of themselves and generate a critical need to establish some new, sexually mature identity, teenagers may look to sex for the things adults are failing to provide. When a girl becomes uncertain of her voice, sex requires no language. Here, her developing sexuality and desire for intimacy seem to her to gain the recognition that is missing elsewhere. And pregnancy, whether deliberate or accidental, can speak volumes to adults who otherwise turn a deaf ear.

Teenagers—and adults who had been pregnant as teenagers—told us they sought from sex some physical closeness and some illusion of intimacy, even though they did not always enjoy the act itself. Some wanted babies so that they could have someone in their lives who would always love them. Our observations were that teenagers, boys as well as girls, often hoped that sex—and sometimes pregnancy and parenthood—would bring them something sorely lacking in the relationships in their lives. The most desperate and deprived hoped for a reason to live, for some shape to their existence. Others sought recognition of an identity apart from the one their parents expected them to attain. We found our own observations confirmed by work done at the Alan Guttmacher Institute, by many professionals who work with teenagers, and lastly and most convincingly by the research published by Carol Gilligan and her associates.

Rates of sexual activity and pregnancy among teenagers in this country soared during the 1970s and have continued to climb. A 1990 study conducted by the Centers for Disease Control (CDC) shows that over half of American high school students are sexually active ("More Teens Having Sex, Survey Says," *Pittsburgh Post-Gazette*, 4 Jan. 1992). The largest increase has been among the youngest teenagers. In 1970, only 4.6 percent of fifteen-year-olds said they had had sex, compared with over 40 percent in 1990. And despite the AIDS scare, fewer than half of America's sexually active teenagers were using condoms during their last intercourse, the CDC found.

Teenage pregnancy is a fact of life in America. More than one million American teenagers become pregnant every year. By age eighteen, one in four teenagers will become pregnant at least once; more than 44 percent will conceive by age twenty, according to the Alan Guttmacher Institute ("Teenage Sexual and Reproductive Behavior in the United States," *Facts in Brief*). Almost half give birth, a few miscarry, and the rest—400,000—account for about one-fourth of all abortions performed each year in the United States. Many teenagers who have not had to decide what to do about their own unplanned pregnancies know someone their age who has.

Parents and other adults who fail to listen and talk to teenagers about sex abandon them to peer pressure and to the prevailing culture. Back in 1957, when the Everly Brothers were singing "Wake Up Little Susie," teenagers still identified with the song's frantic worry about Susie's reputation and purity—even though all Susie and her boyfriend had done was to fall asleep at a drive-in movie. "Good" girls were expected to stay chaste and to guard against giving any contrary impression. Boys had few such worries. Jane O'Reilly, writing in the October 1991 issue of *Mirabella* magazine about her reunion with the daughter she had given up for adoption thirty-two years earlier, said: "In 1958, an out-of-wedlock pregnancy was literally disgraceful. It was almost the only imaginable disgrace (so limited was the range of good or bad behavior for a middle-class girl). . . . I was raised to believe that I was under constant surveillance from a disapproving God and a pitiless social system. 'What will people think?' was a phrase that defined the moral universe."

Then came the 1960s, when chaste reputations, like the double sexual standard, were tossed out with yesterday's bobby socks. Sexuality—primed and propelled by affluence, upheaval, rebellion, drugs, and a new wave of politicized rock and roll—burst across long-standing marital, racial, social, and age-related barriers. But the transformation was uneven. The values reflected in popular culture pulled in several directions at once. In the early 1960s, *Seventeen* magazine's advice column still pondered whether a girl should kiss a boy good night on their first date, but it also worried about the wrong kind of girls, the ones who "put out." By the mid-1960s, the Beatles still wailed "I Want to Hold Your Hand," but Bob Dylan had begun to write and sing about a darker rebellion and the Rolling Stones and Jimi Hendrix honed a harder edge on rock and roll.

Shifting questions about sexual behavior were accompanied by confusion about sexual roles. The post-Sputnik girls had been pushed to achieve in school. Competition with the Russians meant Americans could not afford to waste women's minds. So the 1950s' assumption that early marriage was their best and inevitable fate was cast aside only to reawaken with new intensity the twentieth century woman's dilemmas over marriage and career.

Today, "Wake Up Little Susie" seems quaint. In a popular song of the late 1980s, "Papa, Don't Preach," Madonna boldly proclaimed, "I'm keepin' my baby." No one, not even children in the most comfortable suburbs and secure, intact families, can escape the cultural messages or the risks of today's society.

Isabel Martin

Isabel Martin's plans for the future were firm—or so she thought. She had envisioned an education, a rewarding career, and a stable income. That was what the bright daughters of well-educated, financially secure parents automatically looked forward to in 1979, as they do today. When girls in Isabel's situation get pregnant today, they are no more likely than Isabel was to become teenage mothers. That strong vision of the future will usually outweigh any urge to take care of a baby. In 1973, the year the U.S. Supreme Court made abortion legal nationwide, 280,000 teenagers obtained legal abortions. By 1982 that number had increased 30 percent, reflecting the increased sexual activity among teenagers during the same period. During the 1980s, the number of abortions obtained by women under twenty grew to well over 400,000 per year. Since then rates have leveled off.

As Isabel told her story, she sat in a small cafe in Philadelphia. Her light hair hung in waves around her face. She sat quietly and spoke with little affect. Her parents' divorce had not harmed their finances or Isabel's relations with them, she said. Her mother had a good career as a medical librarian, and her father and his second wife were geologists. Isabel spent equal time with both parents.

When Isabel was 18, in 1979, she and her boyfriend spent the summer with her father and stepmother in Alaska, where they were doing geological research. Isabel was planning to start college that September. "I was being very careful," she recalled. "I mean I was using birth control—a diaphragm and jelly and the whole bit."

But then one evening Isabel went to a nearby Eskimo community to visit a girlfriend. She ended up spending "a lovely night" with the friend's brother.

"I have a very warm physical feeling, still, for that night," she said. Unfortunately, she had left her diaphragm at home in a dresser drawer. A month later, she was back East, feeling sure she was pregnant. Having left behind both her New York boyfriend and the Eskimo boy, she sat peacefully on the porch of her mother's summer cottage thinking about what was going on inside her. "I was just pleased," she recalled. "I quit smoking, at least for a little while. . . . It was a contented feeling to just sort of sit, feel comfortable, and not worry about things." The pregnancy was not confirmed yet, and its potential for changing Isabel's life was still removed.

Then Isabel returned to the city and went to a clinic for a pregnancy test. She could not afford further daydreams. Although she had knowingly gambled with her fate in Alaska and was not entirely certain which young man had impregnated her, she could not deny that a baby would be a serious obstacle on the path she planned to follow. She would be a freshman at New York University in just a few weeks. "I knew I couldn't possibly support a child," she said. "I had no one to do it with. I didn't have any job skills. I hadn't finished school, and there really wasn't any question in my mind what I meant to do."

Yet Isabel admitted, later in the interview, that she had wavered. The Eskimo culture represented an alluring comfort and security that might have been a large part of her dream on the cottage porch. "I had thought about just staying up in Alaska and marrying and living that kind of life. I saw lots of women doing that up there. And babies in the Eskimo culture are adored." In the Eskimo village, she said, there were lots of teenage mothers whose babies were simply folded into the communal family. "You know, they don't care about being married, and it's a very different ethic." That ethic would not expect what Isabel's parents expected of her. "But I decided I didn't want that kind of life. I didn't want to live in the bush as an Eskimo."

Perhaps because of her flirtation with rebellion, Isabel hesitated about telling her mother she was pregnant. When she did, her mother's wishes were clear, and Isabel drew back from any second thoughts. "She really didn't want me to have a child at that point. . . . I think a lot of my decision came from her." Isabel's speech sped up. "I mean, I was thinking the way she was thinking, so a lot of this transferred from her to me, although I don't quarrel with it now. I never disagreed with her. She said 'Look, here's my insurance card. You go down and you do what you have to do.' Isabel's mother had always felt strongly that abortion should be a woman's choice. Isabel did not argue, but when we interviewed her she wondered what she might have done if her mother had opposed abortion.

After the abortion, Isabel kept her feelings tightly controlled. "I felt a pang, but I knew at the time that I couldn't let myself feel guilty about it, because I'd be destroyed." We asked her to explain her strong language. "I knew that I felt guilty or that I *could* feel guiltier," she said. "I could sort of allow myself to feel like an awful person, and if I did, there was no way for me to sort of continue on with my life. . . . So I decided that the reasons that I had for doing what I did were good ones: I wanted to give a child a secure life economically and emotionally. . . . I didn't believe in bringing unwanted children into the world. And I said that all of these reasons, this rational process, was . . . that was how I had to continue to feel." Any thoughts she had had about straying from her parents' world were put to rest as well.

Isabel was twenty-six when we interviewed her. She had left a teaching career to work for a landscape architect, and she was married and the mother of a baby girl. She had had two other abortions before giving birth, and she felt a little defensive. "Abortion is not my method of birth control," she said, although all four of her pregnancies had been unplanned and only one was a birth control failure. She mentioned feeling haunted by the ghosts of her daughter's aborted siblings, but she quickly put such thoughts out of her mind. "You do what you do, you grieve, and then you get on with it," she said. For her, the decision to abort, while serious, was also simple and straightforward. "I agree with *Roe v. Wade*, which I think is lovely," she said. "It just balances the different rights involved as well as possible, given the incendiary nature of the topic."

Isabel repressed her feelings, making them difficult to read. She allowed us, and probably herself, only a glimpse of her reactions to the emotional and moral complexities of the abortion issue. She implied that if she accepted *Roe v. Wade* and women's right to abortion, then consideration of these complexities was only a self-destructive exercise. We were familiar with this kind of thinking. Many women who had supported *Roe v. Wade* politically told us that they were surprised by the mixed feelings and moral doubts they experienced when they personally faced a birth-or-abortion decision. They feared that their ambivalence betrayed their political convictions. These reactions were our first indication that *Roe v. Wade*'s reasoning left something out. Before Carol Gilligan argued that the *Roe v. Wade* decision neglected a caretaking ethic and before Mary Ann Glendon contended that *Roe v. Wade* was too cold and individualistic a policy, women were experiencing a broad gap between their personal experience and their political beliefs.

Women in private crises over unplanned pregnancies, in fact, rarely feel that their rights are at war with those of the fetus forming within them. Isabel sensed a maternal bond when she dreamed on the cabin porch. She dreamed—if only briefly and unrealistically—of joining an Eskimo culture that adored babies, a warm community that would not expect her to achieve but would accept her just for who she was. Then Isabel came back to reality and back to New York City, where she terminated her pregnancy. After that, nothing else she knew about the abortion issue allowed her to accommodate the complex considerations that occasionally tugged at her for attention.

Marian Hogan

Marian Hogan, seventeen when we talked to her in 1989, was a good student from an intact, middle-class family. She, like Isabel, was raised to expect a bright future. Marian's mother, Joan, talked to us for an hour about the values she and her husband tried to impart. Then Marian burst in from school, slinging her backpack and jacket over the back of a kitchen chair. She cut a slice of her mother's peach pie and joined us at the round oak table. Both the pie and the kitchen—a lived-in, homey room with calico wallpaper—reinforced what Joan had stated about Marian's upbringing in a close and stable family.

Marian fits the profile of adolescent girls who give their babies up for adoption, a profile that is similar to those who have abortions. Their sights—like Isabel's—are generally fixed upon a future full of achievement and possibilities that cannot accommodate early motherhood. Since *Roe v. Wade* opened legal abortion as an alternative for such teenagers, most have preferred abortion to adoption. Among teens who do give birth, current estimates are that fewer than 10 percent relinquish their babies. Thus adoption rates have been forced down by two trends: high abortion rates and rising numbers of teenage mothers.

Though the Hogan house sat on a rise in a wealthy Cleveland suburb, it was a modest bungalow surrounded by big vegetable gardens, fruit trees, and a small wood. Marian herself had a wholesome, sweet-faced openness. She blushed as she began, after Joan slipped out of the room, to talk about the boy she met the summer she turned fifteen and got pregnant. It was the first and only time she had had sex. The boy, Jake, was the older brother of a good friend, and Marian had developed a powerful crush on him.

"It wasn't like we really had sex," Marian said nervously. "I mean, I don't know, I don't know. . . . " She played with her fork and looked down at her plate. With some gentle prodding, she was able to explain that Jake had not fully penetrated her, and so she had assumed she was safe from pregnancy. By the time she suspected otherwise, Jake was dating someone else. Marian's period was three months late when she woke up with morning sickness and finally decided to confirm her fears. She went to a Planned Parenthood clinic with a friend. "I was like, you know, 'I have an idea that I am. I'm almost positive that I am. I just want to hear you say that I am.'" Still, when she got the news, she said, "It was shock, and I couldn't walk back down the steps or anything."

Joan thought Marian had allergies or problems with her new contact lenses because her eyes were always red from crying. Marian, who had always felt a little like the bad child in a good family, kept her secret. "At first all I could think about was that I just wanted to have an abortion before anybody knew about it, you know. I just thought I could get on with my life if I had an abortion. . . . I was just hoping that somebody, one of my friends, could take me and just get it all over with one day." But Marian, like so many other teenagers, kept procrastinating. She now thinks it was because she knew in her heart that abortion was wrong. She had always judged girls in school who had abortions and had sometimes even refused to speak to them afterwards. So she kept herself busy with her friends and did nothing.

At first only Jake and the friend who went with Marian to the clinic knew about her pregnancy. Then the friend spilled the news to her mother, Eleanor, one of Joan's best friends. Marian recalled how Eleanor took her aside. "She's like, 'Come on. We're going up to your house now and tell your mom'. . . . You know, she kind of like forced me into telling her."

Eleanor drove Marian home that warm Friday evening and told Joan to sit down. "Marian wants to talk to you. She has a little problem." Marian started to cry, and Joan's first thought was drugs. "Then she said she was pregnant," Joan had told us, her expression replaying how stunned she was. She had never harbored the least suspicion. "I said, 'Tomorrow, first thing you do is go tell the priest. It's not a sin that you're pregnant. It's a sin what you did.'" Remembering, Joan choked up and leaned forward, rubbing her hands over her knees.

The hurt Marian saw in her mother was exactly the reaction she had dreaded during her months of secrecy. Joan was not angry with her daughter, but she was terribly disappointed and she was furious with Jake. "Marian was just a little kid, and my first thought was, it's rape. If it's not physical rape, then it's emotional rape," Joan said angrily. She blamed herself for being naive about the amount of time Marian had spent ostensibly visiting Jake's younger sister. She recalled clues that the children were not being supervised. One morning, after Marian had spent the night with Jake's sister, the day camp where Marian was a counselor called to find out why she was not at work. Joan phoned Jake's house, and his stepmother went and found the girls still asleep at 10:30. "She didn't even know that Marian was still in the house," said Joan, appalled. But by then the summer was over, she said ruefully, and "the damage had been done."

Marian's father also blamed himself for not talking explicitly enough to his daughter about sex. Marian was the third and most worrisome of three daughters. And Joan said: "I always told my kids, 'Don't let anybody touch you. Your body's your own.' I guess I didn't tell them enough. I never dreamed my kids should ever have birth control, especially when they're fifteen years old. Who thinks of that?" Like many parents, Joan seemed to deny the abundant evidence that sexual standards have shifted dramatically since her own youth.

Once the news of Marian's pregnancy was out, the family went into a tailspin for several days. On Saturday, the day after Marian's forced confession, Marian and her mother went to see the parish priest, who told them about a home for unwed mothers. But at home the discussion volleyed between abortion and adoption. Given the future they had always assumed for Marian, no one took seriously the third option—that Marian would bring her baby home to this bungalow. "By the time Monday came around," Joan said, "we decided that . . . she'd have an abortion, she'd go back to school, and it would be all over with." Joan called a local gynecologist to set up an appointment. But Marian was at the end of her first trimester and there was some confusion about whether labor would have to be induced. "I was so confused," Joan recalled. "I just fell down on the couch and I asked God to help me." At that moment, Eleanor walked in with the parish priest. After more talk, Joan decided against abortion for her daughter. "It's just not a natural thing to do," she said firmly. "And then I really came to peace when we decided. I didn't care what people thought. I didn't care who knew, because this can happen to other kids."

For Marian, the biggest hurdle had been telling her parents. She was convinced that if she had really fought to keep the child or to get an abortion her parents would have gone along with her, but she seemed to have been willing to let her mother make the final decision. "She was too young to decide," Joan declared. Marian, in confidence and out of earshot of her mother, agreed. "I think I needed somebody to tell me what to do, you know. . . . I don't know what I would have done, like, on my own," she confessed.

Both before and after Marian told her family, Jake offered to pay for an abortion. But, said Marian, "I just didn't want to talk to him anymore." She had good reason. The other girl Jake was dating also was pregnant, and she, too, decided to relinquish her baby for adoption. Jake joined the Army and left both girls behind with their decisions and his babies. Marian's feelings toward Jake hardened during her pregnancy, and she began to fear that her baby would inherit his red hair.

In her fifth month, Marian moved to a nearby maternity home. "I would never go to school if I was, like, showing," she said, describing her embarrassment among her classmates. She felt more comfortable in the home, in the company of other pregnant teens, even though she had little else in common with most of them. She found it striking that only three of the fifteen girls planned to give up their babies, and they were also the only ones from stable home environments. As the girls shared their life stories, Marian recalled, the ones who were keeping their babies always seemed to tell about some "terrible, terrible things that were going on with their parents. . . . I was like, 'Your baby's going to be going into a life like that?' " Despite Marian's sense of irony, statistics show it is frequently teenagers from the most deprived backgrounds who want to become teenage mothers.

In her ninth month, Marian was back home on a weekend visit to her family when her water broke. Eight hours later, she delivered a healthy baby girl at a local hospital. "I knew all along it was going to be a girl," she said smiling. "I remember the first thing I did was, like, count her fingers and her toes. . . . And then I looked at her hair and said, 'She has red hair!' I couldn't believe it."

Joan remembered that Marian thought the baby was ugly that first day. But the nurses were crazy about her red hair and tied it up in bows. Marian spent two days with her daughter before Rose Macbeth (not her real name), the private adoption intermediary who handled Marian's case, came and took the baby to her adoptive parents. That was the same day Marian left the hospital. "They were probably the worst couple of days of my life," Marian said, blinking back tears. "But I didn't change my mind. . . . I always had my mind set on just what I was doing."

"That baby was family," Joan had said, weeping. "All the time [Marian] was pregnant, you just told yourself that this baby's going to be adopted." Joan cleared her throat, barely able to talk. "But then when she was born, it was really hard to give her up." Marian never talked about what life might have been like if she had kept her daughter, Joan said, as she brought out a stack of pictures of Marian's baby. She pulled out one in which all three of her children posed with the baby in the hospital. Marian was convinced that adoption was the right decision, Joan said. "Not that she didn't want her. . . . She really loves that baby."

A year and a half after the baby's birth, Marian still telephoned and visited Rose regularly for news and sometimes for new photographs as well. She had insisted her daughter be placed in a family where the mother would stay home with her, as Joan has always done, and Marian seemed satisfied with the reports Rose conveyed. Marian knew that the adoptive family skied and went horseback riding, that they dressed the baby well, that they had her baptized, and that they gave her a big birthday party when she turned one. "She just has everything," Marian said proudly. "That's what I wanted to give her is everything, and I couldn't."

Still, Marian felt a longing for the baby who sometimes seemed "right there" in her imagination but was never there for her to touch. Sometimes she stared at Rose when she saw her, because Rose had touched her baby. "She sees my baby and I don't, and I'm her mother," Marian said, shaking her head.

Marian was keeping busy, working a part-time job, going to school, and going out often with her friends. The fact that she was seldom home was causing trouble. Joan was confused by Marian's behavior, even a little panicky. She distrusted her daughter's desire to be out of the house so much. But Marian resented her mother's attitude. "I'm not doing anything like drinking and stuff like that or getting involved with guys again or something. I'm just having fun," Marian said. Besides, she explained sadly, "Whenever I'm out I don't think about my baby, but when my parents make me stay home, you know, I always wish she was here or something."

Marian sometimes heard from some of the girls she met at the maternity home, but she found their news depressing. Two who kept their babies were living with their boyfriends, who physically abused the girls. Another, who gave her baby up for adoption, talked of suicide. "I'm the only one who's doing anything right with her life," Marian told Joan after talking to one of these girls.

Marian's parents and friends made the difference for her, she believed. "Sometimes I think my life is better now than it was even before then," she said. "This year has been, like, so good for me and everything." Her grades were good, she was having a good time, and she planned to apply to colleges in the fall. She wanted to be an elementary school teacher, she said. Her daughter, wherever she was, would be ready for first grade about the time Marian did her student teaching.

A View of the Future

All teenagers in America are at risk for pregnancy, but statistically girls like Isabel Martin and Marian Hogan are relative rarities. Girls who see their future as one full of rich and complex possibilities—maybe college, a career, and financial independence before marriage and a family—usually begin sexual activity relatively late. By their late teens, such girls are likely to have more stable relationships than younger teens and to use birth control more faithfully. If they do get pregnant, they are more inclined to choose abortion or adoption over parenthood. If their bright vision is fixed—and if it is truly their own—they are even more determined to avoid pregnancy in the first place.

At the opposite end of the risk scale are girls for whom pregnancy is deliberate, or nearly so. They frequently are from poor families and have poor academic prospects. Their vision of the future is constricted by the paucity of their experience. They are more likely to start having sex early in their teens, to ignore birth control, and to see motherhood as a rite of passage into a new life. So many studies have examined the external factors that appear to affect American teenagers' decisions about sexuality that one wonders if study has become a substitute for action. According to a concise summary in the Children's Defense Fund's *Teenage Pregnancy: An Advocate's Guide to the Numbers* (Pittman and Adams, 1988), "Poor teens with poor basic skills are less likely to have other more positive life options that make early parenthood an unattractive and irrational choice." Similarly, a 1985 report (Jones, Darroch, Forest, Goldman, Henshaw, Lincoln, Rosoff, Westoff, and Wulf, 1985) prepared by the Alan Guttmacher Institute says:

> In every country, when respondents were pressed to describe the kind of young woman who would be most likely to bear a child, the answer was the same: adolescents who have been deprived, emotionally as well as economically, and who unrealistically seek gratification and fulfillment in a child of their own.

High educational achievement and clear future goals are associated with the level of education achieved by a teenager's parents, since educated parents are more likely to stress and demonstrate the importance of learning and to instill a resistance to the things that interfere with education. On the other hand, very young teenagers who risk their shaky futures with early sex in unstable relationships tend not only to face sexual risks without adequate protection but to engage in other risky behaviors such as drinking and using drugs. Like all teenagers, they feel immortal, but they have less than most to weigh against their own possible demise.

If the roots of every sexual decision lie in the quality of a young person's vision, that quality of vision depends upon the combined circumstances of his or her life. It is a fact of demography and social history in the United States—not an indicator of innate racial tendencies—that blacks and Hispanics are more likely than whites to live in poor neighborhoods with poor schools and high crime rates and to come from poor homes with, in many cases, a single, poorly educated parent. But when whites find themselves in similarly hopeless circumstances they respond in virtually the same ways. According to the Children's Defense Fund (Pittman and Adams, 1988):

> Black, white, or Hispanic, one of every five sixteen- to nineteen-year-old young women with below-average academic skills coming from poor families was a teen mother in 1981. Black, white, or Hispanic, only 3 to 5 percent of sixteen- to nineteen-year-old women with solid academic skills whose families had above-poverty incomes were teen mothers that year.

Besides the quality of their vision of the future, much of what teenagers believe and do about sex is also influenced by what their friends believe and do. In fact, peer example has been cited in some research as the single most important factor affecting the beginning of sexual relations in the United States. In a recent Planned Parenthood poll done in New York, teenagers ages twelve to seventeen cited peer pressure as the main reason they thought teens initiated early sex. Even the idea that boys are not real men unless they pressure girls into sex still thrives among today's teenagers.

One last and only recently explored influence upon adolescent sexual activity and childbearing is independent of the socioeconomic forces we have discussed. This factor is sexual child abuse, which cuts across all social, racial, and economic boundaries, occurring in the most privileged families as well as in the poorest. In every case it profoundly affects a young girl's self-esteem and vision. In a 1989 study conducted at the Pennsylvania State University, Janice R. Butler and Linda M. Burton found that 54 percent of the forty-one rural teenage mothers they interviewed had been sexually abused by age eighteen. The Ounce of Prevention Fund in Chicago, surveying 445 teenage mothers across Illinois in 1987, found that more than 60 percent of them had, at some time, been forced into an unwanted sexual experience. And in 1981 J. L. Hermann reported in her book *Father-Daughter Incest* that 45 percent of the incest survivors in her clinical sample had become pregnant as adolescents.

Emily Edwards

Emily Edwards, forty-one, sat forward on a worn, red leather couch in a private study at the Presbyterian seminary where she is training for the ministry. As she thought back to her teenage pregnancy many years before *Roe v. Wade* made abortion a legal possibility, her elbows rested on her knees. She had a broad, expressive mouth, light brown hair and eyes, and a sincere, almost innocent, expression. She was eager to help, she explained. It was extremely important to her that she make use of the rocky, painful life she has led by helping other women to avoid the same mistakes and hazards she has suffered through. Her voice was smooth and low.

Emily's family life in semirural Indiana was sordid. Her father, an alcoholic, sexually abused her until she was five or six. Her mother, who quashed her own uneasiness with Valium, dismissed Emily's complaints about sexual abuse. She told Emily her father was "just playing."

"On some level, I think she knew," Emily said. "She knew I was affected by my father's sexuality if not that he had abused me." As a little girl, Emily used to crawl onto her mother's lap and put her arms around her neck and kiss her. But her mother's reaction was always to push her away, saying, "Ugh! Don't do that." When she was in her twenties, Emily asked her mother why she had reacted that way. "I always thought you were kissing me because of what your dad was doing to you," Emily's mother told her. "I thought you were kissing me like *that*."

Her parents' marriage was an open battle. The three children, especially Emily, were ammunition. Her drunken father often disrupted the house in the middle of the night and had sex with his wife in front of the children. Emily remembered being very young and nearly convulsed with fear while her parents screamed and battled. "I just prayed. That's how I got to sleep on those nights." Emily looked like her father and was his favorite. She thought her mother picked on her, physically and verbally, to get a rise out of him. Her father stopped his sexual abuse before Emily began school and she repressed it, looking to him for affection despite his flaws. The combination of her father's sexual abuse, the slight hope of his affection, and her mother's coldness seriously damaged her sexual development.

When she was thirteen years old, Emily's parents separated. "There was a sense of relief from the constant turmoil," she recalled. For a year after the separation, the three children stayed with their mother, and their father rented an apartment nearby. The relationships were rocky. "My mother was a controlling woman, and she claimed she couldn't control me. My brother and sister were easier for her to deal with," Emily said. The next year, when Emily was in her freshman year in high school, her mother abruptly announced that she was getting her own apartment and she did not intend to take the children with her. Emily's older sister, Nadine, moved in with an aunt. Emily and her younger brother went to stay with their father, who, she said, "drank and was never home but never sexually abused me again."

During the next year, Nadine began coming by her father's apartment to pick up Emily and take her along to a local drive-in restaurant where older teens "hung out." Emily jumped into cars with Nadine's friends, often ending up beside Howie, a boy her sister's age who was always around. "We would go cruising and racing on a quarter-mile strip, the things teenagers did then," Emily recalled. It was 1966 and she was fifteen years old. She didn't really like Howie, who was four years older than she, but she ended up losing her virginity to him.

"There was no reason for me to get involved with him. In fact, I really never made a decision," Emily said. She wasn't curious about sex, and the three or four times she and Howie had intercourse were unpleasant. "With the knowledge I have now, I can see that what I did was because of the incest I suffered at such an early age. I had no sense of boundaries with a man. . . . If we were sitting by the dam necking and he went further than I wanted him to, my mind raced a million miles an hour—'This is awful, but where do I stop?' I had no idea."

She was afraid if she tried to stop Howie he would reject her. "I couldn't deal with male rejection," she said, even though she had no special feelings for Howie. The idea that Howie might care for her was more powerful to her than the reality that she felt no affection toward him. Again, she traced her feelings to her parents. "I felt more love and affection from my father," even though he was an alcoholic and an abuser, Emily said. "I felt like my mother had cast me to the wolves, and she was one of them. My dad came to my aid when the chips were down. That kind of image of the male figure stuck in my mind."

Emily floundered in school—cheating and failing her classes. When we interviewed her, she had come to think that her pregnancy with Howie had been an unconscious way to serve other purposes. "I wanted out," Emily admitted. "I think I wanted something sure in my life. If I could be sure of my own life and my own family, I thought things would be better. Love would be there."

But by the time Emily discovered she was pregnant she was no longer even seeing Howie. She had felt guilty about the sex and had broken things off. For a while, she was so panicked over the pregnancy that she almost believed her fear could make it go away. It is common for women who have been sexually abused to detach themselves from their bodies, Emily said. It is also common for teenagers to deny a pregnancy. Besides, she didn't know where to turn.

Her father was drinking heavily. Nadine had moved back in with their mother, but Emily was permitted to visit only once in a while. Emily was four months pregnant when she finally told Nadine, who insisted that she tell their mother. Emily resisted. She was still trying to win her mother's affection, despite repeated rejections. "I felt more protective of my mother than of myself," she said. Finally, Nadine took Emily to their mother's apartment and announced that Emily had something to tell her. "I was afraid she would break down and cry, and she did exactly that," Emily said. By the time the news was broken, Emily was almost in her sixth month.

Emily's mother started to talk about abortion, but it was too late. Besides, Emily recalled, "I was probably more certain about not having an abortion than I was about anything in my life. This was my baby, my opportunity to be a better mother than the one I had had, to have love in my life, and to be in control. All that was really important." Emily's mother made it clear she would have nothing to do with raising the child. Emily imagined she would work as a waitress and live by herself with the baby. "I never thought about marriage."

But then Emily's mother called her father, who immediately stormed over to the apartment. It was a warm summer evening, but Emily's mother had to close all the windows because his ranting grew so loud. Emily's father called Howie and demanded that he marry Emily.

"Howie came over. We went for a long ride, and he was very sincere about trying to have a good marriage and raising this child," Emily said. "Once again I was just turning my life over to the control of others. I thought, 'Well he said this, they said that. Maybe this will work.' "

Emily and Howie, little more than strangers, were married just three months before their daughter Melinda was born. Giving birth to Melinda and mothering her turned out to be more rewarding than Emily had ever imagined. During her pregnancy, Emily began reading everything she could about nursing and parenting. She wanted to be the best mother she could.

Howie, however, was a drunk and a drug dealer, and he soon left for California with a gang of motorcyclist friends. He returned briefly, while Melinda was still an infant, and stayed with Emily one night, trying to convince her to bring their daughter to California to live. Emily almost agreed, until she found out he had been having an affair with one of her friends. Howie left again, by himself, and Emily went on welfare, staying in a dark, one-bedroom apartment with a kitchen in the hallway. She was too depressed and isolated to notice what was happening to her.

"After three months, I went to clean out a closet and noticed that I hadn't used any sanitary pads." It hit Emily with a thud that Howie had gotten her pregnant again on his one-night visit. When she called to tell him he tried to claim it wasn't his, but by the time the baby was due he had moved back to try to make a go of it. Howie was bright and could always get good jobs, so Emily was willing to put up with his drug dealing and alcohol abuse. Besides, she felt more comfortable turning over control of her life to someone else than being on her own.

Howie wanted a boy, and both he and Emily thought a boy might help patch up their shaky marriage. But the Justin they had been waiting for turned out to be a Justine, and Howie was furious. He stormed into Emily's hospital room. "When I went down to that nursery and saw 'Girl-Edwards' above the crib, I could've just kicked that goddamned window in," he told Emily. When the nurses brought Justine to her room, Emily wondered if there had been a mix-up. "She was so wild-looking, not pretty like Melinda had been," Emily said. Justine was a wonderful baby, Emily admitted, but "she got the short end of everything. . . . I couldn't open up to her. I just couldn't." As a toddler, Justine slept in a crib in her mother's room. As soon as she would see Emily's eyes open she would jump up to greet her mother with a smile. But her charm failed to melt Emily's heart. "It just made me feel worse because it made me aware of the feeling I lacked. . . . Justine was the one who always showed me unconditional love. If she was in a store and had sixty cents in her pocket, she would spend it on something for me." Justine seemed determined to win her mother's affection, just as Emily had tried to win her own mother's.

Life with two children and a husband she didn't love was pure drudgery for Emily. Finally, after eight months of bitter battles, Howie was gone again, which was both a relief and a disappointment. Emily was eighteen, but she was only vaguely aware of the outside world through a few friends from the old days who smoked pot, dropped acid, and rode motorcycles. It was 1968, the year of the riotous Democratic convention in Chicago and the assassinations of Robert Kennedy and Martin Luther King. The generation gap was widening and the feminist movement was in bud. "To be honest," Emily said, "I was glad that I was not swept up in that because it looked frightening to me."

Instead, Emily was home watching "Sesame Street" and "Mister Rogers' Neighborhood" with her daughters. Her feelings toward Justine mellowed and

Emily began to enjoy both girls, even if her second daughter always had to play second fiddle. "What was actually happening to me was that I was experiencing my own childhood in a healthy way for the first time. In almost all senses, Melinda, Justine, and I grew up together, because I also moved through some very young phases," Emily said.

In their research for *Women's Ways of Knowing,* Mary Belenky *et al.* found that parenthood often "initiates an epistemological revolution. . . . It is as if this act of creation ushers in a whole new view of one's creative capacities." The authors, synthesizing the research of a number of developmental psychologists, write that it is in play that children learn to create metaphors. Play metaphors give way to language, and language is used to develop both an external and an internal voice. As children become capable of using language and other symbols to represent their hopes, plans and meanings, impulsive behavior gives way to behavior guided by longer-term goals. For someone like Emily, playing with her children might have helped her patch together pieces of development that she had missed in her own childhood.

Howie had little to do with the children. He forgot their birthdays and failed to send support payments, but he was worse than just negligent. Every so often he said he wanted to take them out. Emily dressed them up and had them waiting a number of times, but Howie never showed up. "I guess he knew no other way to get to me except through them," Emily said. "He hated me because I could never love him. Most of what he tried to do to me was ineffective, but when he deprived the girls, he knew that would hurt me."

When she was twenty, Emily hit a crisis. She had become pregnant with an older, married man. He had been separated from his wife when they met, and he lived with Emily until, when she was in her eighth month, he suddenly disappeared. He left a letter explaining that he had returned to his wife and son. He made a feeble and baseless claim that the child was someone else's, giving this as the reason for his departure, and he abandoned Emily with her two little girls and a third baby on the way. He never offered financial support.

Emily sank into a deep depression. It was much too late to consider abortion, but she knew she could never handle a third child, financially or emotionally. Finally, she rallied enough to inquire with an agency about placing the baby for adoption. Letting her baby go was a wrenching process, but Emily has come to feel that giving up her third daughter was a wonderful gift to both the child and the couple who have loved her well.

After the adoption, however, Emily's depression worsened. Taking some pleasure in her growing daughters, she gradually emerged. But depression continued to hold her in its grip for several years, through her late twenties, when she was living with a man who had begun to beat her. "I remember saying to him that I couldn't understand his abuse because that had never happened to me before. That's how much I was living in a coma," Emily stated. The relationship ended and Emily's depression grew critical enough to trigger the belief that "something about me needed to change," she said. She began seeing one counselor and then another, traversing a broad terrain of inexpensive or free psychotherapies, from the Adult Children of Alcoholics support group to a clinical psychologist doing her dissertation on sexually abused children. In her thirties, she began to recall the repressed early sexual abuse by her father. She left her therapy sessions shaking and wet with perspiration. But the work proved fruitful. She began to see how the abuse and the deprivations of her childhood had blurred the boundaries between her own body and will and the will of the men whose affection and approval she had sought. Slowly she began to heal.

"I have asked myself again and again how I managed to survive with my sanity, let alone a shred of dignity," Emily said. She has tried to identify the sources of hope that allowed her to climb out of her damaging past and has found very few. But there were enough strands of help and courage for her to weave a lifeline.

Emily pointed first to what she came to call "grace." "There seems to be something within my spirit, a really close connection with God and a belief that He would always take care of me." Emily's private, lifelong relationship with God had begun when she prayed to get through the nights when her parents battled.

Emily also had "a mouth," perhaps the active, less holy side of her "grace." Much more than her siblings, Emily stood her ground and fought back against her parents' abuse, exhibiting a spunkiness that saved her a piece of dignity to build upon.

In addition, Emily said, her daughters gave her hope, although that source was unsteady. "I always thought they were just the neatest things. . . . I always wanted them to have a wonderful mother. I didn't want to give them what I got." She was not always successful, Emily admitted. There were times her strictness strayed into abuse. Her closeness with Justine was only "sporadic." Justine's seemingly endless patience and generosity dried up when she was about ten years old, and a few years later she moved in with Howie, who had matured and settled into a good relationship with his daughters by the time they were teenagers.

Before Emily could tear down the wall between herself and Justine, she had to tear down her own wall of denial about the childhood abuse she had repressed. "Then I was finally able to look at myself and see how I had contributed to what had happened to me and her," Emily said, "and I could see how important she was to me and how ill-equipped I had been to be a parent. She just required me to stretch out, to extend myself, just what anybody needs in a relationship. . . . But all my resentment was projected on her." Emily's daughters have finished college now, and Emily feels close to both of them. Melinda is married and works in public relations. Justine is in law school.

The third thread in her lifeline, Emily said, was that she knew her mind was strong and that one day her intellect might work for her. She remembered two years in elementary school when her mother was hospitalized—first with a nervous breakdown and then with pneumonia—and the chaos at home diminished. Emily got straight A's, felt wonderful about herself, and grew close to a teacher who encouraged her abilities. Even today, Emily said, when her self-esteem slips and she questions her academic skills, the memory of that time and that teacher give her courage.

Emily passed her high school equivalency test while she was pregnant with Justine and slowly earned credit toward a bachelor's degree while working part-time as a sales clerk in a local dress shop. When she finished her undergraduate studies in her late thirties and began breaking through her repression in therapy, Emily felt a fleeting idea begin to take hold. Connections began to form between her personal experience and her studies in her undergraduate major of psychology. Emily began to yearn to work with other women like herself.

Gradually that yearning became a commitment and the commitment a calling. While she was unsure about the logistics of her ministry, Emily knew she had insight and compassion to give. Emily leaned back against the couch in the seminary. "I always thought that my life had been a bitter potion that I had been given," she said, "and I was always hoping the potion would become sweet one day, and it truly has."

Darlene Griffiths

Darlene Griffiths, a couple of years older than Emily Edwards, was the only child of a doting but overworked single mother in a black, working-class neighborhood. She would have a grown son today if her mother had not kept a close eye on Darlene. Her parents were separated. Occasionally Darlene would knock at her father's door, just a few streets away, and get five dollars pocket money. "Ain't you eighteen yet?" he'd ask with an indifferent shrug. Her mother's visits to court had failed to force any regular support from the man who had deserted them. So Alberta Griffiths bore all the responsibility. She worked as a beautician during the day and as a restaurant cashier at night, but her efforts at being a good breadwinner limited her ability to be a good nurturer. Although she was loving and as attentive as she could be under the circumstances, Alberta hardly ever saw her daughter.

In 1965, Darlene would come home after school to an empty house, practice the piano, and listen to Marvin Gaye on the record player. "The way I got pregnant was because [my mother] worked all day, she worked all night, and listening to Marvin Gaye, honey, just got you in the mood," said Darlene, who was a big woman with a deep laugh. But once she began to suspect she was pregnant, Gaye's sounds moved Darlene differently. She listened with tears running down her cheeks. "I was scared to tell anybody, because I was a bad girl. . . . I didn't want to break my mother's heart. She was working hard for me."

Telling the story more than twenty years later, Darlene never even mentioned the boy she had been involved with, but she clearly recalled how the pregnancy had riveted her mother's attention. Alberta noticed that Darlene had bought some oversize dresses and she asked what was going on. The answer was that Darlene, sixteen by then, was more than four months pregnant.

"Well, Darlene, what do you want to do?" Alberta asked.

"I want to finish school, and I want to go to college," Darlene replied.

Alberta questioned whether it made sense to try to do all that with a baby, and Darlene agreed it did not. Besides, she recalled, "I wanted my baby to have a mother and a father." She knew girls in her high school who were having babies and counting on their mothers to help raise them, but Darlene felt her mother had enough of a burden just raising her. "So it was her and my decision that I'd get rid of it," Darlene said.

Though abortion was illegal, Alberta found a way. She inquired among relatives in the small, black community nestled near the smokestacks of a western Pennsylvania glassmaking plant. They gave Alberta the information she needed, and on a Friday night she took Darlene to a house where a wizened woman ushered the girl upstairs and told Alberta to wait on the first floor. The old woman unbent a coat hanger, put red rubber tubing on the end of it, and told Darlene to lie back on the bed and take off her panties. "Don't holler," the woman told the frightened girl. "Don't make any noise."

"And she put that up in me," Darlene said, "and then she pulled out the hanger, and the tubing was up inside and was supposed to abort the baby, I guess." Alberta paid the woman twenty-five dollars and took her daughter home to bed. Darlene remembered labor pains that seemed to last an eternity. Finally, her mother helped her deliver the fetus, which was male, and Darlene passed out from exhaustion. "Don't you ever tell anybody I did this for you because you're not supposed to do this," her mother warned.

On Monday morning, Darlene went back to school as if nothing had happened. Out-of-wedlock pregnancy was more common among black teenagers than white teenagers then, but it still carried a stigma, especially for those blacks with middle-class stature or ambitions. No one had noticed Darlene's belly bulging beneath the loose dresses she had worn to hide it. In the middle of the week, though, she ran home from school because her breasts had begun to leak milk. Her mother gave her tissues to stuff in her bra. After that, neither mother nor daughter ever mentioned the incident. If there were lessons to be learned from the experience, they never talked about them. "It was erased. . . . Sometimes I had trouble figuring out if it was in a dream or if it really did happen," Darlene said with a sigh.

Darlene gazed out the window of her office onto a tree-lined industrial park in central Pennsylvania. Darlene had climbed far beyond the tiny factory town where she was born. She had worked her way up from secretary to a job that she loved as an office manager in a large corporation. She sometimes wondered, she said, what would have happened if her mother hadn't noticed those big shirtwaists in the closet. "I guess I would have had the baby," she said, sighing again. "I mean, I guess I would have waited until it was too late." Instead, she was thirty-seven and childless. She had undergone a second abortion in 1975 after a birth control failure. She had recently entered counseling when we interviewed her in 1986, and she had determined, in what seemed a rational way, that she really didn't want to be a parent. She was considering sterilization. Yet she murmured, "Maybe I should have had that baby." High school friends who had had their babies were "where I'd like to be," Darlene said. Their children were grown and the women had gone back to work. But almost immediately, Darlene shifted her focus again, saying that getting there had cost her friends a mighty struggle. She admitted she could not imagine how she and her mother would have handled a baby, and she shrugged off the passing melancholy.

We spoke to Darlene again when she was forty-one years old. She had decided against sterilization, she told us. She had married and had been trying to have a baby. She was about to begin fertility testing. She paused to marvel at the fact that she might have been a grandmother by now had she given birth when she was a teenager. But in the end, she concluded—without serious remorse—that if she could relive the events of 1965, "I'd probably do it all over again."

Today's Teenage Mothers

Fewer teens who give birth today marry to legitimize their babies as they did in Emily and Darlene's time. Consequently, many end up raising babies alone or with the help, and interference, of their families. In 1988, two-thirds of all births to adolescents occurred outside of marriage, compared with less than one-third in 1970.

Laura Nesbit, Tracy Donatello, and Dora Hooper became teenage mothers in the late 1980s. Like Emily Edwards and Darlene Griffiths a generation earlier, they grew up near the high end of the risk scale, in poor communities where teenage pregnancy was common even in their parents' times. In fact, two of these girls were the daughters of teenage parents. Like many modern teenagers who fit their profiles, these girls began having sex early and were careless about birth control. Their home lives were unstable and unnurturing. There was little possibility that their parents would guide them through the type of renegotiation of relationships that Carol Gilligan says girls seek at puberty. Failing that, all three seemed to use early motherhood, at least in part, as a way to establish a bond with their mothers. None looked forward to the kind of future Isabel Martin and Marian Hogan anticipated, and none of their pregnancies was completely accidental.

Laura Nesbit

Laura Nesbit, who lives in a small, declining factory town in Pennsylvania, became a mother before finishing high school. She had married her boyfriend, Greg, and was expecting their second child.

Laura told us that, although her first pregnancy at the end of her junior year of high school was unplanned, "It was really no surprise." She had used birth control for only the first month of her year-long sexual relationship with Greg. She was not too worried about pregnancy, for it posed no serious inconvenience. Laura and Greg had planned to marry on Valentine's Day in their senior year. Instead, they simply moved the wedding back seven months. "I was happy," Laura said, smiling. "I love kids."

Laura was still happy when we talked with her two years later. She and Greg were living in a public housing project surrounded by a muddy parking lot and a few scrubby trees. We sat in the living room of a unit that was neat, clean, and new but filled with shabby furnishings. Greg could be seen in the family photo hanging above a false fireplace made of cardboard. He and Laura looked sweet and awkward, posed with their baby before a painted backdrop of cherry blossoms. Sunny, sixteen months old, woke from a nap during the interview. She brought toys to show us but otherwise chattered contentedly to herself and let us talk for over an hour.

Like her self-contained daughter, Laura seemed unusually sedate for someone at the normally restless age of eighteen. The only wayward thing about her was her long, teased, auburn hair, its wildness contrasting with her pride in being a traditional wife and mother. Greg, too, took his new family seriously. He was out looking for a job, as he was every day. "Financially, we're not where we want to be," Laura said, "but I've got this little one and a man I love, so I guess I'm pretty happy."

Laura described her daughter Sunny as "something I'll have with me forever, no matter what happens. That makes up for anything I might be missing." But Laura's sense of what she might be missing was limited—by circumstance, choice, or some combination of the two. Laura had been unable to give us directions to her small town because she had never been outside it. Even living in a semirural area, she did not have a driver's license. Although Greg, who is trained to do auto-body work, was searching near and far for work, Laura hoped to remain close to her family. She worried about moving to unknown places where crime was high "with kids bein' stolen and stuff."

In her practical, down-to-earth heart, Laura was sure her family could live comfortably if Greg could earn just six dollars an hour, or about $12,500 a year, which was just over the poverty level for a family of four at that time. "You know, you wouldn't be rich, but you wouldn't be poor either," she said, leaning back against two colorful afghans she had crocheted during Sunny's naps. Her father and stepmother made eighteen dollars an hour between them, true wealth by Laura's standards. The cost of living was low enough in the area that the older couple's income had bought a new house, a car, and a truck—about as much luxury and fulfillment as Laura's imagination could hold.

The springs of a roll-away bed poked out from under the worn cushions on the couch where we sat. There was no television in the tiny unit, and Laura had lived for nearly two years without a telephone until she and Greg had squeezed one into their budget the previous month.

In this small town, teenage pregnancy was almost as prevalent as poverty. Laura was the daughter and the granddaughter of teenage mothers. About one-third of the daughters of poor, teenage mothers become teenage mothers themselves, but researchers are not sure why. Some suggest that their homes are also likely to be troubled by divorce and other stresses that make it more difficult for parents to adequately supervise their teenagers, or that these mothers may indirectly communicate an attitude of permissiveness to their daughters.

Laura's mother, a tenth-grade dropout, had always warned Laura against early pregnancy, just as Laura now planned to warn her daughter. But communication between Laura and her mother had been tense. When her parents divorced, Laura and her brothers ended up with their remarried father as soon as the court would allow each of them, at age twelve, to choose a custodial parent. Then when Laura began to clash with her stepmother, she moved back with her mother and began rebuilding that still shaky bond. She was not completely comfortable in either home.

So Laura got an early start with her own home, choosing to follow her mother's example, not her advice. Laura invited her mother to watch the results of her home pregnancy test. "She was unhappy at first," Laura admitted, "but she loves Sunny now." Indeed, pregnancy and motherhood seemed to have drawn the two closer and bridged their former estrangement. Motherhood fit with Laura's longtime role in her family. Laura's mother had sent her to be a live-in baby-sitter when an eighteen-year-old aunt was abandoned by her husband, and Laura had helped to raise the two children her father had in his second marriage.

The ease with which Laura took to young motherhood was enhanced by the support of her husband. Her happiness, though exposed to the risks of poverty and disillusionment, was nevertheless testimony to the fact that teenage parenthood is not inevitably doomed to failure or resentment. Laura had done well in school, she said, and had completed training in cosmetology after her daughter's birth. She hoped to open a beauty salon, then train to be a nurse when the children were older. Some teenagers aspire to early marriage and parenthood, plan for such a future, and consider it bright. Some will sustain the brightness of that vision and pass it on to their children. Many will not.

Tracy Donatello

Across town from Laura, Tracy Donatello was not happy. Tracy's boyfriend had "dumped" her when he learned she was pregnant. She was living in a trailer with her baby, her parents, and a younger brother when we interviewed her. Though her own mother, like Laura's, had also been a teenage parent, Tracy herself had made no plans for early marriage and pregnancy. She had therefore tried harder than Laura to protect herself against pregnancy, using birth control pills for most of the year she was involved with Earl.

But Tracy's father had found her pills when Tracy was sixteen, and her resolve had vanished. "My mom and dad were so disappointed in me that I was using the pill, so I went off them," she explained. It did not seem to strike her as illogical that she would go off the pill to please her parents but would not stop having sex. She made one further attempt to protect herself, mentioning the possibility of condoms to Earl. But he "wouldn't use anything. He always told me before that if I got pregnant, he'd marry me and we would raise the baby together. I figured I'd get pregnant, but I kept having sex anyway."

In fact, Tracy got pregnant during her first unprotected menstrual cycle. She suspected the truth right away, but "I just kept putting it out of my head." She told Earl several times of her worries, but his response was "No you're not, don't worry about it." She could not dampen her fears, though. Suspecting the flimsiness of Earl's promises, she grew more frightened than she had ever been, withdrawing from family and friends.

"Then I started getting bigger and bigger," Tracy recalled. Rumors floated around school. "I thought maybe I should just run away, because I never knew how my mom would react. . . . We were never that close. . . . She worked all the time. I hardly ever saw her," Tracy said. Not surprisingly, she and her mother had never talked seriously about sex, birth control, or anything else.

Finally, Tracy took a urine sample to Planned Parenthood. When she called Earl to tell him the test was positive, he cursed and hung up. Later, he told his friends the baby wasn't his. He has never seen his son Patrick or taken any responsibility for him.

That same frightening night—at 4½ months pregnant—Tracy finally gathered the courage to tell her mother. Her mother, recalling her own too-early pregnancy, stood in the kitchen and wept. "I felt really bad," said Tracy. "I didn't know what to do. But then she told my dad, and my dad came to me and said, 'I'll help you as much as I can.' "

Tracy was relieved, perceiving no irony in the contrast between her father's shock at finding her pills and his sympathy at the news of her pregnancy. But she knew she still had much to worry about. For a few weeks she considered giving her baby up for adoption but concluded, "I didn't think I could go through with it after nine months." Abortion was never a question. Like many teenagers who are faced with pregnancy, Tracy expressed a stern, self-reprimanding view. "I don't believe in [abortion]. If you're stupid enough to get pregnant, then you have to take responsibility for the mistake—unless you're raped or you're going to die during delivery." Besides, she added: "I always, always loved kids. . . . I always thought, how could somebody do something like that? Why blame it on the baby when it wasn't the baby's fault? It's your own."

Tracy's opposition to abortion was shared throughout the small community where she and Laura lived. In the high school both had attended, where pregnant classmates were a common sight in the hallways, no student was willing, even as devil's advocate, to take the pro-choice side of a school-sponsored abortion debate. According to a local newspaper reporter who had written a series of articles on teenage pregnancy, sentiments in this failing industrial town ran strong against both abortion and adoption. These moralistic attitudes did not extend to premarital sex, however. Like Tracy, Laura, who followed an evangelical faith, expressed no guilt or regret about her early sexual liaisons. And the town's residents, many of them descendants of immigrants from eastern and southern Europe, tolerated teenage pregnancy. A number of girls in each high school class were or had been pregnant by age eighteen. Most decided to have their babies, in part because this was what their friends had done.

Tracy's son, Patrick, had bound her to her own, once-distant mother in ways she found both gratifying and frustrating. As Tracy talked in the cramped, cluttered dining room of her family's trailer, her mother, still trim in her mid-thirties, chatted with a neighbor in the yard. The baby napped in a nearby bedroom. "If I didn't have my mom, I wouldn't know how to take care of Patrick," Tracy admitted, recalling how afraid she was even to bathe him when he was first born. On the other hand, she resents her mother for acting as if Patrick were her own baby. Her dilemma is common among teenage mothers whose babies become absorbed into their families. "Patrick knows if I tell him 'no' that all he has to do is go to my mom and my mom will let him do it." Tracy's feelings were hurt when Patrick, now a year old, wanted grandma, not mom, to rock him to sleep.

Much as Tracy valued the new connection with her mother, she also believed the realities of motherhood and of three generations living together in a small trailer had forced her to grow up fast. "Just like having a little baby doll is what I thought," she said about her vision of becoming a mother. "You don't realize all the money you need for [them], and they get sick and they get teeth and they get up at night." These hard realizations, Tracy said, had given her a sense of purpose she had lacked. "Because before I had him all I did was run around. I never had no responsibility or nothing. It's helped me realize that I have a future, and I have to make something of myself for him." Though she saw the need for direction and discipline, Tracy's ideas still glowed with an unreal light. She talked about a car, independence, college—poignant dreams that were probably beyond the reach of a girl who lacked basic academic skills.

Tracy "didn't like school. It was hard." She still preferred two other big dreams—winning the state lottery and finding a husband—to the toils of academic life, but failing those she did think school might be a long-range answer to the constraints of her life. Tracy was sure her current arrangement was temporary. She wanted to get a job as a bank teller, take night courses to become a child psychologist, and move into her own apartment. Then again, she thought about opening a nursery school, so that she could have Patrick with her all day. Of course there were practical problems about the time and money for training and education, but, well, Patrick had expanded her dreams and ambitions. "When I had Patrick, everything turned around," Tracy said, but she was still not clear just where she was headed.

Dora Hooper

Similar patterns exist sixty miles south of Laura and Tracy's hometown, where Dora Hooper, eighteen years old and black, lives in a Pittsburgh ghetto with her grandmother, two younger brothers, and an infant daughter. What she shares with Laura and Tracy—besides poverty, insufficient schooling, and young motherhood—is a community of peers for whom teenage pregnancy is commonplace. "Everyone in school has babies, two or three," Dora reported with some exaggeration. Many, like Dora herself, have also had abortions. They felt differently about abortion here than in Laura and Tracy's small town. "If you have an abortion, that's just another day," Dora said with a shrug. But later Dora contradicted her nonchalance, citing her own earlier abortion as a major reason for continuing the pregnancy that had given her seven-month-old Shawna.

Dora sat on the front steps of her grandmother's house on a warm summer afternoon. She had wide eyes, a crown of loose curls, and an air of calm authority with the children playing in and around the small yards of the rundown row houses. Shawna dozed in a swing on the tiny cement porch. When she fussed, her mother lifted her down for a feeding. As she gave the baby her bottle, Dora pointed down the hill to where her boyfriend Tony lived. She said she met him at her twelfth birthday party. He was fourteen. They began a sexual relationship right away and had been together intermittently ever since.

Tony, now a part-time student at the University of Pittsburgh, came by at the end of the interview to see Shawna. He had chiseled features, high cheek-bones, and a direct, well-intentioned gaze. As young as Dora was when she first got involved with Tony, she had used birth control pills, at least briefly. She soon cast them aside, however, because of headaches and fears about their side effects with cigarettes. After that, Dora took her temperature and charted her cycles for a while. Then she lost track and simply stayed away from Tony at mid-cycle. She said: "After a year of not using [birth control], I went on the kick 'Well, God's with me. He knows that I don't need a kid, so he'll keep protecting me from getting pregnant.' It stayed that way for four years." Then trouble brewed between Tony and Dora. Some of Dora's friends grew jealous over the couple's long, sunny relationship. They whispered to Tony that Dora was seeing someone else, which made him sullen and insecure. Dora wondered now if it was the stress of their conflict that threw her normally regular cycle off. On the other hand, she thought she might just have been so eager to convince him of her loyalty that she forgot to count the days of her cycle. In either case, she sighed, "It was real stupid, and I got pregnant."

Dora did not include Tony in her decision about that pregnancy. He was angry, especially because he heard about the pregnancy first from one of Dora's girlfriends. He and Dora separated, and Dora went to her mother for help. Although they had an uneasy relationship, Dora knew, "My mother was the only one who could possibly help me if she would see to it in her heart." Dora's mother rallied to her aid, even though her alcoholism had made her unfit to take care of Dora and her brothers on a day-to-day basis. She quickly called other family members to raise the money for an abortion. Her mother's reasons seemed clear. Dora was floundering in school and had been tossed by stormy family relations from one relative's home to another. Dora remembered her mother insisting that "I didn't have a stable place to stay. How could I bring a baby into the world and give her a stable place?" Other relatives chimed in and encouraged Dora to end the pregnancy. So Dora's reasons for having an abortion had to do with her own and her family's concern about her ability to care for a child, not with any bright plans for her future.

"I was scared," she remembered sadly. "I had mixed emotions. I wanted a baby and then I didn't want a baby." Dora was sixteen and so nervous when she went to the abortion clinic that she forgot her mother's welfare card and had to go back home for it. She screamed during the procedure. "It hurt worse than having a baby, and I had her natural," she said, nodding at Shawna. For Dora, abortion was not "just another day"; it was traumatic. She determined not to go through an abortion again. "I made a promise to myself after I did it that first time that I'll never do it again. And I kept my promise," she said with a nod to baby Shawna, dozing again in the windup swing with the sun glistening on her curls.

Having that abortion "was right and wrong," Dora said now, looking back. "Taking a life is wrong altogether. That's the bottom line right there. . . . But it would have been wrong for me to bring a baby into this world and eventually have to put her into a home or something because I wouldn't have been able to take care of her. . . . My family would've took me in, but you have to bend down and do everything that they say. I really don't enjoy that."

Dora seemed not to notice the irony of her comment, which she made on the porch of her grandmother's house with a baby in her lap. Indeed, she complained about living under her grandmother's thumb. But she is an example of how one choice between birth and abortion can affect another, and how a slight change in circumstance can make a big change in the outcome of a pregnancy. A year later, after "taking a chance," Dora was seventeen years old and pregnant again. The same conditions that had ruled against her first pregnancy still existed when Dora became pregnant again, but this time she made her choice herself, without being swayed by family.

Tony's reaction to this second pregnancy was flat. "When I found out that I was pregnant, he also found out that his mom had cancer. . . . It was like the pregnancy went to the side, and I knew what I was gonna do." Dora went ahead with the pregnancy on her own. Tony's mother died during Dora's eighth month, and his hurt was still fresh the day Shawna was born. Dora was at her grandmother's house when her water broke. "I called Tony and said I thought it was time. I guess he was tired or whatever . . . and evil. He told me, 'Tell your grandmother to take you.' I said, 'What do you mean tell my grandmother to take me? My grandmother didn't get me pregnant.' " Later Tony showed up at the hospital but felt too queasy to be with Dora during the delivery. Four months later, Tony's relationship with Dora lay somewhere between Greg's full commitment to Laura and Earl's cynical disregard of Tracy and their child. Tony spent time with both Dora and Shawna and he contributed pocket change for diapers and baby clothes, but his commitment, at least at the time, was partial.

Dora's mother was angry and bitter at first about her daughter's second pregnancy, but the two are closer now. Dora's mother stayed with her through Shawna's delivery after Tony backed out. "I love my mother," Dora said. "I love her to death, and I'm gettin' closer to her now. I don't know if it's because of Shawna or not, but I enjoy it. I've been looking for it all my life."

Dora sounds more like Tracy than Laura, talking about Shawna as a force that can generate a better future. "People say a baby will hurt you. . . . [But Shawna] gives me a lot more to do on my days. . . . She speeds me up; she doesn't slow me down." Dora's hopes challenge her life of turbulence and academic failure. Her father died of a heart attack when she was ten; his death marked the end of the stable, happy family life she had known. Afterward, Dora's mother drew financial support from welfare and Social Security and emotional support from a gin bottle. Now, Dora believed that Shawna had to fill the painful gap left by her father's death before she herself could regain a sense of worth and purpose.

In the eleventh grade, Dora gave up on school after years of despondency and poor performance. She had moved from one relative to another, attending four different high schools. "I didn't feel too good academically," she recalled. School counselors couldn't reach her and she had dropped out.

When Dora became pregnant for the second time she decided to proceed, she said, because of the trauma of her abortion and because an education program for inner-city teenage mothers offered her a chance to return to school. Both her attitude and her academic skills had improved since Shawna's birth, aided by reading glasses she apparently had needed for some time. "All I know is I feel good about myself now. I really do," she said. She had passed her high school equivalency test and she was about to begin courses at the community college. The Pittsburgh in Partnership with Parents and New Chance programs covered her tuition, child care, books, some of her rent, and even bus fare and classes in parenting. So much was taken care of, Dora figured, that, "There's no reason why you shouldn't be able to show up for school."

The program—part of a research project started by Manpower Demonstration Research Corporation with help from the Pittsburgh Public Schools, Magee-Womens Hospital, the Pittsburgh Housing Authority, the YWCA, and local colleges—had drawn an edge of realism around Dora's dreams. She thought about becoming a nurse's aide, a hairdresser, or a social worker, all of which were within reach if she continued her education. "Shawna makes me feel responsible," she said. "I also learned that I have to do for myself. . . . or else I'll end up . . . like my mom," Dora said. What she wanted for Shawna sounded so simple: to say yes to a trip to the zoo instead of responding with what Dora had heard other mothers say: "Oh, no. I don't have money. What do you think welfare gives us?" Like Laura's simple desire for a six-dollar-an-hour job for her husband, Dora's expectations revealed the poverty behind her experiences.

Today, Dora said, looking over at her baby with a glowing smile: "I love waking up in the morning. I'm never sad anymore, because she's always there to make me happy. She's innocent. She's beautiful to me, you know. I just love her, and I know she's one person that will always care about me and love me and I'll never have to worry about her not loving me."

Pregnancy with a Purpose

For each person interviewed here—the affluent as well as the poor—teenage pregnancy was a disruption to her growth, yet it was never without its purpose. Kristin Luker's *Taking Chances: Abortion and the Decision Not to Contracept* explains how women who fail to use contraceptives actually make rational, if not fully deliberate, decisions. Unplanned pregnancies that seem self-destructive, as those begun by teenagers usually do, may be serving other unspoken purposes. For some teenagers, pregnancy is a strategy "to care for themselves, to care for others, to get what they wanted, and to avoid being alone," as Carol Gilligan notes in her prologue to *Mapping the Moral Domain*. Pregnancy can revive a faltering sense of purpose, it can be a rebellion against goals parents have imposed, it can get the attention of too-busy or negligent parents, it can be a plea for help, or it can provide an escape from an unsatisfactory home.

For teenagers from disadvantaged backgrounds, pregnancy may not always be a setback, especially if they are already failing at school. Arline T. Geronimus of the University of Michigan, speaking at the 1990 meeting of the American Association for the Advancement of Science, claimed that teenage childbearing can even have economic advantages for the poor. Teenage mothers get financial and material help from friends and relatives. They enjoy more attention from their own mothers and other family members who help to raise their children. Geronimus, an assistant professor of public health policy, challenged the argument that teenage mothers are less likely to finish school *because* they become mothers, arguing that they are already unlikely to finish school. She claimed that studies of poor, mostly black, inner-city families showed that teenage mothers actually did somewhat better materially and educationally than their sisters who waited to have babies.

But it would be dangerous and irresponsible simply to claim that teenage pregnancy, whatever its outcome, improves lives or accomplishes other purposes. Surely, it is morally misguided to justify the use of pregnancy to create a crisis or to force attention where it has been lacking. And surely it is wrong when a baby must give his or her own mother the incentive to make her life worth living. From any morally mature perspective, children—and therefore pregnancies—are ends in themselves, not merely the means to someone else's ends.

We are then left to wonder how we—as parents and as citizens—can help to provide our fertile youngsters with more productive strategies than sex, pregnancy, and childbearing to get what they so desperately seek. Answers do not come readily or without controversy. The stories of these once-pregnant teenagers give us both hope and clues. They show us how in America's supposedly family-centered culture the family can fail. When it does, we do little to lessen the danger of children tumbling from the nest.

Anatomy of the Problem

In a sense, all teenagers in developed countries come equipped with a common handicap: Their bodies grow up before their hearts and minds do. Better nutrition and health care have lowered the age of puberty for American girls, from sixteen in the late 1800s to about 13.5 in the 1960s and to just over twelve today. Yet there has been no corresponding acceleration in the development of young brains and nervous systems. The result seems to be an increasing gap between the time when teenagers become fertile and the age at which they develop the cognitive and emotional ability to make adult decisions about sex. There is also a widening "courtship gap"—the time between puberty and marriage—in which hormones are flashing ready lights but society provides no sanctioned outlet for sexual urges. While the courtship gap averaged only about two years in the mid-nineteenth century (from puberty at sixteen years old to marriage at eighteen), it now lasts more than eleven years (from puberty at twelve to age twenty-four, the average age at first marriage for women today).

It is encouraging to note that most researchers believe adolescents are neurologically capable of abstract thought and moral reasoning. Most teenagers have developed sufficiently to think sensibly, and many do. Indeed, most teenagers successfully weather the period between puberty and full maturity. But others, in increasing numbers, become sexually active before they are mature enough to handle the physical and emotional consequences. They use sex or pregnancy to act out other problems, they feel coerced into sexual acts they are not ready for, or they fail to keep sex and its possible consequences in perspective with other, realistic long-term goals. The problem is especially critical in the United States.

Teenage pregnancy rates in the United States are at least twice those of other industrialized countries. Teenagers in Western Europe, for example, are sexually active at close to the same ages and the same rates as their American counterparts, but they conduct their sex lives quite differently. In Norway and Denmark, for example, 75 to 80 percent of teenagers use birth control the first time they have intercourse, whereas only 40 percent do so in the United States. Western Europe has lowered rates of teenage pregnancy, just as it has lowered rates of unwanted pregnancy and abortion for the population as a whole. The differences are frequently traceable to the fact that the United States has no centralized health-care system and thus no national policy for preventing unwanted pregnancies. The degree of success in each European nation has virtually no correlation with the strictness of its abortion laws. Instead, what accounts for Europe's success is a complex web of policies, from aggressive sex education and birth control for teenagers to extensive social programs for single mothers. In Sweden, the Netherlands, France, England, and elsewhere, national health-care programs make confidential contraceptive services available to sexually active teenagers free or at low cost. The European medical profession tends to promote the pill and in many places prescribes it without requiring a pelvic examination. Condoms, too, are widely available in Western Europe, not just from pharmacies and clinics but often from vending machines and grocery stores. Although Sweden is the only country with an official, enforced sex education curriculum, other nations convey essential information, too. In the Netherlands, where the Government subsidizes mobile sex education units and where the media extensively cover sex-related issues, teenagers' awareness of contraception is "virtually universal" (Jones, Forrest, Goldman, Henshaw, Lincoln, Rosoff, Westoff, and Wulf, 1985).

Underlying this complex web of policies is a simple assumption: that unwanted pregnancy—especially among teenagers—is a serious public health issue. The morality of teenage sexual activity is not considered. Yet there is an explicit state policy—that pregnancy prevention is preferable to abortion—which many lawmakers and citizens regard as a moral imperative. In Sweden, the liberalization of abortion laws in 1975 was interwoven with programs to provide sex education and contraceptive services for adolescents. The belief, Jones *et al.* (1985) say, was that such services could prevent the need for abortions. In fact, although Sweden's adolescent abortion rates are second only to those in the United States, those rates have declined since the liberalized law and the delivery of services took effect. According to Jones *et al.* (1985), many European countries regard teenage pregnancy and childbearing as "undesirable, and broad agreement exists that teenagers require help in avoiding pregnancies and births."

Ironically, a similar consensus exists in America. Polls show that 90 percent of Americans favor sex education in our schools—including contraceptive and AIDS education—beginning in the early grades. A Harris poll even showed that two-thirds of Americans think that schools should be required to have links with family planning clinics, according to Peter Scales, Director of National Initiatives at the Center for Early Adolescence at the University of North Carolina School of Medicine at Chapel Hill. The problem, according to Scales, is that support is a mile wide and an inch deep. But the price of inability to come together on the problems of teenage sexuality, according to Dr. Michelle Harrison, assistant professor of psychiatry at the University of Pittsburgh Medical School, is that we are abandoning our children.

In an interview with us, Harrison compared teenagers to toddlers, who similarly lack a sense of danger. "Adolescence can be characterized as a time of believing that nothing can happen to you, that the risks are other people's risks," Harrison said. Teenagers experiment with adult behavior while yielding to their still-childish temptations. "So, whether it's speeding [in] cars or smoking cigarettes or drinking or sex without precautions," Harrison said, risk-taking is typical teenage behavior. "The problem is that when the toddler is walking out into the street you can grab him and sweep him up and carry him to safety. The teenager's too big for that."

Besides, when it comes to issues of sexuality, many parents are too naive or too embarrassed to know how early and how frankly the subject needs to be discussed with their children. They may postpone or avoid it, and their silence is deadly. It leaves children open to peer pressure or to mass media messages that typically portray sex as exploitative, whimsical, or without consequence. Parents who dismiss their child's confusion about sex with half-baked platitudes or punitive preaching can invite rebellion. Today, the threat of AIDS makes sexual knowledge a matter of life and death.

Experts agree that parents who listen openly to their children and talk with them—in that order—are telling their children that they love them. By the same token, closing off an important subject like sex can send another message, perhaps that the child is unloved or not loved wholly—that his or her sexuality is somehow beyond the reach of parental love and guidance. As Mary Belenky *et al.* write in *Women's Ways of Knowing,* "It is through attentive love, the ability to ask 'What are you going through?' and the ability to hear the answer that the reality of the child is both created and respected."

An American Solution

The roadblock to solving the problem of teenage pregnancy in America is not so much one of consensus, which Americans have, but commitment, which they don't have. As Peter Scales says, "The problem is that we are not doing a good job of translating support into trust." Americans are much more culturally diverse and geographically separated than the more homogeneous Europeans, and as a result we do not trust each other as much. While some experiments have demonstrated that pregnancy prevention programs can be successful in the United States, many attempts meet head-on with community opposition and die. Scales suggests that all American communities are conservative—but in the best sense. They want to pass on what has worked in the family and what is woven into the social fabric. Therefore, they are understandably uneasy about entrusting something as personal and value-laden as sex education to a public institution, even in part. Successful programs have to be committed to weathering controversy and must even accept it as beneficial. Scales recommends that Americans focus on common concerns, such as worries about sexual innuendo in popular culture, the desire for sexual responsibility in our children, the wish for their good health, and the desire to give them solid academic and social skills. Most importantly, Scales says, successful programs should involve parents even if doing so slows down results. "All the research shows that the more parents are involved, the more comprehensive and successful the results are," Scales says.

Any plans to address teen sex and pregnancy in the United States will have to accommodate our particular national qualities. Programs must acknowledge that this nation is geographically vast and varied in its subcultures and religions.

Imposing uniform solutions upon varied and widely scattered local authorities may be impossible, but consensus regarding broad goals is not, nor is cooperation. When it comes to the interests of teenagers, it is parents who wield the greatest influence, both as voters and as community members. Local programs that respect the different viewpoints within their communities and the wishes of parents to shape their children's values and sex education curricula have every reason to succeed. But, Scales warns, such programs must be tenacious.

An American Model

Tucked away in Gettysburg, Pennsylvania, Maureen Malone quietly runs an innovative pregnancy prevention program that might serve as a model for other communities. Malone, a social worker in the local school district, was influenced by the work of Douglas Kirby, whose five-year study for the U.S. Department of Health, Education, and Welfare indicated that parental involvement and long-term continuity were keys to the success of programs to prevent teenage pregnancy. Malone knew that many parents needed as much education as their kids, at least when it came to talking about sex. They may not think their own parents did a good job with sex education, but they often do not do much better in these changing times.

In 1979, Malone began trying to teach parenting skills to teenage mothers in Gettysburg. She soon decided that "This rushed effort to pick kids up and teach them parenting was a waste of time if they (a) had no self-esteem and (b) could make no decisions." She began, in counseling sessions, to lead the girls back to how they had formed their self-images and their ideas about men and women. Gradually, she came to realize she would have to start long before puberty if she were to change the prospects for high-risk children.

Gettysburg Area School District covers 225 square miles but includes only 2,400 students, virtually all of them white. About twenty girls each year get pregnant, a rate not extraordinarily high but underestimated and disproportionately distributed among the schools' three distinct populations. One segment is made up of the children of academics and professionals who commute to Baltimore and Washington. These nurtured children are considered gifted and few end up pregnant. When they do, they have abortions, Malone reported, and she may never know that they were pregnant at all. At the other extreme are the farm children, who come from families with as many as sixteen children and whose parents may not have finished eighth grade. These children, said Malone, have no goals or aspirations beyond the only life they have known. "They're going to be on the farm. And so they say, 'Gee, I was going to get married at nineteen. So I got pregnant at fifteen, what's the big deal here?' " This group has a very high pregnancy rate, and the conservative values of their community rule out abortion. The middle and smallest student population, the group that also falls in the middle of the risk continuum, is made up of the children of factory workers.

Malone continued her work with teenage mothers, but she also followed up on her idea to start the educational process much earlier. Her immediate inspiration for the program she devised was a television program about the Family Guidance Center in St. Joseph, Missouri, that brought parents together to discuss puberty with their fifth- and sixth-graders. Malone thought the idea was "brilliant," but she also wondered why it should be limited to two grades. "So we decided to start in kindergarten, work all the way up [through high school], and have mothers and fathers." Malone's theory was "that parents are the primary educators of their children. They have so much influence with their values and their choices." And Malone's program is very much about values and choices. What makes the Gettysburg program so interesting is not just that it addresses so many factors that affect teenage sexual decisions, but that Malone listens to all the voices in the community and works with, not against, their concerns. As a result, all but a few parents—mostly Seventh Day Adventists who have religious objections—participate in the program.

In the mid-1980s, Malone began to work in the youngest elementary grades, at first as a volunteer in the local Catholic school and later as a social worker for the Gettysburg area schools. She began by inviting parents to come to the school for two evenings in two weeks. On the first night they came without their children, and some were ready to do battle with Malone over her new sex education curriculum. But Malone quickly disarmed them, explaining what the young children would learn about first—fetal development. "It's usually the pro-life movement that's afraid of [sex education], so when they see what I'm doing, they say, 'Oh, this is great,' " Malone found.

The next week, the parents came back for an evening with their children. They reviewed body parts—including genitals—on a fetal model that, Malone found, was "so unthreatening that everyone just said, 'Oh, this is so cute.' " Then the parents and children talked about the lesson because, Malone said, it is important for children to learn the right anatomical language and to hear their parents use it also. This provides them with a common language and frees them from having to use whatever other language has evolved at home. Finally, the children pretended to interview their parents about childbirth for the *Gettysburg Times*. This activity continued at home, with the family's opening up the baby album and talking about the delivery room and how mom and dad felt when this child was born.

The children reviewed the same material the next day in school. "The first time, they're entertained. The second time, they have questions," Malone said. She has built the program up and repeated the process each semester with increasingly complex material. The kindergartners she started with are now in the eighth grade. Until the fourth grade, most children just want to know about babies—how they get in and how they get out, according to Malone. In fifth and sixth grade, when girls are starting to menstruate, many schools separate boys from girls in health classes. Malone keeps them talking together in the hope that dialogue will overcome the shyness she sees in high school students. When she asks girls of fifteen and sixteen why they haven't insisted that their boyfriends use condoms, they tell her, "Oh, I can't talk to him about sex."

With the eighth-graders, Malone has begun lessons about love and relationships that will continue through high school. Sixth-graders interview their parents about when they first found out about menstrual cycles; seventh- and eighth-graders ask them about their first dates.

A short time before our interview with her, Malone witnessed the difference that the parent-child dialogue has made. She brought together two groups of eighth-graders—one of them from another school district—for a special program about postponing sexual initiation. In workshops, parents and children explored why some young people have sex and others choose not to. Parents and children from the other school district sat stiffly while the students said what they thought their parents wanted to hear: "Sex is a sin" or "It's against God's law." Her own group, said Malone, had been talking over sexual matters with their parents for years. These parents and children laughed and made jokes. "The kids said, 'People have sex because it's fun. . . . It feels good.' They weren't worried that their parents would say, 'Oh, my God. They're going to have sex now,' because they know that it is okay to talk."

The parents, Malone found, have learned to relax; they talk and listen to their children without panicking. "We've been providing adult education to these parents, trying to get them to realize that when their child comes home and starts talking about so-and-so on the pill they don't jump on them and say, 'Are you having sex too? She's your best friend.' The kids just want to talk, just like they want to talk to you about somebody doing something in math class. You're not saying, 'Are you throwing that eraser, too?' You're listening."

The children Malone began to work with in kindergarten are now reaching puberty, so Malone will soon be able to measure how successful her educational program has been in preventing pregnancy. Meanwhile, in Gettysburg's high school, where students have not yet had the benefit of the sex education program the younger students are receiving, Malone has tried a different approach. Students, teachers, guidance counselors, or the school nurse refer boys and girls whom they believe are becoming sexually active, and Malone takes them into a counseling session with one of several teenage parents she has carefully educated about human sexuality and contraceptives. Malone, not wanting to be "just another adult in their face telling them not to have sex," slips out of the room. The teen parents talk about how painfully hard it is to get it back on track and how different their fantasies about sex and love were from the reality. After three years, not one of the teenagers who has received this peer counseling has gotten pregnant.

Malone, who "used to think that all I had to do was invent some [birth control] that could be put in the fountains in the high school," had changed her mind. Dangers such as AIDS aside, she was now convinced that having sex at all can be deeply disturbing to teenagers.

Some of Malone's teenage clientele have had "miserable, miserable experiences." Some girls complained of pain, bleeding, and cramping from sex. Malone advised them to see a gynecologist, but she assumed the problem was simply that they were nervous and unable to produce lubrication. Teenagers often have sex in uncomfortable situations, with most of their clothes on, after very little foreplay. They are cramped in the backseat of a car, or they are afraid someone will walk in. The girl may grant sex as a favor but then worry whether the guy will tell all his friends or will think she is too fat.

Malone tried to convince these girls that sex was not always horrible. "I find myself babbling off the Catholic Church stuff: 'There wasn't a commitment there,' 'You didn't know him,' 'It can be such a beautiful form of communication.'" No adult had explained to these youngsters that sex can range from an animal act to a richly rewarding expression of love. Malone worried that some teenagers were becoming sexually dysfunctional because of their bad adolescent experiences.

Why do these children have sex if it so unpleasant? Malone guessed it is because they felt pressured. Boys had told her they had "to push [the girl]." Date rape is common in Gettysburg, Malone said, but is rarely recognized as such. The girls often blame themselves, saying, "I knew I should never have gone parking with him." Malone hoped the children she has worked with since grade school will be able to avoid these attitudes.

Reducing the Costs

Teenage pregnancy may be a common fact of life in America, but its personal, social, and economic costs are enormous. It can have many long-term ill effects. Many of the 400,000 abortions performed on teenagers each year carry deep emotional and moral pain, and carrying a teenage pregnancy to term is often even tougher. While adoption can be a solution, few teenagers feel capable of surrendering a child they have given birth to. Some who do grieve and wonder for years.

Research into the cost of teenage childbearing has produced shocking results. In 1975, over half the Aid to Families with Dependent Children (AFDC) budget was absorbed by families in which the mother had been a teenager when her first child was born. A 1985 follow-up study suggested that welfare expenditures to teenage childbearers had doubled in the subsequent decade. But welfare costs are only the beginning. Altogether, the support of teenage mothers takes about twenty billion dollars annually—or about two hundred dollars per year out of the pocket of every American taxpayer.

Some might say the only real cure for teenage pregnancy is to reweave the American social fabric and eliminate the pockets of deprivation that are so often associated with the problem. But such sweeping suggestions stymie action. As Lisbeth B. Schorr and Daniel Schorr observe in the introduction to *Within Our Reach: Breaking the Cycle of Disadvantage*, it is not necessary to change all risk factors in order to improve the life of a child. Moreover, says Lisbeth B. Schorr, "The more I looked, the clearer it became that in the last two decades we have accumulated a critical mass of information that totally transforms the nation's capacity to improve outcomes for vulnerable children."

Some kids, Peter Scales points out, have all the risk factors that predict trouble in adolescence and still do not develop any of the problems. "We know the secret," Scales says. He believes the teenagers who escape disaster are the ones who maintain a sense of self-esteem and of competence; the ones who keep at least one close, warm relationship with an adult; and the ones who get lots of positive experience with community institutions. The secret's ingredients sound like the ones that Carol Gilligan has found were missing from the lives of the faltering girls she studied.

The picture is becoming clearer, and Americans are ultimately a practical people. So it seems logical that at some time we will tire of the political harangue over abortion and decide instead to devote our time and our financial resources to reducing the need for abortion—especially among our children.

VICTIMS AND SURVIVORS

The father of psychoanalysis had noticed that many of his hysterical female patients reported a childhood experience of rape or molestation, most often at the hands of their own father. At first the good doctor believed the women. Later he developed the theory . . . that these disturbing reports of childhood assault were fantasies that the child contrived as a defense against her own genital pleasure and her guilty wish to sleep with her father.

Susan Brownmiller, *Against Our Will: Men, Women, and Rape* (1975)

Introduction

Women and girls live their whole lives knowing they are vulnerable to sexual attack, abuse, or harassment. Some learn it early and directly, "at the hands of their own father," brother, uncle, teacher, clergyman, cousin, or baby-sitter. Yet most who are victimized, whether as children or as adults, do not report the crimes against them, and many of those who do meet with disbelief, contempt, or attacks upon their character and motives. Even those who become pregnant as a result of a degrading, violent act are not exempt from suspicion.

That suspicion runs deep, and one major source of it is Freudian psychology—in particular, Freud's repudiation of his "seduction theory," in which he had held that childhood sexual trauma was the universal source of neurosis. Although this theory was received coldly by Freud's medical confreres, he clung to it for some time in view of his patients' consistent reports of incest and molestation. Eventually, however, he reversed himself, declaring that not all neuroses could stem from only one source. Therefore, he reasoned, not *all* the women he treated could be telling the truth. If they were, then unthinkable numbers of good Austrian citizens were raping or fondling their daughters and nieces. It was easier to think that the women who reported such incidents were deluded, and that the source of their delusion was their secret desire to sleep with their fathers. Although Freud continued to view childhood sexual abuse as real, his final position on the question deeply undermined the credibility of victims.

According to Susan Brownmiller, in her landmark book on rape, *Against Our Will: Men, Women, and Rape*, "Men have always raped women, but it wasn't until the advent of Sigmund Freud and his followers that the male ideology of rape began to rely on the tenet that rape was something women desired. The dogma that women are masochistic by nature and crave the 'lust of pain' was first enunciated by Freud in ... 1924 .... " In Brownmiller's view, and in the view of many other feminists, Freud's reluctance to accuse so many respectable Viennese men of sex crimes has led to views of women that have been gravely harmful and persistent.

Yet recent studies tend to affirm the original thesis that so alarmed Freud and his colleagues. We spoke to six social workers and psychotherapists who work with women from destructive backgrounds, and through them we became familiar with findings on the incidence of childhood sexual abuse. In 1986, for example, sociologist Diana Russell, of Mills College in California, surveyed 930 adult women in San Francisco, asking whether they had ever experienced unwanted sexual contact, within or outside their families, before they turned eighteen. Thirty-eight percent said that they had. Sixteen percent said they had been victims of incest (defined as exploitative, unwilling sexual contact with a relative, no matter how distant).

Dr. Jocelyn Tager, a Massachusetts psychologist in private practice, has treated survivors of incest and sexual abuse for sixteen years. In an interview, she stated "I know of fathers who have abused who are physicians, clergy, teachers, businessmen, pillars of the community. Sometimes, after a day of going about my business, it dawns on me that I've probably run into someone who has abused a child. The statistics are just so high—almost 40 percent of all women by the time they are eighteen."

Mary Belenky *et al.* also found evidence of how common sexual abuse has become, or has been revealed to be. Though they never intended to study rates of sexual abuse when they began their research for *Women's Ways of Knowing*, the authors write: "Based on our data, sexual abuse appears to be a shockingly common experience for women. In our sample of seventy-five women, 38 percent of the women in schools and colleges and 65 percent of the women contacted through the social agencies told us that they had been subject to either incest, rape, or sexual seduction by a male in authority over them—fathers, uncles, teachers, doctors, clerics, bosses."

Like any accusation of an offense that has no witnesses, a claim of childhood abuse amounts to the victim's word against the perpetrator's. Usually, it is a girl or woman's word against a man's, and the woman's word is often dismissed, derided, or doubted. Freud, despite the popularity of his theories, cannot be held solely responsible for the tendency to blame and mistrust female victims of sexual assault. Like other harmful ideas about women, Freud's reflect a sense of male superiority that dates at least to biblical times. Western culture is steeped in stories of male domination over women, and such power has been readily manifested in violence.

Examples of such violence abound in this chapter. They represent only a minute, random selection of outrages, but they speak for thousands of stories that are numbingly similar. We know this from the women we have interviewed, the studies we have read, and the professionals who counsel the victims of a kind of violence that is barely acknowledged.

Patterns of denial and reluctance to accuse characterize stories like the ones that follow, often making the facts invisible to anyone but the victims. This chapter talks about victims who do not confront their attackers, abusers who do not regard what they do as wrong, institutions that turn blind eyes to evidence of injury and despair, and people from parents to police officers who are supposed to protect but instead abandon. Certain signs and consequences of such widespread denial—for example, pregnancies conceived in violence, self-hatred, or despair—are regarded as isolated episodes rather than as symptoms of social pathology. The most disturbing cases of abuse that we refer to in this chapter are those committed upon children, even though such cases have come to seem commonplace. Robin Connors, a counselor and former administrator at a rape crisis center in Pittsburgh, believes that the physical and sexual abuse of children may be "epidemic." She points out that early abuse appears in the background of a great many people in certain troubled populations—"I'm talking about people in penal institutions, people in psychiatric hospitals, juvenile delinquents, all kinds of . . . people that are perceived as problematic to society. The incidence [of childhood abuse] is high, very high. [I suspect] that a lot of what has been problematic in our culture . . . really has its roots in childhood abuse experiences, whether it's sexual or some other kind of abuse. If we could really stop child abuse, I wonder what else we could stop."

This chapter, more than any other, is about women whose voices and identities were taken from them by lies and by force, sometimes starting in childhood. All have been victims of violence or cruelty. Some have been physically harmed by intimates or strangers; others have been emotionally devastated. Many have inflicted injury upon themselves. One, a homeless crack addict who was pregnant when we spoke with her, has disappeared since our interview.

A few of these women tried to speak out about the outrages against them but were not believed, while others never spoke out at all. Some groped for words and acts that would make sense of their violent or chaotic lives but could find none within their reach. Others clung to recovery—or sometimes the fantasy of recovery—by a slender thread.

The stories in this chapter harshly exaggerate the themes of earlier ones, in which it is clear that the lives of many ordinary women and girls are filled with multiple forms of disrespect, dysfunction, constraint, or powerlessness. In some of the stories that follow, derogatory views of women explode into rape or incest. Authority figures and institutions often ignore or refuse to believe women in desperate trouble. The women themselves become ill or depressed. Some of those we interviewed and heard about turned to addiction, prostitution, crime, or suicide. What safety nets exist for such women have been woven from little more than dedication and compassion by social workers, volunteers, and sometimes other victims. Some falling women land safely in these nets; more disappear through the holes left by inadequate resources and a lack of awareness. The lost ones end up in prison, insane, on the streets, addicted, or dead.

The effects of physical and emotional trauma on choices between birth and abortion appear in each of the stories that follow. All of these injured and abused women had to decide about at least one pregnancy, and none was truly capable of a sound, healthy decision. Their traumatic, disordered lives raise to an anguished pitch the questions at the heart of this book and the abortion debate—questions of responsibility, care, and the value we assign to human beings and human life. Inseparable from these is the question of power.

Hannah Milevsky

Hannah Milevsky is a beautiful woman of forty-one, with smooth skin, light brown hair, a broad mouth, and high, Slavic cheekbones. She dresses with both simplicity and flair. Her carriage is erect and graceful. It is not until she begins to speak in a deeply personal way that her fragility and pain become apparent. They are her reality, and they have been with her since she was three or four years old. Her confidence, though tentative, is what is new. It wavered several times as she talked with us. Her hands shook as she lit her infrequent cigarettes. Her voice cracked. We sat outside on a summer night, and as the soft light of sunset gave way to darkness, the glare from her kitchen window lit her face and showed the strain of her narrative.

Hannah was born in Philadelphia in 1951 and adopted by a couple who owned a prosperous dry-cleaning business there. She was their only child. Her adoptive father was well known and well liked throughout the city, an affable man who was plugged into broad political and commercial networks through his membership in a fraternal lodge. Her mother was quiet and hardworking. She kept the books for the family business. Both parents came from large families, and Hannah grew up near numerous aunts, uncles, and cousins. Outwardly, her childhood seemed ideal. She lived on a neat, tree-lined, middle-class street and spent her weekends surrounded by an extended family.

At night, however, her mother slept in a twin bed pushed up against Hannah's in the only effort she made to protect her daughter from her husband. It didn't always work. Hannah's first clear memory of abuse is of a night when she was five and her mother had gone on a trip. "This was the first time as a child that I could sleep alone, in my own space, and I wasn't frightened that she left. I remember very distinctly being able to stretch my arms and my legs out without running into another body." Hannah was relishing her space and privacy when her father came in. "Are you all right?" he asked her. "I don't want you to be frightened. You may have a bad dream." She assured him that she was fine, and he left.

Then, said Hannah, "in the middle of the night he came back into the room . . . and I remember him coming in and putting his arms around me. I was half-asleep and I was wondering, you know—what? what? And I woke up and saw Daddy in the bed. I didn't think anything of it, and then he started pulling me. I moved over more on my side so I wouldn't be in the crack between the beds. And he kept pulling me over, pulling me over, and I could feel this incredible—I mean, I felt like I was suffocating. . . . There was a small night-light on and I can remember the striped PJ's and I remember him burying my face [near] his head and then pushing me down further to where his penis was and—this is from the child point of view—there was this thing sticking up. I had no notion what it was, and it scared me. It scared me that I couldn't let go, I couldn't get away from him. And I remember there seemed to be this real fuzzy light in the room and I remember feeling pain, but the visual pictures of what was going on stop there. There are no visual pictures but terrific pain. It was as if somehow my soul had just come out of my body and gone up into this light, and I wasn't there, I was in pieces. I felt like I was in total pieces."

Hannah's rape by her father, on that and several other occasions, lay buried in her mind until she was thirty years old. Her father initiated her forgetfulness himself. The morning after this incident, Hannah woke up alone. Soon, however, her father reentered her room full of solicitous concern. "He said to me, 'You had such a bad dream last night.' " Hannah was scornful and anguished at the memory. She was appalled at "how insidious that situation was. . . . This was a dream, this wasn't real, this never happened. . . . My father would set it up in a very, very clever fashion that denied reality, denied [me] any kind of credence." Even her own pain and blood were not enough to refute him in her mind. She was a small child. He was her father. She was in the habit of believing him.

Hannah still has only spotty memories of the early years of sexual abuse, but she infers from times when she was "too swollen and bruised" to walk that it began when she was only three or four years old. Yet even when she recalled nothing of the rapes, she knew that her father, behind his amiable public persona, was a violent, angry man. Her memories of being beaten up were vivid because the beatings continued well into her teens and "because they were very violent," whereas the rapes had stopped when she started first grade. "I was a very verbal kid," she explained. "I think he was afraid that I might just casually say, 'This is what goes on at our house.' "

This was the first of many times that Hannah was rescued by language, by a voice that she herself did not realize she had. But the rescue was incomplete. She was spared the degradation of sexual abuse only to suffer repeated beatings. And the one time she used her voice to call for help, no one listened.

When Hannah was fourteen, on a night when her father had blackened her eyes and raised welts on her back, she was frightened enough to call the police but unaware that many of them were her father's friends. "They came to the house," said Hannah, "and they basically said that I had self-inflicted [my wounds] in order to get back at my father. And when I stripped my back to show them that there were areas of my body [I could not have reached]—which embarrassed them and embarrassed me no end—they said I was a liar and left. And once that door was closed I nearly got killed. . . . I mean, he had my head in the tub, under water, he beat me and nearly drowned me in my own bathtub."

When we asked where her mother was on this occasion, and on others, Hannah explained: "My mother couldn't cope. My mother wasn't a viable source of anything—of nurture, of protection. I mean, she was just as abusive in other ways as my father was physically and sexually. So . . . there was really nothing there, and outside resources just weren't forthcoming at that time. No one wanted to deal with a white, middle-class family. I mean, this didn't go on."

What Hannah meant by her mother's abusiveness was that her mother would pour out stories of sexual attacks she herself had suffered as a child. She had no sense of what was and was not appropriate to tell a young child, and she frightened Hannah badly with her tales and her acute, lingering fears. She rarely ventured outside the house, and she urged Hannah to stay in as well. She never admitted—to herself or to Hannah—that the dangers at home were worse than those outside. Through her cowed silence brought about by her own victimization, she was complicit with her husband and his cronies among the police.

Since no one would listen, Hannah also fell silent, but she found a more subtle, indirect way to comfort herself through language. Hannah clung to the words of others. "I was always a reader," she said. "That was something that kept me attached to the world. I would go over to Temple [University] and I would pick up syllabuses and go to the library and get the books and read them. I would attend class."

Hannah was seventeen when she started pirating an education from Temple. She was supposed to be in high school but scarcely ever went. Because of an undiagnosed learning disability, she said, "They just assumed that I was pretty stupid, so they stuck me in all these really idiot classes and I was bored out of my mind." Between her boredom and her unwillingness to be seen by friends at school with the frequent marks of beatings on her face and arms, Hannah missed a total of 102 school days her senior year. For what seems a weak reason—that her family had an unlisted telephone number—the school authorities never investigated until she had been absent for two or three months. In the meantime, Hannah said, "I was having a great time at Temple, sneaking into classes, talking to people. It was stimulating, because the people were a lot older."

Hannah never returned to high school. She continued to attend lectures at Temple, and it was there that she met Jonathan, a graduate student in comparative literature. "I became involved with Jonathan and was convinced that I was going to live happily ever after because his vocabulary was better than mine," Hannah said wryly. "The two of us would go to movies and read books, and we'd talk and this wonderful, intellectual—for the first time I had someone I could talk to. In my family, women were supposed to get married, have children, live two blocks away from your familiar home. You know, my father was very resentful of the fact that I read a lot. That really bothered him. . . . I used large words that he didn't understand."

Hannah's forays into the stimulating world at Temple were her first steps toward a final separation from her extended, adoptive family. All along—from the age of eleven or twelve, Hannah said—she had felt "very strongly" that she was a misfit in the family. She daydreamed about her biological parents, imagining "that there was someone out there that liked to read books, that didn't mind big words, that could understand me." Years later, the comforting daydreams turned bitter. "I felt like I had been dumped, you know. Not only did my biological parents not want me, but I ended up getting handed over to these crazy people who abused me. And it seemed that I had no birthing . . . I just had no parents. I was so orphaned and isolated from the rest of the world."

Hannah was drawn to Temple in her hunger for ideas and for a connection to the world from which she felt cut off. She was living less often at home, spending many of her nights at girlfriends' houses, becoming to some extent, she said, "like a street person." She was drawn to Jonathan in her orphan's loneliness, regarding him as the tender parent she had never had, the long-lost "someone . . . that liked to read books."

"I was seventeen," she recalled. "I was very precocious. I knew words, I knew literature, I knew how to dress. But it was like putting on your mother's high-heel shoes and makeup and playing adult." Nevertheless, Hannah became sexually as well as intellectually involved with Jonathan, ignoring for a time the inner voice that warned her something was not quite right.

"I was acting a lot older than I was, and there was that part of [me] saying 'Wait a minute, you're just a kid, this is not what you're supposed to be doing—not at this point'. . . . And there were times when Jonathan was very solemn and the sexual relationship was very, very frightening to me and not a very pleasant experience." In retrospect, Hannah knew she was disturbed not just by sex itself but by the kind of sex she had with Jonathan. "I think he used me, basically. There was no real connection between us . . . I mean, he probably [had] no sense of a person present." Hannah said she felt like an object with Jonathan, but again, looking back, she was not surprised by that. It was what she had been with her father, although at the time she was sleeping with Jonathan she had no conscious memory of her father's attacks.

Though her need for respect and intellectual nourishment blinded Hannah to the unsatisfying and demeaning aspects of her relationship with Jonathan, she said, "the gut, the body knows [what] the heart and the mind can't process." Before her body could inform her mind about what was happening to her, Hannah, just eighteen years old, became pregnant.

Hannah had been using a diaphragm regularly, but, she said, "no one had bothered to tell me that if there was a weight gain or weight loss that would affect the fitting." Because she so seldom lived at home by then, Hannah said:

"I was very poor. I was working as a waitress, I didn't have that much money, so I wasn't eating that well. I lost a hell of a lot of weight, and it doesn't take long for the fitting to get disrupted by that. And [so I found] myself pregnant and I didn't know what I was going to do. I had no idea."

Hannah could not tell her parents at first. Her relationship with them had, if anything, deteriorated over the past year. "If I would come home even five minutes late I would get beaten. I mean, it was at the drop of a hat. A couple of times my father just made me sleep in the vestibule; he wouldn't let me in the house. So I would stay at friends or at Jonathan's. Finally, I just got to the point where I was . . . living a nomadic existence." Hannah's father, moreover, had met Jonathan and hated him—he used "even bigger words" than Hannah did. When Hannah finally did tell her father about her pregnancy, he became violent. "He gave me a few good smacks," she recalled.

When Hannah told Jonathan she was pregnant, he made it clear that he did not want the baby. In fact, his treatment of Hannah changed abruptly and soon bitterly paralleled her father's. Though he had had no qualms about sleeping with her even though she was still a teenager, he turned abusive as soon as sex had consequences. At first, the abuse took the form of humiliating verbal attacks. "He would put me down a great deal in front of his friends. . . . Whatever I had to say was stupid, was infantile. All of a sudden, the whole thing reversed," said Hannah. Jonathan's hostility called deeply into question the sincerity of his earlier show of respect and his long, intellectual talks with Hannah. Had he only wanted to seduce her from the beginning?

Although Hannah feared that a child "born out of this grief was going to be like one gigantic teardrop," she also felt "an incredible, marvelous feeling." The conflict was sharply painful for her, but she was finally swayed by her circumstances. "When you've lived on the streets," she said, "you have to look at pragmatics. You have to say, 'Wait a minute, how do I support myself and my child, at this age, with no formal education and no skills?'" Hannah reluctantly decided on an abortion, but it was 1969 and she had no idea how to obtain one. Jonathan tapped halfheartedly into his network of friends for the names of cooperative physicians, but Hannah was frightened of "back-alley stuff." She knew that in Pennsylvania a woman could obtain a hospital abortion on the recommendation of two psychiatrists, but she did not realize that she needed a referral to reliable sympathizers. Instead of calling Planned Parenthood or another likely source, she called a psychiatric hospital. There, although Hannah was living a rootless life, was only eighteen, had been beaten by her father for years, and had no husband or means of support, she saw two male psychiatrists who thought she was "absolutely a paradigm of sanity. They wouldn't give me the abortion."

Fortunately for Hannah, who now had no choice but to continue her pregnancy, the first true friend of her life soon appeared with the support that made that possible. Her name was Elizabeth, and she was Jonathan's mother. "Elizabeth came in from Chicago, and she was wonderful. She sat down [and] she said, 'What do you want?' She said, 'You know, my son is an adult, I love him very much, but I don't agree with him on this. As a person, I don't know if I like him right now. I don't like what he is doing, I don't like how he's handled this.' She said, 'I know you're very much alone.'"

Hannah described the importance of her encounters with this woman for whom she felt great affection. "Elizabeth was my first role model," she said. "She was successful. She was attractive, bright, competent. My father hated her." Laughing, she said: "He was scared to death. This is exactly what he did not ever want me to become. She would handle him with so much ease, put him down when he was acting like an ass. I had never seen anyone put my father down, socially—any female tell my father to get stuffed. It was a revelation. You know, this man had so much power."

By this time, Hannah was in her fourth month of pregnancy, and she said to Jonathan: "Look, you do what you need to do. I would prefer you doing it with us, but if that's not what you want, then you go ahead and leave, because I don't need this." At about the same time, Elizabeth invited Hannah to come live with her in Chicago until the baby was born. She gave Hannah money and unconditional emotional support. Jonathan was threatened enough by Hannah and Elizabeth's relationship to agree to marry Hannah, and so she stayed with him in Philadelphia.

"I ended up marrying him, basically, so the child would be legitimate," Hannah said. "I mean, for all the craziness in the sixties and seventies, I was still a rock-bottom, middle-class conservative. Don't have a baby without a father. This is what you're supposed to do, even if the father is miserable to you."

Jonathan *was* miserable to Hannah, both during and after her pregnancy. The only change in his behavior came when their son Nathaniel was born. "Jonathan took a look at this child and was absolutely enthralled—after all those nine months being just an absolute miserable monster to live with. When Nathaniel was born he just fell in love with him."

Hannah, however, shouldered most of the responsibility for Nathaniel. Jonathan was still in school, doing poorly but demanding silence and cooperation. "I was trying to keep things quiet and make sure he had time to study,"

Hannah said. "It was Nathaniel he was focused on. After the baby was born it was as if I had just been this wonderful vessel, and then I was the empty vessel. I was just . . . the person that took care of his son, took care of the home."

Before Nathaniel was one year old, Hannah and Jonathan split up. During that time, she met and began spending time with a group of women who had formed a feminist collective. Those with children spelled each other, taking turns watching their offspring. Through them, Hannah grew more painfully aware than ever of how little care and love she had received from any source. Though she continued to escape to the library, she came to realize that the benefits of friendships and intellectual challenge were too thoroughly undermined by her misery at home. She became active in early efforts to establish shelters for abused and battered women, and she learned enough from that work to resist Jonathan when his abuse turned physical. By then, she had friends she could rely on for help.

"Jonathan started beating me, and that's when I said 'I've had it.' I just looked at him and said, 'Listen, my father did this; he was a professional. You're a rank amateur. I'm not dealing with this any more from you or from him, and I'm leaving.'" But despite her strong words, Hannah waited. "I was afraid," she explained. "I was terrified." She could not talk to Jonathan. "I said, 'Why are you doing this?' My friends were saying: 'Why do you put up with this crap? This is ridiculous. Listen to how he talks to you in front of other people.' I found myself dealing with the same situation that my mother dealt with. I didn't have the education; I didn't have the means. It goes back again to social systems. [Help] is just not forthcoming."

Hannah held social institutions in deep mistrust. She had been betrayed or overlooked by the police, by her school, by the psychiatric community, and by the bedrock institutions of marriage and family. She did not know how to connect with sources of help; she did not even believe they existed. She was ashamed to approach anyone. She felt, she said, "like a person who's illiterate. You're so embarrassed and so ashamed of yourself that you haven't done something better in your life." Once again, she was rescued by a few caring individuals.

On a night when Jonathan grew vicious in front of friends and Hannah drew from them the courage to stand up to him, he reacted violently. "I said, 'Look, just knock it off, I don't want to hear this any more,' and he smashed me and I went right across the room." One of the men present stepped in, got Jonathan out of the house, and urged Hannah to keep him out. She did, and soon afterward they divorced. Elizabeth, horrified by her son's behavior, again sent both money and validation. There was enough of each to keep Hannah going.

Hannah was not yet twenty when she left Jonathan. With help, she had been strong enough to break away, but she did not have the confidence to pursue the credentials or career that would free her from her dependency on others. She worked here and there at low-skill jobs, she dabbled in the arts, she volunteered at the women's shelter, but she did not find the satisfaction she dreamed of and she feared setting challenges for herself. Within a year or so of her divorce she met another man, George, who fell in love with her and with her son. George was everything Jonathan was not—respectful, loving, affirming. He waited patiently for Hannah to overcome her mistrust of men and marriage. Finally, she agreed to marry him, and they have been together ever since.

During her eighteen years with George, Hannah has borne another son, taken some college courses, and undergone extensive psychotherapy. It was not until she found a counselor who had also suffered childhood sexual abuse that she was finally able to recall being raped by her father. That was just the beginning of a long recovery that is still in progress. At first she could not absorb the memories that assailed her. She could feel no anger; she wanted George to feel it for her. She could not credit her own perceptions. "I never validated my experience until I told a friend of mine, a very good childhood friend, who told me that my father had tried to rape her, too. I was sitting there talking to her one evening and I said, 'You know, maybe I made this up.' And she came over and started shaking me and crying and she said: 'You know, I've never told you this, but I've got to tell you [now]. Your father was really sick; listen to what happened.' And all of a sudden I realized, my God, I'm still protecting him. I mean, I would rather make myself into some sort of pathological, crazy liar who doubted her own sanity than to really say: 'Look, this guy did this to me. This is my father, and this is what he did.'"

Hannah, whose progress from victim to survivor has been slow and painful, reflected at length on the losses her father had inflicted. She has never loved herself; she has lived her life in fear. She began to redeem the losses with the onset of her first memories ten years ago. Now she is starting again, resuming therapy in an attempt to integrate her intellectual understanding of what happened to her with her emotional reactions to it, which she has never before allowed herself to experience fully. "I've survived," she said. "But you get so enormously tired of just surviving, and I think that the next step has to be a real understanding of what feeling is and what it isn't." To Hannah, and to a great many incest and abuse survivors, that step means reviving and nurturing the child who was so severely harmed. It involves an imaginative and terribly painful exercise in reparenting, an emotional journey into the past whose purpose is to cradle and comfort the child-self who was left abandoned.

This process of reintegrating all the parts of herself is one Hannah believes will take four or five more years. By the time she is forty-five or so, she thinks she may be able to meet challenges with assurance and make full use of the gifts she has in abundance. "I think what happens when you don't take responsibility for those gifts [is that] they kill you. They turn inside and they kill you." The fact that Hannah can see that she *has* gifts may be the biggest gift of all. It is the one thing that has sustained her since she was old enough to read.

In the Absence of Care

Hannah Milevsky's story personalizes the alarming set of statistics with which this chapter opened—the figures on childhood sexual abuse that were uncovered by research and attested to by therapists who work with the victims. As other stories in this book suggest, women abused during childhood may be especially susceptible to unplanned pregnancies, largely because of feelings of worthlessness that prevent the assertive and careful use of birth control or that lead to ill-advised sexual relationships. As we mentioned in the last chapter, studies have in fact shown a link between teenage pregnancy and childhood sexual abuse.

Once a person who has been damaged by child abuse becomes pregnant, how does she decide what to do? According to private therapist Deanna Nilsson, who specializes in the treatment of abused and/or addicted women in the Pittsburgh area, such women "don't feel a sense of power, and usually somebody else makes the decisions about what happens to their bodies— whoever happens to be the most influential in their life at the time. I've never yet met someone who grew up in a dysfunctional family or who has been abused . . . who didn't just feel like scum."

Victimized women who never find help often react to such feelings by forming other abusive relationships and by turning their despair inward in the form of depression or self-destructive behavior. In Hannah's case, poor self-esteem strongly affected the course of her pregnancy. She wanted an abortion because she was afraid and uninformed about options and opportunities. She failed to obtain one for the same reasons. But she was blessed when Elizabeth came along, not only because the older woman rescued Hannah financially but because she respected her and provided her first glimpse of what competent adulthood could look like for a woman. The question in Hannah's case is why no one came to her aid sooner—why the schools, police, and other authorities failed to see or believe her desperation.

Hannah's story is a dramatic example of the immense harm that follows from a virtual absence of caretaking. Her parents not only failed to protect or love her, they tormented her. Institutions and public services offered no relief. Schools and teachers dismissed her as unintelligent. Finally, her choice of a lover who would turn violent seemed almost inevitable.

The next story, about a mother and daughter, also describes an absence of parental caretaking, but in this case the daughter assumed the nurturing role within the family at great cost to her own development. She carried the effects of familial dysfunction into her adulthood, where she finally found the friends and resources she needed to stop the cycle of harm. Her account demonstrates the extent to which one generation's despair—which in this story surfaces most powerfully in an incident involving abortion—can envelop the next, and even the next, unless it finds an antidote in strong human bonds.

Gwen and Sheila Crawford

Abuse and dysfunction had dogged Gwen Crawford's Michigan family at least since her grandparents' time. She herself was never physically or sexually harmed by her parents, but the effects of their alcohol and drug addictions left her with emotional wounds that took twenty-five years to heal.

Gwen's mother, Sheila, suffered even more. She committed suicide in 1975, and Gwen has been left with just enough perspective and compassion to try to piece together her mother's story. Gwen is forty-one—the same age as Hannah—and is a small, soft-spoken woman with a warmth and serenity that have come to her only in recent years. She now lives in a modest Grand Rapids neighborhood, across the state from Flint, where she grew up. She began by speaking to us about a single garish event in her childhood that at the time was laden with fear, anger, sorrow, and far too much responsibility for a ten-year-old to shoulder. Gwen's whole life with her parents was characterized by these qualities, but on this occasion they reached a crescendo.

"It was a summer evening," Gwen recalled, "and my father was out drinking and my brother and I were sitting in the living room watching television. My mother was out of the room for probably forty-five minutes to an hour, and she called me—she left the bathroom and went into her bedroom and she called me in. She asked me if I would go in and clean up the bathroom. She said, 'There's a little bit of blood, I'd like you to clean it up.' And, oh, she did tell me at that time that she was pregnant and that she had lost a baby."

Gwen had long since developed habits of quiet obedience and caretaking. "At ten I was about thirty," she said ruefully. But she was not prepared for the sight that awaited her that night. Sheila had greatly understated what her daughter would find. "I went into the bathroom and there was blood on the floor, blood in the bathtub, blood in the toilet," Gwen said with a shudder. "And I immediately began cleaning it up, and when I got to the commode that's when I really realized what was happening. I looked in the commode and it was full of blood, but inside was a fetus. It was about five, maybe six inches long, and it looked like a baby. . . . I do remember at that point trying to make the decision, what do I do, do I bury this baby or do I flush the commode? And the decision I made was to flush, flush the commode. There was no adult around, and I did that, and after I did that—that was a hard decision to make—I finished cleaning and then went in to talk with her, and by that time she had passed out. She lost an awful lot of blood, but I didn't—ten years old—I didn't realize that she had gone into shock, so I just covered her up and waited for my father to return. . . . He put her in the car and took her to the hospital."

Sheila survived what Gwen later figured out, from overheard bits of conversation, had been a botched, self-induced abortion performed with a coat hanger. At the time, she never questioned the grisly task her mother had assigned to her. She was not aware of how inappropriate such a chore was for a ten-year-old child. It was not until months later, when a horrified neighbor asked Sheila why she had allowed "a little kid" to clean up all that blood, that, she said, "it finally touched me that, yes, this was really an awful thing for a ten-year-old to do."

Gwen's behavior was typical for a child—especially an oldest child—of addicts. Such children tend to become their parents' caretakers and confidants. They hold themselves accountable for everyone's mood, for running the household, and for keeping the family together. They protect their younger siblings, as Gwen did that night by keeping her younger brother out of the bathroom. They unquestioningly assume tasks and responsibilities that are far beyond their capacities. Gwen, for example, was haunted for many years by her decision to flush that aborted fetus away. But at the time, she said: "I don't think it would even have occurred to me to ask my mother what to do. I was very used to making decisions and handling things for myself."

Keeping her own emotions tightly under wraps, Gwen was in no condition to see how desperate and hopeless her mother was. Looking back, she has fitted into place many of the pieces that escaped her notice then. The abortion, she now believes, was only one part of a large, bleak picture.

Sheila had come from an unhappy and destructive family. Her father was an alcoholic, and her parents divorced before she reached her teens. Gwen recalls that there were intimations of incest in her mother's family. She thinks her mother's oldest sister was sexually abused by the alcoholic father. Casting about for the source of her impression, she said: "I probably heard that from my mother, because we had very little contact with her family. I think it was just before my grandfather died, and everyone came to see him except his oldest daughter."

Gwen cannot confirm that there was sexual abuse in her mother's family, but Deanna Nilsson, the private-practice counselor we spoke with who treats addiction in women, drew a tight thread between the incidence of abuse and the many forms of compulsion that people suffer—including alcoholism, drug dependencies, eating disorders, and gambling. Nilsson told us that when she had worked exclusively with women who were addicted to drugs or alcohol, "it was appearing to me, though I haven't kept a really [complete] statistical study, that four out of five of the women I was seeing had been sexually abused." She informally substantiated her impression with an account of some colleagues' experiences. Three other counselors she knew who had different therapeutic specialties had seen the same pattern that Nilsson had. "Marsha started out with a specialization in eating disorders," she said, counting her friends off on her fingers. "Susan and I started out . . . working with addiction. Joanie started out with a specialization in family problems. . . . Why is it that we've all come to the same point?"

The "point" was one at which the four therapists' clients were all dealing with the same issues—"the issues of trust, the issues of boundaries, the issues of who gets to have some power, the issues of how close can be all right," Nilsson said. These are the problems that haunt the victims of abuse. They are also the ones that appear both in Gwen's brief account of her mother's life and in her description of her own recovery from childhood trauma.

Sheila, a high school dropout, had married young and on the rebound in an effort to escape her family. She was eighteen years old. By nineteen she had given birth to Gwen; by twenty-two she had had Gwen's brother. The marriage was unhappy, and the children were, said Gwen, "clearly a bother." Even as a young child, Gwen understood that her mother had never wanted children at all. It was her father, Gus, who had insisted on having a family, probably because he was the youngest of seven brothers and saw fatherhood as "a badge of manhood." Forcing pregnancy on Sheila may have further confirmed Gus's virility, for Gwen recalled that "my mother accused my father of raping her . . . getting drunk and raping her. I don't know if . . . pregnancy was a result of that or not. But children were not by choice." Sheila herself admitted all this to Gwen, not in a punishing way but in an informative one, as if she were confiding in a peer.

The fact that Gwen was her mother's adviser and caretaker from a very early age may have been why Sheila found it so easy to ask her to clean up the shambles in the bathroom. She might not have thought of her small daughter as "a little kid." In any case, Sheila was by that time deeply depressed, addicted to prescription drugs, and empty of hope. She had no way out of her bleak marriage. From time to time she made timid forays into the outside world, but she always retreated again. "She worked occasionally as a clerk or a cleaning lady," said Gwen. "But she couldn't earn her own living. She wanted to leave my father, but she couldn't. Once, she went to live with her mother but hated her too much to stay. . . . I think children were a trap. I believe that she felt that if she didn't have us she could get herself out of the situation."

Sheila's desperation was not apparent to outsiders. She was able to function—which meant keeping up the appearances that were so important in the late 1950s—even during the long unraveling that began the year of her abortion. "She worked very hard to at least present the Ozzie and Harriet–type family," Gwen said. "She was obsessive about cleaning, obsessive about ironing, about all [those] things."

Soon after the abortion, however, Sheila made her first attempt at suicide. She was twenty-nine. By then, Gwen said, Gus's drinking had become public knowledge. He drank every night until he passed out. Despite her mother's accusations of rape, Gwen never saw him become violent. Soon after the abortion, Sheila stopped hiding the facts of her life, though Gwen said she still, "until the day she died," kept her house and yard immaculate.

By the time Sheila died at forty-three she had long been addicted to Valium and other prescription drugs. Her psychiatrist had given her an unlimited prescription, and so the means for suicide was close at hand when she finally gave up. Gwen held the psychiatrist directly responsible, and her anger was validated by Deanna Nilsson, who explained: "There is a tremendous amount of addiction with women . . . where doctors give benzodiazepines—librium, valium, dalmane—all of which are very addictive and are favorites for doctors to use for women particularly. . . . I think that doctors see women as complainers, and they need to fix them and make them be quiet. I think that it's far more that way because a woman patient is more likely [than a man] to say, 'I can't sleep, I'm nervous, I'm anxious, I'm depressed.' "

When Sheila obliterated her symptoms by downing a handful of the pills she had saved, "she had a medicine chest full of drugs," Gwen said bitterly. "Most bottles had her psychiatrist's name on them. At the very least, he should have known that a woman with her history of depression should not have been given an unlimited supply of dangerous drugs."

Except for Gwen's residual anger at Sheila's doctor, most of her grief and bitterness have healed or dissipated. The healing took a long time, but even as a young woman, Gwen took a different path than Sheila did. Though she, too, married young, she did wait until she had finished college. She never wanted to be caught, like her mother, in a trap from which she could not devise her own escape. She feared the helplessness and lack of choices she had seen at the root of her mother's despair, and she admitted to some fears and doubts about motherhood.

Yet Gwen also knew she wanted children, partly, she said, "to create a whole new family." An eight-year struggle with infertility was painful for her, and she rejoices today in the son she and her husband were finally able to have. He is eleven now, and he was born when Gwen was twenty-nine, the age at which her mother aborted. Gwen sensed, strongly and intuitively, a connection between that event and the trouble she had conceiving. "I can't say for sure, but I do believe that scene in the bathroom had such an impact on me that it affected my fertility. I had a lot of ambivalence about having children." About six years after her son was born, Gwen and her husband tried for a second child with no success.

At about the same time that she gave up her second attempt at pregnancy, Gwen was also able to make peace with her past, her mother, and the sadness she had lived with most of her life. "What broke the cycle for me," she said, "was joining a church that is also a community of people. When I walked in, people recognized that I had been wounded. I was surrounded by people who gave their time and energy to me. Through that, I have models of parenthood. I have been parented." When we asked what the stigmata were that made her condition obvious, Gwen said: "I was very, very controlled. There was no spontaneity in my physical being. I was giving a clear message to people to keep their distance. I was good at doing, but not at being. When people tried to get past the barriers I had erected, I was very frightened."

Gradually, a few insightful members of her new church established themselves as trustworthy, and Gwen began to answer their shared confidences with a few of her own. It was through this sense of trust and community that she was finally able to deal fully with the pain of her childhood, particularly with the image of the bloody bathroom and the fetus in the toilet. Her reaction was both physical and entirely spontaneous: she vomited.

"I was angry at my mother for putting me in that situation," Gwen said. "But I was concerned for her as well, and I grieved the death of that brother or sister." As a result of her early experience and her adult religious beliefs, Gwen now feels abortion is "morally wrong." At the same time, she said: "I do think that society does very little to support women who are in my mother's place. I would like to say that I'd like to see abortion be illegal, but at the same time I would like to see more support from the state. . . . It's a hard question." Asked which she would like to see first, Gwen thought for a long moment, clearly struggling for a conscientious reply. Finally she said: "Ideally, I would like to see them happen simultaneously. But if I had to choose, I would like to see more social supports in place first."

Silence and Codependency

Gwen Crawford's mother was, in Gwen's own words, "a typical codependent." Codependency, as it is defined by recovery and support groups for addicts and their families, coincides almost exactly with the defining characteristics that Mary Belenky *et al.* give for silent women. Codependent women have no voice and no powers of agency in their own behalf, they rely on others for their identity and direction, and they cannot define themselves. Thus Sheila, according to Gwen, was "a martyr" who decided that "what she did for other people— she would use that to tie them to her." Suicide was her ultimate act of martyrdom, just one of many ways in which an injured and self-injuring person might try to validate himself or herself through his or her impact on others. Sadly, the ultimate effect is to open the wounds further, until they spread outward like a toxic stain.

The following story in particular drives home the message that the harms people do, to themselves and to others, are self-perpetuating. In D'Anita Corbett's life the causes and effects of harm have become almost interchangeable. It is hard to say where the cycle of harm began for her. To many people, women like D'Anita would be objects of contempt, vilification, or scorn. To those who treat and counsel them, they cause heartbreak.

D'Anita Corbett

When we spoke with D'Anita in the dead of winter in 1990, she was homeless, pregnant, and probably addicted to crack cocaine, yet she was still full of expectations—expectations that had little hope of fulfillment. We met with her in a shelter for homeless women in Pittsburgh. The interview was arranged by the two women who managed the facility, after we talked to them at length about the population of women they served. We call these two social workers by the names Alicia Tanner and Rachel Cunningham because using their real names might reveal D'Anita's true identity.

Tanner and Cunningham explained that D'Anita was not one of their residents, since they were allowed to give bed space only to the mentally ill. Though she spent many of her days in the shelter, she had to sleep wherever she could at night.

Tanner and Cunningham believed D'Anita had become pregnant partly to gain attention from her boyfriend, but D'Anita's own account contradicted their belief. The counselors also told us that D'Anita had virtually no motivation to stay off crack during her pregnancy, whereas D'Anita said she had been clean since before she got pregnant and that her children—a five-year-old and the baby yet to be born—were her source of strength. It is impossible to say for sure whether D'Anita's account was false, only that, despite her apparent openness with us, she had a childlike air of mixed insecurity, fantasy, and bravado that weakened her credibility, especially when it was measured against the experienced, hard-to-fool Tanner and Cunningham.

D'Anita was a pencil-thin, light-skinned black woman of twenty-six, with sandy hair and freckles as fine as grains of sugar. Her seven-month pregnancy was tight and round beneath her loose cardigan sweater. Her French braids descended from a perfect part and were tied at the ends with purple ribbons. She was shy and made little eye contact, but she answered our questions clearly and without elaboration. Throughout our interview, she twirled a small, heart-shaped balloon on a wooden stem. It was blue and pink and said "LUV" in silver letters.

Because D'Anita seemed fragile, and because Tanner and Cunningham had warned us not to probe, we proceeded cautiously. The information she gave us was threadbare in places, and by the time we tried to follow up, hoping to fill in the thin spots, no one knew where D'Anita could be found. So her story is sketchy, with more hints than details in some of its parts. But it is also a compelling commentary on street life and on the forms of victimization that compound poverty and addiction.

D'Anita came from Roxbury, Boston's black ghetto. She was the only child of Rose Corbett, a single mother who bore her at age twenty. Although D'Anita knew her father and spent weekends with him as a child, she was reluctant to talk about him. What she did say was: "He's what you call a rolling stone. He's here, he's there. Every time he came to get me he was with a different woman, or he would take me to different women's houses, and I didn't want to go. I mean, he would come get me, buy me this, buy me that, but he was more with them than he was with me." When D'Anita was eight years old, her father moved to Baltimore, and she seldom saw him after that. Meanwhile, though she and Rose had a prickly relationship, D'Anita never doubted her mother's dedication. Rose worked as a medical transcriber and supported them both on her modest wages, even during an eight-year relationship with a live-in boyfriend. D'Anita's environment apparently was stable, despite the lack of a father, and she finished high school and a course in business.

But D'Anita's life at home was not entirely smooth. She got pregnant at sixteen, when she was in love with a boy named Paulie. "The first time I had sex was with him, and really, that's all he wanted. And then he was gone and I was pregnant." She hid her condition for four months, she said. "I didn't want my mother to know. I thought [she] was going to put me away in a home. I was like, 'I can't tell her, I can't tell her.' "

Finally, D'Anita confided in a cousin, who went with her for a pregnancy test. When it confirmed what D'Anita already knew, the girls went to Rose, who rallied from her initial shock and immediately became businesslike. "She asked me did I want to have it, and I told her no. I really was a child myself, and I thought about going to parties and stuff like that. . . . And she made an appointment for me."

Although D'Anita's decision caused her no struggle at the time, the abortion itself was painfully carried out and left an influential impression. Because she was nearly five months pregnant, she had to enter the hospital for what was probably a saline-induced abortion. "I don't know what it was," she said. "All I know is that it was painful and hurted—it was just like havin' a baby. At the time I didn't know what havin' a baby was like—but to go through that and not have a kid! I just couldn't do that again."

D'Anita was twenty-one years old before she got pregnant a second time. She had a steady job as an office worker, a place of her own, and a boyfriend she referred to only as "Sweet." She had been using birth control pills in her relationship with Sweet, but she "missed some." When the consequence became clear, D'Anita said: "it wasn't a decision, like should I have this baby . . . I mean I wanted to. I was just happy about it. But I was older, I was more responsible."

Sweet ran around with a number of other women during D'Anita's pregnancy and he was lackadaisical about the birth of their son, Bradford. His mother refused to believe that Sweet was the father. D'Anita said, "She'd look at me all strange when I used to go over there." When D'Anita went into labor, Rose called Sweet's mother. "My mother said, 'Tell Sweet that Punkin's in the hospital.' His mother told my mother, 'He's asleep.' My mom cussed the hell out of her. She said: 'I don't give a fuck if he's asleep. Wake him up. Punkin's at the hospital having that baby!' So he came to the hospital looking all simple, and I hated him. I don't know if it was because I was in labor—I just looked at him and I just wanted to spit on him."

D'Anita and Sweet never married or lived together. Their relationship was over before Bradford was born, but Sweet did take his son on weekends, as D'Anita's father had done with her. Apparently, D'Anita went back to work. She said little about the first two years of Bradford's life, skipping ahead to the changes that cost her her job, apartment, stability, earning power, and child.

D'Anita could not explain those changes. Like most people who become addicts, she expected to taste, not to be eaten alive. "Nobody got me curious," she admitted about her introduction to crack. "I did it because I wanted to. I wanted to know what it was like. I mean, it was the thing, it was the high. . . . So I tried it, and I liked it."

After a few months of occasional use, D'Anita said: "It was like I had to get high every day. You can get it for five, ten, twenty dollars. However much I had, that's how much I spent. At the time, I thought that getting high was solving my problems." But D'Anita's problems were just beginning. To support her one-hundred-dollar-a-day habit, she resorted to shoplifting or selling drugs. "That wasn't me," she said about her behavior then. "I don't know who that was. It was a monster. My mother said, 'I don't know what happened to my daughter, but you ain't my daughter.' I was real hurt when she said it to me . . . but I look at the stuff I did . . . dirty stuff, just crazy. . . . "

D'Anita spent some time in jail, but it didn't dent her addiction. Eventually, she had to send Bradford away. "I told his dad to come and get him because I couldn't take care of him. I wasn't doing the things I used to, wasn't spending time with him." Crying softly, wiping her eyes with a flat palm, like a child, D'Anita murmured: "I don't like talking about this. I felt that me asking his father to come and get him was showing how much I did love him—how much I cared. I've seen people drag their kids through that kind of thing. I wasn't going to do that to my son."

Sweet had a secure job in construction, and D'Anita was no longer employed. When she was not scoring or smoking crack, she spent all her time with a new lover, an addict named Rafe. She said the two of them got fed up with drugs. Rafe's mother, who lived in Pittsburgh, was in poor health, and they got the idea of living with her, helping her out, and getting clean at the same time. So they left Roxbury and headed for Pittsburgh. D'Anita took Bradford with her despite her scorn for parents who "drag their kids" through a life run by drugs. She felt sure she and Rafe would kick their dependency.

Their plans soon faltered. D'Anita said they stayed off drugs for a couple of months, but then Rafe got into some trouble with the police in Pittsburgh. He fled to New York, and D'Anita and Bradford stayed on with his mother. Word soon came that Rafe was dead of an overdose, and within another month D'Anita was back on crack. "It was like I stopped caring," she said. "I didn't care, so I guess I used that as an excuse to go get high. I did it for a couple of months."

D'Anita took Bradford and her renewed addiction and left Rafe's mother's house. The older woman, in her grief, had become cold with D'Anita, perhaps holding her responsible for what had happened. "I stayed down at the Salvation Army," D'Anita recalled, "and my son, he didn't like it there, so I called my mom and asked my mom to come and get him, and he's been with my mom ever since." That was exactly a year before our interview, and D'Anita had not seen Bradford since. Her only contact with him was the telephone.

Knowing no one in Pittsburgh, unable to support herself or her drug habit, D'Anita floundered for another six months. She found work through a temporary personnel agency, and she moved from one shelter to another. Then she found a drug rehabilitation program that had a vacancy and she stayed there for six months. That was where she met the father of the child she was carrying. She told us little about him except that he wanted her to live with him and she refused. "I'm not staying with nobody," she said adamantly. "I'm not staying in his mother's house. I've had enough of staying at somebody's mother's. Everything's okay for a while and then they get tired of looking at you. . . . My mom always told me, don't live with no man unless . . . you don't have to worry about somebody putting you out on the street."

This declaration of independence contradicted Tanner and Cunningham's belief that D'Anita had become pregnant largely to tie her boyfriend more closely to her. Had he really asked her to move in with him? Would she really have refused a place to sleep on those cold nights? We did not feel we could ask, given our promise to Tanner and Cunningham that we would not press D'Anita for answers that might be too painful.

D'Anita's plans for her future also contradicted Tanner and Cunningham. D'Anita had visions of keeping her baby (something hardly any homeless women are able to do), having Bradford with her, going to nursing school, and moving into the idealized place-of-her-own. According to Tanner and Cunningham, it was all sadly unlikely. They saw D'Anita, along with many of the pregnant women they counseled, as delusional. "[They] think that they're going to have a house and a car and a job and everything is going to be peachy keen," Tanner said with a sigh. It was as if, through the ordinary act of having a child, homeless women could become like ordinary people; they could create not only a little family of two but a full-blown family life—an American dream. In reality, according to Tanner and Cunningham, homeless and addicted pregnant women have little motivation even to stay off drugs for their babies' sake. Their view was seconded by Anne Holzner, another therapist we interviewed who had worked in a Pittsburgh drug rehabilitation program for addicted pregnant women. Holzner regarded her clients as "the cream of the crop, the rare ones who were willing to cross from being constantly illegal, anonymous, and asocial to, in effect, joining the enemy—facing the authorities, becoming part of social services, committing to giving up drugs." For most pregnant addicts, especially the homeless ones, the hardship seldom seemed worth it, Cunningham said. These were women who had little real hope beneath their delusions. "It's kind of like an acquired taste," Cunningham said. "Your life has been terrible, it's always going to be terrible." In Tanner and Cunningham's experienced eyes, D'Anita did not have the determination to become straight.

By her own account, however, D'Anita had already been straight for eight or nine months. Whether or not this was true, her story was convincing. D'Anita told us she had gone into the rehabilitation program because she was frightened and that she had stayed because "I couldn't keep doing what I was doing. I wasn't doing nothing but going around in circles, that's all—some kind of whirlpool. I stayed there for six months. I haven't gotten high since." She admitted staying clean was not easy but said pregnancy and Bradford inspired her. "I don't know if I would [smoke crack] if I wasn't pregnant. I might and I might not. . . . I just think about my son, 'cause I don't know, if I didn't have my son, I don't know what I would do." She sounded passionate about a nursing career too, and said she planned to start her training that September. "I always wanted to be a nurse," she said. "I like people; I feel sorry for sick people. I watched my grandmother die in the hospital, and some of those nurses, they treated people like they was nothing—you know, those people were sick, dying, and it was like they didn't even care."

If D'Anita's story was false, it was probably less a deliberate lie than a poignant, compelling fantasy, a spinning out of a wish as if a wish could make it so. In fact, when we asked her for details of how she was going to accomplish all her plans—school, housing, a new baby, Bradford, income—in the near future, she could not say. "I don't know, like, when I'll get a place, and I don't know . . . I'm a little too far ahead. It just seems that every time I plan ahead, something happens."

In the meantime, whether she was straight or still hooked, D'Anita could do little but wait for her baby to be born. Without drugs, work, or friends, she told us she spent her days at the shelter, reading or doing crafts. "I read anything, anything that's interesting, just to keep me from being bored. I like trash! Like Jackie Collins, Danielle Steele. . . . I like spooky stuff, too, like Stephen King. Sometimes I go for walks; I'll just be thinking, walking." She also talked to Bradford on the phone, which usually made her cry. "We used to have fun," she said wistfully. "I used to take him everywhere with me. We used to talk and play games, have fun." Several times she said, like a mantra, "He loves his mommy, he always loves his mommy."

D'Anita said she was getting free prenatal care at Pittsburgh's Magee-Womens Hospital, and that she was going to deliver at a home for single mothers. She talked to us about her decision to proceed with this pregnancy, saying that when she went for pregnancy testing, the doctor asked her: "Do you want to have this baby, or do you want to give this baby up for adoption? I couldn't just see bringin' a child into the world and just giving it away. You know . . . you may as well have an abortion if you're going to do that. I just couldn't see myself doing that, even though I'm not in that great of a position right now as far as having my own place and stuff. But that's just temporary, 'til I have this baby."

Though D'Anita did briefly consider abortion, it was really no stronger an option than giving her baby up. It violated her sense of responsibility. She had not been using birth control when she became pregnant because she was having sex so infrequently during her stay at the rehabilitation center. In her mind, because she had not taken precautions she had to accept the consequences. "This is my opinion," she said. "That if a woman lays down in bed with a man, and ... don't have no contraceptive, there's a chance [she's] going to be pregnant. ... I just can't understand how you could say, 'Well, I'm not having this' when you knew, when you did what you did, that you might get pregnant." Had D'Anita gotten pregnant through a birth control failure, she said she probably would have aborted "because the whole purpose of taking the birth control is not to have children."

The Role of Pregnancy in Desperate Lives

Having a sense of responsibility was probably important to D'Anita precisely because she had no outward signs of it—no money, job, home, or child to care for. Being a victim—of addiction, poverty, and lost opportunity—D'Anita had to find some way to think of herself as a survivor. Having a baby was a way of filling the void at the center of her life. According to Alicia Tanner and Rachel Cunningham, D'Anita was rare even in thinking about abortion. "I've been in this business since 1984," Cunningham said. "You know what? I've never talked to a soul here who wanted to have an abortion." She estimated that 20 to 25 percent of the women she dealt with were pregnant. "Out of those, there's not one who considers abortion." She explained: "Homeless women ... are so deprived that they want [their babies]. ... Far better to be pregnant and have something, even for a short time, than to have nothing."

Pregnancy and childbirth, Cunningham continued, represented an achievement to women who otherwise had nothing. Having a baby was a way of "being like everybody else." It was worth doing even if they could not keep their babies afterwards, which was usually the case. "If you have a baby and you don't have a place to stay, obviously the welfare of the child is in jeopardy," Cunningham said. "The institutions will step in and say you can't keep the child." She did not address the question of alternatives that could be provided but are not—for example, why the authorities did not provide housing, child care, and other support instead of separating babies from their mothers.

Tanner told us that homeless women get pregnant for the same reasons more well-off women do. "Let's talk about it in terms of a continuum," she said. "About two-thirds of the women here get pregnant for the same reasons women get pregnant anywhere. Some of the reasons are healthy and some are not." Tanner also said that many of the women she described got pregnant for the same reasons many teenagers do—"intimacy, contact, somebody to love, inadequate information about birth control, all kinds of religious hang-ups about birth control."

But the other major reason homeless women became pregnant, Tanner said, was because they were raped. "A great majority" of women at the shelter were "victims of incest, sexual abuse, sexual assault. The abuse is pretty much a life process, starting early, with an uncle, a brother, a father, or a mother. . . . You know, we have a woman here who has had five children from rape, one of them by her father. She doesn't even remember the births of the children."

Cunningham nodded, adding: "There's a whole crowd of homeless men that prey on homeless women. There's a whole segment of homeless women that pimp off of homeless men in order to get a place to stay, because a place where you can stay with an abuser is better than the street, where you can get abused by everybody."

About the men on the streets, Tanner said, "I suspect that 75 percent of them were abused as kids as well." Such a background is harder to recognize in men, because, as Tanner confirmed, their tendency is to turn their pain outward and inflict it on others, whereas women are more likely to blame themselves, feel worthless, and become self-destructive. "Men end up in the criminal justice system," Tanner said. "Women end up in the psychiatric system. But if the criminal justice treatment system did its homework, they would find out that a significant number of their inmates have been physically and/or sexually abused as children." Citing figures from a number of recent studies, Cunningham added: "The statistics for childhood sexual assault for females used to be one in seven; now it's one in three or four. It used to be, with boys, one in ten, and it's now one in seven."

The amount of child abuse now being revealed by statistics such as these—statistics perhaps still too conservatively estimated—has overwhelming social consequences in Tanner and Cunningham's view. They claim that as many as 80 percent of the homeless women they work with have major mental disorders, and they believe that mental illness can commonly be traced to childhood sexual or physical abuse. Although they readily admit this is an impression and not a systematically documented finding, they nevertheless believe there is a desperate need among homeless women for enlightened therapy that takes seriously the likelihood of childhood abuse.

Unfortunately, Tanner and Cunningham feel very little real therapy is available. "The system has been very slow to keep up with [the statistics on abuse]," Tanner said. "What an abused person needs is three to five years of intensive therapy." What victims often get instead is medication to mask their emotional troubles. If the link between early abuse and later mental illness and criminality is as strong as many social workers and counselors believe, then the social cost of disregarding abuse is staggering: jails overflow, family violence and dysfunction invade more and more households, the ranks of addicts swell, the homeless multiply, and their babies are born into desperate circumstances, often with full-fledged addictions of their own. We do not do well by the victims of lifelong violence; nor, as the next two stories demonstrate, do we do much better by those in better circumstances, who are victimized only once or twice.

Kelly Walker

We interviewed twenty-six-year-old Kelly Walker in 1989 at her mother's home in Rochester, New York, where Kelly had been house-sitting for the weekend. It was a bungalow crowded with antiques, family memorabilia, and the casual clutter of daily life. It felt comfortable and safe—which is how Kelly described her mother.

It was Sunday night, and Kelly expected her mother home soon. In fact, Patricia Walker arrived just as we were leaving. Although we had been careful with Kelly, the interview had disturbed long-dormant feelings about a rape that had left her pregnant seven years earlier. We were relieved to see her mother return, for we had been feeling uneasy about leaving Kelly alone.

Our protective feelings toward Kelly were no doubt heightened by her appearance. Like many of the wounded women in this book, she seemed younger than she was—perhaps because of her evident vulnerability. Though it was June and warm, she was dressed from her neck to her feet in loose, black clothes—a long-sleeved rayon shirt and wide-legged pants. Her light-brown hair was long and wavy, her eyes hazel, her face pale and expressive, an accurate barometer of her emotions. When we were on safe ground with her, she was animated, and color came into her cheeks. When we moved cautiously into tougher subjects, she chewed the inside of her lip, lowered her eyes, and lost her spark.

Kelly had been a nineteen-year-old freshman at a major midwestern university when she became a classic victim of date rape. She disliked both her school and the town in which it was located. Most of the students, she said, "just cared about having a good time. Everyone was just partying and drinking—people my age and younger. There were so many bars downtown and not much else to do, you know."

It is possible that loneliness made Kelly more vulnerable to exploitation, but in fact the situation that led to her rape might not have seemed like a trap even to a more sophisticated young woman, especially not in the years before date rape was widely publicized. "He was in one of my classes," Kelly said about her rapist (she never used his name). "He asked me out, and we went to a bar, and I think we listened to some music. A bunch of people were going over to his house. . . . He shared a house . . . it was a big house, and he had a room upstairs. Some of the people who came with us eventually left. He was asking me a lot of questions about things that, you know, I liked or I enjoyed doing. I just thought they were part of normal conversation. . . . I was flattered that he wanted to know so much about me." She had also been flattered to be included in the group that left the bar together.

Kelly soon learned that her rapist's questions were motivated by more than simple curiosity. As soon as he learned from his interrogation that she was fond of cats, "he said that upstairs his roommate's cat had kittens." Kelly cut short her account and took a deep breath. "My heart's beating fast," she said. "It's sort of frightening. I, I don't like to . . . I don't talk very much about how it all ensued or what he said or, you know, how I was restrained or whatever."

With an effort Kelly resumed her story. She said, "I didn't have [any contraception] to protect me and that, that frightened me a lot." She pleaded with her attacker. "I said, 'I can't, no, I can't, please no, because I don't, this is, I don't want to and I don't have anything to protect me and I'm, and I'm just plain frightened. Just please knock it off and let me go." Implacably, he pinned her down on his bed and forced himself into her, ignoring her repeated, strenuous protests. "He was mean and just . . . of one idea and very insistent," she said, sighing heavily.

The rapist rolled off Kelly and passed out as soon as he had finished. "I was making moves to leave, and he wasn't doing anything," she said. "I looked at him and—there was something wrong with him." Nervously, with a lot of stammering half-thoughts, Kelly said that the young man had a misshapen penis. It looked "crooked" enough to her that she thought he might have been ridiculed by other women, might have been angry, or might have felt that he could have sex only by force. She did not excuse him on those grounds, but like many victims she was able to recognize some humanity in her abuser. "In retrospect," she said, "a part of me feels sorry for him."

Kelly retained an impression of her rapist as "a nice guy." She said he was not good looking but "tall and skinny" and something of "a wimp." That image hung suspended against the brute fact of what he had done to her. He had been nice, nerdy Dr. Jekyll until they had gone upstairs that night to see the fictitious kittens. He had become Mr. Hyde when he "slammed the door and stood against it . . . and his personality changed." Disoriented and frightened, unsure whether anyone else was still in the house, Kelly never screamed for help, a fact that later fed painful feelings of self-blame. The only reason she could give was the fact that they were his friends and "it was his turf," whereas she was "an outsider." She also thought she might have been reluctant to expose a "terribly deformed" part of him to any of his friends who might have been around.

That softer part of Kelly did not subdue her fury, shame, guilt, self-doubt, fear, and hatred. She described all of these feelings to us, fully acknowledging some, downplaying others. She left the rapist's house at one or two o'clock in the morning and ran back to her room at the dormitory. She scarcely left her room for the rest of the term. She did not report the rape, and there was no one she wanted to confide in. "I was just so—just confused and sort of ashamed that, you know, an intelligent person like me could have that happen," she said.

Within a few weeks, Kelly said, "I was having morning sickness and gaining a lot of weight. My chest was getting big. I knew I was pregnant, but it was almost like Rochester was the real world. I was just waiting until I could go home." So she did nothing. "I just denied [the pregnancy] until I came home."

Once she was safely back in her own house, Kelly immediately went to her mother's room and told her everything. Then she sat on the stairs with her younger sister and told her, too. "I think Mom was sitting at the top, and I was in the middle of the stairs with Sue, and we were all crying. . . . I knew I had to do something, because I couldn't . . . couldn't have a baby that . . . that came from a beginning like that and had a—had the face of this person that hurt me and that I didn't even know."

Contact with her mother, who was "strong" and could "always make things better again," lifted Kelly's immobilization. She went to a women's clinic the next day, almost too far along for the abortion she was now frantic to obtain. "I wanted it so bad," she said fervently. "This is the only way it could have been for me, and they made everything—it was such a good, good place. They were helpful and positive and . . . nice, nice people. It was—it was neat."

Kelly's language, almost that of a cheerleader for the clinic, turned solemn as she talked about the abortion, which she felt was both "murder and . . . good, good revenge. . . . I don't think much about the rape part of it." It was the feeling of revenge and the cold necessity of choosing her own well-being over another being's existence that made Kelly feel her abortion was murder. She explained: "I do and I did think about it as a baby, as a living thing, but it was a living thing that I never wanted to see. I mean, I would rather die first." Kelly believed ready access to a safe abortion may have saved her life. "If there had been barriers," she said, "I wonder . . . I think . . . that I would've committed suicide." That possibility seemed more serious than idly speculative, for Kelly returned to it three or four times in the interview, always with some agitation.

Abortion *was* available, though, and according to Kelly: "It was just enough to set things straight and to cleanse me. . . . It got rid of what I wanted to get rid of, and it helped me forget a lot about the rape, too. . . . I don't even think very much about the rape. I don't."

Despite Kelly's denial, the rape still affected her in obvious ways. The cleansing was not as thorough as she wanted to believe. At some level she knew this, for she told us about ways in which her behavior was still affected, seven years later. "I wear clothes that are very baggy," she said. "I wear black all the time. . . . I wear it as a barrier. . . . I don't like to wear shorts, I don't like to wear a bathing suit. I don't blame my body for . . . for what happened to me, but . . . but I don't want anyone to see me unless, you know, I want to be seen."

Apparently, Kelly never did want to be seen. Asked about her relationships with men since the rape, she said, at first, that they were fairly good. But the details were disturbing. She had kept part of herself hidden, in one way or another, from the two men she had been involved with. The first, whom she saw for five years and planned to marry, never knew about the rape. "I never told him, ever. . . . I didn't think that he would understand." Her current boyfriend did know about the rape. "I've known him about five or six months, and I told him *the very first time*—it wasn't even a date! I told him that I was raped and that I had an abortion. . . . I felt like he was more like me, that he could understand and that . . . that my thoughts and secrets were safe with him."

Still, something in Kelly did not feel safe, even with her new boyfriend. As she told us how tolerant he was of her insistence on covering up, even when they were in bed together, she seemed to realize for the first time how difficult that must be for him. "I don't think he really knows what I look like," she said, her voice tightening against tears. "I feel bad for him because I wish I felt better about myself. . . . He must think I'm really—I'm really different, but he doesn't make me feel weird about it. He really accepts me." Crying, Kelly said: "I guess

I haven't come that far. Because even someone I care about that much, you know, I don't . . . don't let him *see* me."

By degrees, and with numerous digressions throughout the interview, Kelly filled in a picture of her ongoing pain over the rape. She struggled with her own freshly revived questions about whether she should have known what her rapist intended, why she did not scream, and why she did not report him. "I wonder who, who he's been with and if the same thing happened to them, or if there were someone before me. . . . The women that can report and can talk and can expose—they save other people from the same thing," Kelly said, sighing. "I was mad at myself. I felt so stupid."

Kelly never sought counseling after the rape. Believing that her abortion had freed her of the rape's destructive effects, she had felt no need for it. Asked how she thought she would have dealt with the rape if she had not become pregnant and if there had been no abortion, she said: "The rape was so negative, and the pregnancy was so negative, and the abortion, the abortion was *the best thing*—that if I didn't have that way of setting things straight again . . . how would I be with men now? I don't know!" Kelly remembered, though, that her first reaction to the rape, before she knew she was pregnant, had been to shut herself up in her room like a wounded animal. Once she missed her first menstrual period, she said, focusing on the pregnancy "was part of my whole tactic [for recovery]."

With that tactic's effectiveness called into question by Kelly's tears and the lingering effects of the rape, we suggested she call a rape counselor. She seemed interested, but we later learned that she did not call. We wonder whether her reluctance to get help is part of older experiences in her life.

Kelly's father left the family when she was sixteen. Her ambivalence toward him and her unwillingness to accuse him emerged along a striking parallel to her feelings about the rapist she was also unwilling to accuse. "He was a good dad," she began, when we asked about her father and her family background. But this "good dad" was often verbally abusive toward Kelly's mother and sister. He spared her, she said, because she shared his interest in sports. She avoided having to take sides during family fights by leaving the room, but in general she felt loyal to her sister and mother. "The three of us were so close. . . . We knew that he had to be touched, he had to be crazy."

Whether he was crazy or not, Kelly's father was a heavy drinker, probably an alcoholic. "He had a good job; he was an executive with a big chemical company, and then he just, he quit and started a series of self-employment kind of things out of our basement." These private ventures were never successful, and her father grew increasingly resentful of Kelly's mother, who "was doing wonderful things with her job."

As her father's self-esteem plummeted, he drank more and more. Finally, he left the family, and Kelly has not seen him since. The last she heard of him, he was in Texas, remarried and the father of a small boy. "I guess—I guess I miss my dad. I seem to go out with men that look like my father," she said with a nervous burst of laughter. "You know, they've got mustaches and round stomachs; they look like my dad. I wonder. I wonder. But, even though I think he's neat, and it was bad that it had to happen, it was *so* good when he moved out—it was *the best thing!* All the negativity was gone, and we three—we were always the family anyhow, he was always just the outsider." Thoughtfully, Kelly added, "I don't think much about him."

Kelly spoke of her father and her rapist in remarkably similar terms. She saw in each of them nice-guy qualities that were belied by their behavior. She claimed she seldom thought about either the rape or her father. She described the same euphoric relief after her abortion (which rid her of her attacker) that she had felt after her father's departure. Although the dysfunction in Kelly's background appears to have been mild compared with other forms of harm discussed in this chapter, her case illustrates how readily a sensitive, compassionate young woman can adopt the incapacitating behavior and self-image of a victim.

The Prevalence of Rape on Campus

In an article entitled "The Scope of Rape: Incidence and Prevalence of Sexual Aggression and Victimization in a National Sample of Higher Education Students," authors M. P. Ross, C. A. Gidycz, and N. Wisniewski report that eight out of ten perpetrators of sexual assaults on college campuses are students and that one in nine college women had been raped. If each victim in this 11 percent of female students had a different attacker, and 80 percent of the attackers were students, it would mean that 8 or 9 percent of male students were rapists or sexual abusers. In fact, 8.3 percent of the men responding to these authors' survey admitted as much. Worse, only 1 percent of these perpetrators understood that their behavior was criminal. Kelly's attacker apparently shared their ignorance. He called her at her home in Rochester two years after the rape and asked her out as if picking up the strand of a pleasant past. She refused him indignantly, but she never accused him of rape or told him she had been pregnant.

Kelly's silence about her rape and her revulsion over her pregnancy are typical. Most victims of sexual assault have profound, mixed feelings of rage, shame, fear, and grief. The discovery of a pregnancy—two or three weeks later, when the worst feelings may have begun to subside—can intensely revive the attack and the terror. Because of this, even some of the strongest opponents of abortion make exceptions in such cases, believing that a woman who has been terrorized must not be forced to carry within her the living consequences of a brutal act.

Because the consequences *are* living, however, many people oppose abortion even in cases of rape and incest, arguing that the sins of the father are not carried in his genes and should not condemn his offspring. It is a sound argument, but one that invokes justice alone and fails to address the trauma of the pregnant woman with compassion. It can be countered with equally sound claims for justice on behalf of the woman—claims that do not always address the innocence of the fetus.

Beyond the debate, however, even some victims distinguish between the act and the consequences of rape. A few proceed willingly with pregnancies that result. Often, they give the babies up for adoption; occasionally, they keep them. In the best of these cases, the women regain their self-respect and control in making and carrying out these choices. In some instances, however, they are prevented from doing so by circumstances or by other peoples' assumptions that a pregnancy engendered by rape can *only* be traumatic. For women like Kelly, being prevented from having an abortion would perpetuate their victimization. For other rape victims, being discouraged from bearing or raising the children of rape has the same effect. This is what happened to Lucy Oates.

Lucy Oates Hilliard

Lucy Oates Hilliard, a tall, angular redhead in her mid-forties, was born in the foothills of the Blue Ridge Mountains and raised without indoor plumbing, electricity, or a telephone. She bathed in the kitchen, in a galvanized steel tub. She attended a one-room school until she entered high school in the nearest large town, seventeen miles away. There, the other students called Lucy and her rural classmates "hicks," and the teachers expected little from them. "They assumed we were all just dumb and unsophisticated," Lucy said.

Defying such assumptions, Lucy became the first in her family to attend college. After earning a degree in library science from the University of Virginia, she returned home to help raise her youngest sisters and to launch a literacy program for her mountain village and the surrounding hill towns. "I was very, very close to my family," she said. "I really tried to be an example, but it didn't matter how hard I tried. Things happened that were out of my control."

Lucy's loss of control over her life began with her rape at age twenty-three, two years after she had finished college. Like Kelly Walker at school, Lucy was lonely at home. She participated fully in the life of her community and her family, but she had no prospects for romance. Few of the young men in her area had even a high school education, and most were married in any case. When a co-worker on the literacy campaign urged Lucy to meet her nephew from Richmond, she agreed. "She kept talking about this great guy and how I should get to know him. . . . I guess he complained about not meeting girls, so his aunt thought of me."

Lucy's friend introduced her to her nephew, Eddie, one night when they were in town for a meeting of a county literacy organization. Eddie invited Lucy to go out after the group adjourned. "I got into his '65 GTO," she recalled. "We went down the street for a five-cent soda and afterward we cruised through the town and out into the country. I thought he was taking me home, but when we got to my house, he took a right and went seven miles beyond it. I thought he was just driving around. Then he parked. I usually started talking real fast when a guy parked the car." At twenty-three, Lucy was still a virgin. "I had fooled around some," she said, "but had never actually had intercourse."

Lucy wondered about her date's behavior, and she felt a shiver of mistrust, but he had been described to her with such praise and pride by his aunt that she never felt genuine alarm, even when Eddie pulled a gun from his glove compartment and laid it without comment on the dashboard. She had grown up with hunters, who always carried firearms in their cars and pickups. She forgot, for a time, that Eddie was not "country."

Soon he began pawing her, reaching under her skirt and inside her blouse. "I resisted," she said. "And I can remember exactly what he said to me then: 'Any woman who has been to college has had sex.'" As if his mistaken opinion amounted to license, Eddie forced himself on Lucy. "He did not make full entry. He ejaculated all over me. My skirt and slip were wet all over. He was angry about that—the fact that he had not made full penetration. He got the gun and went outside the car and walked around for a while. . . . [Then he] drove me home, very fast."

Lucy heated water on a propane stove at home and scrubbed down in the outhouse so she would not wake her family. "I felt ashamed," she told us. "I felt dirty. I felt violated. I was confused. I was bothered about the gun. But I thought I had prevented intercourse. I was relieved that he didn't rape me." She never mentioned the incident to her parents, Eddie's aunt, or anyone else. "This was the mountains," she said. "I didn't want my daddy to . . . go out with a shotgun to defend my honor. And anyway, I wasn't raped."

Lucy thought the incident was over, but its effects had scarcely begun. Within a month, she knew she was pregnant. "I was always real fluid at midcycle," she said, figuring she had produced enough cervical mucus for Eddie's sperm to penetrate where he had not. "I was scared," Lucy said, "but I thought that I could handle it. But I realized that all I had worked for had been thrown away."

Abortion did not occur to Lucy. Not only was it illegal in 1967, but it was remote from her experience. She had heard once about a local girl who had tried to self-abort with turpentine, but that was the only time abortion had come anywhere near Lucy's life. It was not an option. Neither, at that time, was staying at home and braving the disappointment and scorn of her family and neighbors.

So Lucy drove into town to confront Eddie. She found him at home with one of his roommates, getting ready for a party. He asked her to wait outside in the parking lot, and she agreed. Ten minutes later, Lucy said, "his roommate came out and said that he had left. Then the roommate got into my car with me." She let him slide behind the wheel, thinking he was going to take her to Eddie. But when Eddie's friend parked Lucy's car under a bridge, her first nightmare unfolded all over again. "He insisted we were going to have sex. I insisted we were not. He was short, but big and muscular. I finally said, 'No, I'm pregnant.' And he said, 'Well, you can't get any more pregnant, so it won't make any difference.'" He ripped her clothes off and raped her, very forcefully and very painfully. Again, she told no one.

Lucy finally tracked Eddie down and told him of her pregnancy. "Because I didn't want to embarrass my family, I said I was willing to get married," she said. Eddie told her scornfully that he would "never marry a woman who had screwed my best friend." Lucy could see no alternative but to quit her job and leave town. She planned to have her baby, place it in foster care until she could afford to raise it herself, and then adopt it. That way, "no one would know that it was mine."

Lucy withdrew all her savings and drove to Baltimore. She knew the city slightly from an earlier visit, and she felt it was far enough from home that she would not meet anyone she knew. She settled briefly into a rooming house and soon sought medical care. She had to pay all her expenses up front, which wiped out her savings, and then she learned that she would need an attorney to make arrangements for her baby. With no money for legal fees, she counted herself lucky to find a lawyer who would take her case in exchange for baby-sitting and light housekeeping. She lived with his family during the last half of her pregnancy—an arrangement that met her needs but that also kept her within earshot of the attorney's persuasions. Both he and Lucy's doctor urged her to give her baby up, warning her that she would come to hate a child conceived in violence and arguing that a woman alone could never manage with a child. They said the child, "an albatross" to her, would be a joy to a two-parent family who knew nothing of its origins. They even happened to know such a family; in fact, the attorney represented them. Lucy finally consented. "I saw that I didn't have enough money for my first plan," she sighed. She never wondered why these two men, who were so concerned about her financial straits, did not offer to let her pay their own fees over time.

Lucy was told her baby was born healthy and strong. She was anesthetized, so she never saw the birth, never saw the baby, and only later learned from some hospital forms that it had been a boy. She signed the adoption papers three days after the birth, but not before trying to back out of her decision on the way to the courthouse. "I was in the car with two lawyers, the one I lived with, who represented the adoptive couple, and his partner, who represented me. They both talked me back into signing the papers."

Powerless to reverse her decision—or so her attorney told her—Lucy turned with an aching need for comfort to a man much older than she, whom she had met late in her pregnancy. Phil was a friend of the attorney's family, a forty-two-year-old legal historian who taught at a nearby university. He knew about Lucy's rape and pregnancy and did not judge her. Within a month after Lucy's son was born, they were seeing each other regularly. "After what I had been through," she explained, "I wasn't ready to play the dating game and go through what seemed like abuse. Phil seemed like a safe haven."

Lucy married Phil early in 1968, and only then learned how wrong she had been about him. He made it plain from the start that Lucy's task was to do exactly, and only, as he wished, especially in sexual matters. She had thought married couples might have sex two or three times a week, but, she said, Phil wanted sex "all the time, it seemed. And it was a hard, driving, abusive kind of sex." If Lucy attempted to refuse him, he derided, humiliated, or hit her. This went on for three years, until a mild heart attack put an end to Phil's sexual demands. In the twenty years since, he has contented himself with verbal abuse. Today, after suffering a stroke and another heart attack, Phil is an invalid who requires Lucy's constant care and attention, ordering her about as if he owned her very thoughts and will. She stays with him because he needs her.

Once Phil had his first heart attack, Lucy resigned herself to childlessness. She explained sadly, "I didn't want to bring a child into the bad, abusive environment I was in." She filled the void with yearning thoughts of the son she was persuaded to give up, and she told us sorrowfully that she has always regretted that decision.

Had she kept her son, Lucy said, "my family would have had to accept it. My nephew married a girl five days before her baby was born. They all accepted that. And even if they hadn't, I could have made it on my own. It would have been very hard for me; I'm a very family-oriented person. But I would have done it if I'd had to."

Lucy has looked for her son several times in the last dozen years, following leads obtained from groups that help birth parents and their children to find each other. She has proceeded cautiously, not wanting to impose herself on her son or on his adoptive family. When we interviewed her, she seemed both to want and to fear an encounter with him. All this time, she has kept in touch with the lawyer and his family, who have always known the whereabouts of Lucy's son. All they have told her, however, is that she did the right thing for him.

Lucy clings to their reassurances. "My life is very much based on trying to do the right thing," she said. Yet it is the "right things" Lucy has done, from giving up her son to remaining with an enfeebled, abusive husband, that have made her life a misery.

Lucy's positive determination and strength of will were stolen from her by her two rapists, but she might have regained them had she managed to keep her baby. The challenges of facing her family, supporting her child, and keeping her job might have tapped and tested all that was best about Lucy and her up-bringing—her courage, her family values, her confidence in her own abilities. Instead, she was further victimized by well-meaning but ultimately disrespectful attitudes about how a woman would or should react to pregnancy after rape. She was told how she would feel, not asked what she wanted. Weakened by the rapes and the self-doubt they produced, she could not withstand the blandishments of strangers who had other interests than her own at heart. She gave up her child and then immediately gave up the rest of her will and life to a man who arrogantly exploited both.

Any rape counselor knows that a victimized woman needs to regain her sense of control as quickly as possible but that she is unlikely to do so without help. The sad irony is that the very things that make her need help create barriers against seeking it. Lucy felt ashamed and violated. She wanted no one to know of her humiliation. Had she been able to seek solace, she might have gained better counsel than her doctor's and her lawyer's. Instead, with no one to help her reassert her best qualities, those qualities became distorted. They no longer served Lucy, only others. They led her into further abuse and years of longing for the child she had never seen.

Commonplace Crimes and Betrayals

Although the stories in this chapter contain rape, incest, suicide, addiction, homelessness, and neglect, they do not represent all the forms and conditions of trauma that can surround pregnancy and affect the choice between birth and abortion. We have included no stories about AIDS, prostitutes, addicted babies, long-term marital violence, murder, or pregnancies resulting from incest or prostitution. What we have covered is numbing enough. What is more terrible is that severe abuse is either on the rise or is being revealed as vastly more common than anyone has previously thought. The same is true of the milder forms of mistreatment and neglect that run throughout this book— the mundane sexism, dysfunction, verbal assaults, and disregard that infect so many stories of unwanted pregnancy.

Because violent abuse differs only in degree from a more commonplace disrespect for women and their values, we see it as evidence that the bitter controversy over abortion rights masks a more important social failure of care and responsibility. The evidence of that social failure is everywhere, not just in out-of-control pregnancy and abortion rates. Too many teenagers are lost, bewildered, undereducated, fatherless, addicted, and violent—as well as pregnant. Too many male college students are raping their classmates and feeling only triumph or entitlement. Too many parents, dependent on two incomes, have too little time with each other or their children. Too many families are distintegrating or turning viciously on their own members.

Individuals are less likely to think clearly, make sound choices, and act responsibly in a society that does not actively encourage them to do so. Fortunately, the last two chapters of this book provide some instructive contrasts. Its stories are about women who became pregnant by choice, under good circumstances, and with the respect and support of their families and friends, only to be faced with the possibility or diagnosis of a serious medical problem. Many of them had the means and motivation to integrate care with justice, and their decisions provide a reassuring sign that individuals who receive respect and care are likely to apply them in tough circumstances.

7

PROBLEM PREGNANCY

Living with the Odds

Obviously our problems had touched deep emotional wellsprings in many people. It seemed that a fair portion of the human race had chosen sides over a woman out in the middle of Arizona who simply didn't want to give birth to a child who might be hopelessly crippled for life.

Sherri Finkbine, *Redbook* (January 1963)

Introduction

A generation ago, a new mother would awaken groggily from the anesthetic administered during childbirth to ask eagerly about her baby. "Is it a girl or boy? Does it have all its fingers and toes?" And most importantly, "Is it healthy?" As recently as the early 1960s, parents had no sonograms, blood tests, fluid extractions, or genetic analyses to give them a glimpse of their baby's well-being before it was born. Medical science still knew very little about whether a mother's diet or diseases affected the health of the baby she carried. Most pregnant women just crossed their fingers, said their prayers, and hoped for a normal, healthy baby.

But in 1953 James Watson and Francis Crick determined the secret of genes, the inherited, microscopic codes in our cells that determine much of our identity. Watson and Crick discovered that the structure of DNA (deoxyribonucleic acid), the material that genes are composed of, resembled a spiraling molecular ladder twisted into the now-famous double helix. A genetically normal human fetus receives twenty-three pairs of chromosomes from its parents, with one chromosome in each pair contributed by the mother and one by the father. Each chromosome pair occupies one rung of the DNA "ladder," the genetic package that determines whether the child who forms from the fertilized egg will be tall or short; male or female; black, white, red, yellow, or brown; average or otherwise in intellect; musical, athletic, or literary; gifted with its hands or all thumbs.

After the discovery of the double helix, science was still decades away from reading the messages carried by each of these genes. Still, awesome implications were clear. What had been known only by God was starting to fall, piece by precious piece, into the hands of mere mortals. Just what science would eventually be able to tell about the genes of unborn babies was still just vaguely imagined. Nevertheless, the possibility of new scientific breakthroughs hovered around the growing discussion of abortion during the 1960s.

The only well-known cause of genetic abnormality was rubella, or German measles. If a pregnant woman contracted the disease early in her pregnancy there was a 50 percent chance that her baby would be born defective—with cataracts, deafness, heart disease, or mental retardation. For decades before the *Roe v. Wade* decision was handed down, many hospitals routinely aborted women who had come down with rubella. In fact, it was the second most common justification, after a threat to the mother's health, for hospital abortions until the late 1950s, when many hospitals began expanding their criteria. Although the legal justification for such abortions was questionable, few challenges were brought.

The 1967 *Good Housekeeping* poll ("Should Abortion Laws be Eased?") showed that a hefty majority (79 percent) of the magazine's consumer panelists agreed that the law should permit abortion "if the baby is likely to be seriously defective." But just six years before *Roe v. Wade*, when several states were liberalizing laws and many doctors were liberalizing their practices, abortion for known defects in the child was still available only erratically. The women polled by *Good Housekeeping* supplemented their responses to the survey with personal anecdotes. One woman in her eighth month of pregnancy was awaiting "in torment" the birth of a child who had only a 10 percent chance of being normal. Another, the mother of a 2½ year-old child who was deaf because of German measles, wrote, "How I wished then that a therapeutic abortion were legal!"

Even where therapeutic abortions (those performed because of the likelihood of fetal defects) were performed, they were not universally accepted. Dr. James V. McNulty of Los Angeles, a former member of the California Board of Medical Examiners, successfully urged the board to bring charges of unprofessional conduct against nine doctors who had performed therapeutic abortions in San Francisco hospitals during an epidemic of German measles in 1965. McNulty did not openly object to the legalization of abortion—which was then being debated in the California legislature—but to what he saw as the doctors' flouting of a century-old California statute still in effect. The California reform bill that was then in legislative committee was being patterned after a recent

Colorado law that permitted abortion to save the mother's life, to preserve her mental or physical health, or to interrupt a pregnancy when the child was likely to be born with a serious mental or physical handicap. California's governor at the time, Ronald Reagan, had said he would sign the liberalized bill only if it prohibited abortions of defective children. Reagan said, "I cannot justify the taking of an unborn life simply on the supposition that the baby may be born less than a perfect human being."

Reagan took a strong stand on an issue that had already begun to disturb Americans far more than the number of actual cases would seem to warrant. The incidence of women considering abortions because of potential damage to the fetus was minuscule. Medical science had little ability to make prenatal diagnoses yet, but that ability was sure to grow. For many Americans, the opportunity to abort after an unfavorable prenatal diagnosis would be a welcome alternative to suffering both for the family and for the child born without the capacity to achieve full, independent adulthood. But for others, doing away with a potential life because it might be "less than a perfect human being" raised the still fresh specter of the Nazi push for a "super race."

Meanwhile, children and adults already born with handicaps were, for the most part, shoved out of sight. They were segregated in separate schools, housed in institutions, or hidden away by families. The movement for rights for the disabled—which would eventually mainstream many children with disabilities into regular schools and bring many adults out of institutions and into the community—was even further off the horizon than prenatal testing. Many doctors recommended immediate institutionalization for children born with Down syndrome, for example, one of the most common genetic abnormalities. Down syndrome is characterized by an extra chromosome in the twenty-first pair. Such children are usually retarded, but the retardation may be severe or very mild. They may also be healthy or be plagued by a host of problems including heart defects, gastrointestinal disorders, and respiratory difficulties. In the early 1960s, few Americans had any sense of how frequently Down syndrome and other genetic variations actually occurred within the population or how they affected the potential of people born with them. The existence of an abnormal family member was often considered an embarrassment and was seldom discussed openly.

So when a new mother woke up to the news that her baby was one of the unlucky, imperfect ones, she had little way of knowing that the news need not be an unmitigated horror. Little was known, but even less was communicated. Many doctors and nurses still believed their job was to protect the patient from too much bad news, too much pain and suffering. The less said, the better. Even today, information about the developmental effects of genetic abnormalities is often unavailable (see Chapter 8). But in the early 1960s, ignorance was the rule rather than the exception and was sometimes deliberately enforced.

Problem pregnancies differ markedly from other birth-or-abortion dilemmas. They are often the planned and wanted pregnancies of married couples. When such a pregnancy yields a child with a genetic defect or other abnormality, many parents grieve long and deeply. For others, the grief is short-lived and soon followed by complete acceptance. In the 1960s, most couples learned the news only at birth—after the nursery was ready, the baby showers were over, and the family members had only one big question: whether the new baby would be wrapped in a pink or a blue blanket. Neither Hilary Nelson nor Helen Albert knew she carried a child with Down syndrome in 1962. Today each woman looks back on what she might have done had she known beforehand. Each shared with us the complex thoughts and feelings that make them very different, as women and as mothers.

Hilary Nelson

In 1962, Hilary Nelson had two sons and was looking forward to the birth of her third child, who she was sure would be her much-wanted daughter. When she awoke from the general anesthetic back in her room after childbirth, her husband, Dan, told her that she had gotten the girl she wanted, but that their newborn daughter Linda had Down syndrome.

"I was devastated," Hilary said, describing her reaction to Dan's announcement. "I was also repelled that I had carried this severely deformed fetus in my body. I don't know if that's a normal reaction. I'm just telling you how I felt." Hilary saw her daughter only once in the hospital. She was repelled by the sight of her. "I did not feel as if I wanted to hold her. I rejected her. Very definitely." Hilary also had no desire to take the baby home. She and Dan feared their two older sons would be adversely affected by the emotional and practical hardships a child like Linda would cause.

Hilary's disinclination to care for her baby was supported by her doctors, who strongly recommended placing Linda in an institution and did not raise any alternatives. This was common at that time. The standard thinking was that children with Down syndrome were ineducable, that most would be little more than vegetables. Linda's prognosis was doubly poor because she was blinded by congenital cataracts. "The doctor said that she would need total care, and he was right," Hilary told us. The doctor also predicted that Linda "would live to the age of five, *tops*, and he was wrong," she added ironically. Today, at almost thirty, Linda lives in a special-care home. She cannot walk, speak, or see, despite several operations on her eyes; her retardation is severe, she is incontinent, and she is subject to seizures. Whether Linda would be better off today if she had had the benefit of modern techniques now used on children with Down syndrome is forever unanswerable. The combination of Hilary's doctor's advice and her own appalled reaction to her child inalterably set the course of Linda's life.

Hilary had had no suspicion when she was pregnant that anything could be wrong. Amniocentesis had not been available to her. Even if it had been, Hilary was only thirty-two and doctors now recommend the procedure only for women thirty-five and older. Nevertheless, Hilary regrets that the technology arrived too late to change her fate and Linda's. She does not doubt that, had she known about Linda's condition in time, she would have had an abortion.

Hilary's story, told in these stark terms, raises hard questions and touches on much of the controversy surrounding the modern option of aborting fetuses with Down syndrome. What does it say about a woman when she cannot love, or does not want, her abnormal child? What would Hilary have done if Linda's Down syndrome had not been severe and if the child had not been blind? "I'd have done what I did," Hilary told us. "I'd have had tremendous guilt. . . . I don't know if I could have sustained [my decision to institutionalize Linda] if she had had mild Down syndrome. I've often said," she admitted with a rueful laugh, "that I was very fortunate that my Down syndrome child was so severely damaged."

It might be easy—but would surely be misleading—simply to characterize Hilary as unfeeling. As she told us the rest of her story, much of her strong and complex personality emerged, making it clear that she, like the others whose stories appear in this book, behaved in accord with profound, lifelong ideas about herself and her commitments. Hilary took shape in our interview as a woman of great determination, emotion, dedication, and occasional arrogance. But it grew clear that she was not someone whose dedication could be spent on a single afflicted child, even her own. Though she had always identified her primary role in life as that of wife and mother, many of her goals and passions were far more widely focused. Her view of herself was also—until Linda's birth—grounded in the idea that she was someone very special, "one of those very lucky people for whom things were just going to go beautifully."

Hilary is a tall, striking woman with short gray hair swept back off her high forehead. During the interview, she sat within the half-circle of a large bay window, the sun streaming into her living room and lighting the view beyond: a stunning panorama of Chicago's lakeshore. In her elegant, modern surroundings, she seemed far removed from her roots.

While she was growing up in Packingtown, which was behind the slaughterhouses in Chicago and was home to many children of immigrants who were determined to make their way out of poverty, Hilary felt special because her father was literate and well-read, although he had no formal education. He raised his daughters to think they were better than others, and he communicated to Hilary that she was the most special of all. She was set further apart within the family by blond hair and green eyes that contrasted brightly with her sisters' dark coloring.

Of the three sisters, she told us, "I was the only one who graduated from college. I felt pretty omnipotent. I always felt in control—much more in control for that period. In other words, in that era no woman felt completely in control. But within the parameters of being a woman, poor, the daughter of immigrants—I was in control," Hilary laughed. Hilary strongly felt the effects of being on the underside of inequality. She was determined to overcome the vulnerability that prevailed outside the dominant culture, which was male, affluent, and native-born American. In her struggle, she adopted what were almost exclusively male values in her time—determination, a distaste for weakness, and a powerful sense of control over her destiny.

For example, Hilary set firm career goals for herself and stuck to them at a time when few women of any class or culture looked beyond traditional roles. "I always knew I wanted to be a social worker," she told us. She emerged from her background well-equipped for what became her life's work. If people could control their access to social services, Hilary was convinced, they could begin to control their lives. Even in the early stages of her career, before and during the time her children were being born, Hilary had a good network of connections in the field, so she was surprised when she and Dan had trouble finding a private facility in which Linda could be well cared for. "We couldn't find anything," she told us. "The social service department [of the urban, women's hospital where Linda had been born] couldn't recommend a facility for Linda; they didn't know about any." This question of access—to services, facilities, and financial support—eventually became a central theme in all of Hilary's later work. At this time, however, after their difficult search, Dan finally took Linda to a private home outside the city they lived in at the time, where she spent her first five years. "I did go out and visit her," Hilary said. "Dan went more frequently, but I did go a few times."

After finally finding a good facility for Linda, Hilary fell into a deep depression. Much of her adjustment to Linda's birth involved a redefinition of her self-image, a process that distracted her attention from what was going on around her. "I just wasn't really there. That's the only way I can describe it as I look back on that period. I prepared meals and did that sort of thing, but I wasn't really there," she said.

Hilary's sense of specialness was shaken. She had to grow beyond childish notions of herself and gain a "sense of balance," she said. "Unfortunately, for most of us, our growths are caused by pain. . . . So I suppose Linda was a maturing experience." A similar sense of proportion came from Hilary's work and from the environment in which she had grown up. Though she felt she had always been especially blessed before Linda, she also knew that "people were destitute, people had problems. Those things happened to people." Friends asked Hilary if she wondered why fate had singled her out to give birth to this unfortunate child. The question made her realize that "in spite of my feeling that all of life's terrible ugly things [were] going to pass me by, I have to say, I never asked that." A rational part of her always knew that even her specialness had not raised her above life's random distribution of pain.

Hilary said that she emphasized her old sense of specialness as she told her story because, as a social worker, she has met many women who exercise a similar kind of denial. In the years after Linda's birth, Hilary's work with poor women drew her into abortion rights advocacy, and she subsequently counseled clients at an abortion clinic. She told us about one pregnant forty-year-old, not a client but someone she met at a conference, who was on the verge of deciding against prenatal testing because she had already suffered several spontaneous miscarriages and feared the test might trigger another. The woman knew her age put her fetus at risk for a genetic anomaly, but she told Hilary she had seen children with Down syndrome and found them very lovable.

Hilary straightened majestically in her chair. "I said, 'Really?' And I let her have it. I said, 'Let me tell you about *mine*.' And I didn't mince any words. I said, 'How dare you assume that you're going to have, at worst, a lovable Down syndrome child? You may be wiping that kid's ass for the next thirty years.'" Though the woman was taken aback by Hilary's bluntness, she thanked her the next day, saying, "I must have been pretty crazy."

"I really gave *her* a dose of reality, didn't I?" Hilary said with a laugh. She was reminded of an old joke about a farmer with a stubborn donkey. The donkey wouldn't budge at all. The farmer took a slab of wood and whacked the donkey's head. The donkey fell down dead and the farmer said, "That'll teach him."

"I suppose in a way I was being like the farmer with the wood," Hilary said, "but . . . I really felt I had a responsibility not to let her live in this dreamworld. Because she'd had six or seven pregnancies that ended in disaster, she was willing to say 'I'll have a cute Down syndrome?' It was like me being special. I'm going to have a cute little perfectly normal girl. Well, I mean, that's bullshit. It doesn't work that way."

Hilary seemed to argue that a woman needs to strike a proper balance between an immature and dreamy sense of "specialness" and a whack in the head by reality. But the argument is ultimately unsatisfying. Even mature women can vary widely in their attitudes about risk-taking. Hilary assumed that the woman at the conference had not taken a true account of her risks. But if we weigh that woman's attitudes and risks—her history of miscarriage, the incidence of induced miscarriages associated with amniocentesis, her willingness to raise a child with Down syndrome, the chance of any genetic anomaly, and, specifically, the risk of a baby as seriously damaged as Linda—the woman's calculations may have been perfectly realistic for her.

The toughness and arrogance that characterize Hilary in her own stories are also troubling because they are not softened by compassion for her child. Hilary sees Linda's birth as "my personal little tragedy." And so it is. But it is surely Linda's tragedy, too. The very qualities that Hilary developed in order both to survive and prevail may also have prevented her from truly caring for Linda. "I'm a very responsible person," Hilary said. "She's my daughter. I want her to have the best care possible. But I can't say that I feel toward her as a mother." Out of a deep sense of duty Hilary insures that others take care of Linda, but she cannot give her daughter what Hilary herself would say is every child's birthright: a mother's love.

Had Hilary herself had access to prenatal diagnostic tests and abortion, she would have ended her pregnancy. Still, she acknowledged that if Linda were born today, things might be different for her. Perhaps the eye surgery would have been successful. Perhaps current, more advanced knowledge about care for the retarded and the handicapped would have raised her potential. "But it's still a lousy situation," Hilary asserted. "The handicapped *are* better off, if they have the means. Access, access. Access to me is a key word in all of this." Who has access to the sometimes limited supports for retarded children is often, Hilary believes, a matter of class, awareness, timing, and economic standing.

Moreover, although more and more children with disabilities are being mainstreamed in the schools today, most of the daily, time-consuming stimulation and care of such children usually falls to their mothers, whose other interests and ambitions often must be shelved. Hilary pointed out that the women's movement, which has encouraged women to be less self-sacrificing than their counterparts in past generations, has largely coincided with the movement for the rights of the handicapped. This places any woman faced with a Down pregnancy in an uncomfortable position. Most, as other stories to follow demonstrate, are still uncomfortable with putting their own interests first, and hardly any are as unapologetic as Hilary when it comes to doing so. Hilary's bluntness and candor are products of her upbringing, her social work, and her activism for abortion rights. Hilary's strong views on abortion reflect her larger world view that human beings have a profound obligation to take life by the horns and maintain as much control as possible, a view shared by many of the pro-choice activists Kristin Luker studied in *Abortion and the Politics of Motherhood*. And like her fellow advocates, Hilary tends to be threatened by those who profess views that contradict her own.

Hilary's shield against maternal compassion might have been a matter of emotional survival for her. The specialness she felt as a young woman was not just an immature attempt to escape life's tragedies; it was also a valiant attempt to overcome her own vulnerabilities. To give in to maternal feelings for someone as needy as Linda could have pulled Hilary back into everything she had struggled to overcome in "being a woman, poor, the daughter of immigrants." Had she truly bonded with Linda, she might have felt Linda's irredeemable "female" dependency, her hopeless paucity of resources, and the permanent oppression of her handicap. For someone with Hilary's determined mettle, the pull of maternal feelings could have met a wall of fear—fear that the pull could destroy her long fought-for control. Psychiatrist Jean Baker Miller associates such fears with men in her book *Toward a New Psychology of Women*, but they can be equally true of women who, like Hilary, have adopted some of men's protective mechanisms. The threat of emotional attachment can be, as Miller says, the threat of psychic annihilation.

For most women we spoke with who had undergone amniocentesis, however, their choice was prompted by more than just a need to control their own lives. While the limits of their physical and emotional resources were a major consideration, they also expressed concern for a damaged child's quality of life and the child's effect on his or her siblings. If arguments are to be made for and against the legitimate use of prenatal testing, they will not rest solely—for most women—on the mother's needs or desires. Many people argue that the burdens placed on the nuclear family by the birth of a child with special needs should be eased by a community more supportive than our society is today. The more difficult questions, ones which modern society can no longer sidestep, are "What quality of life is worthy of our protection and nurturing?" and "When is abortion more merciful than birth?" Since amniocentesis became a common option in the 1970s, women have explored these questions with painful reality and responsibility.

Looking back, Hilary Nelson has no doubt what she would have done had amniocentesis revealed Linda's condition before she was born. On the other hand, Helen Albert, whose son Simon was born in 1962—the same year as Linda Nelson—cannot say what her decision would have been. Like Linda, Simon's genes carry an extra twenty-first chromosome, but in other ways, Simon and Linda are as dissimilar as their mothers' reactions to them.

Helen Albert

Helen Albert was in her early forties when her son Simon was born in 1962. Her story coincides chronologically with Hilary's and provides some important counterpoints. Helen already had two healthy daughters, and she awoke from the anesthetic she had been given during Simon's birth expecting the same joyful announcements of health and gender that had greeted her twice before. Instead, she was met with the nurses' silence. She knew something was wrong, yet when she saw Simon she noticed nothing. "I didn't see Down. To me he didn't look Down syndrome. It never occurred to me."

Helen was distressed by the way her husband and the doctors and nurses were acting, and her distress served only to deepen their secrecy. The more she wept, the more they decided she was not ready to hear the diagnosis. "I was such a wreck," she remembered. "Everyone else knew." After three days of silence, Helen's doctor finally told her merely that her baby would be a slow learner. She recalled his saying, "Some people put slow babies in institutions, but I don't think you would do that." Helen took Simon home, though she still did not know specifically what was wrong with him.

"When I went back for a four- or five-week exam," she told us, "they still hadn't said. So when the doctor was out of the office, I looked in my folder."

It was only then that Helen discovered her son had Down syndrome. Once she knew, her obstetrician and pediatrician reassured her about Simon's condition. They did not mention the possibility of health problems or the long-range implications of his possible lifelong dependency. Instead, they stressed how sweet and lovable children with Down syndrome are, and they told Helen that Simon would be an easy child to raise and that he would need no extra care.

Their prediction seems overly optimistic since even today it is almost impossible to diagnose how severely a newborn is affected by Down syndrome. On the other hand, Helen's doctors' predictions were no more irresponsible than that of Hilary Nelson's doctor, who said Linda probably would need total care and only live to the age of five. Helen's doctors, like Hilary's, failed to refer her to any resources for retarded children or their parents. What was unusual for that time was the doctors' assumption—implicit in the fact that they did not recommend institutionalization—that Simon would be better off at home. What was common was their patronizing treatment of Helen. Kept in the dark for her own "protection," Helen was also denied her own voice. How could she make known her own reactions, articulate her concerns, or consider what was best for her son and her family if she was not given the information she needed?

When Simon was about eighteen months old Helen took him to a nearby hospital that was doing tests on several babies with Down syndrome. The babies were doing fine, the staff told the women; the mothers were a wreck. The staff suggested that the mothers start a support group. "That was the biggest help," Helen said. "Until then I felt sorry for myself, but I found I was better off than some." Helen, for example, had the unwavering support of her husband, whereas the husbands of two women in her group had walked out after their babies were born. A third mother gave up her baby in order to save her marriage. "She paid a nurse to take him," Helen recalled, "so that, as a baby, he would at least be held." Still another mother had been advised to leave her baby at the hospital for four weeks before deciding whether to keep him. Deprived of the opportunity for important early bonding, she nevertheless went back to get him when the month was up. That baby turned out to be the highest-functioning of any in the group. He now works at a fast-food restaurant and lives almost independently.

Like Hilary, Helen had been depressed after giving birth to a child with Down syndrome. Her participation in the support group with other mothers who had babies with Down syndrome was the first thing to pull her out of her doldrums. "It was just so important to hear someone else say all the same things that you were feeling and you were going through."

Simon himself, though he never talked until he was over three years old, is also a high-performer, with an IQ of 76, a measurement that places him in a "borderline" category. His IQ is only four points below the "low-average" range and six points above the category called "mentally deficient." This is both a blessing and a curse. Until just before this interview, Simon worked in a sheltered workshop and attended a recreation and socialization program afterward. He outstripped most of his peers in these programs, which meant he had few friends among them, and he was bright enough to be frustrated by his shortcomings. He wanted to date normal girls, his sister told us, but they rejected him, subtly or overtly, as many normal people did. "He's incredibly sensitive," said his mother. "He just knows. If he met you he'd know if you were really listening or just dismissing him."

Simon's acute awareness made him lonely. A worker in his recreational program told the family that, one day, after attempting something he could not manage, Simon stomped angrily down the corridor muttering, "Damn that extra chromosome!" The worker said, "Simon knows a lot more than we give him credit for." Simon's sister believed he would be happier if he were less intelligent and less aware. Some experts speculate that psychological problems will be among the last to be recognized and treated as persons with Down syndrome gradually become "normalized" within our society.

Helen never thought about placing Simon in an institution, perhaps in part because of her doctor's assumption that she would not want to do so. Helen also felt lucky to have the full cooperation of her family in Simon's upbringing. "You could never find better sisters than my girls," she said. Helen never felt either of her girls was hindered by Simon. They and their friends were always kind to him. "And Simon never had any health problems at all. We always said he was our healthiest child." Nevertheless, she added, "It breaks your heart that his future won't be what it should be."

Had Helen been offered amniocentesis during her pregnancy with Simon she is not sure what she would have done. "I've asked myself that question hundreds of times. I don't know if I can ever answer it because Simon has turned out so well. We just can't imagine our family without him." On the other hand, Helen said, "there've been a lot of worries and heartache, particularly about his future—at least until recently." In 1991, Simon went to live in a state-supported group residence with other high-performing retarded adults. He became much more independent than he had been at home. He learned to deposit his paycheck, withdraw the cash he needs, and spend it according to a budget. Helen and her husband now feel at peace that Simon will be secure and independent after they are gone.

Though Helen could not say whether she would have chosen amniocentesis, she has advised her daughters, one of whom now has two children, to undergo prenatal testing. She said she would not try to influence their decision if the results were bad, though. "It is never easy. It's a very difficult thing to decide."

Helen was now no more willing to pass judgment on women who decide to abort babies with Down syndrome than she was willing to judge women in her generation who institutionalized their children. She knew she had been lucky. A supportive family had been the most important element in her success with Simon, but almost as important had been the network of other parents and the range of public and private services, including the group residence and workshop where Simon was now living and working. "Today there is more help available than there was when Simon was born," Helen said. There is also less stigma. Where once there was shame, now there is more openness. "Today, you can go out and say, 'Yes, I had a Down's syndrome child.' In my day, you didn't admit that until you absolutely had to."

Science and Social Attitudes

Hilary Nelson and Helen Albert's stories both demonstrate the lack of social awareness and resources for families to whom a child with disabilities was born. Even a woman as socially and professionally resourceful as Hilary Nelson had to search hard for quality care for her daughter. Helen Albert had to stumble upon the comfort she needed. In Hilary Nelson's experience as a social worker, she had found that access to private and public social services, even to other parents in similar circumstances, was often a matter of who you were and whom you knew. Too often, access was made difficult by class, economics, or ignorance, and families were left to fend for themselves. The message both Hilary and Helen heard was that few people cared. The message they received from the medical community and the community at large was that some babies were too odd, too needy, and too threatening to our sense of control. Some babies were not expected to be welcomed or wanted.

This nation loves to tell the story of its rugged individuals, who overcome adversity with courage and wit. It is a good story that serves our national character well. But if it is not softened with a sense of compassion, it can imply a lack of respect and care for those among us who will always be needy, despite their greatest efforts. In 1962, when Linda Nelson and Simon Albert were born, many experts felt it was best to keep such people out of sight. Today those attitudes have given way to policies that mainstream people with disabilities into our schools and communities. If such changes reflect an increase in our compassion and understanding, surely we have never needed it more than now, when we face the power to keep some disabled people from being born.

Since the mid-1960s, when medical science began to make amniocentesis available on an experimental basis, people have not had to accept, so power-lessly, the roll of nature's dice in their hopes for a normal, healthy baby. Increasingly, the odds could be challenged. Science did not wait for society to decide how it would use this ability to diagnose genetic imperfections in the unborn child. There was no historic precedent to guide parents, physicians, and ethicists in the choices now available. Yet the unfolding story would surely be affected by society's attitudes and behavior toward the less-than-perfect who were already living.

In the same year Linda Nelson and Simon Albert were born to families who had no way of knowing beforehand that their babies would be less than perfect, a genetically normal child was conceived in Arizona. It would not remain normal for long, however, and its unwitting mother was about to become the first test case for prenatal diagnosis in the court of public opinion.

Sherri Finkbine

Sometime during a night in May 1962, Sherri Finkbine woke up severely nauseous. "After you've had four children, you don't need your family physician or a frog test to tell you you're pregnant again," she wrote in a January 1963 *Redbook* magazine story, "The Baby We Didn't Dare to Have."

She told her husband Bob, who smiled placidly. "That's nice, dear," he said and went back to sleep. "Bob loves children, and sometimes I think he wouldn't mind if we had twenty of them," Sherri wrote. The Finkbines had two boys and two girls, ages two to seven. Both parents were originally from the midwest and the young couple now lived in Phoenix, where Sherri, thirty, hosted a local television show for children. Bob, thirty-one, coached and taught history at a suburban high school. On their first date, as students at the University of Wisconsin, they had gone to see a movie about a crippled child. Sherri had wept during the final scene as the child, with his legs locked in braces, walked haltingly toward the camera. She was embarrassed by her emotional display, but Bob was impressed with her sensitivity.

A few years later, their first daughter, Terri, was born with a congenital hip deformity. She spent most of her first year in a formidable metal and leather brace that ran the length of her leg and hooked onto a leather strap around her waist. An iron bar forced her legs apart. "We took the brace off only for baths," Sherri recalled. "I suspect she had some of the longest baths in history." Terri fully recovered, but Sherri thought the painful memory of that experience had a bearing on the Finkbines' decision about their fifth pregnancy.

Soon after she discovered she was pregnant in 1962, Sherri developed sharp chest pains. Her doctor attributed the pain to nerves. He prescribed tranquilizers, which eased the condition. When the pills ran out, Sherri found two bottles of another tranquilizer, which had been prescribed to Bob when he was in London leading a tour of teenagers.

"It seemed silly to get my prescription refilled when there were plenty on hand," Sherri figured, "and a tranquilizer was a tranquilizer." She took thirty or forty of Bob's pills over the next month and a half. Few, if any, medications carried special warnings for pregnant women in those days, because little was known about the potential harms. But the first evidence was beginning to surface, and it was not, unfortunately, emerging from a laboratory. Bob's tranquilizer, thalidomide, had been widely prescribed throughout Europe, and while Sherri was pregnant, thousands of birth deformities were being traced to the mothers' use of the drug.

It was mid-July when Sherri first read about thalidomide and its effects in the *Arizona Republic*. The infants were being born with a malformation called phocomelia. Most of the sufferers had flaps instead of arms; some had shortened and twisted legs. In some cases a child was without limbs, was missing an ear, had a flattened nose, or had a permanently paralyzed face. The U.S. Food and Drug Administration had blocked distribution of the drug in the United States. Still, some pills, like Bob's, had made their way into the country. Not long after Sherri's doctors confirmed that Bob's pills were indeed thalidomide, a mother in New York bore a thalidomide-deformed baby who died forty-one minutes later.

The night before Sherri and Bob went to see the obstetrician about their options, they talked for long hours about life and death. They thought about the prospect of a baby born without arms or legs "—a human vegetable. His life—or her's—would be a living death. . . . Did we have the right to condemn a human being to that kind of existence? Would he be grateful to us someday, when he reached maturity, for giving him life? Or would he look about him at people with arms and legs, at children running, at boys and girls walking hand in hand, and curse us for letting him be born?"

Sherri and Bob thought about their other four children and what would happen to them if much of the family's time and money "would have to be lavished on the helpless one, and the others would be cheated of part of their birthright. Did we have the right to do that?" They thought about all the time and energy they had devoted to Terri's disability when she was their only baby. With this baby there would be no hope of recovery.

Sherri, nearly hysterical with worry, looked down the next seven months of pregnancy as if she were "standing at the edge of a great black pit." On the other hand, she knew nothing about abortions except that "women died and crooked doctors went to jail because of them."

The next day, the doctor wasted no time. He leafed through a medical journal and handed Bob an article about the tragic crop of malformed children in Europe. Although the doctor urged her not to look, Sherri saw the clinical photographs of the naked babies without arms or legs. One had only a head and torso. The doctor recommended that Sherri undergo a therapeutic abortion, explaining that they were quite safe for the mother when done under proper conditions by a competent doctor. He assured the couple that the hospital's review board would approve their application. It was Saturday. The abortion was scheduled for the next Thursday.

Arizona law allowed hospital abortions only to save the mother's life. Although the hospital board maintained strict secrecy regarding their decisions, its grounds for granting the Finkbines' request were surely psychiatric. In Arizona, as in many other states with similar laws, hospitals routinely bent the legal language to protect women from hardships and possible breakdowns that could result from the birth of a deformed infant.

Ordinarily, Sherri Finkbine's abortion would have passed unnoticed, like the other eight thousand to ten thousand hospital abortions performed around the country in 1962. Instead, it became front-page news, triggering the first national debate about what had become a relatively common, albeit largely invisible, practice.

On Sunday morning, the day after visiting their doctor, while Bob painted the patio, Sherri called J. Edward Murray, the managing editor of the *Arizona Republic*. Murray's daughter had gone to Europe with Bob's tour and his son was taking Bob's history course. Murray was not in, so Sherri explained her situation to his wife and said that she wanted to thank the newspaper for alerting her to thalidomide's disastrous consequences. "Then I had a thought," Sherri recalled. "Perhaps, I suggested to Mrs. Murray, the paper might like to carry another story about the drug in order to make sure that women who hadn't seen the earlier publicity would be warned in case they too had taken thalidomide." Almost immediately, Sherri got a call from the paper's medical editor, Julian DeVries, who was working on a series about thalidomide. He asked a few questions and assured Sherri her name would not be used.

On Monday morning, the *Arizona Republic* carried a front-page story with a box around it: "Pill Causing Deformed Infants May Cost Woman Her Baby Here." The story went out on the wire services. Within hours, DeVries was getting calls from the *New York Times*, from NBC, and from newspapers in London and Australia. Amid the flurry of interviews with clergymen and doctors, news sources also carried a somewhat veiled threat from the county attorney to prosecute the Good Samaritan Hospital, where Sherri was to have her abortion.

On Tuesday, Sherri's doctor told her the operation had been postponed. The hospital, squirming under the glare of publicity, had decided to preempt the county attorney by filing suit in Arizona Superior Court, naming the state of Arizona, the state attorney general, and the county attorney as defendants. The hospital hoped to bring about a declaratory judgment that would force the court to make abortion legal in the state. The lawsuit made Sherri Finkbine's name public.

Reporters and photographers besieged the Finkbine home. A headline the next day read: "Abortion Case Mother TV Star Here." The story covered nearly the entire front page. The family's telephone clamored ceaselessly; the house was filled with television crews and their cumbersome gear. "By noon I was so jittery that I felt as if I'd blow apart," Sherri said.

That afternoon the doorbell rang, and a uniformed security guard from the hospital came to tell Sherri she was to report to Good Samaritan. The hospital staff had been unable to reach her by telephone. Sherri immediately drove to the hospital. In a matter of moments she was registered as Mrs. Jane Doe, shown to a private room, given an injection and put to bed. "The doctors and lawyers had decided, both for the sake of my nerves and because of the impending hearing, that I had best be placed out of reach of the reporters," Sherri said. She did not say whether the doctors and lawyers had asked if she *wanted* to be removed from her home and family, given an injection, and put to bed. It is not clear whose interests were actually being served.

The hearing was held on Friday—the day after the abortion was supposed to have taken place—and on that Monday the judge granted the state's request to dismiss the case, allowing Mrs. Finkbine to proceed with the operation without a court review. The hospital, however, once again fearful of damaging publicity and possible prosecution, now refused to perform the abortion. Sherri left the hospital on Tuesday, and she and Bob applied for passports. At home, the telephone continued to ring constantly. Bushels of letters and telegrams brought messages of support and denunciation. Some offered to adopt their baby if they would let it be born. Others sent curses, curative herbs, or religious medals.

Eager to obtain an abortion before the second trimester of pregnancy, when a more risky Caesarean operation would be required, Sherri and Bob soon flew to Stockholm, greeted by reporters at every stop. The Swedish procedure was complicated, and the hurdles were especially complex for foreigners. Only about 15 percent of American applications were approved. Sherri had to undergo interviews and tests with psychiatrists, social workers, gynecologists, and a radiologist. The resulting reports, as well as X-ray evidence, were presented to a ten-member medical board, which then weighed the merits of Sherri's claim that her child was in grave danger. One doctor told her: "This intense procedure will prove good for you in the long run. The burden of decision is no longer yours alone. Wise and thorough medical people will now share your burden. You are in their hands."

After nearly two weeks of examination, waiting, and praying, the Finkbines got the call that the abortion had been approved. "I cried. All the terrible tightness in me broke and I felt a blessed release," Sherri said. The next day, after the procedure was completed, she awoke from the general anesthetic and found Bob standing by her bed. He told her again and again through the anesthetic fog that the baby *had* been deformed. The doctor who had performed the abortion explained: "It was not a baby. You must think of it as an abnormal growth within you. It would never have been a normal child."

When the Finkbines returned home, Sherri lost her on-air television job, but the station gave her a position in which she helped to plan, write, and produce new local programs. Bob, too, held onto his work despite some pressure against him. In the end, Sherri Finkbine said, her only regret was that her situation had unleased so much bitterness. "We respect beliefs different from our own even while we ask that others respect our right to believe differently. I believe God does not knowingly send children into the world to suffer. If God had wanted me to have a malformed baby, He would not have given me the power to prevent it. Hadn't God's will already been tampered with by a man-made pill that crippled His finest work—a child?" A little over two years after Sherri published the story of her abortion ordeal, she gave birth to her fifth child, a healthy girl, in February 1965. She and Bob went on to have a sixth child, another daughter.

She wrote that she hoped her family's ordeal had helped to focus public attention on stronger safeguards against dangerous or unproven drugs. Surely that was accomplished. She also hoped her tragedy would hasten "the day when our nation, advanced and enlightened in so many other respects, will take a fresh, unprejudiced look at its abortion procedures." A decade after Sherri wrote those words, the United States Supreme Court swept away all major restrictions on abortion in its *Roe v. Wade* decision. But two decades after *Roe v. Wade,* many Americans have questions about just how "advanced and enlightened" we have become concerning abortions.

Opening Pandora's Box

For decades before Sherri Finkbine's abortion, hospitals across America had routinely terminated pregnancies because of possible prenatal damage to the child, usually in cases involving rubella. Only two things were really new in the Finkbines' situation. First, their case introduced a new understanding of how fragile the fetus's development is and the extent to which its system is interlaced with its mother's. Eventually, pregnant women would learn to be wary of a long list of possible hazards, from alcohol and cigarettes to aspirin and cold medicines. Second, their crisis brought the quiet practice of hospital abortion into the public limelight.

The picture that emerged left many disquieted. During the 1940s and '50s, discussion on abortion had scarcely existed. In the absence of information, the popular view was that abortion was performed by stealthy, back-alley opportunists on promiscuous single women, who often died or became sterile as a result. In the public's mind, abortion had always been associated with illicit sex. Sherri Finkbine, however, was a married woman who wanted a child and was virtually innocent of any part in the hand fate had dealt her. One could not dismiss her agony—as some did in cases of sexual promiscuity—by saying that she deserved it.

On the other hand, there was the potential child to consider. One popular magazine ran a story about the thalidomide scare that included a full-page picture of an armless German girl, a beautiful child with artificial arms and mitten-like hands connected to a harness of metal and leather. Should such a child never have been born? Who had the right to decide?

When Sherri Finkbine called the *Arizona Republic*'s managing editor that Sunday morning, she inadvertently opened Pandora's box. But if she had not done so, someone else would have played Pandora's part. Editors and news directors all across the country knew immediately that her story was front-page material. Their news instincts told them that the issue would rivet public attention. When Sherri Finkbine's name became a household word, so did the word "abortion." The volume of letters and telegrams testified, as Sherri herself said, that her experience indeed "touched deep emotional wellsprings."

The Finkbines' case not only broke the silence on hospital abortions and thereby shattered simplistic views of the issue, but it also sparked public debate on the morality of aborting potentially deformed infants. Some people continued to resist the sad complexities of considering the child's quality of life. But Pandora's box would never be shut again. Simplistic answers would continue to prove unsatisfying. At the time, the more thoughtful saw it was impossible to wholly champion either Sherri Finkbine or the fetus she carried without denying their claims upon each other and robbing the issue of all its moral nuances.

According to Sherri Finkbine's own account, she herself denied little. If she ended the life of the baby she carried, it was not for a lack of love or responsibility. She believed more deeply in that baby's right to die than she did in its right to live. But it was neither right that ultimately swayed Sherri's decision. It was her love and sense of responsibility for all her children, including the one she carried, that led her to think abortion was the best among her hopelessly inadequate choices. Many who wrote to the Finkbines disagreed with their standards and held up others they found superior. Some, for example, believed that innocent life was too sacred ever to be taken. This is a belief honored by time and many institutions. But in a culture that often had hidden away, isolated, and abandoned its less-than-perfect children as if they were shameful, it was not Sherri Finkbine who deserved the blame for questioning the sanctity of life. She and her family had acted with all the love, care, and conscience they could muster. American society could not say the same.

8

CHALLENGING THE ODDS

We may think it too farfetched to believe that young couples in the future might actually choose whether to continue a pregnancy on the basis of genetic tests that predict a child's incapacities, deficiencies or susceptibilities in the distant future. But social mores change rapidly in the face of new technology. The advent of techniques like amniocentesis and more recently chorionic villus sampling for just a limited number of chromosomal defects has led to an explosion in prenatal testing in the last decade. As a result, pregnancies are routinely terminated today for reasons that would have left previous generations aghast. Genetic counselors say it's not unusual to encounter young couples who, for whatever reason they may formally state, are actually seeking a prenatal test solely to determine the sex of the fetus. And sociologists say younger couples today are showing an increasing tendency to expect—and demand—only 'perfect' children.

Jerry E. Bishop and Michael Waldholz,
*Genome: The Story of the Most Astonishing Scientific Adventure of Our Time—
The Attempt to Map all the Genes in the Human Body* (1990)

Introduction

Today, sonography allows a pregnant woman to peer into a video screen and see the fuzzy contours of her unborn child's fingers and toes—as well as its kidney, bladder, brain, spine, and the chambers of its tiny, beating heart. Even before a mother can feel her baby's first soft flutterings, she can watch it kick, wiggle, and somersault deep within her. Levels of serum alphafetoprotein (AFP) in the mother's blood can indicate whether her fetus might have a neural tube defect such as spina bifida. Amniocentesis and a newer prenatal test called chorionic villus sampling (CVS) can analyze the fetus's chromosomal makeup, revealing or ruling out many genetic birth defects. Thus, months before delivery a woman can, if she so chooses, call upon modern medical technology to learn much about her unborn child's health and even to discover its gender.

Amniocentesis is performed on more than 300,000 American women each year, or in about 5 percent of all pregnancies. The test involves the withdrawal and analysis of a sample of amniotic fluid from the placental sac surrounding the fetus. A hollow-bore needle is inserted into the mother's abdomen when she is in about the sixteenth week of pregnancy. The genetic diagnosis is usually completed by the eighteenth week, close to the date when abortion becomes both more dangerous and, in some states, illegal. The CVS test, which carries a higher risk of miscarriage, is conducted on tissue taken from the newly forming placenta and permits genetic diagnosis by the ninth week of pregnancy. Because both tests can precipitate a miscarriage, they are generally recommended only for women over the age of thirty-five, when the rising risk of genetic abnormalities is considered higher than the chance of a spontaneous miscarriage. As amniocentesis has become safer, some centers now recommend it for women in their early thirties. Couples who are morally opposed to abortion rarely accept these tests' risks, however, because the only "remedy" if prenatal diagnosis detects a defect is to terminate the pregnancy.

The crystal ball of prenatal testing is also limited by areas of obscurity and even total darkness. For example, while in most cases diagnosis is definitive, prenatal testing cannot always say how severe the effects of an abnormality will be. In more unusual cases the test results themselves are puzzling because of the rarity of the condition they reveal or even because of laboratory errors. Furthermore, both looking and choosing not to look within technology's magic glass can impose heavy moral, emotional, and practical responsibilities on expectant parents. Deciding what to do if a glimpse into the crystal ball reveals misfortune can have devastating consequences, yet the glass offers no help in weighing the profound moral questions an abnormal diagnosis can thrust upon two stunned and grieving parents. On the other hand, deciding not to look within the glass at all can lead to the birth of a child who will live with unrelenting pain and hardship. Thus the mere availability of the crystal ball compels parents to weigh powers that once belonged only to God or nature. Whether couples exercise those powers or not, they can impose a challenge that seems far greater than the human capacity to respond.

The technological futures predicted in Aldous Huxley's *Brave New World* and George Orwell's *1984* are here. But it is not Big Brother—or the state— that controls the scientific breakthroughs that revolutionize our sexual and procreative lives, as Huxley and Orwell had feared. Instead these changes are dawning in an era of privatization. Rules of the market and individual decision making prevail. In the United States, at least, the government has stepped back from regulation. *Roe v. Wade* has placed abortion beyond state intervention and put it in the hands of the pregnant woman and her doctor. By extension, then, the tools of decision making, such as prenatal testing, also belong to these two individuals, not the state. But while the *Roe v. Wade* decision assures the *right* to a private decision, it does not require *responsibility* of either the woman or her doctor. It does not specify what they should consider or even that they meet except during the procedure itself. By contrast, as we have mentioned in earlier chapters, abortion laws in most other Western democracies explicitly balance access to abortion with both individual and social responsibilities.

In the previous chapter, we saw Hilary Nelson and Helen Albert's obstetricians take two very different positions regarding their patients' babies born with Down syndrome. Hilary's doctor advised her to institutionalize her child immediately; Helen's took a stance more unusual for those times and urged her to keep her son at home. But both doctors imperiously prescribed solutions for these mothers. It was standard at that time for doctors to decide unilaterally what was best for their patients.

Then, during the 1960s and '70s, the patients' rights movement rose up against such paternalism, especially among obstetrician/gynecologists, who had been especially guilty of it. Medicine gradually adopted a more professional, if less personal, demeanor, helping patients to make informed decisions of their own. But disseminating information concerning abortion has been a politically, morally, and emotionally sensitive issue. Some segments of the pro-life movement, for example, have promoted legislation that would require doctors to "counsel" abortion patients by showing them graphic pictures of abortions or models of developing fetuses. Responsible medical professionals have recoiled from coercing or intimidating patients. Many believe that if the patient is fully alert and the doctor has no reason to suspect she is being coerced by a partner or parent, then she requires no further information than a clinical description of her options. In fact, although doctor and patient are specifically mentioned as partners in the *Roe v. Wade* ruling, doctor-patient contact may be limited to the ten minutes or so it takes to perform the procedure in the thousands of abortion clinics that have sprung up in *Roe v. Wade's* wake.

Although some clinics do require that each patient meet at least briefly with a counselor, the medical profession has largely shrugged off its part in abortion decision making. Most medical schools deal only superficially, if at all, with questions about the doctor's role in abortion. And although continuing-education seminars on ethics are popular with practicing physicians, abortion is not high on the agenda in such programs. Dr. John Coulehan, former associate director of the Center for Medical Ethics at the University of Pittsburgh Medical School, explained why. "You see," he said, "generally speaking, the women involved [in abortion choices] are competent to make their own decisions." Medical ethics currently focuses more often on right-to-die issues, where treatment decisions sometimes must be made for unconscious or incompetent patients.

A patient's competency, however, depends on the accuracy of her information. Every woman in this chapter faced some possibility that the baby she carried might be defective. Some chose to glimpse inside the womb, while others waited for birth to reveal its secrets. Whatever they decided, they desperately needed complete, accurate information at every step of the process. They needed knowledgeable professionals who could hear their wishes and concerns without imposing their own. Some stories in this chapter reflect the best of modern American medicine. Some of the women we interviewed told of caring, well-informed professionals, who guided them—without pushing—through what technology could and could not reveal. Others told us much of what is wrong with American medicine—the lingering practice of well-meaning paternalism as well as the hurried, uncaring attitudes of doctors, nurses, and counselors who judged their patients, treated them cruelly, or simply failed to give them the information they needed. In this small sample, there seems to be a pattern of bias among those who represented the worst side of medicine. They had a squeamishness about abnormality, a distaste for risk, a tendency to push prenatal testing and therapeutic abortion, and a lack of compassion for the needy and dependent.

Modern science has brought these families' stories into being, and their plots are as new as the technologies that deliver them. Little wonder, then, that so many of these couples floundered in the face of such weighty decisions. Sometimes family and friends rallied with support; sometimes they backed away in confusion. Sometimes the medical professionals served honorably; sometimes they failed miserably. Some responses were inappropriate, reflecting a tendency to react instead of to listen. Couples received sympathy for a child with disabilities when they themselves felt joyful about the many abilities they saw. Others were subjected to a false cheerfulness—"You can always have another"—when they needed to grieve a baby they had aborted.

Only the couples themselves—the parents or would-be parents—consistently and successfully struggled to comprehend the responsibility modern science had thrust upon them. Every woman in this chapter carried a child that she and her husband had planned for and wanted. What these couples had conceived in love and deep wanting was not an abstract fetus or tissue mass; it was their child. From the time the pregnancy was confirmed, they had begun to love a baby, the real flesh and blood forming within the woman as well as the dream they could not yet see or touch. Perhaps their dream was compromised, but they still responded as parents. And it was as parents that they acted, with all the love and concern, joy and grief that came with their decisions.

It is not surprising, then, that while the cases that follow are neatly divided between women who gave birth and women who chose abortion, the factors in each decision, and the consequences that followed it, bridge that gulf. Threads of guilt, self-doubt, sorrow, courage, and respect for the beauty and sanctity of birth crisscross these cases, often tying them together with extraordinary compassion and understanding.

Down Syndrome: Definitive Diagnosis— Uncertain Prognosis

A genetically normal human fetus receives twenty-three pairs of chromosomes from its parents, with one chromosome in each pair contributed by the mother and one by the father. Down syndrome, the most common cause of mental retardation, is characterized by an extra chromosome in the twenty-first pair. When amniocentesis or CVS renders a diagnosis of Down syndrome, it is unambiguous. What is ambiguous is how severely the child will be affected by the syndrome in a given case.

The older a woman is when she conceives, the greater the chance that her baby will have Down syndrome or another congenital problem. At age twenty, the risk is one in one thousand for all genetic abnormalities, one in two thousand for Down syndrome. At age forty, her odds for bearing a Down syndrome baby are one in one hundred.

Today, thanks to greatly improved resources and methods of care and education, the futures for children with Down syndrome are brighter. Just how much brighter is difficult to assess, though. Older studies showed the average IQ of a person with Down syndrome was about thirty-five. Today the average is thought to be between fifty-five and sixty-five. Some persons with Down syndrome have even been measured at one hundred, which is considered the normal average. But the use of IQ measurements with Down syndrome is disputed, because the test fails to measure Down syndrome's particular peaks and valleys of ability. While many Down children are slow to develop verbal ability, for example, they may be quite proficient readers. Down children with IQs as low as thirty-two have been taught to read with good comprehension.

But social worker Hilary Nelson, who told about her adult, institutionalized Down syndrome daughter in the previous chapter, maintains that despite such progress: "It's still a lousy situation. The handicapped *are* better off today, if they have the means." And having the means is not guaranteed.

Although fewer children with Down syndrome were institutionalized during the 1970s, many parents still got the same message Hilary and Dan Nelson got in 1962—that their daughter would be little more than a vegetable. When Jason Kingsley was born in 1974, the obstetrician minced no words. "Your son is a 'mongoloid,' " he told Jason's father, Charles Kingsley, forty-five years old. "He will be severely retarded. Do not let his mother see, feed, or form an attachment to him. Put him in an institution immediately; tell everyone he died. Then go home and have another child."

Fortunately for Jason, his mother Emily, thirty-four years old and a writer for the children's television program "Sesame Street," saw a normal, beautiful baby. "The little I'd been told about chromosome imbalance," Emily said in a 1982 article in *Family Circle* (Fein), "sounded so mysterious. . . . I felt almost as if my baby had been kidnapped by some sorcerer and replaced with a creature from another planet whose chromosomes had no relationship to ours." Later she came to realize that of course Jason's chromosomes were made up of the genes she and her husband had contributed. He simply had an extra piece of that heritage.

"No one I knew had ever had any contact with a Down syndrome child. What do you do when there's no one to talk to—take the phone book and look under R for *retarded*. . . . or M for *mental?*" But some progress had been made since Hilary Nelson and Helen Albert had had to search for their own resources twelve years earlier. The hospital's genetic counselor did visit the Kingsleys, and she told them that children with Down syndrome have a good chance for development though early infant education programs. That advice encouraged Emily and Charles to give it a try.

It was Emily's brother who referred them to the Mental Retardation Institute in Valhalla, New York, near their home in Westchester County. Teachers there helped the Kingsleys discover that a stimulating program could be part of daily life, much as it is with genetically normal babies. A trip to the grocery store became an opportunity to identify foods by color and shape. Containers became stacking blocks and noisemakers. Bathing and dressing were times for naming body parts.

Jason sat up at eight months and began walking at eighteen months. When he was two years old, he was enrolled in a preschool program sponsored by the Westchester branch of the Association for Retarded Citizens (ARC), a national organization with support groups and infant stimulation programs. There he learned to dress and feed himself, and he became toilet trained. At four, Jason started to read and transferred to a local Montessori school for a richer academic environment. At eight, he was reading on a fourth-grade level.

Jason has appeared on "Sesame Street," and Emily wrote the television movie "Kids Like These" about children with Down syndrome in the mid-1980s. Both kinds of exposure helped to raise public consciousness about the near normality of many people with Down syndrome. Today there is even a popular television program in which one of the actors has Down syndrome. The prophecy that a child with Down syndrome would be nothing more than a vegetable had been a self-fulfilling one for most of these children and their families. Institutionalization made it come true. Unfortunately, the myth lives on. Advocates for children with Down syndrome believe many medical practitioners, including obstetricians, are ill-informed about radical new findings in recent research and literature about Down syndrome. In turn, expectant parents who are told they carry a child with Down syndrome and new mothers who have given birth to one may also be ill-informed about their child's prospects.

Moreover, as we mentioned in the last chapter, mainstreaming children with handicaps often means that the daily, time-consuming stimulation and care they require falls to their mothers, whose other interests and ambitions may have to be curtailed. The conflict has not gone unrecognized. Barry Mitnick, father of a child with Down syndrome and book review editor for the periodical *Down Syndrome: Papers and Abstracts for Professionals*, has written that time management is one of the biggest problems facing families with such a child (Mitnick, 1988). Yet most parents of children with Down syndrome willingly took on the job of caring for them because they are self-educated advocates for their children, facing inadequate community support.

Today Mitnick and others report that services for these children have improved because their success has been so overwhelming. Even so, Mitnick told us in an interview, research on Down syndrome, the most common genetic variation, remains "astonishingly small," and educational and job training opportunities for the older adolescents and young adults are "atrocious." According to Mitnick, Americans like to believe the myth that we are a generous people doing all we can. This way, our shortcomings can all be blamed on the victim. When persons with disabilities do not achieve, the public often assumes it is because they lack the capacity.

If we stood back from the myth, what would we see? The United States has the most liberal abortion laws among Western democracies, yet it lags far behind most others in social welfare policies for persons with disabilities. It has a health care community that is often uninformed and perhaps even uninterested in the potential of persons with Down syndrome. It would appear, as Mary Ann Glendon has pointed out about our policies toward children in poverty, that we have decided to solve the problems of persons with Down syndrome by choosing to abort them rather than to fully fund enlightened research and social programs that would allow many of them to become productive citizens. Such a grim story, Glendon has said, is not one Americans like to believe about themselves.

Jackie Kolar

If Hilary Nelson, who was repulsed when her daughter was born with Down syndrome in 1962, stands at one end of the spectrum of maternal reactions to a child with Down syndrome, Jackie Kolar stands at the other. Though each woman was raised by immigrant parents in a religious household, their childhood experiences and their widely divergent priorities as adults led them to opposite poles of feeling and action. Of the two women, Jackie is the more sympathetic in some ways, yet her story, too, centers on the painful question of a child's suffering and a mother's reaction to it.

When Jackie Kolar became pregnant when she was thirty-six years old, she knew her age put her at risk for a baby with birth defects. She also knew exactly what she would do about it. When her obstetricians brought up the question of prenatal testing, she asked if any new medical breakthroughs allowed problems detected by the tests to be treated in utero. The answer was no, so Jackie turned down the test. "I think that's just the kind of person I am," she said. Indeed, when we met her, she seemed entirely at peace with herself and her three children: Anita, five years old; William, three years old; and Tammie, nineteen months, who was born with Down syndrome.

Jackie is personally opposed to abortion, and she was not interested in having amniocentesis just to gain information about her baby's health before its birth. "I like surprises," Jackie said, smiling. "I wouldn't even want to be told the sex of the baby. I think that's the fun of it, when the baby's delivered and the doctor says, 'Oh, yes, it's a boy' or 'It's a girl.' "

But not all the surprises at Tammie's birth were happy ones for Jackie and her husband, Bill Duffy. "The delivery of Tammie was really great," Jackie recalled with a smile. "It was what I call 'textbook perfect.' " Jackie's biggest worry had been whether she could deliver vaginally after William's Caesarean birth, but such concerns dwindled in the face of much larger ones. "A baby can come out your ear, as long as the baby is normal and healthy," Jackie said, "and Tammie really wasn't."

The first thing Jackie noticed was that her newborn's tongue protruded. "And I thought, oh, that's cute. That's just like her cousin Bernadette, who always stuck her tongue out. . . . And I looked at her eyes, and they looked a little bit slanty, and I thought, uh oh, there's something the matter here. In the back of my mind, the Down syndrome question was there because of my age."

Within a few minutes, Jackie and Bill's pediatrician was in the delivery room examining Tammie. She congratulated the couple but then told them she suspected their child had Down syndrome, a diagnosis later confirmed by lab tests. "I just answered—I know what I said—I said, 'I'm not surprised, because I thought so too,'" Jackie recalled. "That was about it. We just said, 'Well, give us Tammie and we'll just get on with things.' I think we cried a little bit right then but not a whole lot." In fact, Jackie felt she did not cry enough for the long-faced nurses who came around to her room for the next couple of days.

Jackie, whose dark permed curls fall softly to her square jaw, had known for a long time that she opposed abortion and that she accepted the possibility of giving birth to a handicapped child. "I think our reaction was kind of matter-of-fact, because it's something that I had considered a long time ago," she said. As a freshman in college, Jackie had told a pregnant friend that she would help her in any way that she could, except in getting an abortion. "I don't think at that time it was anything that I had really thought out, but I think it was just something—a feeling that I grew up with, that I really respected life. . . . You know, it's not that I'm a religious fanatic, or I'm a fanatic pro-lifer; I'm not. I think I feel those things in my heart, but it's not something I would impose on anyone," Jackie said. Neither does she feel comfortable with groups that publicly support the right to choose. She herself strongly supports the women's movement, for example, but has never felt that she could join the National Organization for Women (NOW) because of its stand on abortion.

Jackie's parents came from eastern Europe. They settled in an eastern Pennsylvania coal town and raised Jackie and her brother with the fundamental values of hard work, cash on the barrel, close family ties, and solid religious faith. Jackie, a practicing Catholic, nevertheless shook off the idea that her religion dictated her views. She was convinced she would have the same beliefs even if she had had a different religious upbringing. Her belief, she said, is simply in the sanctity of life from the moment of conception.

Jackie had an abundance of traditionally feminine qualities. She was a nurturer, a patient and uncomplaining caretaker not only of her children but, at different times, of her parents as well. She seemed not to have questioned or in any way rebelled against her upbringing; to the contrary, she embraced her past as she embraced the demands made upon her in the present.

When we interviewed her, Jackie was routinely caring for her father, who suffered from Parkinson's disease, and she and Bill were remodeling the basement of their bungalow in suburban Detroit so that her father could move in when his condition deteriorated. Jackie had also nursed her dying mother through her final bouts with ovarian cancer while her first child was still an infant.

"I think my mother's illness and subsequent death prepared me for everything and anything that could happen to me in life. My mum showed me how to live and she showed me how to die," Jackie said. "She let me take care of her in a way that didn't embarrass her and it didn't embarrass me." Jackie remembered running downstairs to her bedridden mother with a warm washcloth. "She yelled at me: 'Jackie, you're running down the steps too fast. You're gonna get hurt.' I just loved it, because here she was still being my mother, still telling me what to do, but yet I was taking care of her." Her mother died just a few hours later.

"My mum chose life," Jackie said, referring to her mother's bravery and good humor even in the face of death. "I think that's what God wants us to do. He wants us to choose life. I guess that's why we had Tammie and kept her and wouldn't even consider doing away with her, because that's the way my mother lived, my father lived."

Jackie had an undefined sense during her last pregnancy that her baby might have Down syndrome. Many of her friends were having babies relatively late in life, and she thought it was bound to happen to someone. Nevertheless, she told us: "I didn't even speak about it to Bill. I don't even think we said, 'Well, what if this baby has Down?'" Once Tammie was born, Jackie, unlike Hilary, never asked, "Why me?" Instead she thought, "Why *not* me?" If someone she knew was going to have a mentally retarded baby, Jackie felt she would be the best one to handle it. "I just knew that this baby would be so accepted and so loved that it wouldn't make any difference."

Despite their own ready acceptance of Tammie, Jackie and Bill at first ran into some barriers in acquiring the information they needed in order to raise her. While she was in the hospital, Jackie remembered: "I kept asking the nurses for information about Down syndrome. 'Do you have any pamphlets? Do you have any books? Can I go to the library here?' They said no, that the library was just for the professional staff. The social workers wouldn't come to speak to me, because they had to have the laboratory report and that would take a couple of days. I was disappointed that they didn't put me in contact with ARC, the Association for Retarded Citizens, right away. We were surprised that the hospital staff wasn't more prepared to handle a case like this."

Another couple we interviewed had a similar experience after an amniocentesis told them they were going to have a daughter with Down syndrome. A blue-collar couple from Pittsburgh, Carole and Sam Thompson had decided to go ahead with the pregnancy, although they knew virtually nothing about Down syndrome. Frantic for information, Carole and Sam went to the library, where outdated clinical books told them their baby would be sickly, have a bad heart, and probably not live beyond the age of thirty. The pictures in these books frightened them. Carole's obstetrician sent them to the genetics department at a large women's hospital. When Carole and Sam asked to be put in touch with another family with a Down syndrome child, the counselor there referred them to a woman fifty miles away. Carole and Sam assumed Down syndrome must be rare if the closest case was so far away.

Access to the information they so desperately needed might never have come at all if Carole and Sam had not moved into a new home. On moving day, Carole introduced herself over the back fence to her new neighbor, Eleanor, who eyed her belly and asked when her baby was due. Carole felt tears come to her eyes. "I said . . . 'I just found out I have a Down child.' She said, 'Oh, don't feel bad, let me introduce you to my daughter. She's eight years old and has Down syndrome.'" Eleanor gave them books, more modern and hopeful than the ones the library had had, and she told them about the Association for Retarded Citizens, which had support groups and infant stimulation programs right in their community. When Carole and Sam met Eleanor's daughter, their feelings about the pregnancy changed profoundly. "I said, 'If this is what it's like, I'll take it,'" Carole told us. "She was so precious." Indeed, their image of their unborn baby changed from one of sickliness and hopeless retardation to one of health and potential. They regained the hope and expectation that the diagnosis of Down syndrome had shattered.

Jackie and Bill's problems with access to information were fortunately short-lived. Soon, they were given a book that got them off to a good start, and, Jackie stressed, "both the pediatrician and the obstetrician were wonderful. The pediatrician said, 'I want to find you the best infant stimulation program in the area.'"

Jackie admitted that she had never really given any thought to how much work a baby with Down syndrome would require, and Tammie's special needs profoundly changed the lives of everyone in their family. Nevertheless, Jackie had no regrets. It was hard for her to understand how anyone could abort something "so human" as a baby with Down syndrome. "I guess I wouldn't be totally honest in saying that [Tammie's condition] didn't make any difference, but it didn't make a whole lot of difference to us. It was almost a test of my convictions. I just felt that I had this pact with God in that, you know, this is the way I felt and I would never do anything about it, and sure enough it happened. And I just had to be true to my word, my feelings, my convictions. And I hope that I am."

"The tragedy of Tammie," Jackie continued, "is not necessarily her Down syndrome, but all the other medical health problems that come with it." With a sigh she said, "Tammie has a complicated history for a nineteen-month-old. It all started with her heart murmur, which was detected immediately." Tammie was born with a hole in her heart and a mitral valve problem that required surgery. Doctors hoped to delay the operation, but when Tammie's condition grew worse, at 4½ months, they decided to operate. "Tammie almost died. Bill was told that she wasn't going to make it. You wonder, how do you bury a child? In a couple of seconds you play the funeral scene out in your mind." Tammie pulled through, though. "We had our miracle with this baby," said Jackie with a smile.

Sadly, the miracle was followed by a host of other problems for Tammie. "She became badly anemic, and we had to correct that. Then she started getting infections. One infection after the other—a sinus infection, ear infections, stomach viruses—that started when she was six months old and culminated with a case of pneumonia at about ten months and continued on and on. We were told she had restricted airways. She would aspirate food into her lungs and get infections that way. She had a suck-swallow coordination problem. She had a breathing problem. It looks like she has asthma. She still has these problems to a lesser degree. They're manageable now."

Daily management of Tammie's problems were not easy, however. If Jackie and Bill wanted to go out they had to call two baby-sitters, one for Anita and William and a registered nurse for Tammie. At one point, on top of her regular exercises in mental stimulation (developed by the ARC), Tammie required eighteen applications of medicine per day and several administrations of physical therapy. By the time of our interview, she required ten medications, including a saline mist blown in her face four times a day with a bronchodilator to open her airways. She was usually on an antibiotic and an antihistamine, which was sprinkled from a capsule onto her food. Her food was usually a thickened "sludge" that she was unlikely to aspirate. Even her milk had to be thickened.

Sometimes the pressure caused by Tammie's health problems needed a release valve. Over one Thanksgiving, when Tammie had to be given prednisone to help her breathe, the additional medication proved the last straw. Tammie hated the taste of the drug, and Jackie had to give her a cola syrup afterward to keep her from throwing it back up. "It's a horrible medicine to take, and it's a horrible medicine to give," Jackie said. She had to sit on Tammie to get it into her. Bill helped when he could, but finally Jackie's seemingly limitless patience broke.

"I said, 'I have to leave the house,' " she remembered. "It was the day after Thanksgiving. I said: 'I want to do what everyone else in the world does after Thanksgiving—they go shopping.' I just wanted to join the masses. I wanted to lose myself in the crowd and be just like everyone else."

Jackie and Bill did their best to maintain a normal family life. The older children helped with Tammie's medication, and they were learning sign language to help her overcome the slow speech development that is frequently a problem for children with Down syndrome. They helped with the infant stimulation exercises, and, Jackie said, "They really have been [Tammie's] best teachers."

But sometimes life was not normal, Jackie admitted. "We make lots of trips to the hospital and lots of trips to the doctor, and we spend a lot of time medicating her and blowing bronchosol mist in her face," she said. The older children seemed to accept Tammie's needs as part of the family routine. "They never complain like, 'Ah, hurry up, mum, and get that over with.' "

Before Tammie was born, Jackie already had decided to abandon her career temporarily in order to be with her other children. She had worked as a sports trainer at a local university, "something that I really enjoyed doing," she said. But after the two children were born, she said, "I found that I was starting to not like my job. I thought I would always work outside the home, and that this is what people did these days." But Jackie found it impossible to assure quality time with her children at the end of each hectic day. "I've never been an anxious person, but I became anxiety-ridden. I couldn't eat. I had a lump in my throat all the time. I just wasn't doing well at all, at home or on the job. . . . It just took me a long time to realize that I didn't want to work outside the home any more, that I wanted to come home and be with the kids full time."

Bill gave his support, but Jackie hesitated to quit her job, particularly because of the income loss. "We bought this house on two incomes," she said, glancing around the three-bedroom bungalow they owned on a wide lot in the suburbs. "I don't know how we're doing it, but we are. Things just kind of work out. I don't feel that I've made a lot of sacrifices as far as not buying things and having things."

Nevertheless, Tammie's medical problems bit into the family income, Bill admitted. So far, though, it had not been more than they could handle. "I've been fortunate," he said, "to have a job and have insurance coverage" that has paid for most of the medical expenses. Whatever hardships there were, Bill added, they were far "outweighed by Tammie, the little kid. That's . . . payment enough for incurring many greater financial hardships."

Jackie and Bill hoped that Tammie would eventually be able to live independently. Advances in the treatment of people with Down syndrome have allowed more of them to approach independence, but most will always require a group-living situation with some supervision. It is too early to tell where Tammie's intelligence falls. In any case, Jackie and Bill expect that, after their deaths, Anita and William will continue to look out for Tammie.

Jackie and Bill have no regrets about their decision against prenatal testing and abortion. Indeed, they were prepared to risk having another handicapped child. When Tammie was just over a year old, Jackie became pregnant again, by accident. Once more, she and Bill had decided against prenatal testing, but Jackie miscarried. A laboratory study revealed the fetus had a chromosome abnormality. Although he and Jackie had not consulted a geneticist, Bill is now convinced that their risk for problems is much higher than the statistical average. "So that's really changed my outlook," he said. In order to provide a full life for the children they have now, he explained, "I think that having any more kids is something that we're not going to attempt to do."

Natalie Murdoch

Natalie Murdoch and her husband, Richard Meyer, planned carefully so that the birth of their second child would coincide roughly with their daughter Amanda's third birthday. The story of their second pregnancy contains elements of all the other stories in this section on Down syndrome, but its outcome and its effects on Natalie were wholly different.

Natalie was thirty-four when she conceived, and she would have been thirty-five at delivery. This meant the risk of Down syndrome had just drawn even with the risk of a miscarriage caused by amniocentesis. Natalie was not sure whether she wanted to undergo the test.

Natalie and Richard planned carefully for everything in their lives. All the furnishings in their remodeled home on the eastern edge of Cleveland have been carefully selected for function and aesthetics. The couple thought and talked about major decisions, closely examining their reactions and anticipating the effects of change before acting. In this, their approach was vastly different from Jackie and Bill's willingness to risk profound change.

"We spent a lot of dinner time just talking about amnio for almost four months," Natalie said. She and Richard went to genetic counseling, and, with no history of genetic problems on either side of their family, finally decided to forego amniocentesis unless an alphafetoprotein (AFP) test indicated a higher-than-average risk of Down syndrome. AFP levels in maternal blood serum can, in addition to indicating neural tube defects, refine the statistical chances that a child will have Down syndrome. Unless Natalie's AFP test increased her age-related odds, which were one in 350, she intended to refuse further prenatal testing.

"Part of the debate that we had for four months was that I really was terrified about having a needle stuck into my 4½-month pregnant stomach," Natalie said. Another factor in her aversion to the test was the idea of choosing abortion in her second trimester if the results of the amniocentesis were bad. Although she had already had a very early abortion when she was in college and was still very pro-choice politically, Natalie said: "I knew that I would feel very differently about it this time around. I had some moral reservations about a late abortion. With the first abortion I had never had a full-term pregnancy. But now I *knew* what a baby was like at 4½ months. I had been through it, I had read all the books."

Natalie's AFP level slightly *reduced* her risk of having a baby with Down syndrome, from one in 350 to one in 367, and she informed her doctor that she had decided against amniocentesis. When the doctor very gently asked why, Natalie explained her fear of the needle used in amniocentesis and her uneasiness about terminating a pregnancy in the fifth month. "And then," Natalie said, "she posed the question in a way that I don't think Richard and I ever did in all the months we debated it. She said: 'Would it be more difficult for you to terminate the pregnancy at this point or to raise a child with Down syndrome for the rest of your life?' And I just started to cry 'cause I knew what the answer to the question was, but I wished I didn't feel the way that I did."

When Natalie decided to proceed with amniocentesis after all, Richard was relieved. "I had always felt that the amnio was the right thing to do," he said, "and had never quite felt like I could come out and actually say that, because a lot of Natalie's fear was about the procedure itself. That was something she had to go through and not me. So it was easy for me to sit back and talk about the risks and benefits when I was the person who wasn't taking any of the risk and didn't have to face getting stuck with a needle."

Natalie was in her seventeenth week when she went into the hospital for the procedure she had feared so much. That part, she told us, "was a piece of cake." But Natalie was not to emerge from the test without confronting a worse fear—one that was revealed in her ultrasound test. The first sign of a problem was the intensity with which the physician conducting the ultrasound test peered repeatedly into the screen. With him was an entourage of other medical personnel, staring with him.

"I didn't think much of it," Natalie recalled, "because it's a teaching hospital, and they always have entourages of people. But they just kept pressing on my stomach and redoing the sonar." Finally, her doctor whispered to her that the baby's head looked too large. When Richard questioned the doctors further, they told him there was about a 20 percent chance that the measurement reflected hydrocephalus, a condition characterized by excess fluid in the cranium. Yet, there was an 80 percent chance that it was merely within the range of error for the sonar equipment. That seemed reassuring, but the odds that something was wrong with the baby had suddenly gone from one in 367 to one in five. The doctors wanted to redo the cranial measurement in three weeks. The amniocentesis results were expected in four weeks.

During those three weeks before the next ultrasound test, Natalie and Richard, who works for the county health department, searched the literature for information about hydrocephalus. They learned that it could range from a treatable condition to one that would prove fatal soon after birth. They decided, said Richard, that, "if there was any real chance that surgery could correct the baby's problem, we would go ahead and not terminate the pregnancy."

The next day, as Natalie was feeding Amanda a late Sunday breakfast, her doctor called. The amniocentesis results had come back early. Natalie and Richard's baby had Down syndrome. Natalie, telling this part of her story, began to cry. Richard, too, had been stunned. After all their research on hydrocephalus, he had almost forgotten about the amniocentesis test. Ironically, there was no relationship between the seemingly abnormal ultrasound reading and the diagnosis of Down syndrome.

Natalie and Richard knew immediately that they would terminate the pregnancy. To some, their decision to abort a baby with Down syndrome might seem inconsistent with their willingness to keep one with hydrocephalus. Natalie tried to explain their thinking: "We knew if the child had Down, the child had Down. Yes, there were varying degrees of Down and varying abnormalities that were associated with it, but there was no hope that this child was ever going to have anything but Down. There was no way of curing it or lessening it, which we understood there to be with hydrocephalus."

Natalie's doctor repeatedly invited questions and asked Natalie if she and Richard were sure about their decision, but Natalie assured her that she and Richard were unwavering. Natalie and Richard's attitude toward the range of possibilities for children with Down syndrome contrasts sharply with Jackie Kolar's. Jackie, after learning that it was not possible to cure genetic problems either in utero or after birth, refused amniocentesis, certain that she and Bill would love and accept whatever child they were given, regardless of how severe any handicaps might be. Natalie, in response to the same information, chose abortion rather than risk the kind of suffering Jackie and Bill's daughter Tammie has endured. "I know all of the things about how a seriously handicapped child brings a lot to your life that you wouldn't get otherwise," Natalie said. "A seriously handicapped child takes a lot from your life that you wouldn't otherwise have to give," she added. "I think life is difficult enough as it is. It didn't make sense to us to start [a baby] out with a severe problem, to go into it knowing."

Along with their unwillingness to burden a child with a handicap whose severity could not be known ahead of time, Richard and Natalie were also afraid that raising such a child might deprive Amanda of necessary time and attention. Richard explained, "I guess we knew that a Down child would require, at best, constant care from us, and that would take a great deal away from Amanda."

Their careers were another consideration. "Both of us are in jobs that are a lot more than jobs. They're things that we do because we believe in the work," said Richard, who works in public health. Natalie is an architect. Both jobs require commitments of time and emotion, which they willingly give. "All those things would have been affected by a life of caring for a Down child," Richard said. Natalie thought she would probably have to quit her job—one of the things a handicapped child could take from her life.

Natalie entered the hospital for an abortion two days after she took the devastating call from her doctor. Doctors injected the amniotic sac surrounding the fetus with a saline solution. Then, Richard and Natalie waited nearly twenty-four hours for the contractions that would allow her to expel the dead fetus and placenta. Their sorrow was compounded by anger at the nurses, who seemed unsympathetic. Finally, at 6:30 in the evening, the day after the saline injection, and after hours of contractions, Natalie felt a sudden release of pressure. The nurse told her her water had broken, and she took the bedpan to empty it. "Richard turned to me," Natalie recalled, "and said, 'I think you just had the baby.' And I said, 'Well, it sure felt like more than just water to me.'" Richard left to corner the nurses, who confirmed that Natalie had delivered the fetus. By then, Natalie was too physically and emotionally drained to become angry.

Richard asked to see the baby. He had been caught up in Natalie's trauma and had been unable to indulge his own feelings until then. Alone in an empty room with his dead baby boy, Richard wept. He was still overcome when he returned to Natalie's room. "It was stunning to me because I've known him for a long time and I've never seen him cry," Natalie said.

Natalie herself had thought she would not want to see the baby, but she changed her mind. She had worried about the possibility of a mix-up in lab results, and seeing the baby put her worries to rest. "As tiny as he was, it was very clear that he had Down. I mean he was very tiny, but he had deeply webbed fingers and his ears were set very far back and his eyes were wide apart. . . . I mean, there was no question that that baby really did have Down."

When she returned home from the hospital, Natalie wanted to cut herself off from the world. "I just wanted to go in a dark cave and not have to deal with anything at all," Natalie said. She felt guilty. A social worker who had counseled her in the hospital suggested that Natalie participate in a pregnancy loss group. Natalie followed that advice for a while, but she could not identify with the other women, who felt guilty after losing babies through miscarriage or stillbirth. No one else had gone through an abortion. Natalie said: "I just wanted to scream: 'You don't know anything about guilt. You didn't do any-thing.'"

Richard felt very little guilt. "What I did feel, often, was angry that nobody really understood what had happened to us," Richard said. "Not angry at them, but angry at the way society treats this sort of thing. You know, I think that the world seems to be about evenly divided into two camps. One camp is the people who think that any kind of abortion, including the kind we had for genetic reasons, is a sin and probably ought to be a crime, and the other camp thinks it's sort of a convenient medical procedure. But nobody really responded to it like a great personal tragedy for Natalie and me. That's not part of the public debate."

Richard admitted the physical reality of being pregnant made the emotional impact more intense for Natalie. "I felt that baby kicking," she said, and it took her much longer to recover. During the year that followed the abortion, Natalie continued to grieve and feel guilty as she passed a number of anniversaries: the baby's due date, the dates of the bad news, and the date of the abortion. When we spoke to her, she was pregnant again. "Our chances are much higher now that we've had a Down fetus," Natalie said. "For some reason they don't understand, once you have a Down baby, the recurrence rate goes to one in a hundred—bingo—for all ages."

Natalie asserted that her and her husband's decision to abort their Down syndrome fetus was the right one and that they would do the same thing again. But her conviction was weakened somewhat by the fact that she had decided to proceed differently this time, opting for CVS instead of amniocentesis. The test is done as early as the eighth week and delivers results in days, thus allowing a first-trimester abortion if chromosomal abnormalities are diagnosed. "My best guess," Natalie said, "is that if the CVS were not available . . . I don't think I would have tried to get pregnant again." Natalie said she was not, in fact, prepared to repeat a second-trimester abortion. "You're starting to get to the point where the fetus could live, possibly, outside the womb," she pointed out. She said she would still abort her current pregnancy if she had to, but she would not have felt the baby kicking or heard its heartbeat. "While I think that what we did was right, it was emotionally more difficult because the baby was becoming more human as it got older," she said.

A few weeks after our interview, Natalie's CVS revealed that she was carrying a girl in normal health. She was relieved but still not able to put all the pain and guilt of her abortion behind her. It was not until that baby was born six months later that Natalie seemed at peace—with herself and with the newborn daughter who would not exist except for the loss of the tiny fetal boy with Down syndrome.

Richard encapsulated their experience, saying thoughtfully: "I think if it had been some years earlier, when amniocentesis wasn't available, and we had had a Down child come to term . . . we would have done our best to raise the child and give it all the love we could. I think we could have done a good job of raising a Down child. But we had the choice. One of the good things and one of the terrifying things about technology is it gives you that kind of choice."

No Clear Boundaries

Today, women who are at risk for bearing babies with Down syndrome can learn whether that risk is reality in time to cancel it through abortion. To some women, the option is full of hubris, and they refuse it on moral, religious, or emotional grounds. But prenatal testing and the availability of abortion allow other women, some of whom might not otherwise chance an abnormal pregnancy at all, to increase the chances that the children they bear are healthy. To them, the option is indispensable. It comes burdened with a dilemma, however, because a diagnosis of Down syndrome, definitive as it is, offers an incomplete prognosis. What the diagnosis says is that the child, though diminished in his or her capacities, can live, but that his or her quality of life or degree of suffering cannot be known in advance.

The dilemma thus begs the question, where does one draw the line when it comes to abortion? The lack of clear boundaries can be either a relief or a frustration to expectant parents, depending on how capable they feel when it comes to making crucial decisions. Some, like Jackie Kolar, know exactly where the bounds of their own actions lie: at the clear divide between life and death. Jackie never felt willing or able to say that a life of possible pain was not worth living. Natalie, who aborted a baby she knew had Down syndrome, was less certain. When she thought about getting pregnant again, after her abortion, she said to Richard: "With the Down baby we went into [the pregnancy] not expecting a problem, having had no problems before. What happened, happened. It was out of our control. Now we know the risk." Going into a pregnancy knowing the risks seemed morally precarious to Natalie.

Natalie believed she had made the right choice when she decided to abort her baby with Down syndrome, but she recognized that such a choice could not be carried out without piercing pain and doubt. Neither, in fact, can the opposite choice, especially if it sentences a child to lifelong hardship. What the choice involves, after all, is the powers of life and death, and even the wisest humans can never be wholly certain that they have exercised such power righteously.

Uncertain Diagnoses

It rarely occurs to a woman who elects to undergo amniocentesis that the test could yield unclear results. But the test, for all its technical sophistication, is crude compared to the complexity and sophistication of the scrap of nature it examines. In the last step of the diagnostic process, a laboratory employee takes a collection of photographs of cells, cuts them, and then pastes them into karyotypes, pictures of paired and ordered chromosomes. If all is in order, the assembled picture lines up twenty-three pairs of chromosomes, from number one, the largest, to number twenty-two, the smallest, followed at last by the sex chromosomes—XX for a female and XY for a male. Down syndrome is called a trisomy twenty-one, although actually it is not a full third chromosome attached to the normal pair but two chromosomes and an extra piece of chromosome at position twenty-one. As we have seen, the diagnosis of genetic abnormality is usually relatively clear-cut. The prognosis for the potential is not.

In some cases, however, even the diagnosis is unclear. In a rare case, the laboratory itself can create the error. In other cases, the genetic anomaly is so rare that geneticists are unable to predict just what it means. In such cases, the stunned parents are left in a lonely and awful darkness that the light of science has not, so far, been able to penetrate.

Rebecca Lewis

Rebecca Lewis, a psychologist, could never see herself as a patient and selfless mother to a seriously handicapped child, nor did she believe she would ever impose upon an unborn child the possibility of intense, lifelong suffering. "I remember talking about this years ago, in an idle sort of way, with a woman I once worked with in a bookstore. She was strongly anti-abortion, and she said that if she ever got pregnant in her late thirties she would have amniocentesis but not an abortion. She would just want to be prepared for any problems the baby might have. I couldn't begin to understand her position. I always knew it was a big responsibility to get pregnant at all when the risk of genetic problems was high. I also never doubted that for me that responsibility would lie in abortion," Rebecca said.

Rebecca's discussion in the bookstore, however, had been abstract because Rebecca had reason to believe she was infertile. "I'd had a complicated menstrual history—no periods until they were induced in my late teens, sporadic ones thereafter. I eventually went on the pill, not for birth control, but to 'prime the pump' as my doctor so wittily put it. When I went off the pill—because my ovaries were swollen—was when I got pregnant that first time." The pregnancy, however, was implanted in a Fallopian tube and required emergency surgery.

One tube, an ovary, and the ectopic pregnancy were all removed. Afterward Rebecca began having regular periods, "but—I think partly because of incompetent medical advice—I never thought I could get pregnant. And even though I was careless about birth control I still didn't get pregnant."

When Rebecca conceived again at thirty-eight years old, the pregnancy was therefore a great surprise. Although she had thought she was reconciled to childlessness, her long-suppressed desire to be a mother surfaced in an uprush of joy and a determination to proceed with the pregnancy. "My husband, Paul, had never wanted children," Rebecca told us as she settled back into a large wing chair in her New York office. Her shiny, dark-brown hair contrasted sharply with her ivory skin and with the muted rose of the chair's upholstery. "He was not thrilled that I was pregnant. I was. Had it been his decision alone, he might have chosen abortion, but there was no way I could even think about that. I wanted that baby. I was prepared to raise it alone, if I had to. Paul soon realized the depth of my feelings, and he came around. He really began to accept and enjoy the idea that we were going to be parents."

Rebecca now speculates that deep within herself she may have known otherwise. "Twice, early in my pregnancy, although I went about by day in a cloud of joy and disbelief, I woke up sobbing at night. That had never happened to me before. Once, I dreamed very specifically that there was something wrong with the baby. The next time, I dreamed that a friend had died. I realize now that she was the closest friend I had at that time who was a mother. I think that dream foreshadowed the death of the mother in me. At the time, though, I shrugged off the dreams and the crying at night. I thought it was hormones. Maybe it was."

More objective signs of trouble came weeks after Rebecca's dreams, when her doctors attempted to perform an amniocentesis. "The first two times they tried," she remembered, "there wasn't enough fluid. And they told me that the baby looked small for its gestational age. I was worried, especially after the second attempt, but they did tell me that it might mean nothing." Rebecca was eighteen weeks pregnant when a third attempt at amniocentesis succeeded. The results came in five weeks later.

"I called my doctor's office," she remembered, frowning and shifting in her chair. "I was very, very nervous. But when he told me that they had found this puzzling irregularity, I went into total denial. The test results were ambiguous and rare. They didn't know what they meant, so I was just determined that they meant nothing serious." Over the following weekend, before Rebecca and Paul could consult with the geneticist at the hospital, Rebecca spent hours looking

up everything she could on genetics. She devised frantic and elaborate explanations for how this anomaly could be trivial, "but I don't remember a single
detail anymore," she said, shaking her head in disbelief.

What amniocentesis had revealed was that Rebecca's baby—a girl—carried extra genetic material on the long arm of one of the second chromosomes.
When Rebecca and Paul saw the geneticist on Monday, she told them that the
condition was called "partial trisomy two." According to Rebecca: "She told us
that the manifestations of this problem could be benign or serious. They didn't
know which. All they could do was search the world literature for another case
of partial trisomy two with the exact same amount and location of extra
material." Rebecca and Paul left their session with the geneticist knowing that
the literature might yield nothing and that they might never know for sure what
to expect from their baby's anomaly.

The geneticist, though, had still not been reassuring. She thought that the
chance of serious problems was very high. "She was very clinical, very cold,"
Rebecca recalled. "I was in shock, all my carefully constructed explanations in
ruins, but I remember thinking that her work must be difficult, that she must
find it hard to talk to parents about such dreadful things. I tried to express that
to her, and she just gave me the blankest stare. Total incomprehension."

Rebecca held onto her composure until she and Paul were outside the
hospital. Then, on the way to their car, she said: "I suddenly heard the oddest
sound coming from my throat. I had never made such a sound before in my
life—a kind of high animal whimpering. It was beyond my control. A woman
looked at me in the parking lot, and she might as well have been a different
species."

While the geneticists were searching the literature, they also ran blood
tests on Rebecca and Paul to examine their chromosomes. In advance of any
results, they suggested three possible explanations for the baby's irregularity.
The first was that either Paul or Rebecca carried exactly the same anomaly and
that this "family marker" would indicate the baby should be normal. This was
a very remote chance. The second possibility was that one of them had a
"translocation of chromosomal material" that was passed on to the baby. That
would probably be very serious. The third and most likely chance was that Paul
and Rebecca's chromosomes would prove normal, which would mean the baby
had a spontaneously duplicated "triple dose" of genes on the affected chromosome. It would also mean she was likely to be severely handicapped, both
physically and mentally.

Rebecca and Paul had to wait another week before they learned that the third situation was the one they confronted. "The odds were very great that the baby was going to be terribly handicapped, but it still was not a certainty, and we knew it might never be. The literature search might find nothing. We had decided, during that awful week of waiting, that if we didn't get any more information, we were going to abort. But accepting that decision seemed impossible. I would wake up at four every morning in terror. How could I agree to the death of what I had so deeply wanted? What if the odds were wrong, and the baby was healthy? I was panic-stricken."

Rebecca's panic was deepened by the fact that she was now twenty-four weeks pregnant, and the law in the state where she lived then prohibited abortions for reasons of genetic abnormality after that date. She was afraid she would have to abort right away, before the literature search could be completed. "I asked my doctor about this, very tentatively. I hardly dared call attention to how far along I was. But he said, very firmly, 'No one is going to force you to carry a baby that has serious problems.' I was so relieved. It was a bitter relief, but it was real."

Another equally bitter relief came a few days later. The geneticists had at last found a nearly identical case of partial trisomy two, written up two years earlier in the journal *Clinical Genetics*. The article described a baby girl who had been born a month early with multiple heart and kidney defects, severe brain anomalies, and physical malformations of the face, skull, chest, and genitals. She had died at twenty days old of cardiorespiratory arrest. "What an awful irony," Rebecca said, "to be in a position where news like that can offer some comfort. But we knew then that abortion was the thing to do."

Rebecca and Paul arranged for a saline-induced abortion the next day. They said goodbye to their baby that night, their hands on Rebecca's swollen belly. "I remember saying to a friend, 'All I know is, I have to kill my baby,'" Rebecca said. "It never felt like anything else to me. I was so aware of her death."

Paul stayed in the room all night with Rebecca, feeling helpless and horrified. They each wept from time to time. Rebecca's labor and the delivery of her small, doomed daughter were mercifully short. Her doctors had told her it took an average of thirty-four hours from the administration of the saline injection until delivery. Rebecca delivered after seventeen hours. "At one point," she said, "when I had no idea I was near the end and was in a lot of pain, I asked for something to relieve it. I got a shot of Demerol, which let me sleep through the contractions for an hour or so. I woke up with the baby half out of me. Paul called the nurses—who had never so much as checked on me in all those hours—and they hustled the fetus out of the room in great haste. Then I delivered the afterbirth and fell asleep exhausted." Rebecca's ordeal, though shorter than she had expected, was nevertheless lonely and traumatic.

Rebecca was apprehensive about other people's judgments throughout the whole process of making her decision and recovering from the abortion. She did not understand why, however. She had never regretted her decision or really wavered in making it, no matter how awesome it seemed. "I deeply regretted having to make that decision," she said, "but once it was made, I never wanted to change my mind. So it puzzled me why I was so afraid of what people would think. I went quite crazy for awhile when I would anticipate judgments, or imagine people gossiping about me, or read rabidly anti-choice letters to the editor in the newspaper." One such letter, Rebecca recalled, maintained that the conception of an afflicted child was "God's will," which abortion defied. "I don't understand how people can be so sure of God's will," Rebecca told us. "I could say it was God's will that gave me the means to make a decision. But what I really believe is that I had to look for what was most godly in myself: my conscience, my love for my baby, my desire to keep her from pointless suffering."

Rebecca emphasized that her family and friends gave no grounds for her fears of judgment. Support came from every direction and in every form. "It was only gradually that I began to realize what was wrong," Rebecca told us. "I felt enormous guilt. I did not feel guilty about what I had done but about being human and having limited vision. I wanted right answers, and there were none. I wanted to know that what I had done was right, and the best I could know was that for me it was less wrong than the alternative. I had had to choose between killing my baby or watching her suffer for whatever span of life she could have. Neither of those could possibly be a right choice."

Rebecca was profoundly aware of the magnitude of her decision. She came out of her experience with a deepened belief in the necessity of legal abortion. "I would never have guessed how overwhelming a choice can be. But in the midst of choosing I also thought, with incredible passion, no one has the right to tell me this choice is not mine to make. That choice stretched me to my moral and emotional limits. No one else would have known how far I could stretch, would have loved my unborn baby as much, would have struggled so hard." Rebecca went on to explain that she thought the moral acceptability of abortion, which, she said, "will be debated till the end of time," was a separate issue from the right of women to decide that moral issue for themselves, in the privacy of their conscience. "Some people will abuse the right to choose," she acknowledged, "but I believe worse abuses come out of denying that right."

Rebecca's abortion occurred almost six years ago. As soon as she had recovered physically, she and Paul began trying to conceive another child, an effort that took 2½ years to bear its fruit—a healthy son named Max. "Accepting the impossibility of right answers resolved my guilt," Rebecca told us, "and having Max resolved my grief. He's three years old now, and there are still times when his existence astonishes me as much as it did when my doctor first plopped him on my stomach."

Rebecca's feelings about abortion have remained constant. Having had a full-term pregnancy, and having given birth to a healthy child, simply gave her the other half of the experience—the joyous part. Pausing for a moment, Rebecca then went on to say: "Since Max's birth, I've had to put my mother in a nursing home. She has Alzheimer's disease, and she's had a couple of strokes. She's helpless, bedridden, hardly there at all. I don't think she knows who I am anymore. Could I knowingly give birth to someone who might be like that at the beginning of life? I can't imagine such a thing."

An autopsy, in fact, showed that if Rebecca's daughter had been born alive, she probably would have been like Rebecca's mother at the beginning of life. There is some chance she might have survived, because her heart, unlike that of the baby referred to in the literature who died at three weeks old, was normal. Her abnormalities, however, were severe and would have left her profoundly disabled. "The list of abnormalities on the autopsy report was half a page long," Rebecca said. "I don't know if she would have survived, but I do know she would never have lived."

Undetectable Dangers

Amniocentesis normally yields a clear picture of a fetus's chromosomes, but a perfect picture does not guarantee a perfect baby. Even with all its forty-six chromosomes in perfect order, a baby can still be severely damaged by things that happen to its mother during gestation. It has been thirty years since thousands of European babies were born with deformities caused by their mothers' being given the drug thalidomide, and medical science has taken long strides toward understanding the delicate relationship between the pregnant woman and the developing life she carries. We now know that ingesting drugs and alcohol, smoking, being exposed to radiation and toxins, and using some kinds of birth control can endanger the fetus.

Physicians have an ethical responsibility to inform pregnant women of potential dangers, and pregnant women have an ethical responsibility to protect their babies. But such responsibilities are not always met, nor are the lines of danger and responsibility always clear. What is clear from all the cases in this chapter is that if women are going to be able to take full responsibility for the decisions they make concerning pregnancy, they have to be given that authority and all the information that is known.

Jeanne Zebert

Jeanne Zebert and her husband, Bill, were high school sweethearts from a small town in Missouri where they now own a home. They had waited to marry until Jeanne finished nursing school. Most of their friends had married much earlier and at age twenty-seven already had children who no longer needed training wheels on their bicycles. Jeanne and Bill, however, seemed unable to conceive. They had been trying for five years to have a child. Infertility tests had been unable to determine the reason for their lack of success.

Then, one February, Jeanne's period was late by just three or four days. She and Bill let their hopes rise only slightly because they had already been disappointed so often. Before they could learn whether Jeanne was indeed pregnant, she started to feel a tight knot of pain in her abdomen. She became nauseous, the pain grew severe, and she began vomiting bile.

Jeanne immediately recognized the symptoms of appendicitis. She went to the emergency room where she worked as a nurse, in a hospital about ten miles outside St. Louis. The staff examined her white blood cell count, which, despite her symptoms, was not high. Appendicitis seemed unlikely, so the doctor on duty ordered X rays to check for a bowel obstruction. Jeanne objected, explaining that she might be pregnant. A urine test for pregnancy was negative, but Jeanne pointed out that it was probably too early for pregnancy to show up on a urine test. She had blood drawn for a more accurate pregnancy test, but the sample had to be sent to St. Louis for processing.

Meanwhile, the doctor insisted on the X rays. "Your life is at stake here," he told her. By then the pain was excruciating, so Jeanne consented. She had two abdominal X rays and one chest X ray for which her abdomen was left unprotected. No bowel obstruction was found. The surgeon asked for permission to operate and found that it was Jeanne's appendix that had caused the problem after all. After her appendectomy, Jeanne was given painkillers and antibiotics to protect against infection.

Although the St. Louis laboratory normally processed blood pregnancy tests within hours, four days went by before Jeanne's results were returned. They were positive. "I was panicky," Jeanne recalled as she sat in the lunchroom of that same hospital, where she still works. A few light-brown curls that matched the freckles on Jeanne's nose peeked out around the edges of the blue cap she still wore after assisting in surgery that morning. Her voice and hazel eyes were steady and sure, but she only pushed at her food with her fork. She said that the year-old memories were still painful.

Jeanne's surgeon immediately advised her to have an abortion, given her exposure to radiation and medications. "He told me I could always have another baby," she said sarcastically. The surgeon's partner, who had been trained in gynecology, recommended that Jeanne see an obstetrician-gynecologist in St. Louis. Jeanne and Bill made an appointment and took with them a list of all the procedures and dosages that had subjected the fetus to risk. But the obstetrician Jeanne recalled, was "very iffy and unconcerned." She and Bill found his answers imprecise. He said there were indeed risks, but in his professional opinion no pregnancy was entirely safe. They left his office disappointed and confused.

"We discussed it. We wanted a baby so bad, but we didn't want to bring one into the world with problems," Jeanne said. The surgeon's advice to abort weighed heavily on their minds.

Jeanne went to her Catholic parish to see the priest, "an older man from the old school," as she described him. His opinion was unequivocal. "You take what God gives you," he told her. "Don't you dare get an abortion." She was prepared to go against his advice, but her conscience was troubled.

Jeanne called the obstetrician in St. Louis and told him that she and Bill had decided to have an abortion, even though they were still filled with doubts. He did not address the couple's uncertainty. He told Jeanne to come in that evening and he would perform a suction procedure in his office. She told him she did not want it done that way, insisting, "I want to go into the hospital as an outpatient and have a DC&E [dilation, curettage, and evacuation] procedure." The doctor replied, "If you don't want the abortion, then don't get it." Jeanne hung up on him.

Jeanne's surgeon's partner, however, agreed to do the procedure she wanted. They set a date, but he also listened to her doubts. She and Bill had hoped for a child for a very long time. Now they had conceived, but the medical advice they had received so far gave them no real indication of whether this child would be healthy.

"I always pray a lot, but at that time I was praying every spare minute about what to do. I even bargained with God," Jeanne said. She believed her prayers were answered at about ten o'clock the night after she had arranged for her abortion. Her phone rang, and it was a physician she did not know. "I feel that God sent Dr. K. to us that night," she said.

The doctor was an obstetrician and a friend of Jeanne's surgeon's partner. He said to Jeanne, "Dr. P. was under the impression that you really don't want this procedure done," and he offered to obtain all her hospital records and consult with radiation and genetic specialists at the women's hospital where he worked. "I can try to get you some more precise information on which to base a decision," he told her.

When all the reports were in, Jeanne and Bill met personally with the specialists. While the exposures to drugs and radiation had indeed put their baby at some higher risk for birth defects, the statistics were definitely in Jeanne and Bill's favor. Jeanne and Bill finally had the information they needed. They decided to go ahead with the pregnancy.

The pregnancy turned out to be no easier than the decision to continue it. Jeanne worried nonstop. Her personality changed. She demanded perfection of her co-workers and barked at her husband for the slightest infraction. If she and Bill saw families with young children, the sight would bring tears to their eyes. Handicapped children made them nervous. They began to convince themselves that they had to prepare for the worst. They became obsessive about protecting the baby they already feared was damaged. Bill refused to have intercourse. Doctors assured him several times that sex would not hurt the child, but Bill remained unconvinced. For her part, Jeanne began to count grams of vegetables and milk every day. She refused to touch alcohol, coffee, or tea.

While demanding precision and control in her own life, she became jealous of friends to whom the simple miracle of a normal child had come so easily. Few of the other women in their circle of friends had careers, so Jeanne and Bill were materially better off than most couples they knew. But when a friend complimented Jeanne on their beautiful home, Jeanne snapped back, "You know I would give all this up in a second for your two healthy children."

"But, Jeanne, you're pregnant," the startled friend replied.

"I know," Jeanne said, "but I'm not going to have a healthy child."

Jeanne, like many infertility patients, had felt her identity as a woman was called into question by her seeming inability to conceive and give birth. The possibility of a child with birth defects exacerbated her feelings of inadequacy.

"If I couldn't have a normal pregnancy and a healthy child, then I wasn't really a woman. That was just how I felt," she said.

Despite her doctor's continual reassurance that everything was proceeding as it should, Jeanne and Bill's uncertainty about their decision weighed heavily on them. They were still full of apprehension at three o'clock one fall afternoon when Jeanne's water broke on her way to work. She called Bill and told him to meet her at the hospital. Because no contractions had begun, Jeanne's doctor ordered the administration of drugs that would stimulate labor. Jeanne resisted. She had become extremely cautious about taking any medication. "But for some reason, once that labor really began, all our worries were forgotten," she said, smiling.

Jeanne's labor was painful but quick. At eleven o'clock that night, she was taken from the labor suite to the delivery room. Her doctor was coaching her through her pushing when his attention suddenly sharpened and he motioned her to stop. "Just pant for a few minutes, Jeanne. Don't push," he told her. He sent a nurse to run back to the labor suite to bring Jeanne's glasses. "You don't want to miss seeing this," he said with a grin. A short while later he placed a wiggling baby girl on her stomach. "You couldn't have a healthier-looking baby," he told her, and he confessed that despite all his reassurances during the pregnancy, he too was relieved.

While Jeanne and her husband are delighted with their daughter and their decision to have her, their confidence in the medical profession was permanently shaken by their experience. The seemingly casual way in which the surgeon immediately advised Jeanne to abort her long-awaited pregnancy appalled her. "I still see that man around the hospital," she said grimly. "He saw that I continued the pregnancy and never said anything to me. I can't bring myself to look him in the eye, I'm so angry." On the other hand, Jeanne holds the doctor who delivered her baby in the greatest esteem for his thorough care and concern. For many women, a pregnancy is a precious and important matter, Jeanne said. "Abortion shouldn't be treated as if it were a tonsillectomy," she said.

Technology: Blessing or Nightmare?

Miscarriage is nature's way of destroying the "mistakes" of conception. Any infant conceived with a chromosome abnormality has more than a 75-percent chance of being spontaneously aborted before the twelfth week of pregnancy. This raises the question of whether prenatal testing and abortion simply augment nature's own selection process.

We have stumbled into an era of wondrous reproductive technology that promises—and threatens—even more amazing breakthroughs in the near future. For example, researchers are now perfecting a technique for testing a baby's genetic makeup from the tiny number of its cells that circulate in the mother's bloodstream. Such a test, while not yet perfected, could make prenatal genetic testing inexpensive and practically risk-free for mothers of all ages. Another test, which so far has been performed only on laboratory rats, may eventually allow couples to flush out a newly fertilized egg for genetic testing before implantation. Yet another experiment may someday lead to a test on the mother's eggs before fertilization, thus allowing any egg carrying a defective gene from the mother to be discarded before a perfect one is fertilized with the husband's sperm and then reimplanted in the woman.

In their 1990 book *Genome: The Story of the Most Astonishing Scientific Adventure of Our Time—the Attempt to Map All the Genes in the Human Body*, Jerry E. Bishop and Michael Waldholz predict that genetic testing for fertilized eggs that have not yet been implanted will be widely available to couples within a decade or two. Some couples may be eager to use it—or the analysis of the mother's unfertilized eggs—if it allows them to circumvent the morally charged issue of abortion.

The authors describe a "swelling cascade of gene discoveries" that will soon allow us to trace the genetic markers that predispose an infant to "colon and breast cancer, Alzheimer's disease, multiple sclerosis, diabetes, schizophrenia, depression, at least one form of alcoholism, and even some types of criminal behavior." No one knows how long the list of human defects carried on the genes may grow. These discoveries hold hope for marvelous treatments and correction of these defects, but they also carry frightening potential. Bishop and Waldholz speculate that insurance companies and employers may wish to avoid financial liability by weeding out people with risky genes. Ethicists are already discussing the dark possibilities of "genetic discrimination" and "genetic labeling."

So far, however, the only widespread use of genetic screening has been prenatal testing. Since that door is already open, there is good reason to believe that doctors will soon be able to supply couples with much more information. Parents might be able to learn not only whether their child will have a crippling or life-threatening disorder but whether he or she has a predisposition to a mental or physical disease that may or may not develop. Bishop and Waldholz point out that the advent of amniocentesis and CVS for a limited number of chromosomal defects has led to an explosion of prenatal testing and the subsequent termination of pregnancies, developments that would have astounded previous generations. Over the next decade, newer, safer tests will combine with a wider array of information about the fetus's genetic makeup. When that happens, prenatal testing could change pregnancy as much as the pill is seen by many to have changed sex. Even when the pregnancy is planned and wanted, a positive pregnancy test, today and in the future, might not mean a commitment to having a baby any more than sex is considered a commitment to marriage. Couples may have trial pregnancies—much as they now live together in trial marriages—to choose the kind of baby they want.

Even people who have supported the unrestricted right to abortion admit that the implications of this technology trouble them. In a 1987 survey reported in *Medical World News*, for example, eight out of nine prenatal diagnostic clinics surveyed reported that they occasionally encountered couples seeking prenatal testing solely to determine the sex of the fetus. About 60 percent of the geneticists surveyed reported that they either tested such couples or referred them to a clinic that would. The magazine did not report what these couples intended to do once they learned the sex of fetus, but members of some cultures—in their native countries and here in the United States—are believed to be using amniocentesis and CVS to eliminate female children because of a cultural preference for males. While parents in those cultures may love their daughters, religious and cultural traditions often make a female child both a social and an economic liability.

Is modern medical technology a Pandora's box whose spilled secrets outstrip our wisdom in dealing with them? Are the benefits of those secrets canceled by the fact that they can generate further problems, questions, and even tragedies? Have we started down a slippery slope toward the rationalization that some genetic characteristics—even those of sex and eye color—are more desirable than others? Does the desire for a "super baby" lurk even in some people who would be disgusted by attempts to create a "super race"?

Answers do not come easily to responsible people. Technology did not represent a simple solution to a simple problem for anyone in this chapter. Instead its benefits came mixed with compromise and moral uncertainty. The uncertainty surrounding decisions based on prenatal testing will undoubtedly grow for both individuals and society. In a sense, we are like the four children in C. S. Lewis's *The Chronicles of Narnia*, who stumbled through an old wardrobe into another dimension of time and space. Like those children, we will be forever changed by the new world we enter and whatever wonders it reveals to us. But the adventurous youngsters in Lewis's story came to rule Narnia, and we, likewise, will shape this new world in accordance with the values and priorities we bring to it from our old one.

Perhaps the slippery slope is a proper metaphor for where we are headed, but perhaps not. It is foolhardy to try to predict how our society will cope with scientific advances to come. What is more profitable is to examine how we are coping with what we have been given so far. Are we becoming the people we want to be? If we begin by looking at the stories of individuals, such as the couples in this chapter who made choices, we see reason for hope.

Individual Stories of Hope

For the most part, the couples interviewed here engaged in authentic struggles of conscience. As we said earlier, they all saw themselves as the loving parents of a baby who existed both in its still-forming flesh and in these parents' dreams of what it would become. Turning over what scraps of information they were given, most of these couples struggled with some of life's most profound questions. They weighed what qualities of life made it worth living and what they wanted from and for a baby.

Those who chose not to seize upon the new technology saw the power it unleashed as inappropriate. They did not want to make choices or to undertake actions that they felt belonged only to nature or to God. Yet, their restraint was itself a weighty choice. These parents in effect had to decide on behalf of their unborn children whether the risks of birth defects were worth chancing or whether lives of potential pain and limitation were worth living. Of course, all lives are ones of potential pain and limitation. Our challenge is where to draw the line.

Those who would avoid drawing lines at all believe in the sanctity of all life. They argue that life itself cannot be qualified. This position, embedded in the traditions of our culture, is attractive in its simplicity. Yet it is unlikely that such a value will ever gain universal acceptance. Abortion to end the life of a fetus who would become a seriously ill child has been widely accepted by many thoughtful people for decades. Besides, there is no precedent in our society for setting aside a technology because of its potential hazards, especially not one that so many see as beneficial.

Those in this chapter who drew their own moral lines were humbled by the power they took into their hands. Some decided against too much risk, too much potential for pain, or a life that they saw as little more than a slow death. Most chose abortion with as much love for their children as those who gave birth.

Every woman brought to her decision everything that had shaped her—from her childhood teachings to all the feelings and reasoning she could muster as an adult. Each showed a special, feminine strength—an ability to cooperate and to see the relatedness and interconnectedness of life that has been discussed by several of the scholars cited in this book. In other words, most mothers explored the full implications of their decision for themselves and for their children. Yet after their decision, they continued to see their connection to the considerations they had set aside in making their final choice. They were able, after a painful decision, to express to us a profound respect for those who had taken an opposite course.

The soft sound of such appreciation and understanding goes almost unheard in the shrill political debate, yet it was expressed in some way by every woman who had experienced a problem pregnancy. Each had respect for the miracle of conception. None underplayed the significance of interrupting the body's determined march toward birth, including those who had done so. Neither did anyone deny the serious consequences of having a child with disabilities. Every woman interviewed for this chapter, including many whose stories do not appear here, expressed a deep understanding for others in the same situation who had made another choice. Their respect for each other is a hard-won, humanizing force that allows for disagreement while acknowledging common ground.

The Larger Picture

There is an ominous gap between the values and conscientiousness of parents whose individual decisions have weighed heavily upon them and the sometimes callous indifference of the larger society. Across this great divide, the institutions of law, medicine, education, and social services send messages about what America values among its people, and those messages greatly affect those in the throes of private decision making.

Until recently, ours was a society that shielded itself from children who were born with disabilities. Doctors, carrying messages from the larger society, advised parents to put their children with Down syndrome in institutions to protect us all from our fears of neediness, incapacity, and differences. No one ever pretended these institutions were created to benefit those inside them. They protected those of us on the outside. When Emily Kingsley's obstetrician advised her husband Charles to tell everyone their son Jason had died, he told the Kingsleys something very frightening about how society would treat the baby they regarded as precious.

Some parents still get that message when their child is born with imperfections, but attitudes have improved greatly in the last two decades. In the early 1960s, the more socially conscious Scandanavian countries first put into practice the concept of "normalization," which holds that all persons should be aided and supported to live as normal a life as possible within the community. In this country, it has been some parents and people with disabilities themselves who have vastly broadened our awareness and pushed our institutions to expand services, opportunities, and protections. Yet no one would pretend that all the fears and harsh judgments are gone.

In 1984, for example, researchers at the University of Kansas asked a group of twenty- to forty-year-olds to imagine that they were parents who had just given birth to a child with disabilities. On the whole, Beach Center research coordinator Dr. Patricia Barber said in an interview, these would-be parents felt that if the child was capable of being happy and could communicate, then they would feel that the child's life would be worthwhile and that they would receive the rewards they wanted from parenting. But they worried that society would expect much more. Almost immediately, Barber said, participants started reacting protectively against the social stigma. They worried about what society would do to them and to their imaginary children.

If individual parents and even would-be parents seem to react with such thoughtfulness and compassion, then how can our society as a whole be accused of making such harsh judgments? Isn't the United States—or whatever is meant by "society"—the sum of the individuals within it? The choices we make individually shape the kind of people we are, but they are not the same as the ones we make collectively or those we make through institutions.

The court ruling that governs our abortion laws is not one we made collectively, yet it both reflects the way we tend to think as Americans and helps to shape that thinking. The technology of prenatal testing was introduced in the United States almost simultaneously with the 1973 *Roe v. Wade* decision. Although amniocentesis had been available experimentally since the late 1960s, it was only when *Roe v. Wade* made widespread selective abortion possible that prenatal testing became routine. The Supreme Court decision provided no guidance about the use of this new technology, however. While it established the right of the woman and her doctor to select abortion, it said nothing about the value of the pregnancy or the potential child, however healthy or imperfect he or she may be.

As we saw at the end of Chapter 2, no one, not even reform advocates like Dr. Alan Guttmacher, was prepared for the sweeping changes that *Roe v. Wade* brought to social policy. Yet *Roe v. Wade* fit neatly into an already imbalanced world where the ideals of justice and rights largely dominated those of responsibility, caring, and connectedness.

Roe v. Wade also fit neatly into the medical community, the social institution that would deliver legal abortion into the private lives of millions of American women. New prenatal technology combined with the patients' rights movement, the feminist movement, and the American value of rugged individualism to encourage the medical community to focus only on narrow medical indicators, despite the enormous social and moral implications of amniocentesis and other tests. Few medical practitioners evaluated the human ends this technology was to serve, and no one asked them to do so. In most abortion decisions, as medical ethicist Dr. Jack Coulehan pointed out in an interview, the patient is competent and therefore is assumed capable of making her own choice. The doctor's—or genetic counselor's—job is to inform the patient of her options and refrain from imposing his or her values. But we have seen how faulty and inadequate this communication process can be.

In research for her book *The Tentative Pregnancy: Prenatal Diagnosis and the Future of Motherhood*, sociologist Barbara Katz Rothman found that most women at risk for birth defects or abnormal fetuses were encouraged by their doctors to undergo amniocentesis. In general, Rothman says, medical professionals recommend seeking out information that might reveal disease or abnormality. Rothman cites one study conducted in 1973, when most genetic counseling was still being done by physicians, that showed that 85 percent of physicians considered it important to see that counseling achieved the prevention of disease or abnormality. Sixty-four percent of physicians felt they should guide patients toward an "appropriate" decision.

Today, non-M.D. genetic counselors have taken on much of this work. These counselors are more likely to feel that they should be nondirective. In other words, they try to present information without telling the patient or client what to do with it. How these counselors carry out their work, however, may not be quite so morally neutral.

Rothman found that most genetic counselors told patients, in a session prior to amniocentesis, what the test could tell them and what the risks were. They did explain what Down syndrome is, sometimes with pictures, and what neural tube defects are, making frequent reference to March of Dimes poster children. They briefly explained what amniocentesis could and could not reveal, without getting into rarer genetic variations, such as sex chromosome abnormalities, that might upset the patient. Some mentioned the possibility of abortion, some did not. Thus, genetic counselors, Rothman concludes, can consider themselves nondirective because they do not push women toward abortion, which they see as a purely personal decision. But they view the issue of choosing amniocentesis as morally neutral. Deciding whether to enter the decision-making process by gathering information is not widely recognized as a moral dilemma itself.

Most counselors, therefore, felt that the way they presented information about the amniocentesis test could subtly pressure for the test without violating the nondirective nature of the counseling. When Rothman asked counselors about potential disabilities that might show up in a prenatal test, for example, she expected them to make important distinctions—between problems associated with mental as opposed to physical impairments and mild as opposed to severe retardation. Instead, the counselors talked as if the same problems would arise in the same degree for all parents of genetically abnormal children. The counselors cited demands on the parents' time, issues of dependency, monetary concerns, and concerns about an uncertain future. Of course, as Rothman points out, these are concerns in the raising of a normal child. But the counselors did not portray these factors on a continuum. In general, the picture was one of either good news—a normal genetic reading—or very bad news, especially if the genetic variation involved mental retardation. Rothman found that counselors tended to paint the darkest possible picture of retardation—a drooling ten-year-old in diapers, for example—when in fact only a very small proportion of the retarded are never taught to communicate or use the toilet.

With rare exceptions, these counselors, who steered their clients toward some questions and away from others, believed that amniocentesis and selective abortion are favorable developments that expand women's options. Only one counselor among the twenty-five Rothman interviewed said she would not have an abortion herself for any reason. Of the other twenty-four counselors, all said they would abort in cases of severe retardation and all but three in cases of mild retardation.

The counselors' attitudes varied sharply from those of the women they counseled, even from those who chose prenatal testing. Their patients, like the women in this chapter, were much more willing to consider moral gradations. Out of sixty women Rothman talked to who underwent amniocentesis, almost all said they would have aborted if the test indicated severe retardation, but less than half said they would do so in cases of mild retardation. So, as Rothman points out, while the diagnosis of Down syndrome may be a clear indicator for abortion in counselors' eyes, it may be full of ambiguity for their clients.

What is troublesome in the way that doctors and counselors advise patients is not so much what they do as what they fail to do. When they fail to value a fetus, no matter how damaged or defective, they diminish what would-be parents have come to love and cherish. When they patronize by deciding, without *listening*, either what the patient should do or what she should know, they diminish the patient herself. When they abdicate their responsibility to help in the decision making process because the woman has the right to decide with or without the information they provide, they diminish their profession.

Technology and Human Ends

Dr. Jean Baker Miller, psychiatrist and author of *Toward a New Psychology of Women*, laments the lack of human connection in modern institutions. "There is a widespread concern about our inability to organize the fruits of technology toward human ends; it is, perhaps, the central problem of the dominant culture," Miller writes. But human ends, as we have said earlier, have traditionally been considered female concerns. And, like the women who have asserted them, these human concerns have generally been dismissed as trivial.

With technology out of control, Miller writes, we can no longer afford to brush aside human ends. The very future of the planet is at stake, she claims. She contends that the "characteristics most highly developed in women and perhaps most essential to human beings" are suppressed by the dominant male culture because it is afraid of its own soft, "feminine" underbelly of vulnerability, emotion, and connectedness to others. If women in particular and feminine values in general do not assert themselves more prominently, however, our society may be brought down by the social and psychological consequences of its continuing imbalance.

Our scientific and medical institutions have handed over the revolutionary technology of prenatal testing, but we are not quite sure what its human ends are to be or even what problems it is supposed to solve. Are amniocentesis and selective abortion supposed to rid nature of her "mistakes" when she fails to do so? Surely that smacks too much of race purification to be socially acceptable. If the aim is to prevent the suffering of children, how could we ever set an acceptable standard? Who is to say what quality of life is worth living? On the other hand, many parents would object to the notion that selective abortion is justified merely to save them from the hardship of raising a child with disabilities. Often the child's potential suffering and its effect on other children are paramount concerns. Much of women's ethical framework is based on the goodness of giving and caring for others. When Rothman raises such questions and dilemmas in *The Tentative Pregnancy,* she concludes that women who must make choices within the current social environment are ultimately left with the unpleasant task of selecting who will be victimized and how.

Lore Reich Rubin, a psychiatrist and psychoanalyst in private practice in Pittsburgh, argues that people's decisions, as well as their ability to question them, are very much affected by ideologies. And ideologies, she adds, change like fashions. "It used to be that you could say, if the child is mentally retarded: 'You should put it in an institution. You know, you should think of yourself,'" Rubin said in an interview. "But nowadays, you're supposed to dedicate your whole life to that child." At first glance, these two viewpoints appear to be opposites. In fact, both are part of the same way of thinking, one that pits the interests of the individual mother and child against one another. It is a way of thinking that so pervades American values and policies that we are often blinded to its narrowness. It is an immature way of thinking, if we measure it against the scale of ethical and intellectual development put forth by Mary Belenky *et al.* It is the thinking of what Belenky *et al.* call a "subjectivist knower," who still sees her interests as being in competition with those of others. Women who are more ethically and intellectually mature describe their relationships with others as interconnected in a web or net, not as a tug-of-war. "In the complexity of a web," Belenky *et al.* write, "no one position dominates over the rest. Each person—no matter how small—has some potential for power; each is always subject to the action of others. It is hard to imagine other ways of envisioning the world that offer as much potential for protection to the immature and the infirm." In women's "different voice," Carol Gilligan tells us, mature morality is "conceived as a problem of inclusion rather than balancing claims."

The story we Americans tell in our abortion and family law, in our social policy, and in the policies of many of our institutions, is a story that we love to tell. It is all about individual liberty, self-reliance, and a tolerance for diverse points of view. But, as comparative law specialist Mary Ann Glendon rightly claims, we have told that story too often to the exclusion of other stories. We no longer moderate it with a sense of duty and charity. We have begun to translate the ideology of tolerance into a posture of neutrality toward most controversial issues. The right to be let alone has become the practice of leaving others alone. At some point, our favorite story began to drift toward one that Americans do not mean to be telling—one about selfish indifference, isolation, and nihilism.

We cannot escape the technology that has been thrust upon us, nor can we afford to sidestep the dilemmas it sets before us by placing all the burden on the individuals who use it. We need to listen to the voices of care and responsibility among us. If we are a truly great people, these voices will not diminish our commitment to rights and justice but enhance it. We see that sort of moral sophistication in some of the couples whose struggles fill this chapter. If, for example, America embraced the caring ideal that all children deserve an opportunity to reach their fullest potential, we could find ways to prevent the pitting of mothers and children against one another. Indeed, we are beginning to see such a shift among the policies and institutions that touch children with disabilities and their families. The mainstreaming of the disabled in our schools, communities, and workplaces represents a shift toward public sharing of responsibilities. The education of our children is a burden we have shared publicly for a long time. We only recently began to include all children in the educational process, when we recognized that we must encourage everyone's potential and see beyond disabilities. In turn, policies such as these carry a message about what we value back to those who worry about the chances for children they bear.

As a society, we have to have faith in individuals and their ability to choose what is right, even though they will sometimes choose wrongly. The belief that individuals are capable of sound choices is the basis for democracy. The private struggles in this chapter, for the most part, reinforce that belief. There is little indication that we are traveling on a slippery slope to the day when parents will routinely abort babies with the "wrong" hair or eye color. But as long as we say through our public policy that the fetus has no value, we offer little evidence to the morally malnourished among us that anyone cares if they do abort for these reasons. Individual decisions are shaped by information and by the values and resources of the larger society. Freedom of choice has meaning only within a society that nourishes its citizens, encourages healthy development, and broadens options. We cannot afford to be a society that abandons people, fails to inform them, closes off their options, and makes their choice a hollow one. The policies, attitudes, and values of the medical community, the government, and other private and public institutions can both support individual choice and cushion its harsh realities, just as justice and human rights can be tempered by mercy and responsibility.

CONCLUSION

The Human Face of the Dilemma

The quality of mercy is not strained,
It droppeth as the gentle rain from heaven
Upon the place beneath. It is twice blest;
It blesseth him that gives and him that takes. . . .
It is an attribute to God himself,
And earthly power doth then show likest God's
When mercy seasons justice.

Portia, in *The Merchant of Venice*, by William Shakespeare

Like the moment when the ambiguous figure shifts from a vase to two faces, the recognition that there is another way to look at a problem may expand moral understanding.

Carol Gilligan and Jane Attanucci, "Two Moral Orientations: Gender Differences and Similarities"

In the life-or-death courtroom struggle between the Venetian merchant Antonio and the moneylender Shylock, the concept of mercy is introduced by Portia, a woman disguised as a man. Her direct plea for Antonio's life fails, however, when Shylock insists on the pound of the merchant's flesh that is due him as payment on a debt. Portia must then resort to arguments that are even more legalistic than Shylock's. If he refuses to be merciful, she reasons, he must at least be exact, taking neither more nor less than one pound of flesh and spilling no blood in the process. Shylock has no choice but to abandon his quest for blood justice.

Though Portia averts injustice and saves Antonio's life, her passionate plea for mercy fails to produce much of it in the court. Shylock backs down only grudgingly, and then he in turn is found guilty of plotting against Antonio's life. He is ordered to forfeit all his wealth, which to him is the equivalent of life. Half must go to Venice as a penalty for threatening a citizen, the other half to Antonio as the intended victim. Shylock, in effect, is charged an eye for an eye.

The quality of mercy in this outcome is very much strained, not only by the legalistic attitudes but also by the racial and sexual biases that prevailed in Shakespeare's time and inevitably colored his work. Although Shakespeare might have developed the character of Shylock as a complex and redeemable soul, he remains, for the most part, a one-dimensional villain simply because he is a Jew. Despite some indication that Antonio may soften toward Shylock, the prevailing view of the moneylender is scornful and condemnatory. The views of women that are represented in the play are no less biased. Had Portia appeared before the court simply as herself—a woman, the wife of Antonio's best friend— she would have been evicted. Without her disguise and her ability to address the court on its own terms, using a language associated more with men than with women, she would never have been heard at all. When she spoke in her own voice on behalf of mercy, it was as if her words were Greek.

Modern women, too, have had to adopt the language of the male-led culture, even on a matter as quintessentially female as birth and abortion. Both the courts of law and the court of public opinion in the United States have argued social dilemmas in terms of rights, justice, and the sanctity of the individual for so long that scarcely anyone questions that exclusive standard. When other moral concerns are introduced, they are at first disorienting. Like Portia's plea for mercy, they seem out of place, at odds with standard procedure. In *The Merchant of Venice* the moment of disorientation is never resolved, for Portia is forced to accept the prevailing values of the court. Yet her speech about the God-like quality of mercy remains, after four hundred years, the play's most memorable and frequently quoted passage. Clearly, it represents a human ideal. If today we can elevate mercy to the same level as justice, we may discover a new and broader moral vision.

Carol Gilligan and Jane Attanucci's article "Two Moral Orientations: Gender Differences and Similarities" suggests that the examination of women's moral development and behavior can create such a vision. These authors refer to a familiar optical illusion in which the black figure of a vase is dominant and only a closer look reveals that its contours are formed by the pale profiles of two human faces. Gilligan and Attanucci draw an implicit parallel between the optical illusion and the standard practice in psychological research of studying men without looking at women. The sudden inclusion of women in research is like the moment in which the background of the illusion jumps out at the viewer.

Focusing the Lens

Once a viewer has seen the complete picture of the vase and the two faces, he or she can never again recapture the old way of seeing. The black-and-white images move in and out of view, becoming first background and then foreground, but neither can disappear. This is how, in writing this book, we have come to see the public and private aspects of the abortion issue. Our interviews have shown us the human faces in the dilemma so clearly that they can never drop from our sight. What we see in them is that the problem of birth and abortion is never entirely a matter of rights and justice, nor is it entirely a matter of responsibility and care. Concern for the woman and concern for the fetus are not incompatible but integral to the heart of the abortion dilemma.

Yet, in conducting our research, we had our own moment of disorientation before we could integrate and understand the images we were seeing. We had collected fewer than half the stories we uncovered in our research when we began to understand that private decisions took place somewhere beyond the debate. Although the people we talked to asked themselves a variety of conscientious questions in their search for a sound decision, these questions seldom, if ever, included the tediously familiar, unanswerable ones: when life begins, whether the fetus has rights, whether the woman's claim to autonomy outweighs a fetus's claim to life. Instead, as readers know by now, the questions had to do with caretaking expressed in terms of relationships and circumstances as well as financial, emotional, or spiritual resources. Did the woman love the man with whom she had become pregnant? Would he stay with her? Could she love the baby? Could she live with herself if she had a child and turned it over to strangers to raise? If she kept her child, could she care for it properly? Did she have marketable skills, an education, income? Would she ever acquire them if she went ahead with her pregnancy? Would the birth of another baby jeopardize the welfare of her existing children? Would the child be born with serious abnormalities? Would it suffer more than it would thrive?

Given the complexity and diversity of the stories we were gathering and the richly variable detail in which they were told to us, our effort to articulate the patterns we were seeing in them was greatly aided by the works of other researchers—Mary Belenky, Carol Gilligan, Jean Baker Miller, Kristin Luker, and their colleagues. Their studies, by focusing directly on women rather than regarding women in terms of findings about men, brought into sharp relief images that had gone unnoticed in the field of psychology—evidence of rich values that were formative for women and that had to do with community, interdependence, and the need for human beings to care for one another. As we have stressed throughout this book, these values had not appeared in studies of men, whose moral criteria were based primarily on autonomy, logical reasoning, the weighing of conflicting rights, and the blind dispensation of justice. Though men also weighed questions of responsibility and caretaking, those concerns remained in the background, undifferentiated, until the new insight into women brought them into the open for both sexes. In the meantime, both women and men were measured according to values that often contradicted the ones women had learned to honor. Not surprisingly, women fared badly by this measure. Their behavior and concerns tended to be dismissed as naive, morally underdeveloped, insubstantial, or irresponsible.

Such views of women and their actions have flourished in the hostile climate of the abortion debate. Women who do not use birth control are seen as ignorant or careless. Women who have abortions, especially for practical reasons, are unfeeling, selfish, and anti-life. Women who proceed with pregnancies they cannot afford are martyrs or welfare queens. Women who oppose legal abortion are anti-feminist prudes; women who favor it are somehow both promiscuous and, in their worldly ambition, man-hating. Unfortunately, women themselves hold many of these stereotypical views.

Such biases represented to us the mire in which the debate—and the interests of women and children—had become stuck, each passionate faction ranting at the other but neither making progress. We knew, from what our interviews revealed, that something important was going on in private decisions. Once we adjusted our lens in accordance with insights provided by several feminist psychologists and scholars, we recognized the moral considerations we were hearing about as central to decisions about birth and abortion. These considerations were present across the diversity and complexity of the cases we were gathering—and they were not the considerations that ran the public debate.

The Dangers of Imbalance

We also saw the question of birth or abortion as one in which a balance must be struck between the two moral standards we have discussed throughout this book—the caretaking standard that women tend to consult and the justice standard that is more typical of men. Because our culture has been led and shaped mainly by men, it has listed heavily toward the standards that men have been raised to promote. The effects of this imbalance are unmistakable in the legal and political controversies over this complicated issue. As we argued in Chapter 3, *Roe v. Wade* established a right to abortion without promoting an equal—or any—measure of respect for the fetus. A major effect of this was to polarize this nation over the fetal rights that were thereby dismissed. Sustaining the discussion exclusively in these terms has created many false dichotomies. The interests of women and fetuses are pitted against each other instead of being seen as intricately interwoven. People who urge compassion for women feel at odds with others who urge compassion for developing life, and both sides disregard the irony of compassion laced with fury and mistrust. Finally, women are divided, within and among themselves, over the relative importance of their domestic and public roles. Too often, they are made to sacrifice or shortchange one or the other because the private and public spheres of life compete.

Yet imbalances appear also in the realm where the more typically feminine standards prevail. We saw imbalance in the confusion, lingering grief, and unresolved ambivalence that characterized many stories, and we regarded this disproportion as the sad, private counterpart to the polarization and anger that the public debate has generated. In the personal sphere, an overemphasis on care and connections left wounds that sometimes failed to heal. They were inflicted when women or girls assumed inappropriate responsibilities, became involved with exploitative men, denied their own interests, kept silent about crimes against them, or were pushed by other people into unsound choices. They were inflicted when women with little sense of autonomy or self-esteem neglected birth control because their emotional neediness outweighed their desire to avoid pregnancy. Such women were also unable to hold men account-able for contraception. They became pregnant because they wanted to test the strength of a man's commitment or because they wanted to prove their fertility or because they longed for the affirmation that many pregnant women receive from those around them.

In all these failings and missteps, we gradually came to see the distortion or betrayal of the moral standard that is based on caretaking and relationships. Yet it was still the standard on which these women relied. Even their mistakes were described to us in the language of human interconnectedness and respon-sibility. Some women carried pregnancies to term because they saw them as their due after a failure to use birth control, "If you were responsible enough to have sex," said one of our subjects, "then you are responsible enough to raise your own child." Other women had babies or abortions to please their mates. Still others admitted that they depended on mothers, lovers, or friends to make their choices for them. "When it was all over," one woman told us, "I said, yeah, the abortion was for the best of everybody else involved. But I don't know if it was for me. A day doesn't go by that I don't think of it."

Seeking Moral Maturity

Carol Gilligan's work characterizes moral maturity as a state in which the standards of both justice and care are weighed and finally balanced. In the studies she conducted with Jane Attanucci, the two found that about one-third of their male subjects and one-third of their female subjects strove for this balance in resolving moral dilemmas. Gender differences showed up only among the subjects who focused on one moral standard at the complete or partial expense of the other. In these cases, the women were more likely to overbalance toward caretaking, the men toward justice.

The stories in this book support Gilligan and Attanucci's insights. They show, in the context of one moral problem, that many women do consider relationships and responsibility first. They also show that this puts women at special risk in a society that disrespects or subordinates them and relegates their highest priorities to at best a secondary position. As we have noted more than once in this book, the women who have been most hurt, degraded, or confused seem younger than their years. They lack confidence, they lack a strong voice, they fear the loss of relationships more than the loss of identity, and they depend on others to define themselves. In seeking relationships and connection without an equal and balanced commitment to their own and others' rights and self-determination they lack clarity, objectivity, and judgment. They more readily become pregnant without meaning to, and they more readily take direction from others in deciding what to do about it. The evidence suggests that a great many unwanted pregnancies—perhaps even the majority of them— can be traced to women's fears, poor self-esteem, victimization, or insecurity, all of which interfere with safe, careful sexual behavior. For example, over 60 percent of the unplanned pregnancies people told us about were the result of birth control misuse or neglect on the part of one or both partners. The United States has the highest incidence of unintended pregnancy among Western democracies, and the Alan Guttmacher Institute estimates that about 57 per- cent of them occur among women not using contraceptives ("Abortion in the United States," *Facts in Brief*, 1991).

The stories in this book also show—though less directly—the male bias toward autonomy that Gilligan and others have noted. Just as many women's decisions reveal a distortion of the caretaking standard, many men's actions in these stories represent a slide from individuality into plain selfishness and irresponsibility. Repeatedly, the women we spoke to told us of men who engaged in sex with no particular fondness or respect for their partners, men who refused to use birth control but nevertheless walked away once the women became pregnant, and men who pressed their own preference for birth or abortion without considering the woman's choice. And of course, there were the rapes. Fortunately, other stories in this book confirm the possibilities of balance and maturity on the part of both women and men:

Anna Jacobi spoke in Chapter 3 about her painful disagreement with her husband, David, over the fate of an unplanned pregnancy. She wanted an abortion; he desperately wanted the baby but did not attempt to coerce her. Aware of her influence over David's happiness and concluding that his reasons and desire were stronger than her own, Anna continued the pregnancy, not reluctantly but with a feeling of relief and rightness. The costs were temporary and acceptable to her, requiring her to postpone but not to sacrifice her plans to return to school. The benefits, a daughter and a deeper intimacy in her marriage, were more lasting.

Maxine Bonner, whose story appears in Chapter 2, feared the loss of both her job and her parents' approval as a result of her out-of-wedlock pregnancy in the early 1970s. She decided on abortion, which had recently become legal in New York. At the last moment, however, she changed her mind, suddenly willing to pay whatever it would cost her to have her baby. Today, she marvels at how empty her life would be without her son.

Denise Gage, who had self-righteously proceeded with her first pregnancy at eighteen, aborted her fourth in her early thirties, grieved and humbled by necessity. The abortion she described in Chapter 3 was her own, fully explored, painful choice, made by weighing all her priorities: her desire for another child, her need for an education that would end her dependence on an unstable husband, her determination to provide both emotional strength and material support for her three other children. The struggle for balance was so difficult for Denise that she believes it broadened and sensitized her entire moral outlook. She no longer makes snap judgments about other women's decisions about pregnancy, or about anything else, since she has experienced the full brunt of the complexity and pain that can confound easy answers.

Daniel and Sidney Callahan, mentioned in Chapter 1, have been married for thirty-seven years and have raised six children together. They regard each other with the deep-running respect and affection that such a long shared history often engenders. They also disagree profoundly over the question of abortion. Daniel is pro-choice, Sidney pro-life. They have discussed and debated the matter both in private and in public for many years, each admitting that the other's views have humanized the face of the opposition. Their accommodation of this deep difference between them speaks loudly for the balance of care and justice.

These people, and others throughout the book who reached sound, balanced choices, meet a standard of moral maturity that integrates not only justice and caretaking but also inner knowledge and the wisdom to be found in the insights of other people, publications, institutions, and ideas. Such receptivity enables us to recognize that moral strength and clarity come not only through weighing the concerns, experiences, and principles of others but also through learning from them.

Since we believe unplanned pregnancy arises most often from a lack of balance and self-definition, it is not surprising that many of the women portrayed in this book typify these qualities. Women who have attained a degree of moral maturity are unlikely to become pregnant without meaning to and are therefore unlikely to show up in a sample such as ours (except in our chapters on problem pregnancies). Women with a healthy sense of identity and maturity are usually either consistent and careful in their practice of contraception or they abstain from sex if pregnancy would be unwelcome. If their contraceptive fails, they have at their command the means for sound decision making. If they want a child and can see their way past obstacles, they will proceed with their pregnancies. If they do not want a child or the obstacles are insurmountable they will abort, often with anguish over the loss of the pregnancy and the loss of their sense of control. To such women, abortion may be a lesser evil, but it is still an evil. It is never a positive choice, only a negative one.

For these reasons, we speculate that abortion may truly be a last resort for women who have worked hard to achieve and act with integrity. The only worse outcome for an unplanned pregnancy would be one that was coerced—either by laws that made a painfully chosen abortion illegal or by society's failure to help a pregnancy go forward.

The Social Challenge

As a nation, we have remained less morally mature than many of our private citizens in addressing the troubling matter of abortion. While individuals have struggled for ways to respect and accommodate differences, to balance personal autonomy with regard for others, and to understand that both birth and abortion challenge the best that is in us, our public disagreement has persisted in furious invective. Our only hope for replacing diatribe with genuine dialogue lies in listening carefully to people who have struggled with real-life ambiguities and complexities—even people who have erred or misjudged. They speak in different terms than those that characterize the debate; they apply a different standard. Theirs are the human faces in the optical illusion. They never say that justice is unimportant. They simply say that care counts, too.

We think most Americans are prepared to listen to these private stories, because a majority have already expressed an intuitive grasp of the need for balance. Their desire both to see abortion remain legal and to see the abortion rate enormously reduced implicitly relies upon both the justice standard and the standard of responsibility and caretaking. Most Americans have been at a loss to reconcile these two desires, largely because the public debate has portrayed them as forever incompatible. But the stories here have indicated otherwise.

We even have some hope that a few members of the most vocal factions in the debate will be able to listen to these stories and to each other. If they can focus briefly on the importance of relationships and community, they may understand that true dialogue does not require them to give up their political views or the strength of their beliefs. Sidney and Daniel Callahan have known this for many years. A few passionate activists in Fargo, North Dakota, discovered it on at least one occasion in 1986.

Fargo had been a city profoundly at odds over abortion since 1981, when a women's clinic there became the first freestanding facility in North Dakota to perform abortions. Anthropologist Faye D. Ginsburg went to Fargo to interview activists on both sides of the issue. The result was an important book entitled *Contested Lives: The Abortion Debate in an American Community.* The goals of Ginsburg's research, which closely parallels our own, were to witness "this critical 'backstage' setting for the national abortion drama, to get a sense of the specific shape and impact it has at the local level, and to understand the abortion controversy from 'the actor's' point of view."

Near the end of Ginsburg's work in Fargo, a number of activists formed a group called Pro-Dialogue, whose purpose was to bring women from both sides of the controversy together in the hope of finding some shared concerns. The group had read one of Ginsburg's articles, but the main impetus for dialogue had come out of the North Dakota Women's Conference in 1984, at which women in the Democratic party had been divided over their official stance on abortion. Ginsburg quotes from the minutes of Pro-Dialogue's first session:

> As we talked and *listened* that night, we discovered some *very* important common
> ground. We wished that women would not be faced with pregnancies
> —that they couldn't afford,
> —that at times they weren't ready for
> —by people they didn't love
> —or for any of the many reasons women have abortions.
> That common ground gave us something concrete . . . a goal we could work toward
> together. . . . Here we were in—as [ABC] called us—'The Community Ripped
> Apart by Abortion' and we were: talking, listening, discussing, agreeing, disagreeing,
> and reaching consensus. We were: Picketers of Abortion Clinics and Patient Advo-
> cates who walked with women through the picket lines to the clinics.

One of the women who had protested outside Fargo's clinic changed her approach, but not her convictions, after the Pro-Dialogue meeting. She reported: "I picketed the clinic because I wanted to help the women going there—but I can see that's not how they perceived me. I still care about the women and want to help them, but I know picketing isn't the answer for me" (Ginsburg, 1989).

This woman had listened. Her feelings about abortion did not change, only her actions did. The picketing she had no doubt undertaken in the service of rights and justice turned out to violate the caretaking standard. What she had intended as a form of helpful communication she later perceived as confrontation, and so she gave it up.

We in this country also need to understand how others see us. We, too, need to give up confrontation if we want to perceive the human face of the abortion dilemma. We may find, in dialogue instead of debate, that we are not as divided as we think.

The purpose of this book has been to stimulate such dialogue, not to predict its outcomes. It is far beyond our scope to recommend specific policy changes or to delineate a common ground that can be discovered only through common cause. Nevertheless, we believe there are pathways to a shared purpose and a richer understanding of the abortion question and of one another. It is clear to us that legality is not the question. Women will always have abortions, legal or not, as long as women get pregnant without wanting to. The real challenge, therefore, is how to prevent most unwanted pregnancies and how to deal more positively with the ones that occur. We offer the following questions as ones where exploration might help us to meet this challenge:

- How might laws and policies be reconfigured to demonstrate concern for both women and the value of developing life? What combination of changes, brought about in what order, might accomplish that?
- How might we support aggressive research into better male and female

contraceptives? What are some ways we might overcome the prevalent idea that women should bear virtually all responsibility for birth control?

- Should we promote greater sexual responsibility among men by consistently establishing paternity and enforcing child support as European countries do? Are there additional ways of holding resistant men accountable?
- How might schools, churches, community organizations, and even pro-choice and pro-life groups help parents talk honestly with their children about sex and sexual responsibility? Are there programs that can serve as models for such an effort?
- How can children best be educated, from an early age, about the great responsibilities of sexuality and parenthood? Can the effects of negative family experiences—divorce, neglect, abuse, addiction, etc.—that often lead to early sexual activity be eased by social policies or by education programs?
- What can teenagers do to turn peer pressure around so that children feel less compelled to become sexually active at an early age? Can rock stars, athletes, actors, and other popular role models convey the message that abstinence is okay? Can teenagers who have been there—either by having abortions or by becoming a single parent—counsel their peers against too-early sexual activity and against birth control misuse?
- Could grass roots action help unplanned but wanted pregnancies go forward in individual communities? Would broader national policies—such as family or maternal allowances, subsidized housing, affordable but high-quality child care, job training, and even a national health program—help more women proceed with pregnancies that they wanted to keep?
- What kinds of changes in adoption policies might encourage pregnant women to proceed with their pregnancies and feel confident about finding the right family to adopt their babies? What do adoptive parents need to understand about the birth mother's reality and needs? What should they be able to learn about the natural parents' medical histories, history of drug or alcohol use, level of education, or socieconomic background?
- Should pregnant women be offered help from the state if they agree to have their babies and place them for adoption?
- Should women considering abortion be offered counseling, in a neutral

setting, that would simply provide them with some principles and models of balanced decision making? Should such counseling try to make sure that women's decisions are not unduly influenced by other people?

- Should men who have impregnated women without intending to also be offered counseling sessions?
- Should state and federal legislatures officially acknowledge the importance of pregnancy, childbirth, and families and work toward policies that would make abortion—whether it remains legal or not—truly a last resort for pregnant women? What might these policies look like?

These questions can all be traced to a single motivating question that we need to ask women who are making decisions about sex, birth control, pregnancy, birth, and abortion. It is the same question that Mary Belenky *et al.* place at the heart of successful childrearing: "What are you going through?" This question is also at the heart of the caretaking standard that our public discussion and national policies regarding abortion have overlooked. If, as we have barely begun to do in this book, we could ask it of everyone touched by the abortion issue—women who neglect or misuse birth control, parents who feel helpless to communicate with their teenagers, mothers who have surrendered their babies for adoption, people who have aborted because they have no health insurance or jobs, teenagers who have sex even though they do not enjoy it, women raising babies they never wanted, children of unloving parents, couples considering prenatal testing, and countless other women and men—then, inevitably, the paths toward common ground would open up. Our concepts of both justice and care would broaden until each encompassed the other, and we would keep the human faces of a profound moral dilemma plainly in view.

REFERENCES AND
RELATED READINGS

"Abortion Attitudes: Case by Case" (graph). *New York Times*, 26 April 1989.

"Abortion Comes Out of the Shadows." *Life*, 27 Feb. 1970, 20–27.

"The Abortion Dilemma." Report from the *Institute for Philosophy and Public Policy* 10 (Spring 1990). College Park, MD: University of Maryland Press.

"The Abortion Epidemic." *Newsweek*, 14 Nov. 1966, 92.

"Abortion: Searching for Common Ground." *Hastings Center Report*, July/August 1989, 22–37.

"Abortion in the United States." *Facts in Brief*, 11 Feb. 1991. New York: The Alan Guttmacher Institute.

Arditti, Rita, Renate Duelli Klein, and Shelley Minden, eds. *Test-Tube Women: What Future for Motherhood?* Boston: Pandora Press, 1984.

Belenky, Mary Field, Blythe McVicker Clinchy, Nancy Rule Goldberger, and Jill Mattuck Tarule. *Women's Ways of Knowing.* New York: Basic Books, 1986.

Bengis, Ingrid. *Combat in the Erogenous Zone.* New York: Alfred A. Knopf, 1972.

Berkin, Carol Ruth, and Mary Beth Norton. *Women of America: A History.* Boston: Houghton Mifflin, 1979.

Bernard, Jessie. *The Future of Motherhood.* New York: The Dial Press, 1974.

Bettelheim, Bruno. *A Good Enough Parent.* New York: Vantage Books, 1988.

Bishop, Jerry E., and Michael Waldholz. *Genome: The Story of the Most Astonishing Scientific Adventure of Our Time—The Attempt to Map All the Genes in the Human Body.* New York: Simon and Schuster, 1990.

Bonavoglia, Angela, ed. *The Choices We Made: Twenty-five Women and Men Speak Out About Abortion.* New York: Random House, 1991.

Borg, Susan, and Judith Lasker. *When Pregnancy Fails: Families Coping with Miscarriage, Stillbirth and Infant Death.* Boston: Beacon Press, 1981.

The Boston Women's Health Book Collective. *The New Our Bodies Ourselves.* New York: Simon and Schuster, 1984.

Brown, Helen Gurley. *Sex and the Single Girl.* New York: Bernard Geis Associates, 1962.

Brownmiller, Susan. *Against Our Will: Men, Women, and Rape.* New York: Simon and Schuster, 1975.

Butler, Janice R., and Linda M. Burton. "Rethinking Teenage Childbearing: Is Sexual Abuse a Missing Link?" Unpublished paper. The Pennsylvania State University, State College, PA, 1989.

Byrd, Robert. "Teen Sex Soars Despite AIDS Warniñgs." *Pittsburgh Post-Gazette*, 5 Jan. 1990, p. 1.

Calderone, Mary Steichen, ed. *Abortion in the United States: A Conference Sponsored by the Planned Parenthood Federation of America, Inc. at Arden House and the New York Academy of Medicine.* New York: Hoeber-Harper, 1958.

Callahan, Daniel. "An Ethical Challenge to Prochoice Advocates: Abortion and the Pluralistic Position." *Commonweal*, 23 Nov. 1990, 681–687.

Callahan, Sidney, and Daniel Callahan, eds. *Abortion: Understanding Differences.* New York: Plenum Press, 1984.

Cargan, Leonard, and Matthew Melko. *Singles: Myths and Realities.* Beverly Hills: Sage Publications, 1982.

Cohen, Marshall, Thomas Nagel, and Thomas Scanlon, eds. *The Rights and Wrongs of Abortion.* Princeton, NJ: Princeton University Press, 1974.

"Conversation with Mary Ann Glendon, Harvard University Law Professor." Host Bill Moyers. Producer/director Kate Roth Knull. *A World of Ideas.* PBS. WQED, Pittsburgh. 25 Sept. 1990.

Cook, Edith Valet. "The Married Woman and Her Job." National League of Women Voters, 1936. Cited in "Dangers to Jobs Seen for Married Women," *New York Times*, 24 May 1936, sec. 6:2.

Dash, Leon. *When Children Want Children.* New York: William Morrow, 1989.

David, Henry P., Zdenek Dytrych, Zdenek Matejcek, and Vratislav Schuller. *Born Unwanted: Developmental Effects of Denied Abortion.* Prague: Avicenum, Czechoslovak Medical Press, 1988.

Davidson, Muriel. "The Deadly Favor." *Ladies' Home Journal,* Nov. 1963, 53–57.

Davis, Maxine. "Have Your Baby." *Good Housekeeping,* June 1944, 45ff.

Davis, Nanette J. *From Crime to Choice: The Transformation of Abortion in America.* Westport, CT: Greenwood Press, 1985.

D'Emilio, John, and Estelle B. Freedman. *Intimate Matters: A History of Sexuality in America.* New York: Harper and Row, 1988.

Ehrenreich, Barbara. *The Hearts of Men: American Dreams and the Flight from Commitment.* Garden City, NY: Anchor Press/Doubleday, 1983.

Ehrenreich, Barbara, and Deirdre English. *For Her Own Good: 150 Years of the Experts' Advice to Women.* New York: Anchor Press/Doubleday, 1978.

Ehrlich, Paul R. *The Population Bomb.* New York: Ballantine, 1968.

"The Ethics of Abortion." *Time,* 15 June 1957, 93.

Fein, Elaine. "We Could Not Give Up on Jason." *Family Circle,* 26 Oct. 1982, 40ff.

Feinberg, Joel, ed. *The Problem of Abortion.* 2nd ed. Belmont, CA: Wadsworth, 1984.

Feuerstein, Reuven, Yaacov Rand, and John E. Rynders. *Don't Accept Me as I Am: Helping "Retarded" People to Excel.* New York: Plenum Press, 1988.

Finkbine, Sherri, with Joseph Stocker. "The Baby We Didn't Dare to Have." *Redbook,* Jan. 1963.

Fitz-Gibbon, Bernice. "Woman in the Gay Flannel Suit." *New York Times,* 29 Jan. 1956, sec. F:12.

Francke, Linda Bird. *The Ambivalence of Abortion.* New York: Random House, 1978.

Friedan, Betty. *The Feminine Mystique.* Twentieth anniversary edition. New York: W. W. Norton, 1983.

"Gains for Birth Control." *Newsweek,* 13 Dec. 1965, 94.

Gay, Peter. *Freud: A Life For Our Times.* New York: W. W. Norton, 1988.

Geddes, Donald Porter, ed. *An Analysis of the Kinsey Reports on Sexual Behavior in the Human Male and Female.* New York: New American Library, 1954.

Geronimus, Arline T. "Teenage Pregnancy, Myth or Epidemic?" Panel discussion at the annual meeting of the American Association for the Advancement of Science, New Orleans, 16 Feb. 1990. As quoted by Charles Petit in "Researcher: Pregnancies Help Poor Teenage Girls." *Pittsburgh Post-Gazette,* 17 Feb. 1990.

Gerson, Kathleen. *Hard Choices: How Women Decide about Work, Career, and Motherhood.* Berkeley: University of California Press, 1985.

Gilligan, Carol. *In a Different Voice: Psychological Theory and Women's Development.* Cambridge, MA: Harvard University Press, 1982.

Gilligan, Carol, and Jane Attanucci. "Two Moral Orientations: Gender Differences and Similarities." *Merrill-Palmer Quarterly* 34 (3) (July 1988): 223–237.

Gilligan, Carol, Nona Lyons, and Trudy J. Hammer, eds. *Making Connections: The Rational World of Adolescent Girls at Emma Willard School.* Cambridge, MA: Harvard University Press, 1990.

Gilligan, Carol, Jane Victoria Ward, and Jill McLean Taylor with Betty Bardige, eds. *Mapping the Moral Domain.* Cambridge, MA: Harvard University Press.

Ginsburg, Faye D. *Contested Lives: The Abortion Debate in an American Community.* Berkeley, CA: University of California Press, 1989.

Gitlin, Todd. *The Sixties: Years of Hope, Days of Rage.* New York: Bantam Books, 1987.

Glendon, Mary Ann. *Abortion and Divorce in Western Law.* Cambridge, MA: Harvard University Press, 1987.

Glendon, Mary Ann. *The Transformation of Family Law: State, Law, and Family in the United States and Western Europe.* Chicago: The University of Chicago Press, 1989.

Hayes, Cheryl, ed. *Risking the Future: Adolescent Sexuality, Pregnancy and Childbearing.* Washington, D.C.: National Academy Press, 1987.

Herman, J. L. *Father-Daughter Incest.* Cambridge, MA: Harvard University Press, 1981.

Hochschild, A. R. "The Woman with the Flying Hair." *Swarthmore College Bulletin,* Dec. 1991.

Howe, Louise Kapp. *Moments on Maple Avenue: The Reality of Abortion.* New York: Warner Books, 1986.

Hymowitz, Carol, and Michaele Weissman. *A History of Women in America.* New York: Bantam Books, 1978.

Jones, Elise F., Jacqueline D. Forrest, Noreen Goldman, Stanley K. Henshaw, Richard Lincoln, Jeannie I. Rosoff, Charles F. Westoff, and Dierdre Wulf. "Teenage Pregnancy in Developed Countries: Determinants and Policy Implications." The Alan Guttmacher Institute's *Family Planning Perspectives,* March/April 1985, 53–63.

Jones, Elise F., Jacqueline D. Forrest, Stanley K. Henshaw, Jane Silverman, and Aida Torres. "Unwanted Pregnancy, Contraceptive Practice and Family Planning Services in Developed Countries." The Alan Guttmacher Institute's *Family Planning Perspectives,* March/April 1988, 53–67.

Kaledin, Eugenia. *American Women in the 1950s: Mothers and More.* Boston: Twayne Publishers, 1984.

Kerby, Phil. "Abortion: Laws and Attitudes." *The Nation,* 12 June 1967.

Kinsey, Alfred C., and the Staff of the Institute for Sex Research at Indiana University. *Sexual Behavior in the Human Female.* Philadelphia: W. B. Saunders, 1953.

Kirby, Douglas. *Sexuality Education: An Evaluation of Programs and Their Effects.* Santa Cruz, CA: Network Publications, 1984.

Kitchell, Mark (producer/director). *Berkeley in the Sixties.* With Mario Savia and Tom Gillin, 1990.

Kolata, Gina. "Fetal Sex Test Used as Step to Abortion." *New York Times,* 25 Dec. 1988, sec. A:1.

Koss, M. P., C. A. Gidycz, and N. Wisniewski. "The Scope of Rape: Incidence and Prevalence of Sexual Aggression and Victimization in a National Sample of Higher Education Students." *Journal of Consulting and Clinical Psychology,* 55, 162–170.

Lader, Lawrence. *Abortion.* New York: Bobbs-Merrill, 1966.

Lader, Lawrence. *Abortion II: Making the Revolution.* Boston: Beacon Press, 1973.

Lader, Lawrence. "First Exclusive Survey of Nonhospital Abortions." *Look,* 21 Jan. 1969, 62–65.

Lader, Lawrence. "Let's Speak Out on Abortion." *Reader's Digest,* May 1966, 82ff.

Lader, Lawrence. "The Mother Who Chose Abortion." *Redbook,* Feb. 1968.

Lochridge, Patricia. "Abortion is an Ugly Word." *Woman's Home Companion,* March 1947, 4–5.

Luker, Kristin. *Abortion and the Politics of Motherhood.* Los Angeles: University of California Press, 1984.

Luker, Kristin. *Taking Chances: Abortion and the Decision Not to Contracept.* Los Angeles: University of California Press, 1975.

McDonnell, Kathleen. *Not an Easy Choice: A Feminist Re-examines Abortion.* Toronto: The Women's Press, 1984.

McLaughlin, Steven D., Barbara D. Melber, John O. G. Billy, Denise M. Zimmerle, Linda D.

Winges, and Terry R. Johnson. *The Changing Lives of American Women*. Chapel Hill, NC: University of North Carolina Press, 1988.

Mead, Margaret. *Male and Female: A Study of the Sexes in a Changing World*. New York: William Morrow, 1949.

Medea, Andra, and Kathleen Thompson. *Against Rape: A Survival Manual for Women: How to Avoid Entrapment and How to Cope with Rape Physically and Emotionally*. New York: Farrar Straus and Giroux, 1974.

Messer, Ellen, and Kathryn E. May. *Back Rooms: Voices from the Illegal Abortion Era*. New York: St. Martin's Press, 1988.

Miller, Jean Baker. *Toward a New Psychology of Women*. 2nd ed. Boston: Beacon Press, 1986.

Millett, Kate. *Sexual Politics*. Garden City, NY: Doubleday, 1970.

Mitnick, Barry. "Asking Questions About Down Syndrome." Review of *Down Syndrome: A Resource Handbook*, by Carol Tingey, ed. *Down Syndrome*, Jan. 1989, 5–8.

Mitnick, Barry. "The State of the Art: What We Don't Know About Down Syndrome." Review of *New Perspectives in Down Syndrome* by Siegfried M. Pueschel, Carol Tingey, John E. Rynders, Allen C. Crocker, and Dianne M. Crutcher, *Down Syndrome*, April 1988, 4–8.

"More Teens Having Sex, Survey Says." *Pittsburgh Post-Gazette*, 4 Jan. 1992, p. 2.

Neustatter, Angela, with Gina Newson. *Mixed Feelings: The Experience of Abortion*. Dover, NH: Pluto Press, 1986.

O'Reilly, Jane. "Mother and Child Reunion." *Mirabella*, Oct. 1991, 148ff.

Ounce of Prevention Fund. *Child Sexual Abuse: A Hidden Factor in Adolescent Sexual Behavior: Findings from a Statewide Survey of Teenage Mothers in Illinois*. Chicago: Illinois Department of Children and Family Services, 1987.

Palmer, Greta. "Your Baby or Your Job." *Woman's Home Companion*, Oct. 1943.

Peck, Ellen. *The Baby Trap*. New York: Bernard Geis Associates, 1971.

Pittman, Karen, and Gina Adams. *Teenage Pregnancy: An Advocate's Guide to the Numbers*. Washington, D.C.: Children's Defense Fund, 1988.

Prose, Francine. "Harvard Professor Carol Gilligan Tracks the Psychological Development of Girls as They Enter Adolescence." *The New York Times Magazine*, 7 Jan. 1989, 23ff.

Rich, Adrienne. *Of Woman Born: Motherhood as Experience and Institution*. Tenth anniversary edition. New York: Norton, 1979.

Rothman, Barbara Katz. *Recreating Motherhood: Ideology and Technology in a Patriarchal Society*. New York: W. W. Norton, 1989.

Rothman, Barbara Katz. *The Tentative Pregnancy: Prenatal Diagnosis and the Future of Motherhood*. New York: Penguin, 1987.

Russell, D. E. H. *The Secret Trauma: Incest in the Lives of Girls and Women*. New York: Basic Books, 1986.

Scales, Peter. "Teen Pregnancy Prevention: A Community Approach." Address to the Adolescent Resource Network, Monroeville, PA, 25 Oct. 1990.

Schorr, Lisbeth B., with Daniel Schorr. *Within Our Reach: Breaking the Cycle of Disadvantage.* New York: Doubleday, 1988.

"Sex Among Teenage Girls Has Risen Sharply Since 1985." *The Pittsburgh Press,* 5 Jan. 1991, sec. A:2.

Shaevitz, Marjorie Hansen. *The Superwoman Syndrome.* New York: Warner Books, 1984.

Shriver, Eunice Kennedy, and Alan F. Guttmacher. "When Pregnancy Means Heartbreak." *McCall's,* April 1968, 60ff.

"Should Abortion Laws be Eased?" (poll). *Good Housekeeping,* Oct. 1967, 12ff.

Sidel, Ruth. *Women and Children Last: The Plight of Poor Women in Affluent America.* New York: Viking Press, 1986.

Sontheimer, Morton. "Abortion in America Today." *Woman's Home Companion,* Oct. 1955.

Spock, Benjamin. *Baby and Child Care.* New York: Pocket Books, 1976. Originally published as *The Common Sense Book of Baby and Child Care,* Duell, Sloan, and Pearce, 1945.

"Teenage Sexual and Reproductive Behavior in the United States" *Facts in Brief.* New York: The Alan Guttmacher Institute.

Tribe, Laurence H. *Abortion: The Clash of Absolutes.* New York: W. W. Norton, 1990.

Ward, Jane. "Don't Have an Abortion." *Reader's Digest,* August 1941, 17–21.

"The Wed and the Unwed." *Newsweek,* 7 April 1958, 92.

Whitelegg, Elizabeth, Madeleine Arnot, Else Bartels, Beronic Beechey, Lynda Birke, Susan Himmelweit, Diana Leonard, Sonja Ruehl, and Mary Anne Speakman, eds. *The Changing Experience of Women.* Oxford, England: Martin Robins, in association with the Open University, 1982.

Wilson, Sloan. "The Woman in the Gray Flannel Suit." *New York Times,* 15 Jan. 1956, sec. F:12.

"Women: The Road Ahead." *Time* Special Issue, Fall 1990.

Zaccharias, L. (1969). "Age at Menarche." *New England Journal of Medicine* 28:868.

INDEX